THIRD EDITION

CRIME

IN CANADIAN CONTEXT
Debates and Controversies

WILLIAM O'GRADY

OXFORD
UNIVERSITY PRESS

OXFORD
UNIVERSITY PRESS

Oxford University Press is a department of the University of Oxford.
It furthers the University's objective of excellence in research, scholarship,
and education by publishing worldwide. Oxford is a registered trade mark of
Oxford University Press in the UK and in certain other countries.

Published in Canada by
Oxford University Press
8 Sampson Mews, Suite 204,
Don Mills, Ontario M3C 0H5 Canada

www.oupcanada.com

Library and Archives Canada Cataloguing in Publication
O'Grady, William, 1959-, author
Crime in Canadian context : debates and controversies / William
O'Grady. – Third edition.

(Themes in Canadian sociology)
Includes bibliographical references and index.
ISBN 978-0-19-900508-6 (pbk.)

1. Criminology--Canada--Textbooks. 2. Crime--Sociological aspects--
Textbooks. I. Title. II. Series: Themes in Canadian sociology

HV6807.O47 2014   364.971   C2013-907178-4

Cover image: Gary Roebuck/Alamy

Oxford University Press is committed to our environment.
This book is printed on Forest Stewardship Council® certified paper
and comes from responsible sources.

Printed and bound in Canada

2 3 4 — 17 16 15

Contents

Preface

Crime in Canadian Context, third edition is an introductory-level textbook that will provide students with a concise yet thorough review of criminology in Canada today. The book focuses on significant issues and questions that bear upon the discipline today, while remaining sensitive to classical material that was so central in shaping the early days of criminological research. The text is written in a style that is accessible for students taking a criminology course for the first time.

Readers will come to recognize early that the study of crime incorporates several different theories and methods, yet professional criminologists, such as the author of this book, tend to be selective in their range of approaches while conducting their own research. However, the endorsement of any particular perspective is arrived at after many years of reading books and scholarly articles and engaging in conversations and debates with colleagues. One should take time and careful consideration before endorsing one particular theory or perspective about crime. Students will note that this book is written to avoid promoting one particular approach over others. The various perspectives are presented in a critical yet even-handed fashion so that readers can more easily decide what approaches they find engaging, interesting, and most compatible with their world views. Some readers may discover in the subject matter reasons for further study at a more advanced level.

Crime in Canadian Context takes the reader on a relatively short journey designed to cultivate the types of critical-thinking skills necessary for successful learning at the post-secondary level. Indeed, asking a lot of questions about ideas and not accepting "knowledge for knowledge's sake" is a large part of what academic training is about. I hope that this book, and the criminology course that you are taking, will enhance your overall learning experience.

Outline of the Book

As is evident in the Contents, a standalone chapter devoted exclusively to gender and crime is absent. Instead, issues about gender have been incorporated throughout the entire book. The decision to do this is based on the fact that an ample amount of material on gender and crime has accumulated in the discipline over the past quarter-century and, fortunately, can be incorporated into most topics. Also, rather than including a separate chapter examining the correlates of crime, factors such as age, gender, race, and social class have been discussed throughout the text in their proper theoretical or substantive contexts.

The opening chapter considers how crime is defined. It then proceeds to discuss the role that the mass media play in representing crime to society. The reader is also introduced to the classical literature on crime, the skewed influence of mass media on public perceptions about crime, and the theory of moral panics.

Chapter 2, with updated statistics, provides an overview of the core methods that criminologists rely on to measure crime and to conduct empirical research. The strengths and weaknesses of official police statistics, self-report studies, victimization surveys, and observational studies are reviewed. Since criminology is a social science, researchers do everything possible to ensure conclusions drawn about the nature of crime and crime control are valid and reliable.

Chapter 3 is the first of three chapters devoted to criminological theory. Beginning with pre-scientific thought and early religious doctrine that considered much abnormal behaviour to be the result of a generalized force of evil, the reader is then presented with early biological explanations that suggested crime was due to a wide range of physical abnormalities. Recent research linking genetic abnormalities with gang involvement and weapon use are also presented. The role that psychology has played in the study of criminal behaviour is also examined. This will include a review of the classic work of Freud, social learning theory, and research on psychopaths.

Chapter 4 explains the ways in which the sociological approach to crime differs fundamentally from non-sociological conceptions of criminal behaviour. Because sociology is concerned with the way people function within groups, early sociological explanations for group behaviour are looked at first. The development of sociological research has been paralleled by development in criminological research, and the concepts sociologists try to test empirically have been researched by criminologists as well. Some of these foundational concepts are examined: social disorganization, anomie, economic deprivation, reaction formation, control theory, differential association, labelling, critical (Marxist) theory, and feminist critical theory.

Chapter 5 focuses on more recent developments in criminology. The specific theories introduced include the general theory of crime, general strain theory, rational choice theory, the life course approach, environmental criminology, and actuarial criminology.

Chapter 6 tackles the issue of crime and social exclusion—a concept of social inequality that originated in Europe—by examining particular groups in Canadian society who are either at a high risk to offend or are prone to criminal victimization because of their excluded status. Issues surrounding homeless youth, gang members, Aboriginal people, women who experience partner violence, and victims of hate crime will be explored.

Not all crime takes place within marginalized and excluded groups in society, and Chapter 7 explores wrongdoing by people within organizations who are economically powerful or that enjoy privileged social status. Crime that occurs within corporations, governments, police departments, religious groups, and other organizations is given attention in this chapter. The topic of "green criminology" is also introduced in this chapter.

In Chapter 8 the reader is introduced to the law-and-order approach to crime as well as to the structure and organization of the Canadian criminal justice system. The law-and-order approach to crime control is critically assessed by focusing on research concerning the police, the courts, and the correctional system. The reader is introduced also to harm reduction, restorative justice, and the debate around the legalization of drugs.

The last chapter concludes with a review of the main issues raised throughout the book, a brief commentary about the role that criminology plays in the field of criminal justice policy, and future directions in the field.

It is my goal that this book will inform students about the key issues and debates in the field of criminology and, at the same time, challenge "common-sense" perceptions about the nature of criminality and crime control.

Acknowledgments

The third edition of this book would not have been possible but for the help and support of several people. I would like to once again thank Lorne Tepperman who first encouraged me to become involved in this project. I would also like to thank the many students and faculty at the University of Guelph who, in their own way, helped me think through the set of core issues in criminology that appear in this book. I am also grateful to all the people at Oxford University Press Canada for their interest and enthusiasm in developing a third edition of this text. Special thanks go to Tamara Capar, my developmental editor. My gratitude goes out to the anonymous reviewers who provided thoughtful feedback on the manuscript for this third edition. Thanks also to Ashley Depaola for her assistance in updating the statistics in Chapter 2. Finally, I would like to thank my wife, Grace Ollerhead, for her continued love and support.

1 Crime, Fear, and Risk

Learning Objectives

After completing this chapter students will be able to:

◎ Understand the objectivist-legalistic and social-reaction approaches to defining crime.

◎ Outline the ways in which crime is depicted in mass media.

◎ Recognize the relationship between public fear of crime and how crime is depicted by mass media.

◎ Understand the term *moral panic* and be able to provide examples of how social reactions to crime may be subject to moral panics.

◎ Critically evaluate the moral panic framework.

◎ Understand the term *moral regulation*.

Introduction

After reading this book, you will realize that it is common for criminologists to disagree with one another. Many opposing viewpoints exist within the discipline, but defining crime is a topic that, arguably, splits the discipline down the middle. While several different definitions of crime can be identified in the research literature (e.g., Henry & Lanier, 2001) it would be fair to say that the majority of these conceptualizations can be captured under one of two broadly based approaches: the objectivist-legalistic position or the social-reaction perspective. This chapter begins by reviewing these two viewpoints in addition to providing examples that show how crime is subject to social definition. Research is reviewed that shows the way crime is represented by the mass media, and the impact that the media has on public perceptions about crime is described. The concept of moral panic is introduced, along with research that has used this idea to highlight the role that the media play in constructing, setting parameters, and representing crime in society.

The Objectivist-Legalistic Approach

Often referred to as a "value consensus" or "normative" position, the **objectivist-legalistic** standpoint understands the definition of crime to be factual and precise. This point of view typically defines crime as "something that is against the law." Such a conceptualization essentially views crime as a violation of legal statutes, where criminality is limited to its legal construction. In Canada, this viewpoint would hold that the study of crime should be restricted to what is contained in **The Criminal Code of Canada**. Tappan, an oft-cited and early adherent of this approach, argues that crime is an intentional act in violation of the criminal law that is subject to penalization by the state (1947, p. 100). Laws are simply widely shared customs and beliefs that, over time, become codified into legal statutes.

From this perspective, the proper focus of criminology or, for that matter, the goal of criminologists is the analysis of the "rule-breakers" in society. For this reason, the primary question that stems from the objectivist-legalistic viewpoint becomes, "What are the causes of criminal behaviour?" Since the definition of what is considered criminal is, for the most part, defined by legal statute, the goal of criminology is a quest to understand why people break the law. To obtain a good sense of how much crime actually exists in any society at any particular point in time, one would simply turn to the facts: official crime statistics.

Those who endorse the objectivist-legalistic approach to the study of crime are no doubt aware that a considerable amount of behaviour takes place in society that may not be against the law but, nevertheless, may cause people harm. Examples of extra-legal behaviour include lawyers who do not adequately represent their client's best interests, some forms of insider trading, and physicians' malpractices that permanently damage or cause the death of their patients. While adherents of the traditional legalistic approach would not deny that people become victims in these types of circumstances, the perpetrators are not violating the **criminal law**. Until such time when society deems these offences to be criminal, such behaviour is not the proper realm for the study of **criminologists**.

Several theories of criminal behaviour are informed by the objectivist-legalistic approach. These theories range from biological to psychological to sociological explanations of offending. In fact, scientific criminology that focuses on biological causes of criminality originated from this definition of crime. The work of biological determinist Cesare Lombroso (1911), which will be described later in this book, is a good example of a theory of crime that is informed by the legalistic definition of crime. Studying inmate populations, Lombroso argued that these individuals were biologically inferior to those from the non-criminal population. Later, when psychological theories played a more dominate role in the discipline, the focus continued to be a search for the causes of crime by examining individual pathology and personality defects. Cleckley's (1964) work on psychopathology exemplifies the perspective where serious criminals—for example, serial killers—were thought to lack the ability to feel shame or guilt. To be sure, several influential and recent sociological theories of crime also employ the legalistic framework. For example, Gottfredson and Hirschi (1990) suggest that crime is based on a **social consensus** and that those who break the law do so because they lack self-control. Law is regarded, therefore, as the proper guideline in differentiating acceptable from illegal behaviour. In short, crime and crime control are considered to be objective phenomena.

Canada's criminal justice system is very much modelled on this objectivist-legalistic approach. Although the various stages and institutions in the Canadian criminal justice process (policing, courts, and corrections) will be presented in Chapter 8, it is important to now briefly introduce and discuss the concept of law within a Canadian context.

Criminologists find it useful in making the distinction between three types of law: administrative, civil, and criminal. **Administrative law** is a form of public law that governs the relationships between individuals and the state by regulating the activities of organizations dealing with matters such as unemployment insurance, labour relations, and landlord and tenant relations. Violation of these laws generally results in penalties such as warnings or fines imposed by quasi-judicial tribunals. **Civil law** relates to arrangements between individuals, such as property disputes, wills, and contracts. The purpose of criminal law, which is another form of public law and is of course of great interest to the objectivist-legalistic tradition, is to ". . . punish certain acts that have been declared to be threats to the established social order" (Boyd, 1995, p. 267).

In Canada, *Criminal Code* violations generally fall into three different categories: crimes against the person (e.g., homicide and sexual assault); property crime (e.g., theft over $5,000 and breaking and entering); and offences that are considered to be just plain wrong, even though there is no obvious victim (e.g., living off the avails of prostitution and using illegal drugs). Violators of criminal law can face much more punitive sanctions (e.g., incarceration) than rule-breakers of administrative and civil laws (e.g., fines).

To be found guilty of most criminal offences in Canada, in legal terms, an individual must have committed an "evil" act (*actus reus*) and have an "evil" mind (*mens rea*). For many *Criminal Code* violations, linking these two concepts together is unproblematic. Take the example of an individual who walks into a hardware store and intentionally walks out with a $2,000 snow blower without paying for it. In this scenario the *actus reus*, taking a snow blower without paying for it *and* intending not to pay for it (*mens rea*) are both present. However, there are other situations where connecting the two concepts can be more complicated. Consider another example where an RCMP officer discovers an illegal drug in the luggage of a woman waiting at an airport for her flight to depart. While the *actus reas* is evident (being in possession of an illegal drug), if the person has no knowledge of the presence of the drug—and in court convinced a judge that she was telling the truth—then there would be no *mens rea*—no intent to possess the illegal drug. When it comes to these principles of criminal law, it is important not to overlook the fact that children under 12 and the "insane" are considered unable to form *mens rea* and are therefore not held criminally responsible for their actions.

This brief discussion of Canadian law has obviously only scratched the surface in presenting the depth of analysis that is required to fully understand the system of law in Canada. However, as a criminology student, it is important to gain a basic level of understanding about the structure and operation of the Canadian criminal justice system in addition to realizing that this system is premised by the notion that crime is defined primarily in legalistic terms.

Crime and Social Reaction

Taken at face value, the **objectivist-legalistic** approach appears to be straightforward enough: Crime is what is defined by legal statutes, and the purpose of criminology is to find out what causes crime so that policy-makers can implement the initiatives required to combat this social problem.

Until a few decades ago, there really was not a great deal of debate about the way crime was defined by the criminological community. This acquiescence quickly changed with the development of labelling theory in the 1960s (Becker, 1963), and later by the various "critical criminologies" (Taylor et al., 1973) of the 1970s that questioned the objectivist-legalistic approach. Concern was awakened because people had come to see that such a narrow definition of crime assumes that legal definitions reflect widespread social consensus about what is deviant in society (Hagan, 1991, p. 7), and anyone could see that society was anything but consistent in its definitions of deviancy.

Labelling-theory theorist Howard Becker argues that social groups *create* **deviance** by making the rules whose infraction constitutes deviance and then by applying those rules to particular people to label them as outsiders (1963, p. 9). For Becker "deviance is not a quality of the act the person commits, but rather a consequence of the application by others of rules and sanctions to the offender. The deviant is one to whom that label has successfully been applied; deviant behaviour is behaviour that people so label" (1963, p. 9). In other words, the label is the social reaction to deviancy. However, in a complex society one cannot assume that what is regarded as deviant by the law has been arrived at by universal agreement or social consensus.

At the time, Becker's way of thinking was considered controversial, and no wonder that it was. According to what is sometimes referred to as "hard" **labelling theory**, no act—even murder or rape—is inherently criminal. If society does not create the criminal label, then there is no criminal act; crime and deviance are considered to be social constructs. The theory refers to the manner in which individuals and groups create their perceived reality. As a methodological approach, its application involves looking at how social phenomena are produced, institutionalized, and put into practice by humans (Berger & Luckmann, 1966). Adherents of **social constructionism** focus on the processes through which social problems, like crime, are defined and responded to. To this end, crime is not to be understood as an objective condition, but rather as a function of the claims made by individuals or groups who seek to turn a set of conditions into a social problem (Loseke, 2003).

The idea that crime is socially constructed typically produces a more holistic understanding of crime and deviance as elastic in society. If crime is primarily socially constructed, we must at least be alert to the fact that while criminal behaviour is generally regarded to be deviant behaviour, it certainly is not the case that all deviant behaviour has been defined as criminal.

Consider the example of sexual assault. In Canada, sexual assault constitutes both a crime—punishable according to the *Criminal Code*—and an act of social deviance—as the widespread consensus in Canada appears to be that sexual assault is harmful and that such behaviour should not be tolerated. However, other behaviours that are generally considered to be socially deviant—for example, not flushing a public toilet after defecating—are reacted to with repugnance and deemed socially deviant, but by no means does such a behaviour represent a criminal act nor is it punishable on the basis of a legal statute. Consider also behaviours that may be in violation of administrative laws, and subject to a penalty like a fine, but that until recently were not considered by many Canadians to represent a serious social harm. Municipal bylaws prohibiting smoking in bars or restaurants, now in place across Canada, are examples of administrative laws and do not fall under the auspices of criminal law. Even though a business may be subject to a fine for a smoking violation, the behaviour would not result in the merchant's having a criminal record.

In essence, social deviance is a continuous variable, that is, deviance is best understood as being an elastic concept or as a "continuous scale that ranges from the most to the least serious of acts in any given society" (Hagan, 1991, p. 30). The interesting question that arises, then, is why are some behaviours regarded simply as social deviance, other behaviours as breaches of administrative statutes, while a select number of behaviours reach into the criminal realm?

A logical response to this question would be to point out that behaviours deemed by society to be "criminal" are based on concepts of harm or of socially injurious behaviours, like murder or sexual assault, where it is clear that an individual or social harm has been inflicted. This appears to be a reasonable claim. However, as those who endorse the social-reaction position point out, not all dangerous behaviours that hurt people are against the criminal law. Take the earlier examples of professional malpractice that take place in the legal, medical, and financial services professions. Moreover, certain behaviours that do not appear to be particularly harmful to society are, in fact, against the criminal law and can lead to serious punishment. The possession of illegal drugs provides an example of this latter point. There is neither at present widespread consensus in the research literature on the behavioural and long-term health effects of cannabis use nor are there any known records to indicate that marijuana use can lead to death from overdose; yet the possession of marijuana for non-medicinal purposes is against the law in Canada. Furthermore, anyone found guilty of possessing cannabis faces the possibility of spending a considerable amount of time in prison. Even though the Canadian courts rarely punish marijuana offenders to the full extent of the law, especially for possession of small amounts of the drug, the fact remains that the maximum penalty for marijuana possession (more than 30 grams) in Canada is five years less a day in custody (Controlled Drugs and Substances Act, 2005).

This example not only suggests that the level of social and individual harm may not be directly linked to the severity of punishment imposed by society for other criminalized behaviour, but it also alerts us to the idea proposed by the **social-reaction** perspective that many rules and laws are not endorsed by all segments of Canadian society. The way in which so-called deviant behaviour is understood and reacted to is more largely a reflection of how a society is structured than it is an indication of any pathological traits inherent in those who are labelled as criminals. To argue that crime is socially defined points us in a direction where the meaning of crime can vary across social and cultural contexts. Several examples could be used to illustrate how this is the case. Among the more interesting are laws meant to regulate the distribution and use of drugs. While the violation of drug laws in Singapore can lead to the death penalty or to caning, in other countries drug laws are much less strict. Marijuana is legal to purchase in the Netherlands and one may smoke cannabis openly in certain licensed establishments such as the "coffee shops" of Amsterdam.

Infidelity is another example that shows how the moral regulation of behaviour differs between cultures. Even though adultery in Canada is commonly defined and responded to as "deviant behaviour," by no means is it against the law to cheat on one's spouse. Therefore, in Canada, there are no formal punishments imposed for those guilty of such acts. This, however, is not the case in Iran ("Stoning to death in Iran," n.d.) where, since the establishment of Islamic law, the state has enacted specific laws to deal with adultery that include flogging and death by stoning:

> The penalty for adultery under Article 83 of the penal code, called the Law of *Hodoud*, is flogging (100 lashes of the whip) for unmarried male and female offenders. Married offenders may be punished by stoning regardless of their gender, but the method laid down for a man involves his burial up to his waist, and for a woman up to her neck (article 102). The law provides that if a person who is to be stoned manages to escape, he or she will be allowed to go free. Since it is easier for a man to escape, this discrimination literally becomes a matter of life and death.

The social-reaction perspective has remained influential since its origins in labelling theory. Not long after labelling theory was introduced, attention shifted away from the study of why people violate **social norms** to why certain behaviours are labelled as criminal or deviant. This was achieved by investigating the processes by which laws are created or reformed. For example, "conflict criminologists" or "critical criminologists," who operate under the assumption that society is in a constant state of divergence, argue that laws come into being within the context of social conflict. So, like the labelling theory perspective, their focus is not on the traits of individual law-breakers, but on the entire law-making process. The context of social conflict leads the researcher beyond the labelling perspective's narrow critique to examine the dynamics and power imbalances that exist between different groups in society. More specifically, critical definitions of crime generally pay heed to such concepts as social class, race, and gender. For example, the critical position would point out that much of the crime reported on the front page of newspapers or in other news sections usually involves street crime, often being committed by working-class individuals. However, the crimes of the powerful, such as corporate crime, are much more likely to appear in the business section of newspapers. This discrimination based on class suggests, of course, that the crimes committed by the economically powerful are to be taken less seriously than street crime. However, as the critical position points out, there is good reason to believe that crimes committed by the powerful are far more costly to society than crimes committed by the powerless. The point, then, is that the two types of crime are subject to different values in different classes of society and, hence, are subject to different definitions.

A recent perspective in criminology that fits well with the social-reaction position is found in a body of literature that has been influenced by the work of Michel Foucault and his writing on **moral regulation**. According to this viewpoint, and in keeping with the social-reaction definition of crime, the social regulation of behaviour is not based on widespread social consensus but on moral regulation: a social process that defines what is right and what is wrong in society, encouraging certain forms of behaviour while discouraging others. The process by which behaviour is encouraged or discouraged is mediated by a complex system of social institutions that reward and punish people. While conflict theory views law-creation essentially as a process whereby the powerful—usually economic and political elites—impose their will on others (in the form of norms, values, and ultimately laws), the way that power is understood by moral regulationalists is not so straightforward. While moral regulationists see law-making in terms of judicial power, they do not think populations follow rules simply because of the fear of consequences that would come to bear by getting caught and punished. Rather, other processes, or "discourses," are at play in society that serve the function of what could be described as social discipline.

For the Foucauldian school, these forms of discipline are of paramount interest (Corrigan, 1990). Modes of regulation often included in the study of moral regulation usually imply social controls exercised on low-consensus crime and non-criminal deviance. These social controls affect social group-ings such as drug users, prostitutes, exotic dancers, homosexuals, and the poor. One of the more interesting aspects of the moral regulation perspective is that it introduces the idea of self-regulation. That is, it carries the social-reaction perspective of crime and deviance one step beyond laws, lawmakers, and the implementation of direct force and authority to the individual's appropriation of his or her choice of moral behaviour. The moral regulationist maintains that people are self-regulated; that people's identities are socially shaped through "self-appropriation of morals and beliefs about what is right and what is wrong, possible and impossible, normal and pathological" (Rous-maniere et al., 1997, p. 3). In keeping with the social-reaction perspective, the moral regulationists are careful to point out that the researcher must ask, "Whose morals are being regulated, and by whom?"

Even though self-regulation is occurring in society, the criminologist must recognize that groups who are officially morally regulated by the society often resist the efforts by the law to control their behaviour. In this context, one needs to understand the role of the state and how regulation operates in almost every form of state activity from who gets into the country (immigra-tion and citizenship) to how families are defined (taxation) to how the justice system functions. While moral regulation is not confined to the role played by the state, much research in this area does centre on examining the state and how socially appropriate behaviour is defined by the state and is subject to the state's regulatory efforts. The viewpoint of moral regulationists is very much in keeping with the social-reaction perspective; they are not interested in why people are poor, homosexual, or drug users, but simply in how and why groups are controlled, as well as in the ways groups resist that control.

Two examples of Canadian research that has been informed by the social-reaction approach will now be discussed. The first concerns actions that took place early in the twentieth century in British Columbia; the second involves events that came to a head in Ontario in 2000.

Prior to 1908, the use of heroin and other opiates was not subject to crim-inal sanction in Canada. In fact, in the late nineteenth and early twentieth centuries, heroin and cocaine were common ingredients in many tonics and elixirs (Carstairs, 2005). However, after a series of events pertaining to drug use among the Asian community that occurred in British Columbia at the turn of the century, the Canadian Opium Act was enacted and opiate use across the country was legally censured. What is interesting from a social-reaction standpoint about the creation of such an Act is that there really was not any solid evidence at that time to support the assumption that society in general was concerned about this type of drug use, or that great numbers of people were being adversely affected by the use of opium (Boyd, 1991). (This is not to say that contemporary medical research would support the social consensus of that period.) Without social consensus, how did such a law come to be passed by the Canadian Parliament? Becker's notion of **moral entrepreneur** has been used to attribute the passage of the Opium Act to enterprising individuals or groups, rather than to a societal consensus on the perils of opiate use.

In response to a riot that arose from a labour demonstration that spread to the streets of Vancouver's Chinatown, Deputy Minister of Labour Mackenzie King travelled to British Columbia to investigate. While in Vancouver, King met with Asian merchants—including some who were the proprietors of opium dens—whose properties had been damaged by the rioters and who were seeking financial compensation from the government. During his investigation, King also met with a small number of business people and clergy who were upset by the existence of the opium trade in British Columbia. According to Solomon and Green (1988), King had four main concerns as the result of his visit: (1) opium-smoking was becoming more popular among white people, (2) the Chinese were making vast profits in the opium trade, (3) opium trade was in violation of provincial pharmacy legislation, and finally (4) as a Christian nation, Canada had to set an example for an international campaign against opium (Solomon and Green, 1988, p. 91). The elimination of the "opium menace" became the primary focus of King's early political career. Under his leadership, Parliament enacted its first prohibitionist drug policy. The 1908 Opium Act "made it an indictable offence to import, manufacture, offer to sell, sell, or possess to sell opium for non-medical purposes, but prohibited neither simple possession nor use" (ibid., p. 92). Ostensibly, the passage of the Act had more to do with political opportunism than with a crystallization of custom or a call from the "voice of the people." Today, a century later, simple possession of an opiate in Canada can result in a 25-year prison sentence and the social burden of a serious criminal record.

A more recent example of how laws emerge even when they may not represent the voice of the people concerns legislation that was put into place in Ontario a few years ago (similar legislation was introduced in British Columbia in 2004). The Ontario Safe Streets Act (OSSA) came into effect in January 2000. The law prohibits various forms of panhandling and acts such as "squeegee-cleaning of windshields" at roadway intersections. While the law is a provincial statute and, therefore, not within the federal jurisdiction of the *Criminal Code*, it nevertheless gives police in the province the power to ticket anyone who is involved in squeegee-cleaning or "aggressive" panhandling. The passage of this law has given rise to considerable controversy and debate, much of which took place in the Ontario legislative assembly prior to the Act. Moreover, the constitutionality of the law has been challenged in Ontario courts (Hermer & Mosher, 2002). Those opposed to the law argue that the streets are no safer since the passage of the legislation and that the OSSA also discriminates against the poor and criminalizes homelessness. In fact, research prior to the Act showed that homeless youth who were engaged in squeegee-cleaning in Toronto were less involved in crime and in serious drug use compared to a group of homeless youth who were not involved in squeegee-cleaning (O'Grady et al., 1998). Despite being aware of this research, in addition to not having any systematic evidence suggesting that squeegee cleaners were making the streets of Ontario unsafe, the Conservative government under the leadership of Premier Mike Harris proceeded to pass this law.

Similar to the passage of the Opium Act almost 100 years earlier, some commentators insist that efforts to control the activities of this behaviour had more to do with politics than with the social harm posed by squeegee cleaners and panhandlers. The passage of such legislation can be understood within the context of the political agenda of the Ontario government during that time period. This political agenda manifested itself, argue Hermer and Mosher (2002), through a pervasive discourse that emphasized the "disorder" and threat that was created by those who were not surviving in the economic social order provided by the government; they were not considered to be self-sufficient. Certain "disorderly people," many of whom were assumed to be dependent on state support, were scapegoated because of their perceived lack of ambition and laziness. The argument was that unless efforts were made to impose limits on these sorts of individuals, they would eventually bleed the Ontario taxpayer dry (ibid.).

At the time, the passage of this law carried a powerful message, since Ontario citizens were increasingly being depicted as either the givers or the takers: the "Ontario taxpayer"/"Ontario citizen" versus the "welfare cheat," the "squeegee kid/aggressive beggar," the "coddled prisoner," or the "violent youth." There are those who contribute to society and those who do not. Discipline is seen to be required for those who do not pull their fair share, and this took the form, argue Hermer and Mosher, as the "get-tough approach" of the OSSA. And discipline was indeed applied. Since the passage of this law charges for panhandling have soared. For example, from 2000 to 2010 the total number of charges increased from 710 to 15,324—over a 2000 per cent increase! (O'Grady et al., 2011: 9). Not surprisingly, the police estimate that over 90 per cent of panhandlers they encounter have "no fixed address" (CBC News, 2007). In other words, the vast majority of tickets are handed out to homeless people. However, it would be interesting to know just how many homeless people pay the fines that they receive. At the same time, very little is known about the way in which the system deals with offenders who do not pay these fines.

These two examples of law-making clearly point out how political imperatives can underlie how social deviance is produced. Equally, the reasons why the Opium Act and the Ontario Safe Street Act were made into law also illustrate how the classification and regulation of deviant behaviour is by no means based on social consensus or accurate information. In both cases, there was

1 Crime, Fear, and Risk   **11**

scant evidence to support the contention that society was in dire need of protection from the activities of opium addicts or of squeegee cleaners.

What, then, is crime? Well, it depends on which definition of crime one chooses to endorse. For the criminologist, important implications reside in the definition accepted in terms of the types of questions that will be posed and in the method that will be used in the effort to answer them. If one endorses an objectivist-legalistic definition, then it is quite likely that questions about the causes of crime will be at the forefront of analysis. On the other hand, if one endorses a social-reaction perspective, questions will be addressed that include law-making processes and how crime and deviance become socially constructed.

As the reader will observe in the following chapters, many of the major debates in criminology are rooted in issues pertaining to the definition or meaning of crime. In practical terms, the sociological analysis of crime is keenly conscious that any definition or meaning given to different types of crime and criminals cannot be taken for granted. This lack of agreement may be frustrating for a student who would like to get straight to the facts about crime in society. However, as the next section of this chapter attests, developing an understanding of the meaning of crime that extends beyond the resources provided by "common sense" will not only deepen our understanding about crime and criminals, but also stimulate public dialogue about how crime can best be addressed by society.

Media Portrayals of Crime in Canada

While it is impossible to provide one, straightforward, and agreed-on sociological definition of crime, it is feasible to turn to a locus that does tend to portray crime in a much more uncomplicated and definitive manner: the mass media. Since the 1960s, studies of mass media, particularly of television and of the press, have shown how they play an integral role in how the general public understands the social reality of crime, and why it is crucial to consider these media in understanding how crime is defined in society.

Generally speaking, crime is defined by the media on a basis that is very similar to the objectivist-legalistic viewpoint. In most **media accounts of crime** (both "news" and programmed entertainment) crime tends to be defined primarily as events associated with personal fear and risk in which violence is not only commonplace, but its victims are sympathetically portrayed and who are often let down by a judicial justice system perceived as being too soft on criminals. While important differences do exist among the various forms of mass media—for example, between newspapers and television—crime reports have in the past and continue to play a prominent role in news content; estimates of the proportion of total news items devoted to crime coverage have been noted as high as 25 per cent (Surette, 1998, p. 62).

Whether through politicians talking about how, if elected, they will "get tough on criminals" or in dramas depicting crime scene investigations, crime is depicted in the mass media as an ever-present part of our culture.

A well-established body of literature has examined the treatment and presentation of crime in the mass media. The two well-accepted findings that have come from this research are, first, that public knowledge about crime and justice is derived largely from the mass media (Surrette, 1998), and second that the way crime is portrayed in the media differs considerably from how crime is measured and defined officially, in the official statistics, for example. For some time, scholars have pointed out the generally weak relationship between societal concerns and media presentations about crime and official crime rates (Erickson, 1966; Fishman, 1978; Hall et al., 1978; Best, 1989). Within a Canadian context, a study of youth crime by Sprott (1996) showed that while 94 per cent of youth crime reported in the press focused on youth violence, according to court statistics less than 25 per cent of youth crime is violent—much of which entails relatively minor assaults.

Box 1.1   Debates and Controversies

New Media and Crime Awareness

Young people today may find it difficult to imagine an era when there were no televisions, video games, computers with Internet access, cellphones, iPods, Facebook, or Twitter. Not only have advances in electronic equipment made it simpler to be entertained and to communicate with one another, such technology also exposes Canadians to outlets that transmit information about crime and violence. According to a study undertaken by the Canadian Radio-television and Telecommunications Commission (CRTC), use and consumption of these technologies is on the increase:

- In 2010, Canadians could access 1,208 different radio services.
- In 2010, 11.5 million Canadian households subscribed to television services offered by broadcasting distributors.
- In 2010, there were 716 television services available to Canadians.
- Canadians watched an average of 28 hours of television per week in 2010.
- The amount of time Canadians spent online increased between 2009 and 2010: anglophones spent 17.1 hours online per week, up from 14.1 hours in 2009, while francophones spent 12.5 hours online, up from 11.8 hours.
- In 2010, there were 25.8 million wireless telephone subscribers, an increase of 8.5 per cent over the previous year (CRTC, 2011).
- In 2011, there were 16.6 million Canadian who used Facebook (Oliveira, 2011).

The above research raises questions about the power and ability wielded by the mass media in shaping public understanding about crime and in manipulating viewers' ideas about the appropriate responses for addressing the problem. Without a doubt, the exposure of Canadians to these images of crime is pervasive, as Internet use rises from year to year and just about every Canadian household has at least one television set and watches it, on average, 26.8 hours per week (CRTC, 2007).

There is good reason to believe a change has been made in the way crime is depicted in film, television, and the press. A study in England by Reiner and Livingstone (1997) found a decrease in the number of portrayals of property crime, but a steady rise from the 1950s to the mid-1990s in treatments of violent, sexual, and drug-related crime. This analysis concluded that, on the basis of how crime is depicted in the media, society has come to feel more threatened by interpersonal violence and mayhem.

The media are primary sources of information about crime that the public relies on. Moreover, the way in which crime is presented in the media does not often correspond to the picture of crime that is painted by official police statistics. According to research, both of these realities are well-accepted. However, there is much less agreement in the research literature about the *effect* that media have in terms of instilling fear of crime in the public. The relationship between the ways the media depict crime and how the public fears crime is neither simple nor direct. For example, one might think that viewers who are exposed to crime in the media on a regular basis would be more fearful of crime than people who watch little television, yet according to the research literature the relationship between a person's levels of exposure to the mass media and their fear of crime is multifaceted.

First, it would be unreasonable to assume that audience members are passive recipients of television, which arguably is the most dominant form of mass media. Sacco (2000) cites the work of Williams and Dickinson (1993), who suggest that television news consumers are actively involved in giving meaning to what appears on their screens. This meaning doubtless is informed by individuals' past experiences and by their own predispositions to interpret what crime means for them. For years, the notion persisted that the media acts like a hypodermic needle, whereby a dose of information is injected to an unsuspecting public who then become directly affected by such a dose. For some decades this notion has been criticized by mass media researchers (e.g., Lazarsfeld et al., 1968) as an overly simplistic model. The mass media are not the public's only sources of information about crime, and other experiences may come to bear on fears and anxieties. Research has shown that the news about crime that travels through interpersonal networks is more likely to induce fear than news that travels over the airwaves of the mass media (Berger, 1995). To learn, for instance, about crime through the experiences of a neighbour whose home has been broken into is more persuasive and elevates fear more than hearing about a home invasion in a city that could be 3,219 kilometers away. Research by Dowler (2003) has shown that survey respondents who were regular viewers of crime dramas were only slightly more likely to fear crime than non-regular viewers. Factors such as gender, age, income, and perceived neighbourhood problems and police effectiveness were much better predictors of fear of crime than was media consumption.

One of the prime data sources for crime and media research has been the newspaper. Examining hard copies or microfiche transparencies of newspapers is not only laborious work, but it also assumes that there exists a one-way vertical communication from the news outlet to the reader. The only opportunity for readers to share their views with other readers was to write letters to the editor or submit short opinion pieces. However, as Jacklin (2009) points out, since most major newspapers today are online, the idea of one-way communication is becoming an outdated way of looking at the press. Figure 1.1 provides a useful illustration about how the Internet has changed the relationship between newspapers and their readers.

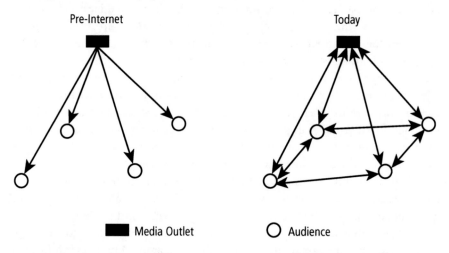

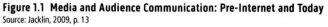

Figure 1.1 Media and Audience Communication: Pre-Internet and Today
Source: Jacklin, 2009, p. 13

Because of this two-way vertical communication, a reader today can quickly add his or her thoughts below the text of an article in the form of a short commentary. Audience members can also horizontally communicate between each other in a public forum by commenting on material. In this way readers can write commentary that either endorses or criticizes content that appears in the press, which can then be responded to by other readers. Hopefully it won't be long until research becomes available that will tell us whether or not this important technological development has altered the way in which the public understands and interprets the meaning of crime as it appears in the mass media.

Even though the idea that the media have a direct influence on public fears about crime is a dubious one, there is reason to believe that the media are capable of distorting public understandings about crime and its control. For instance, in the news media the police can appear to be more effective in apprehending offenders than they actually are. Take the example of illegal drug "busts." In recent years, the media have often presented images of police raiding indoor marijuana-growing operations. The scene is familiar: police clad in white, disposable lab coats are captured by television camera crews as they remove large amounts of marijuana and growing equipment from suburban homes, apartments, or other buildings. Often the news clip concludes with a presentation of a cost estimate of the street value of the drugs seized in the operation. While police may have been effective in destroying the particular grow-op in question, any reference to how effective in general the police are in controlling levels of illegal drug production, distribution, and consumption is seldom made. In other words, the public is left with the impression that the police are doing their jobs wonderfully well and that the entire problem of illicit drug production is under control.

Box 1.2 — **Debates and Controversies**

Can't Always Believe What You Read

The story below, attributing a face-eating attack of a homeless man in Miami to *bathsalts*, made headlines all around the world in the spring of 2012. When the story first appeared it was reported that police had shot and killed a man who had stripped a homeless man of his clothes and allegedly began to eat his face while high on bathsalts (a synthetic drug). The attacker soon thereafter came to be known as the Miami Cannibal. However, not long after the incident had taken place, when an autopsy was performed on the body of the deceased attacker, it was determined that there *were no bathsalts at all in his system*. However, the autopsy did reveal that cannabis was detected in the in body of the assailant and that he had a history of mental illness. The story reveals the power that that an unsubstantiated media account can have on shaping government drug control policy, with the complete absence of scientific study of a new street drug.

***

OTTAWA—The Conservative government is moving to ban a controversial street drug linked to the grisly attack in Florida in which an assailant chewed off a portion of a man's face.

    The government plans to regulate MDPV, a key ingredient in the drug known as "bath salts," Health Minister Leona Aglukkaq told a news conference Tuesday.

Continued

"This action shows our government's commitment to protecting the health and safety of Canadians from this dangerous substance," Aglukkaq said.

"This action helps give law enforcement the tools they need to keep our streets safe from this new and emerging drug that ruins lives and causes havoc in communities across the country."

The drug, which resembles a harmless bath additive, has gained notoriety since the vicious May 26 attack in Miami, where police shot and killed a man who tore his victim's face apart with his teeth.

It's not clear why 31-year-old Rudy Eugene—a man described by family as a sweet person who didn't drink much or use hard drugs—suddenly attacked Ronald Poppo, 65, alongside a busy highway, apparently without provocation.

Surveillance video from a nearby building shows Eugene pulling Poppo from the shade, stripping and pummeling him before appearing to hunch over and then lie on top of him.

A witness described Eugene ripping at Poppo's face with his mouth and growling at a Miami police officer, who shot and killed the attacker.

Media reports suggest police and medical experts believe the bizarre attack was fuelled by MDPV, which police say is marketed as a form of ecstasy.

Aglukkaq says the government intends to add the drug to the Controlled Drugs and Substances Act, placing it in the same category as heroin and cocaine.

Once the changes are approved, activities such as possession, trafficking, possession for the purpose of trafficking, importation, exportation and production would be illegal unless authorized by regulation.

Aglukkaq said the changes would also allow law enforcement agencies to take action against suspected illegal activities involving these substances.

Experts say the drug mimics the effects of certain stimulants, causing agitation and increased heart rate and blood pressure — as well as paranoia, hallucinations and aggressive behaviour.

Source: Canadian Press, 2012a.

Research by Sprott (1996) suggests that the promotion of misconceptions like these have a real impact on what the public believes should be done to confront crime. For example, from population surveys we know that the public thinks that most youth crime is violent. According to Sprott, this false belief leads to the public's opinion that, in the case of youth crime, youth court dispositions are too lenient. When asked to indicate what kinds of cases the respondents were thinking of when youth crime comes to mind, most of those who thought that youth court dispositions were too lenient were thinking of a very small minority of cases: those involving seriously violent repeat offenders. Respondents also had very little accurate knowledge of the operation of the youth court in Canada; they underestimated the severity of dispositions available to the court under the law. The public also believed that the courts were much more constrained than they are in their ability to transfer youth cases to adult court. The view that youth courts are too lenient can best be thought of as a general "belief," more linked to general views about crime and the criminal justice system than to genuine knowledge or to facts about youth crime and the youth justice system. Thus, not only does this study show that the youth crime coverage in the press does not correspond to the "statistical reality" of youth crime, it also shows that media coverage can promote public pressure for more punitive measures to deal with youth who come into contact with the criminal justice system.

Crime and Moral Panics

There is no doubt that media play an important role in constructing crime. Sociologists have developed concepts, therefore, that are intended to better describe the role that communication plays in producing social knowledge about crime. One idea that has been commonly used by criminologists since the 1970s and that is increasingly making its way into public/journalistic discourses about crime is the notion of a "moral panic." This section of the chapter will review the origins and meaning of the concept, in addition to reviewing research that has focused on media representations of crime in an effort to show the complex interplay between how crime is defined *and* reacted to by society.

Influential to this day is a relatively early study by Stanley Cohen (1973), who examined the impact the media play in shaping how crime was defined in England during the late 1960s. Not only did the media exaggerate and distort a series of events that began with a stone-throwing incident between the youths of two subcultures (the mods and the rockers) at a seaside village, but the local merchants and the police played an important role in creating what was to become, in Cohen's terms, a **moral panic**:

> Societies appear to be subject, every now and then, to periods of moral panic. A condition, episode, person or group of persons emerges to become defined as threat to the societal values and interests; its nature is presented in a stylized and stereotypical fashion by the mass media; the moral barricades are manned by editors, bishops, politicians and other right-thinking people; socially accredited experts pronounce their diagnoses and solutions; ways of coping are evolved or (more often) resorted to; the condition then disappears, submerges or deteriorates and becomes more visible. Sometimes the object of the panic is quite novel and at other times it is something that has been in existence long enough, but suddenly appears in the limelight. Sometimes the panic passes over and is forgotten, except in folklore and collective memory; at other times it has more serious and long-lasting repercussions and might produce such changes as those in legal and social policy or even in the way the society conceives itself. (Cohen, 1973, p. 9)

Local merchants who equated youthful wrongdoing with commercial losses lobbied for action so that the fears these youths represented could be controlled or alleviated. All sorts of subsequent youth misbehaviour was taken as evidence that postwar youth in Britain were out of control and were, therefore, in need of increased discipline and surveillance. Each event was portrayed by the media as part of the mods-and-rockers phenomenon, and the police were arbitrarily stopping, questioning, and sometimes arresting youth who were identified through their appearance as belonging to one of these so-called deviant subcultures. Because of the media exposure, the social reaction posed by the threat was evidenced in the British House of Commons where certain members of Parliament recommended that stiffer penalties be levied to control this outbreak of youth crime.

A number of subsequent studies emerged incorporating this sort of moral panic logic. Interestingly, as in Cohen's original study, much of the targeted activities involved threats posed by youth. For example, there have been studies on moral panics associated with drug use among Israeli youth (Ben-Yehuda, 1986); satanic cults (Jenkins & Maier-Katkin, 1992); serial killers (Jenkins, 1994); muggers (Hall et al., 1978); gangs (McCorkle & Miethe, 2002); and date-rape drugs (Moore & Valverde, 2003). One of the more interesting and well-documented moral panics that occurred in the United States and that is particularly interesting and worthy of a detailed discussion was the 1980s "crack epidemic," which played an important role in what was to become America's "war on drugs."

Crack cocaine began making the headlines in the mid-1980s when claims were made that the drug was responsible for a growing number of deaths and overdoses. Crack cocaine is a less expensive and more potent form of cocaine hydrochloride. Research shows that the effects of crack are more intense than that of powdered cocaine, but the effect is not as long-lasting (Cheung et al., 1991). Consequently, the drug is considered to be more dependency producing than powdered cocaine and, as a drug typically sold on the street in relatively small quantities, it was gaining popularity among young people and economically marginalized populations.

Triggered by the cocaine-related deaths of college basketball star and top NBA draft pick Len Bias and of comedian John Belushi (*Saturday Night Live, Animal House,* and *The Blues Brothers*), large segments of the American mass media covered these and related stories that dealt with the drug and how its presence in America was having devastating consequences. Commonplace at the time was film footage of feeble, innocent "crack babies" in hospital wards (infants of mothers allegedly addicted to crack cocaine) and professional video recordings of film crews who followed federal drug enforcement officers into public housing projects of inner-city black neighbourhoods in search of crack dealers. In fact, the 1986 CBS documentary *48 Hours on Crack Street* received critical acclaim for showing the extent of the crack cocaine problem within inner-city poor neighbourhoods. Experts were warning not only of the exorbitant costs associated with treating "crack babies," but also of the lucrative dealing in crack that encouraged some disadvantaged youth to drop out of school and work as street runners and street-level dealers. Indeed, the money earned by such work surpassed any wages that could be earned by unskilled youth participating in the formal, low-wage service-sector economy.

What is particularly interesting about these events, as Reinarman and Levine (1989) point out, is that not long before the 1988 presidential election more than 1,000 stories on crack appeared in the American press. In fact, at the time, the CBS documentary *48 Hours on Crack Street* was the most-watched documentary in television history. It would appear that some politicians were using the public anxiety around crack that was generated by the media to serve their own political interests. Not only were politicians trying to score points by denouncing the drug and all those who used it, but allegations were made that a main reason why the American economy was becoming less competitive internationally was rampant levels of drug use among American workers. Citing statistics about worker absenteeism and other indicators of worker output, random and in some cases mandatory drug-testing policies were put into place as a means of combatting this supposed drug problem. It is widely accepted by many sociologists that concern over crack cocaine served as the catalyst for the American "war on drugs" that is still being fought today.

For the above sequence of events to be identified as a "moral panic," evidence must be available that calls into question the factual basis of the claims being made. Claims, for example, that crack was highly addictive were, and are, misleading (Currie, 1993). In fact, a study by Canadian researchers Cheung et al. (1991) provided evidence to suggest that while it is true that some individuals who use crack cocaine end up having dependency problems with the drug, the majority of people they interviewed who had experimented with cocaine did not become addicted to it. Moreover, as it turns out, medical research has shown that concerns that "crack babies" would be plagued by birth defects and learning disabilities was also misleading and prone to exaggeration during the period when they were being expressed (Robert, 2002). However, this moral panic around drug use in the United States had important implications, not only in terms of the momentum that the war on drugs received in garnering financial resources for police enforcement ($15 billion in 2010 according to the Office of National Drug Control Policy in the United States), but also to the large numbers of people—mainly black males—who are being incarcerated for drug offences. In fact, in 2011, of the 1,433,741 sentenced male prisoners who were under state and federal jurisdiction 465,100 (32.4 per cent) were non-Hispanic white, 555,300 (38.7 per cent) were non-Hispanic black, and 331,500 (23.1 per cent) were Hispanic (Carson & Sabol, 2012, p. 7).

Moral Panics in Canada

The moral panic perspective also has informed research on the subject of how crime is defined and reacted to in Canada. One such example stems from a study that was undertaken in Newfoundland. During the mid-1980s, worry was mounting in that province about an apparent rise in crime, particularly violent crime, especially murder and armed robbery. According to Statistics Canada, levels of violent crime in Newfoundland had increased by nearly 40 per cent over a 10-year period. This increase was said to be among one of the greatest for any Canadian province over this same time period (O'Grady, 1992, p. 2). Groups such as the St John's Board Of Trade, some clergy, union leaders, academics, women's groups, and the police all were offering their views about why Newfoundland was suddenly becoming a more violent society, in addition to suggesting what could be done to stem this tide of mayhem. Typical to other studies of moral panics, a **"folk devil"** emerged within this discourse and was deemed responsible for the rise in crime: unemployed male youth.

Even though official levels of unemployment historically have been higher in Newfoundland than in other Canadian provinces, during the early to mid-1980s the unemployment rate was extremely high, around 20 per cent. Rates for youth were even higher, and some communities reported levels of youth unemployment that exceeded 30 per cent (Felt & Sinclair, 1995). A good example of how the frustrations and blocked opportunities of these youth were seen as being tied to crime is expressed by a witness to the Newfoundland Royal Commission of Unemployment:

> I see the young people in our community getting very upset and possibly there could very well be a sudden rage of the people towards the Government, and maybe in our community, towards whatever groups of people they see as being in authority, which are seemingly not doing anything to help. It's like a time bomb which is very soon, I should think, ready to explode. . . . The correlation between crime and unemployment is a reality. Many individuals find themselves in a rut. As long as the present unemployment situation continues, the crime rate will continue to rise due to the poverty cycle and the social and psychological effects that this cycle has upon the individual. (Clarke, 1986, pp. 1, 2)

However, after testing the assumptions of these claims, O'Grady (1992) found that there was a discrepancy between actual changes in official crime rates and the concern directed toward the level and character of crime in the province. Levels of violent crime had not increased in the province in any meaningful way, even though sentences for some violent crimes, such as armed robberies, imposed by the judiciary had become more severe. In fact, a major explanation for the 39 per cent rise in the violent crime rate was largely the result of changes in record-keeping and initiatives placed on police by the government to lay assault charges in "domestic disputes."

Not only was the moral panic caused by the uncritical examination of crime statistics and increased media attention, but Leyton, who also examined violence in Newfoundland during this same time period, found that the fear of crime was in part generated by the role of interest groups in the province such as politicians, government agencies, professional associations, and social action groups, who had "discovered" violence and used it to further their own interests (Leyton, 1992, p. 191). To quote Stanley Cohen, "The worse the crime problem becomes, the more professional growth can be justified" (Cohen, 1985, p. 177).

More recent studies of moral panics in Canada have incorporated the concept of risk society. The concept of risk can be traced to the writings of Ulrich Beck, a European social analyst who argues that deep changes to economies, cultures, and social life are a conspicuous feature of global societies. Because of these changes, traditional institutions and social constructs have been transformed and the effect has been an increase in feelings of insecurity (Beck, 1992). Certainties of life have been replaced by a state of risk, fear, self-consciousness, and vulnerability (Pile, 1999).

In an attempt to integrate the moral panic perspective with notions of risk, a study was undertaken by Doyle and Lacombe about the anxiety over pedophilia in British Columbia. The authors document the frenzy that occurred in that province during the late 1990s over a Supreme Court of British Columbia ruling that struck down the possession provision of the child pornography law. Censuring the possession of child pornography was deemed an invasion of freedom of expression and privacy, according to a judicial ruling. Even though it remained illegal to produce, make, or distribute child pornography, the judgment ruled that it is not illegal to possess such material for private use. Following this ruling, the press, the public, politicians, teachers' unions, and other groups voiced their outrage and concern over this ruling (Doyle & Lacombe, 2003, p. 286). The common concern expressed was the connection between child pornography, pedophilia, and child sexual abuse. According to Doyle and Lacombe, at the centre of the controversy was "folk devil" Robin Sharpe. Sharpe, a 65-year-old gay male who lived in Vancouver, was targeted not only for being a child pornographer, but also as a pedophile. While not confessing to have been involved in sexual activity with children, Sharpe did point out to the media that sex between adults and children was a long-standing practice in society. Not only were these views widely publicized in the mass media, but a poster campaign was waged in his Kitsilano neighbourhood depicting Sharpe as a menace to society. While the media and others overlooked many aspects of his life that would have "normalized" the man to some extent, Sharpe not only was depicted as a freak, but was made a scapegoat (ibid., p. 287).

For Doyle and Lacombe, Sharpe's unsympathetic treatment needs to be understood as part of a larger moral panic around child abuse, pedophilia, and child pornography. In fact, the authors state that Canada is currently "engulfed in a moral panic around pedophiles" (ibid., p. 304). The authors point out that there has been a sharp increase in the number of alleged cases of child abuse that have been reported to the authorities since the 1970s, even though such reports are not to be taken as indicative of a "real" increase in the incidence of such behaviour in society. Such an increase in reported cases, in addition to the proliferation of media cases about abused children, has served to heighten social anxieties over such abuse. The authors contend that this attention is associated with rising levels of public awareness and concern over this behaviour. Coupled with the notion presented by "experts" that the consumption of child pornography leads to pedophilia and with the development of the child as an "icon" in present-day society, it should not have been a surprise that the case of Robin Sharpe as folk devil evolved as it did.

Moreover, Doyle and Lacombe argue that the proliferation of news media and other new technologies provides more sources in society to alert the public about crime, danger, and risk. In effect, with more channels available from new satellite television technology and the rise of the Internet, fear of crime in society is enhanced and promoted. These sources depend on advertisers for their revenue and are motivated to attract viewers and listeners to purchase the advertisers' products. Such sources are not regulated or limited in their production of attention-catching "news." The overall effect of this wave of advertising about criminal behaviour is that criminals have become objects of generalized abhorrence and anxiety and for whom stricter controls and punishments are exacted. Box 1.1 on page 12 is a typical example of Internet material related to this theme.

A review of the literature indicates that most attention to crime that has been analyzed according to the moral panic perspective has focused on males. Until recently, public anxieties about crime have not involved folk devils who happen to be female. This situation, however, changed in Canada during the mid-1990s. Research by Barron and Lacombe (2005) explain—in what they call the **nasty-girl phenomenon**—that a new breed of female criminal has emerged and is being portrayed as on the rise in the mass media. Citing the examples of Karla Homolka, who was imprisoned for 12 years in connection to the sexual murders of two Ontario teenage girls (in collaboration with Paul Bernardo), and the events surrounding the beating death of Victoria, BC teen Reena Virk by seven female teens in 1997, Barron and Lacombe argue that public anxiety around girl violence is beginning to mount. Not only were teenage girls thought to be increasingly violent, but the numbers of teenage girls who were getting involved in violent crime was thought to be on the rise.

Nasty Girls was the title of a CBC television documentary that first aired in 1997. The program investigated teenaged girls' experiences of violence and imprisonment. Barron and Lacombe make the case that this program was a reflection of Canadian society's concern that it had entered into the era of the nasty girl. The documentary juxtaposed the modern teenaged girl, who is shown to be fighting at school, with a young girl from the 1950s, who was dutifully helping her mother with domestic chores. The idea that girls of the past were obedient and respectful to adult authority, whereas girls today are becoming just the opposite, is a theme that is commonly featured in the construction of moral panics. While not focusing on female crime per se, in a book entitled *Hooligan: A History of Respectable Fears* that focused on newspaper accounts of crime and youth in England dating back to the nineteenth century, Pearson (1983) argues that present-day concerns about deviant youth are not unique: Evidence of such concern is longstanding, as is the idea that in the past society was a more caring and civilized place.

Box 1.3   Debates and Controversies

The Murder of Tori Stafford Case

The newspaper article below reporting on the court case of the slaying of Tori Stafford in 2009 that involved Terri-Lynne McClintic has been suggested by some commentators as evidence to support the assumption that the character of female crime in Canada has become more violent in recent years.

McClintic's shoes found after Tori Stafford's death

The shoes that Terri-Lynne McClintic says she wore when Victoria Stafford was killed were the focus Wednesday at the first-degree murder trial of McClintic's former boyfriend.

McClintic testified earlier at Michael Rafferty's trial that after Tori was killed north of Guelph, Ont., he instructed her to throw her shoes out the car window on a side road.

Rafferty, 31, has pleaded not guilty to first-degree murder, sexual assault causing bodily harm and kidnapping.

A woman who lives in the area testified today that in about early April 2009—the month Tori was killed—she was taking a walk on Sideroad 6 near her home north of Guelph and found a pair of white basketball shoes with blue trim and another single shoe.

Lillian Metcalfe says she threw the single shoe out and took the pair of shoes home and washed them, intending to donate them to Goodwill. On May 30 she gave them to police while they were canvassing the area and McClintic later identified them as hers.

Continued

The jury saw the blue and white Shaq basketball shoes as they were entered as an exhibit at the trial today.

Told officer shoes were in her house

Metcalfe also said there was a car's back seat in the same area of the side road for a while. She mentioned it to police since she had heard they were searching for Rafferty's back seat, but by May 30 it was no longer there. She then told the officer about the shoes and he asked her to describe them, Metcalfe said.

"I said, 'Well, I think I can do one better than that,'" Metcalfe testified Wednesday. "'I have the shoes in the house. Would you like to see them?'"

Tori's remains were found partially clothed in a field near Mount Forest, further north of Guelph, more than 100 days after she went missing April 8, 2009.

McClintic testified that after Tori was killed Rafferty went to great lengths to cover up their crime, including hiding Tori's body under a rock pile, reversing over tire tracks to make them less distinguishable, providing McClintic with a change of clothes, discarding the clothes they were wearing as well as the murder weapon and throwing out the shoes.

"He turned his lights off and pulled onto the sideroad," McClintic testified earlier about their actions following the murder. "He said, 'We need to get rid of our shoes,' so I believe I tossed my pair of shoes out the car window. He gave me a pair of shoes to wear and he put on a different pair of shoes as well. Then we drove off."

Rafferty then drove to a car wash in Cambridge, Ont., where they hosed down the car and shampooed the interior, McClintic testified.

Trial to resume on Friday

McClintic is already serving a life sentence after pleading guilty two years ago to first-degree murder. The trial heard from her as the central witness in the case over two weeks, with questioning largely focusing on inconsistencies in her story.

When she first confessed and when she later pleaded guilty, she said it was Rafferty who killed Tori using the hammer. But she testified at Rafferty's trial that it was she who wielded the hammer.

The Crown alleges Rafferty and McClintic abducted Tori outside her elementary school and drove her to a rural area more than 100 kilometres north, where she was raped and violently killed.

The trial is not sitting Thursday, but resumes Friday with what the Crown says will be "quite a full day."

Source: The Canadian Press, 2012b.

The documentary moves on to show the metamorphosis of the good, "sweet" girl of the past to the violent criminal of the present. The harmful effects of modern popular culture—gangsta rap, sexualized music videos, and teen fashion magazines—are depicted in the documentary as the culprits for the rise of the nasty girl, the new female folk devil of the 1990s. Barron and Lacombe point out that, like other analyses of moral panics, the fears about nasty girls do not correspond to the official statistics that measure the nature and level of young female crime in Canada. For example, the authors point out that the sharp rise in violent crime by young female offenders has more to do with a rise in minor assaults, such as pushing and slapping, than a rise in the number of seriously damaging crimes, such as murder. In fact, this point has been supported in recent research by Doob and Sprott (2004), who have argued that the main reason why the proportion of female younger offenders who have been found guilty in Canadian youth courts in relation to males has increased in recent years is largely the result of the smaller number of males who have appeared in court, not because there has been a landslide of females appearing in court.

Barron and Lacombe then go on to claim that the social construction of the violent girl is linked to a societal backlash against feminism. Quoting Schissel (1997), they write: "[t]he 'sugar and spice' understanding of femaleness is often the standard upon which young female offenders are judged, and, in effect, the images of 'bad girls' are presented as . . . sinister products of the feminist movement" (Barron and Lacombe, 2005, citing Schissel, p. 107). Similarly, they argue that what troubles society most about the violent girl is that she has come to represent the excesses of the changed social, political, and economic status women have gained through their struggles for equality since the 1960s. The media, they contend, have "sensationalized the spirit of girl power by positing it as the cause of girl violence" (Barron and Lacombe, 2005, p. 58). Girl power, the source of social anxieties, is the real nasty here; the moral panic over the nasty girl is an outcrop of a desire to return to a patriarchal social order characterized by gender traditionalism and conformity.

Box 1.4   **Debates and Controversies**

Fear and the Blogosphere

The following Internet blog relates to the public perception of fear raised by Doyle and Lacombe (2003). Not only does the Internet alert the public to the dangers and risks associated with child abuse, but the medium is also a forum whereby members of the public can voice their perceptions that these crimes are becoming more prevalent in society and that action is needed to deal with the perceived crisis. Notice that no comparative statistics of any kind are offered, nor does the writer indicate what "gummint report" he refers to. This example shows how public anxiety can be transmitted to the public without much debate over the authenticity of the statistics used in the blog.

Continued

More Common than Cancer: The Sexual Abuse of Kids Has Gotta Stop

So there I am, tooling along on page 2 of this gummint report, when all of a sudden these words hit me like a Mike Tyson gut-punch out of the blue.

"Most disturbing is that one of every seven victims of sexual assault (or 14% of all victims) reported to law enforcement agencies were under age 6."

My eyes search for typos. Then I put down the report and walk around outside for a minute, because I want to give that particular sentence the chance to reconsider.

When I sit down again, the words are still there, bunkered down on the page, refusing to move.

14% of sexual assault victims are under age 6??!!

I grab the calculator. According to the National Violence Against Women Survey, which was co-funded by the US Department of Justice and Centers for Disease Control and Prevention, about 300,000 women are raped each year. Take 14% of that, and you get—are you ready for this?—42,000 girls who are raped before they hit second grade every year!!!!

WHUMMMMFFFF!!!!

I've read a lot of horror stories since I started looking into the issue of men's violence against women. But this one bit of research prose is enough to make me re-process lunch.

I glance out the window at the kids playing in the neighborhood. I think of the girls in my son's kindergarten class a few years ago. I summon up some Kodak moments of my seven nieces. And then I close the cover on this report. And I sit there, dumbfounded.

If this report is on the money . . . if my crude number-crunching is within walking distance of the proverbial ballpark . . . there's only one thing to say: I CAN'T BELIEVE WE'RE NOT TALKING MORE ABOUT THIS!!!!!!!!

Source: Shaw, 2006.

Criticisms of the Moral Panic Perspective

While the concept of moral panic is useful for understanding how crime can be exaggerated and distorted and to concerns about the broader social order, the concept has not been without some criticism. The moral panic framework has been criticized on the basis that it often does not pay enough attention to the fact that all social reaction is not the same, and that audiences today are more sophisticated and less likely to be manipulated by the media than perhaps was the case in the past. For example, McRobbie and Thorton believe that while certain segments of the media exaggerate and distort crime, this is not to suggest that the mass media should be treated as a homogenous entity. They argue that opposing viewpoints are often expressed when it comes to issues related to crime, law, and order. The police, the press, and governing parties do not necessarily operate in a concerted campaign; there is often some organized and articulated opposition (McRobbie & Thorton, 1995, p. 154).

An example of this point can be found in a study by Ericson and Voum-vakis, who looked at the coverage given by Toronto newspapers to attacks on women in the 1980s. They found that considerable variation in how these assaults were reported and commented on existed among the *Globe and Mail*, the *Toronto Star*, and the *Toronto Sun*. A more recent example can be found in the wake of a Boxing Day shooting that took place in downtown Toronto in 2005. A 15-year-old girl was killed and six other people were injured by gun-fire on normally busy but safe Yonge Street and on the threshold of one of the city's venerable department stores. An opinion column in the *Toronto Star* was headlined, "There's no going back to what we once were." Columnist Rosie DiManno (2005, p. A6) muses that her "hometown has become unrecogniz-able, angry, and malevolent." The popular columnist further laments that a "culture of nihilism and reckless wrongdoing has caught up with us" where Toronto could be headed for an "irreversible ruin, a place of besiegement by crime and wicked malaise." Words such as these are certainly in keeping with the moral panic perspective in terms of the role that media can assume in playing to the public's anxiety about the threat posed by the perceived growth in ruthless handgun violence.

However, on the very same day, in the same edition of the same news-paper, and only a few pages after the DiManno column, the main editorial of the *Toronto Star* took a completely different slant on this tragic event, oppos-ing the view held by DiManno. While the editorial denounces the crime as a "senseless" and "intolerable" act, it also notes that despite the high-profile murders in 2005, the number still was short of the "record of 88 killings in 1991." The editorial continued by maintaining that "Toronto is far from being 'just like any big American city' or another 'Dodge City' as some critics would have us believe. The streets are not out of control" (*Toronto Star*, 2005).

Since the time of that well-publicized shooting, other hand-gun shootings have occurred in public places in Toronto. For example, in 2012 there were three that drew much attention. One was a food-court shooting that killed 2 in the Eaton Centre on Yonge Street. A second was a gangland style execution-type shooting that took place on a restaurant patio in Little Italy during a televised World Cup soccer game. And perhaps the most notable was a shoot-ing at block party that killed 2 and injured 22 in August of that year. During the aftermath of these shootings the press was often quick to connect them to broader sense of social malaise, but at the same time reports were also issued in the press suggesting that, statistically, Toronto is one of the safest large cit-ies in North America in which to live.

Moore and Valverde (2003, p. 307) have also challenged the moral panic framework on the basis that understanding social change is not advanced by simply pointing out that "X or Y fear is not justified by crime statistics." By emphasizing only that fears about crime are irrational—that is, that crime statistics may be declining while fear and anxiety is increasing—one is

Easy to Find in Toronto...

Political cartoon by Theo Moudakis. Reprinted with permission—Toronto Star

suggesting that the only remedy to the problem would be a more informed public. However, Moore and Valverde point out that "[r]ational information and aggregate data don't necessarily counteract moral panics" (ibid.). Rather, they propose that

> [c]ampaigns to stamp out this or that moral evil, we argue, aren't reducible to or completely explained by popular ignorance and unconscious fears, and will not disappear with the application of solid information. No doubt ignorance and unconscious motives are present in popular discourses; but we believe it is high time to get away from the notion that the populace is in the grip of irrational myths and that only the enlightened philosophers (or critical sociologists) can save the world through reason and accurate facts. (ibid., p. 308)

In their analysis of the panic surrounding the "date-rape" drug Rohypnol, Moore and Valverde argue that it is more important to study the "format than the content of the claims made by various information providers" (ibid.). Informed by a Foucauldian approach to risk management, Moore and Valverde argue that youth are exposed to a mix of messages and formats about date-rape drugs—scientific, statistical data from experts; personal anecdotes as well as moralistic sensational accounts—and perhaps borrowing from the early work of the famous Canadian mass communications expert Marshall

McLuhan, Moore and Valverde argue that significance needs to be given to the "medium" in which these mixed messages are presented as a tool for better understanding moral panics and moral regulation.

Despite these criticisms, the moral panic perspective is a useful way to think about how and why public anxiety about crime surfaces in the way that it does. We are living in a period where information technology is expanding rapidly and many people believe that society is increasingly in need of protection from the risks posed by crime. Criminology can provide insight into the various media in which crime messages are produced for public consumption; as the public embraces that technology, the messages and public response to them will pose substantial, but interesting, challenges for future criminological research.

Conclusion

The main objective of this chapter has been to introduce the reader to the idea that meanings and definitions about crime are subject to debate. Which definition of crime is adopted can have important implications for the framing of the types of questions that criminologists ask. The objectivist-legalistic framework normally relies on legal definitions of crime and considers the criminologist's task to be an explanation of how and why rule-breaking occurs in society. Criminologists working with definitions of crime informed by the social-reaction perspective are more interested in knowing about the ways in which society reacts to those who have been targeted and labelled as rule-breakers. Their emphasis is on the structures and processes associated with rule-making, not rule-breaking.

This chapter has also revealed the role that the mass media play in framing crime within our culture. It was shown that it is too simplistic to suggest that watching television has a direct bearing on public fears and anxieties about crime—especially in the Internet age. However, since the media generally define crime according to a police-informed, legalistic perspective, it is not surprising that law-and-order responses dominate public and political discourses about the remedies required to confront crime. The moral panic perspective is one example of an alternative to mainstream or common sense understandings about crime. The moral panic framework shows how the media, in conjunction with various claims-makers and experts, can amplify or even distort the risks posed by certain types of crimes or criminals. Images about crime that appear in the media cannot be assumed, therefore, to represent fully the social "reality" of crime.

Where, then, can one turn to obtain a more accurate picture or a truer measure of the level and character of crime? To answer this question, the next chapter will present the main tools that criminologists use to measure crime. Even though the four empirical methods that are reviewed in the following chapter offer a more systematic understanding of the extent and character of crime, in the end, how we as a society come to measure crime is very much dependent on how crime is defined.

Critical Thinking Questions

1. Considering the two definitions of crime presented in this chapter, discuss using current examples which perspective seems to best represent how each of the mass media depict crime in Canada today.

2. How has the Internet changed the relationship between newspapers and their readers?

3. What is the significance of *mens rea* and *actus reus* in determining guilt in a criminal case?

4. Describe examples, other than the ones presented in this chapter, of how certain types of crime have been reacted to that can be interpreted on the basis of a moral panic.

Suggested Readings

Carstairs, Catherine. (2005). *Jailed for possession: Illegal drug use, regulation, and power in Canada 1920–1961*. Toronto, ON: University of Toronto Press. This social history of drug use in Canada examines drugs in the context of drug users, regulators (including the medical profession), social workers, and the police. The book raises a number of issues that are in keeping with the social-reaction perspective discussed in this chapter.

Cohen, Stanley. (1990). *Folk devils and moral panics: The creation of the mods and rockers*. Oxford, UK: Blackwell. This is an updated edition of Cohen's original analysis of moral panics. In the Foreword, Cohen comments on theory and research on moral panics that have appeared in the research literature since the book was first published in 1973.

Jewkes, Yvonne. (2004). *Media and crime*. Thousand Oaks, CA: Sage. Jewkes has written an accessible review of important media and criminological debates about the ways in which the mass media construct images of crime in society.

O'Grady, William, Patrick Parnaby, and Justin Schikschneit. (2010) "Guns, gangs and the underclass: A constructionist analysis of gun violence in a Toronto high school," *Canadian Journal of Criminology and Criminal Justice* 52 (1): 55–77. This article is a social constructionist account analyzing how the print media reported the shooting of Jordan Manners on 23 May 2007 at C.W. Jefferys Collegiate Institute in Toronto.

Websites and Films

Marijuana Party
www.marijuanaparty.ca
    The materials on this website exemplify debates and arguments used by interest groups in efforts to lobby the Canadian government to reform marijuana laws.

The Homeless Hub

www.homelesshub.ca

> The Homeless Hub is Canada's largest collection of online research on homelessness. The site deals with a range of issues about laws that have been initiated to curtail the presence of squeegee cleaners and "aggressive" panhandlers on Canadian streets. The site also contains video clips and links to other websites that pertain to issues of homelessness in Canada and other countries.

Quadrophenia (1979). A film set in 1964 based on a rock-opera album of the same name released by the English rock band The Who in 1973. The film deals with the clashes in the 1960s between the mods and the rockers and was the basis of Cohen's book on moral panics.

Dark Crystal (2005). A CBC documentary about the drug crystal methamphetamine. After watching this documentary think about whether or not the portrayal of the drug and its users fall under the category of a moral panic. You can read about the documentary at www.cbc.ca/fifth/darkcrystal/facts.html.

Reefer Madness (1938). A film that depicts the effects of marijuana in an extremely exaggerated fashion. Today the film is generally regarded as a propaganda film produced for the prohibition of the drug in the United States. In 2005 *Refer Madness: The Movie Musical*, starring Neve Campbell, was released as a spoof of the 1938 original. You can read more about the movie at www.archive.org/details/reefer_madness1938.

2 Measuring Crime

Introduction

The previous chapter reviewed the complexities involved in defining crime within its social context. Chapter 2 builds on this awareness while examining an issue that has claimed the attention of criminologists and policy-makers for some time: the measurement of crime. Even if there were complete agreement about the meaning or definition of crime (an unlikely scenario), measuring crime would not be a simple task. By no means do we have a completely satisfactory method even for counting crimes. By examining official police statistics, victimization surveys, self-report surveys, and observational accounts this chapter will introduce the debates and controversies dealing with the measurement of crime, with a focus on the strengths and weaknesses of each technique. Chapter 2 also addresses such important questions as, "Is violent crime in Canada on the rise?" With an emphasis on homicide, this chapter considers the legal definition of homicide in Canada and reviews homicide statistics from the time in 1962 when they were first systematically collected. Finally, Canadian homicide rates will be compared to the rates of homicide in other industrialized countries.

As we have noted, mass media are the principal resources Canadians rely on for their knowledge about the level and character of crime, and the ways in which crime is depicted by mass media often distort or even exaggerate what can be known about crime. Criminologists often point out that the images constructed by the media do not match "reality." But just what is **empirical reality**, and how is it measured?

Generally speaking, an empirical investigation refers to the systematic collection of observable data. For example, the criminologist may ask questions such as, "What forms of crime are the most common in Canada?" or "How many of these events are brought to the attention of the police?" Answers to factual questions such as these, however, are more thorny and difficult to answer than might be expected. If information used to measure crime is not accurate, then what are we to make of statements that purport to explain these data? Criminology is not just about collecting the "facts." The systematic study of crime also entails understanding criminal events. For example, if we are confident about data showing that homicide rates in Canada are lower than they are in the United States, the next logical step would be to explain *why* these differences exist. In short, criminology is not simply about describing the nature of crime in society, it must explain and *understand* the nature of crime using the most reliable and valid information possible. However, as the following discussion confirms, there is no one technique available that can successfully fulfill this need.

Official Statistics

In attempting to understand the "real level of crime" the first place to turn is the **Uniform Crime Reporting (UCR) system**. While methods and resources vary, most countries around the world go to considerable lengths and expense to measure crime within their geo-political borders. By and large, all official crime-reporting systems rely on reports of crime by the police. For this reason, the way crime is measured falls under the objectivist-legalistic definition introduced in the previous chapter. In theory, whatever crime comes to the attention of the police is reported *by* the police to their government's statistical agencies. In the United States, the Federal Bureau of Investigation (FBI) is responsible for counting crime across the nation. In the United States, the origins of the Uniform Crime Reporting system can be traced to 1929, when the International Association of Chiefs of Police met and decided that a reliable, uniform crime statistics compilation was needed. In 1930, the FBI was commissioned with the task of collecting, publishing, and archiving those statistics. Today, several annual statistical publications, such as the all-inclusive *Crime in the United States*, are produced from data provided by nearly 17,000 law enforcement agencies across the United States (FBI, n.d.). In the United Kingdom (England and Wales) the **British Home Office** is responsible for assembling and releasing crime statistics.

Crime data in Canada have been systematically collected on a national basis since 1962. While Canadian information about crime—especially homicide—was reported by the police and was available to the public prior to 1962, it was not until then that police forces in Canada were required by law to submit statistical crime reports to Canada's statistical agency, the Dominion Bureau of Statistics (now Statistics Canada). Today, the **Canadian Centre for Justice Statistics** (CCJS) in Ottawa is the division at Statistics Canada responsible for gathering and analyzing the reports submitted by police from across the country. On an annual basis, these reports are released to the public in the form of media releases, annual reports, and website updates. In Canada about 1,200 separate police detachments, representing about 230 police forces, submit crime data to the CCJS.

UCR data are crimes *known by the police to have taken place*. This includes the following three general categories: violent crime, property crime, and other *Criminal Code* violations. Within each of these categories several differing offences are accounted for. A detailed breakdown of these offences can be found in Table 2.1.

Since the inception of the national crime-reporting initiative in 1962, police detachments from across Canada have been required to submit a Uniform Crime Reporting Aggregate Survey to Ottawa, which is basically a tally sheet used to count offences within police jurisdictions. However, some Aboriginal police forces in Canada do not respond to the survey. According to Statistics Canada, these typically are very small communities and serve less than half a per cent of the Canadian population. For these forces, obviously, estimates of reported crime cannot be produced. The UCR form collects summary data about more than 100 *Criminal Code* offences.

More recently, in order to collect more detailed information on each incident, including data on victims and accused persons, the **UCR2 Survey** was developed. In this alternative method of data collection, a separate statistical record is created for each criminal incident and it is known as an "incident-based" reporting system. This system of respondent-reported, incident-based data began in 1988. According to Statistics Canada, this survey introduced certain efficiencies for police services and lowered response burden by removing or simplifying UCR2 (Sauvé, 2005).

Crime data from police departments are submitted monthly on machine-readable forms, normally within two weeks after the end of each month's reporting. It is important to know how crime is actually counted in these reports. While UCR data represents "crime known to the police," this is not actually what is being counted. In fact, and this is clearly made known by Statistics Canada, there is at least some level of *alleged* law-breaking behaviour that does *not* appear on these records for the simple reason that the UCR Survey classifies incidents according to the *most serious offence* (MSO) occurring during the incident—generally interpreted as the offence that carries the longest maximum sentence under the *Criminal Code*. In categorizing incidents, violent offences always take precedence over non-violent offences. Take, for example, an incident involving both a breaking-and-entering offence and

Table 2.1 Police-Reported Crime for Selected Offences Canada, 2010–11

Type of offence	2010[r] number	2010[r] rate	2011 number	2011 rate	Per cent change in rate 2010 to 2011	Per cent change in rate 2001 to 2011
	number	rate	number	rate	per cent	
Total crime (excluding traffic) – "Crime Rate"	2,094,875	6,139	1,984,916	5,756	–6	–24
Violent crime						
Homicide	554	2	598	2	7	–3
Other violations causing death[1]	100	0	78	0	–23	–49
Attempted murder	668	2	655	2	–3	–19
Sexual assault – level 3 – aggravated	179	1	140	0	–23	–22
Sexual assault – level 2 – weapon or bodily harm	402	1	398	1	–2	12
Sexual assault – level 1	21,795	64	21,283	62	–3	–19
Sexual violations against children [2, 3]	3,684	11	3,822	11	3	n/a
Assault – level 3 – aggravated	3,481	10	3,486	10	–1	15
Assault – level 2 – weapon or bodily harm	51,955	152	50,184	146	–4	5
Assault – level 1	175,289	514	172,770	501	–2	–19
Assault police officer [4]	15,913	47	11,943	35	–26	31
Other assaults	3,281	10	3,097	9	–7	–34
Firearms – use of, discharge, pointing	2,017	6	1,936	6	–5	–20
Robbery	30,478	89	29,746	86	–3	–13
Forcible confinement or kidnapping	4,301	13	3,774	11	–13	35
Abduction	449	1	402	1	–11	–46
Extortion	1,578	5	1,525	4	–4	–17
Criminal harassment	21,315	62	21,690	63	1	1
Uttering threats	76,347	224	71,945	209	–7	–28
Threatening or harassing phone calls	21,604	63	20,341	59	–7	–42
Other violent *Criminal Code* violations	3,830	11	4,597	13	19	9
Total	**439,220**	**1,287**	**424,410**	**1,231**	**–4**	**–16**
Property crime						
Breaking and entering	197,058	577	181,217	526	–9	–42
Possess stolen property [5, 6]	30,275	89	21,496	62	–30	–28
Theft of motor vehicle	92,505	271	82,411	239	– 12	–56
Theft over $5,000 (non-motor vehicle)	15,649	46	15,153	44	–4	–35
Theft under $5,000 (non-motor vehicle)	527,509	1,546	497,452	1,443	–7	–32
Fraud [7]	89,830	263	89,801	260	–1	–7
Mischief [8]	340,090	997	315,977	916	–8	–15
Arson	12,234	36	10,378	30	–16	–35
Total	**1,305,150**	**3,824**	**1,213,885**	**3,520**	**–8**	**–31**

(continued)

Table 2.1 (continued)

Other *Criminal Code* offences

Counterfeiting	815	2	620	2	−25	−68
Weapons violations	15,038	44	14,471	42	−5	0
Child pornography [9]	2,218	6	3,312	9	40	209
Prostitution	3,020	9	2,459	7	−19	−57
Disturb the peace	119,913	351	117,476	341	−3	17
Administration of justice violations	178,135	522	177,159	514	−2	2
Other violations	31,366	92	31,304	91	−1	−29
Total	**350,505**	**1,027**	**346,621**	**1,005**	**−2**	**2**
***Criminal Code* traffic violations**						
Impaired driving [10]	87,231	256	90,277	262	2	−2
Other *Criminal Code* traffic violations	55,615	163	55,938	162	0	29
Total	**142,846**	**419**	**146,215**	**424**	**1**	**8**
Drug offences						
Possession – cannabis	56,853	167	61,406	178	7	16
Possession – cocaine	7,325	21	7,392	21	0	23
Possession – other drugs [11]	9,761	29	10,352	30	5	97
Trafficking, production or distribution – cannabis	18,363	54	16,548	48	−11	−26
Trafficking, production or distribution – cocaine	9,873	29	10,251	30	3	37
Trafficking, production or distribution – other drugs	7,047	21	7,215	21	1	41
Total	**109,222**	**320**	**113,164**	**328**	**3**	**14**
Other federal statute violations						
Youth Criminal Justice Act	11,957	35	11,619	34	−4	−44
Other federal statutes	20,767	61	21,344	62	2	0
Total	**32,724**	**96**	**32,963**	**96**	**0**	**−22**
Total – all violations	**2,379,667**	**6,973**	**2,277,258**	**6,604**	**−5**	**−21**

ʳ revised
1. Includes, for example, criminal negligence causing death.
2. Sexual offences against children is a relatively new crime category with only partial data available prior to 2010 therefore the per cent change from 2001 to 2011 is not shown.
3. Includes sexual interference, invitation to sexual touching, sexual exploitation, and luring a child via a computer. Excludes incidents of child pornography due to limited information on victim characteristics.
4. In 2010, a system anomaly resulted in some non-peace officer assaults being coded as peace officer assaults in 2010. Comparisons between 2010 and other years should be made with caution.
5. Includes trafficking and the intent to traffic stolen goods.
6. In 2011, the UCR survey was modified to create separate categories for possession of stolen property less than or equal to $5,000, and possession of stolen property over $5,000. As a result, incidents of possession under $5,000 may now be reported as secondary offences when occurring in conjunction with more serious offences, leading to a decrease in the number of possession of stolen property incidents reported in 2011.
7. Includes identity theft and identity fraud.
8. Includes altering, removing or destroying a vehicle identification number (VIN).
9. Due to incorrect reporting by a police service of incidents of child pornography from 2008 to 2011, the data originally contained in this report have been suppressed and revised data were made available on July 25, 2013 with the release of 2012 crime statistics.
10. Includes alcohol- and/or drug-impaired operation of a vehicle, alcohol- and/or drug-impaired operation of a vehicle causing death or bodily harm, failure or refusal to comply with testing for the presence of alcohol or drugs and failure or refusal to provide a breath or blood sample.
11. Includes precursors and equipment.

Note: Counts are based upon the most serious violation in the incident. One incident may involve multiple violations. Data for specific types of crime are available (in most cases) beginning in 1977. Rates are calculated on the basis of 100,000 population. Per cent change based on unrounded rates. Populations based upon July 1st estimates from Statistics Canada, Demography Division.

Source: Statistics Canada, Canadian Centre for Justice Statistics, Uniform Crime Reporting Survey.

an assault. In this scenario the event would be recorded and counted as an incident of assault, not as a break and enter and not as both offences. As a result of the MSO-scoring rule, less serious offences are undercounted by the aggregate survey. While the incident-based survey allows the recording of up to four violations per incident, thus permitting the identification of lesser offences, not all police detachments in Canada submit these data because of its phased implementation. However, as of 2008 these data are based upon information reported by police services covering 98 per cent of the population of Canada (Taylor-Butts, 2010).

Yearly counts of crime in Canada are reported both as *absolute numbers* and as rates. Data produced by the Canadian Centre for Justice Statistics are standardized on the basis of differences in populations across Canada. For instance, because the total population in Canada has been increasing steadily since 1962, any meaningful understanding of relative change over time in levels of crime must standardize these absolute numbers by calculating **crime rates**. Furthermore, provincial populations vary considerably in Canada, and rates allow us to compare relative differences in crime levels among Canada's 10 provinces and three territories. The way in which annual homicide rates are standardized is illustrated in the simple formula below:

Number of police-reported crimes × 100,000 ÷ population = Crime rate
Canada's population: 33,476,688

Using the homicide and population data above, the Canadian homicide rate for 2011 is:

598 homicides = 1.78 per 100,000 population

Not only does the UCR system illustrate the methods that government agencies, such as Statistics Canada, use to count behaviour that is defined as criminal, it is possible to examine levels of police-reported crime in Canada over time. Since all police departments across the nation are required to submit data to Ottawa, it is possible to compare crime rates between provinces, cities, and smaller municipalities. Table 2.2 shows a selection of crime incidents and rates for Census Metropolitan Areas (CMAs) in 2011.

Even though the way in which crime is defined and measured varies from country to country, it is possible to compare some forms of crime—most notably homicide—between different nations. Since homicide is—and has been for some time—defined similarly in Canada, the United States, and England and Wales, it is possible to compare homicide rates between these three countries over time. Homicide in Canada is considerably lower than in the United States, but rates in Canada are higher than they are in England and Wales.

Table 2.2 Police-Reported Crime Severity Index, Census Metropolitan Areas (CMAs), 2011

Census metropolitan area [1,2,3]	Population number	Total Crime Severity Index index	Total Crime Severity Index per cent change 2010 to 2011	Violent Crime Severity Index index	Violent Crime Severity Index per cent change 2010 to 2011	Non-violent Crime Severity Index index	Non-violent Crime Severity Index per cent change 2010 to 2011
Regina	222,125	124.5	−6	123.5	−18	124.9	0
Saskatoon	277,504	118.7	−8	134.5	−14	112.7	−5
Thunder Bay	119,999	107.3	−4	128.7	−8	99.1	−2
Winnipeg	767,277	107.2	−7	173.8	6	81.6	−16
Kelowna	182,239	97.4	−14	86.0	−11	101.8	−15
Vancouver	2,424,544	94.5	−7	98.3	−9	93.1	−6
St John's	188,653	93.3	−7	74.7	−16	100.5	−4
Brantford	140,267	92.2	−7	84.5	−10	95.2	−7
Edmonton	1,198,397	89.4	−13	105.9	−2	83.0	−18
Abbotsford–Mission	177,866	87.9	−11	72.4	−19	93.9	−9
Halifax	408,000	87.4	−9	111.7	6	78.1	−16
Montreal	3,924,554	80.9	−2	97.7	0	74.5	−3
Saint John	103,412	79.2	−14	91.3	−6	74.6	−17
London	499,637	79.0	−4	70.5	−5	82.3	−4
Greater Sudbury	162,892	78.9	−7	78.7	−8	79.0	−7
Victoria	362,264	71.3	−17	70.9	−15	71.4	−17
Saguenay	145,506	71.1	−3	55.2	−5	77.2	−2
Moncton	138,607	68.8	−5	68.2	−7	69.1	−4
Trois-Rivières	149,761	67.9	−3	46.2	4	76.3	−4
Calgary	1,270,927	65.8	−14	72.1	−11	63.4	−15
Hamilton	737,330	65.2	−8	75.8	−5	61.2	−9
Gatineau [4]	311,644	63.6	−8	68.1	14	61.8	−15
Kitchener–Cambridge–Waterloo	530,248	62.9	−7	69.5	0	60.4	−10
Windsor	331,284	62.5	−5	59.8	−7	63.5	−4
Peterborough	123,094	62.2	−8	60.2	−8	62.9	−8
Sherbrooke	190,154	60.7	−11	49.3	4	65.1	−14
St Catharines–Niagara	445,363	60.7	−13	48.0	−16	65.6	−13
Kingston	161,350	59.5	−5	48.1	−12	63.9	−3
Barrie	200,602	58.3	−3	49.2	−2	61.7	−3
Ottawa [5]	946,835	57.9	−5	63.9	−6	55.6	−4
Toronto	5,783,398	54.9	−5	84.7	−3	43.5	−6
Quebec	759,446	52.2	−6	46.8	−8	54.3	−6
Guelph	126,106	47.0	−7	48.2	8	46.5	−12
Canada	**34,482,779**	**77.6**	**−6**	**85.3**	**−4**	**74.7**	**−7**

1. A census metropolitan area (CMA) consists of one or more neighbouring municipalities situated around a major urban core. A CMA must have a total population of at least 100,000 of which 50,000 or more live in the urban core. To be included in the CMA, CMA adjacent municipalities must have a high degree of integration with the central urban area, as measured by commuting flows derived from census data. A CMA typically comprises more than one police service.
2. CMA populations have been adjusted to follow policing boundaries.
3. The Oshawa CMA is excluded from this table due to the incongruity between the police service jurisdictional boundaries and the CMA boundaries.
4. Gatineau refers to the Quebec part of the Ottawa–Gatineau CMA.
5. Ottawa refers to the Ontario part of the Ottawa–Gatineau CMA.

Note: Data on the crime severity indexes by census metropolitan area are available beginning in 1998.

Source: Statistics Canada, Canadian Centre for Justice Statistics, Uniform Crime Reporting Survey.

Despite the fact that official police statistics are widely available and easily accessible, especially since these data are available online from Statistics Canada, this source of information about crime has long been recognized as problematic if they are taken to represent an *accurate* and *true* count of crime in Canada. There are a number of important reasons why official police statistics should be treated with caution. First, most crime that comes to the attention of the police is *reported in the first instance by the public*. There are many reasons why many criminal events may not be reported to the police. Data from victimization surveys—information collected over the phone from households sampled and asked to report experiences associated with being victims of crime—tell us that many victims feel intimidated by those who have offended them, particularly if they know the offender personally. In these cases, the victims feel that reporting the incident to the police could jeopardize their personal safety. Scenarios such as this are particularly evident and noteworthy in cases involving intimates. For a number of good reasons, women in intimate relationships may not call the police for fear of retaliation. In fact, a call to the police may trigger an immediate physical assault. Also, recent research has shown that women who have experienced violence in the home from their partner may wish that the perpetrator could be removed from the household, but do not necessarily want the offender to be arrested and perhaps face incarceration. This has been shown particularly to be the case in situations where women are economically dependent on their abusers (Dobash and Dobash, 2003).

Box 2.1   ## Debates and Controversies

The Police-Reported Crime Severity Index (PRCSI)

Unhappy with the use of the crime rates as the standard measure of crime and violence in Canada, in collaboration with a group of criminologists and policy workers from the community, the Canadian Centre for Justice Statistics has recently developed a measure that takes into account the severity of crime. The **Police-Reported Crime Severity Index (PRCSI)** was introduced in 2009 and tracks changes in the severity of police-reported crime. Data from this new measure are contained in Table 2.2. According to Canada's federal statistical agency:

> In the PRCSI, each type of offence is assigned a weight derived from actual sentences handed down by courts in all provinces and territories. More serious crimes are assigned higher weights, less serious offences lower weights. As a result, when all crimes are included, more serious offences have a greater impact on changes in the index.

Source: Statistics Canada, 2009a.

Other times crimes are not reported to the police because the public feels that very little, or perhaps nothing, would be accomplished by having the police involved. Take, for example, a hypothetical case of bicycle theft. Bicycle theft, according to the *Criminal Code*, is "theft under $5000." Consider the scenario where an individual finds that her bicycle has been stolen and contemplates reporting the theft to the police. However, upon realizing that her home insurance deductible is set at $500, and the stolen bicycle is worth much less than this amount, there really is no point in making a claim and reporting the incident to the police—especially if there is little reason to hope that the bike would be recovered by the police.

Other reasons why the public fails to report illegalities to the police have to do with the fact that many people consider certain offences as trivial matters and would not likely report such behaviour to the police. Consider, for instance, a situation involving two young men who got into an argument and then started pushing and shoving each other. It would be unlikely that an event such as this would come to the attention of the police if neither individual was physically injured by the altercation. However, an incident like this one, according to the *Criminal Code*, would constitute a common assault.

It is also quite possible that many incidents that are defined as crimes occur but do not come to the attention of the police because a person may not realize that he or she has been a victim of a crime. For example, an individual may have given money at his or her home to a canvassing individual thought to be collecting for a legitimate charity. But, in actuality, the canvasser was an imposter and pocketed the donated money. Unless the activities of the dubious individual were brought to the victim's attention by the media, neighbours, or the police, there is little likelihood that the victim would have realized that he or she was duped by such a fraud.

Even crimes of a more serious nature may not be reported to the police if citizens feel that reporting such activity would cost time and money, or that reporting would not lead to an arrest or conviction. For that matter, and this has been substantiated in victimology research, in some instances the public may not report crimes to the police because they may fear or distrust the police or even the judicial system (Jones et al., 1986). All of the above examples serve to illustrate why crime may or may not be reported to the police.

The volume of crime a police force tallies and reports to the Canadian Centre for Justice Statistics may also be a function of the size and resources of the force. This is particularly evident for offences pertaining to prostitution or drug-dealing. Since these types of crime often require proactive policing, the resources that police departments commit to the enforcement of such activities can have a direct bearing on the amount of crime that makes its way into the record books. For example, a police department may be suspicious of certain activities taking place at so-called massage parlours located in the suburbs of a large metropolitan city. However, unless the police feel that there is a need to be proactive and rigorously enforce Canada's prostitution statutes—perhaps because of public complaints—there is a strong likelihood that these sorts of crime would not be subject to investigation or arrests. Similarly, since police exercise discretion while on the job, certain cases may be deemed less serious and may not be acted upon and, therefore, never make their way to Canada's annual statistical crime summaries.

The way in which crime is defined can also affect the official crime rate. Legal definitions of crime vary over time. Legislative changes in the wording of laws may cause new behaviours to be classified as "illegal," while at other times changes in legislation can eliminate behaviours from crime statistics. The rise during the mid-1980s in sexual offences provides an example. In 1983 Canadian rape laws were broadened to **sexual assault** laws. As a result of these legal changes, sexual assault referred to any form of sexual contact without voluntary consent. Beginning in 1983, the evidentiary requirement for penetration was also abolished and a wider array of sexually assaultive behaviours fell under the purview of criminal law. Acts such as kissing, fondling, vaginal intercourse, anal intercourse, and oral sex were defined as sexual assault if voluntary consent is not involved. Since the previous rape laws were not defined as broadly as the new sexual assault laws, and since levels of other forms of sexual assault were generally greater than levels of rape had been, the statistics showed that sexual crimes in Canada spiked dramatically over a one-year period from 1982–3. One needs to understand that because of these legislative changes the definition of the crime had changed, and the statistics from prior years were not strictly comparable with statistics following the legislation.

A more recent example of legislative changes leading to a reduction in official measures of crime can be seen with the repeal of the Young Offenders Act and the implementation of the **Youth Criminal Justice Act** (YCJA) in 2003. According to the Canadian Centre for Justice Statistics, there was a 20 per cent reduction in youth court cases over the period 2002–4. Between 1999 and 2002 there were 86,300 youth court cases on average annually in Canada, while in 2003 the number had declined to 70,465 (Carrington & Schulenberg, 2005). The substantial dip in numbers of youth going to court is not indicative of a change in behaviour among Canadians aged 12–17. In fact, there is good reason to believe that the substantial fall in the number of young Canadians appearing in court was caused by the 20 per cent of YCJA cases that received one of the new sentences (reprimand, intensive support and supervision, attendance centre order, or a deferred custody and supervision order) that were designed to keep first-time offenders away from the traditional court system (Moyer, 2005). In this situation, the law appears to be achieving its intentions of reducing crime. According to research by Bala et al., (2009) the Youth Criminal Justice Act has succeeded in significantly reducing the rates of use of court and custody without increasing police-recorded youth crime. These authors also note that there continues to be some regional variation in rates of use of youth courts and custody, as rates of youth court cases dropped the most in Ontario and Atlantic Canada but no change occurred in the Prairie provinces.

Even though police-reported crime statistics have been collected systematically in Canada since 1962, for the reasons mentioned above this information must be treated with extreme caution if this source is used as a barometer for measuring the incidence of crime in Canada.

Self-Report Surveys

Prior to the late 1950s, most empirical research in criminology relied on official records of the police, courts, or correctional institutions. Due in part to the described limitations imposed by these measures of crime, additional techniques have been developed. The best-known of these are self-report surveys. **Self-report surveys** are questionnaires that seek anonymous reports from respondents about offences they have committed over a selected period of time. The obvious intention of this technique is to capture information about crimes that may not have come to the attention of the police. In addition, these surveys normally seek information about the demographic characteristics of participants, such as age and gender profiles. Additional questions to these surveys are included so that explanations about the causes of crime can be tested or developed. The information gathered from crime surveys, therefore, is meant not only to describe the nature and extent of crime, but also to explain it.

Prior to the modern self-report survey, most information about crime relied on police or correctional institution statistics. Most of these data concluded that crime was primarily a lower-class phenomenon, engaged in mainly by young males. In fact, many well-known social psychological and sociological theories that attempt to explain crime—which will be introduced in Chapters 3 and 4—are grounded in data that were obtained by these types of official records. However, because we know that a considerable amount of behaviour defined as crime does not come to the attention of the police and, therefore, is excluded from the official statistics, one must ask about the extent to which these explanations are based on suitable information.

The use of self-report surveys can be traced to about the middle of the twentieth century. Porterfield (1943) conducted one of the first self-report surveys to appear in the criminological literature. This survey compared official juvenile court records of 2,049 delinquents in Texas, with nearly 350 self-reports from a sample of college students in the same state. Porterfield discovered that every college student admitted to having engaged in the same sorts of illegal activities as the delinquent group, yet few of the students had ever been charged by police. While researchers may have suspected that these disparities were taking place in America, it became evident not only that people were quite willing to report their indiscretions to researchers, but also that the idea of low socioeconomic status being tied to delinquency was disputable (Thornberry & Krohn, 2000).

The popularity of self-report surveys was further inspired by the work of Short and Nye (1958). In what is often taken to be a landmark study in this area, Short and Nye paid considerable attention to the methodological issues involved in the empirical study of juvenile delinquency, such as sampling, scale construction, reliability, and validity. Continuing Porterfield's focus on the relationship between delinquent behaviour and social status, Short and Nye failed to find any statistically significant relationship between crime and social class. These findings were important because, like Porterfield's, they challenged the conventional wisdom of the day that crime was somehow connected to low socioeconomic status. In fact, Short and Nye found relatively few differences between crime and the socioeconomic status of the adolescents' parents they surveyed. These results posed a significant challenge to the validity of police-reported crime and the statistics that they generated. Findings from this research on self-reporting also gave reason to question many of the causal theories of crime, particularly those that linked crime with poverty and material disadvantage. This new method of measuring crime gave reason to believe that the juvenile justice system, for example, may be using what criminologists refer to as "extralegal factors" in making decisions concerning youth who are targeted by police. In other words, these findings raised the possibility that the reason why lower-class individuals are overrepresented in police-reported crime had less to do with actual levels of criminality among them and more to do with issues pertaining to policing practices, including possibly discrimination as to who was policed.

To construct a valid and reliable self-report survey is no simple task and involves a number of important steps. One of the first considerations concerns the issue of sampling. Sampling is a process of systematically selecting units (i.e., people) from a population so that generalizations can be made about the larger population by studying the characteristics of a smaller group. A probability sample is most desirable in survey research. While there are several different types of probability samples, the simple random sample is the easiest to understand and is the one used as a model for other techniques. In simple random sampling, a researcher has a list of an entire population (e.g., all cases investigated by the Alberta Securities Commission from 1990–2005) and randomly selects elements from this group using a mathematical random procedure. This means that a researcher is able to study this smaller group and is able to make inferences to a larger one. A common question often asked in survey research is how large a sample should be. While statisticians have developed techniques and formulas to determine an appropriate sample size for a given population, a general rule is the larger the sample the better. A good example of a large self-report survey is the **Canadian General Social Survey** (GSS). This is a large population survey that has been ongoing in Canada since 1985. Over this time the GSS has surveyed

Canadians on a wide number of issues, including family and work life, education, use of information technology, and criminal victimization. More than 19,000 Canadians were interviewed in the 2009 General Social Survey.

It should be pointed out that, given the nature of the populations criminologists are interested in examining, it is not always possible to have a complete and accurate list of an entire group of people. For instance, researchers who work with homeless populations find it virtually impossible to draw simple random samples (e.g., Hagan & McCarthy, 1997). There are two fundamental reasons why this is the case. The first is a definitional matter: Who are homeless youth, for example? Definitions range from "those who sleep outside in places such as transit shelters and under bridges" to "persons residing in homeless shelters" to "those who move from place to place staying with relatives and friends" (a group sometimes referred to as "couch surfers"). While the circumstances and living conditions of these three groups vary considerably, different research has recognized each as constituting a homeless population. In short, since there is no simple, straightforward definition of "homelessness," the concept is difficult to measure.

Second, even if there were an agreed-on definition of homelessness, putting together a complete list of such a population would not be possible because homeless individuals do not have permanent addresses, nor do their names regularly appear on voter lists or in telephone directories—the sorts of lists that researchers often rely on to draw random samples of "conventional populations." For these reasons, researchers rely on other sampling techniques, such as snowball and quota samples, where no claims are made about statistical randomness.

For some time, self-report surveys have been the subject of some criticism, most of which pertain to issues of **reliability**—the extent to which a measurement procedure produces the same results on repeated trials—and of **validity**—the accuracy of a measure in relation to the concept that one is attempting to measure. The most obvious problem with these surveys is the fact that participants are not obliged or forced or coerced to tell the truth. Since it is standard practice in self-report research to guarantee subjects anonymity, there is no way a person's identity can be linked to their responses. Hence, there is also no way of safeguarding the truth. Consequently, it is possible that those who have committed a crime may not divulge such information on a self-survey. On the other hand, there is also the possibility of exaggeration, or of embellishing the amount of criminal activity in which one actually may have been involved.

Besides bald-faced deception, other forms of invalid data may be given unintentionally on self-report surveys. For instance, self-report crime surveys normally ask respondents to report criminal involvement (e.g., illegal drug use) over a specified period of time (e.g., one year). Because of memory loss or other reasons, respondents may offer inaccurate reports of their behaviour.

Some have been critical of self-report surveys because they neither ask questions about the more serious forms of crime (Hindelang et al., 1979) nor include many high-risk offenders among their respondents (Elliott & Ageton, 1980). This point is particularly evident in self-report research on youth and delinquency where data are collected only from samples of school-aged youth. As was mentioned earlier, much of this research has failed to reveal social class differences in levels of criminal behaviour. Instead, explanations for youthful offending have tended to rely on the personal bonds and attachments that these youth have with parents and other adult authority figures. The limitation of this research and of the theory that has been generated from it is its basis on samples that often exclude youth who were absent from class on the day when a survey was administered. Besides missing information from youth who are inclined to skip school, these classroom surveys also omit students who either have been expelled or have left school altogether. In fact, in Canada, 18 per cent of youth drop out of school—even though many return to school by the age of 24 (Bowlby & McMullen, 2002). In response to the problem of not having representative samples of youth in school-based surveys, researchers have gone to "the streets" to collect self-report data from samples of youth who do not attend school. This task has been undertaken mainly by studies that have focused on street-involved and homeless youth. Unlike their high school counterparts, street-involved youth are more likely to commit crimes, in addition to being involved in more serious offences (Hagan & McCarthy, 1997). Interestingly, this research has also shown that the reasons for this offending are not adequately explained by the sorts of factors that account for the more mundane deviant activities that are engaged in by youth who are captured in classroom surveys (Hagan & McCarthy, 1997; Gaetz & O'Grady, 2002; Tanner & Wortley, 2002). Factors related to economic, physical, and psychological deprivation must be included in explanations of why these marginal youth are involved in crime.

Even though self-report research has made concerted efforts to deal with sampling issues, another factor that must be attended to is that of deception. Ensuring that respondents tell the truth is difficult to safeguard, regardless of the composition of a sample. However, depending on how a survey is designed, it is possible to select responses of participants who may not be telling the truth. For example, a self-report study that examined the use of sexually explicit material among a sample of Canadian university students found that a small number of respondents reported accessing sexually explicit material in excess of the total hours that they claimed to spend online per week. Nineteen students from a total of 526 were dropped from the study because this discrepancy gave the researchers reason to believe that they had not taken the survey seriously or had not paid careful attention to the questions or to their answers (Byers et al., 2004). Researchers may take precautionary measures against deception by crafting their questionnaires to detect dishonesty and by engaging in careful analyses.

Because of the kinds of improvements that have been made to self-report research designs over the years, many analysts now rely on the self-report method as a tool to collect information about crime and other sorts of behaviour in the population. While critics are correct in pointing out the inherent problems with self-report surveys, research has shown that despite these limitations the tool can produce valid and reliable findings if careful consideration is given to issues of sampling and to the challenges inherent in deception (Thornberry & Krohn, 2000).

A good deal of self-report research has been undertaken in Canada. One of the best-respected and longest-standing studies in the self-report field is the biannual study carried out in Ontario by the Centre for Addiction and Mental Health (CAMH). Every two years since 1977, CAMH has carried out drug surveys using large samples of elementary and high school students in Ontario. The Ontario Student Drug Use Survey (OSDUS) is a population-based survey of Ontario students in Grades 7 to 12 and is the longest ongoing school survey in Canada. This self-report survey is conducted with the intention of identifying trends in student drug use. In more recent years, the survey has also asked questions about mental health (e.g., depression), physical activity, and such high-risk behaviours as violence and gambling. Normally, the OSDUS surveys about 6,000 students in more than 100 elementary and secondary schools across Ontario. Figures 2.1 and 2.2 show how patterns of student drug use in Ontario have changed from 1977 to 2011.

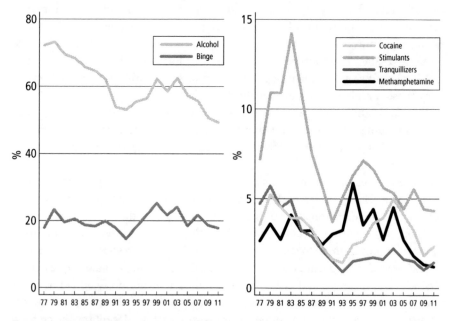

Figure 2.1 Long-Term Drug Use Trends, 1977–2011, Pattern 2
Source: Paglia-Boak et al., 2011.

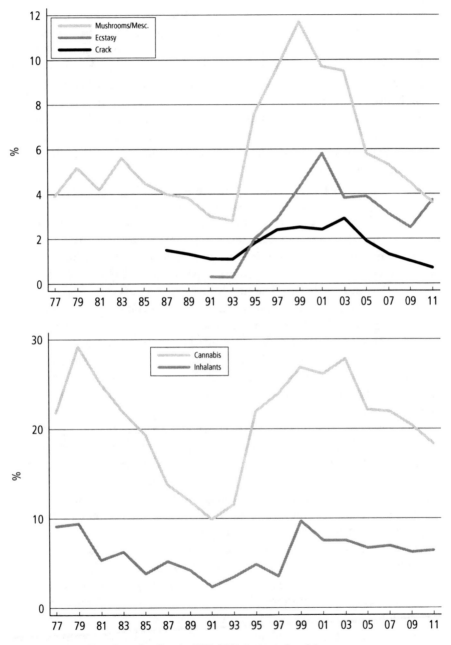

Figure 2.2 Long-Term Drug Use Trends, 1977–2011, Patterns 3 and 4
Source: Paglia-Boak et al., 2011.

Victimization Surveys

The most recent technique for measuring crime is the **victimization survey**. These instruments were developed first in the United States in the 1960s and were initially implemented in Canada in 1981 with the Canadian Urban Victimization Survey (CUVS). Since that time Statistics Canada has conducted national victimization surveys as part of the General Social Survey (GSS). These surveys differ from UCR data and self-report surveys in that they collect information on the victimization experiences of individuals, usually sampled at the household level. Over the years, crime victimization surveys have consistently revealed that a large number of crimes do take place that for various reasons do not come to the attention of the police. In fact, for many types of crime, these tools provide a much more accurate measure of criminal activities than do UCR data.

In 1981, the Canadian Urban Victimization Survey randomly sampled 60,000 Canadians over the age of 16 in seven major cities. Over the telephone, respondents were asked to recall any criminal victimization experiences they had experienced during the past calendar year. Participants were asked to report victimization experiences in the following areas: assault, sexual assault, break and enter, car theft, theft of personal property, theft of household property, robbery, and vandalism. The survey revealed that less than 42 per cent of personal and household criminal victimizations had come to the attention of the police in 1981. One of the most revealing findings of that early survey was that 62 per cent of sexual assaults go unreported in Canada. More recent Canadian victimization surveys have revealed similar results. For instance, the 2009 General Social Survey revealed that 31 per cent of criminal incidents came to the attention of the police, down from 34 per cent recorded in the previous 2004 survey (Statistics Canada, 2010).

Not only are respondents in victimization surveys asked to report their experiences of victimization and whether or not they reported it to the police but they are also asked to provide information about each incident, including why they may or may not have reported the incident to police, and how they were affected by the event. Demographic information, such as the age, sex, marital status, and the number of children living in the household, was also collected in the 1993, 1999, 2004, and 2009 surveys.

Because the GSS and the CUVS are carried out over the telephone, there is a finite amount of time that a respondent can be expected to be kept on the line speaking to an interviewer. As a result, these types of surveys are limited in terms of the number of questions respondents can reasonably be expected to answer. This is becoming increasingly problematic as most Canadian households are constantly being bombarded by irritating telephone calls from telemarketers and other telephone surveys; the Canadian public is becoming less tolerant of what are perceived to be invasions of time and privacy.

While large-scale national victimization surveys are useful for uncovering crimes that have not been reported to the police, they have been criticized because they are not able to focus specifically on those populations who may be the most vulnerable to crime. According to probability theory, every household in Canada with a landline telephone has an equal chance of being selected for participation in a victimization survey. The problem with this design is that these types of research instruments are unable to provide useful information about victimization in what are often described as "crime hot spots" where levels of victimization are well above the national average. Such hot spots often include communities where there is a high concentration of socially disadvantaged people. In fact, the 2004 GSS survey revealed that individuals who live in households with incomes of less than $15,000 per year are 1.5 times more likely to be a victim of a violent crime than individuals living in higher-income households (Gannon & Mihorean, 2005). However, because national surveys like the GSS are based on random probability samples, only a relatively small number of individuals from crime-prone communities are included in these national surveys. This provides a barrier to those who wish to get a stronger sense of the dynamics within these higher-risk communities. In recognition of this problem, research by Jones et al. (1986) carried out a local victimization survey in a high-crime neighbourhood in Britain. This survey found levels of victimization for some offences were far greater than national data provided by the British Crime Survey. Not only are local surveys useful in gaining information about levels of criminal victimization in particular communities and how these levels may differ from provincial or national averages, but their results also have implications for service provision in these communities, including the police, assaulted women's help lines and shelters, and other social service agencies.

A similar study has been carried out in Canada by DeKeseredy et al. (2003), who surveyed more than 325 people in a public housing community in eastern Ontario. The results of this local victimization survey showed that "public housing residents were much more likely to be victimized by most types of predatory crime than are members of the Canadian general population" (DeKeseredy et al., 2003, p. 44). For example, public housing residents were three times more likely than those surveyed in the GSS to report that someone broke in or attempted to break in to their residence. These results show that the more vulnerable people are socially and economically, the more likely they are to be harmed by predatory crime.

Another Canadian small-scale victimization survey carried out by Gaetz (2004) also focused on a marginalized population. In a study where 208 homeless youth (ages 15–24) were interviewed, Gaetz revealed findings similar to the study undertaken by DeKeseredy and colleagues. Examining six types of victimization, Gaetz found in almost every category that homeless youth reported more victimization than a sample of similarly aged youth who had been surveyed in the 1999 GSS. The GSS survey noted, for example, that 12 per cent of youth (ages 15–24) had been the victim of an assault in the past year; the corresponding figure for the group of homeless youth was 62 per cent. It should not come as a surprise that these two studies found that levels of criminal victimization are far greater among groups of people who face social and economic exclusion. This theme will be picked up and explored in more detail in Chapter 6.

Both national and smaller-scale victimization surveys face certain problems that are difficult to rectify. First, surveys such as these are dependent on the ability of respondents to accurately place their experiences of crime in the proper time frame. This problem may occur both in terms of placing certain events further back in time than they actually took place, as well as situating other events further ahead in time than they actually took place. Criminologists refer to this problem as "telescoping," which refers to a respondent's mistaken specification of when an experience of victimization occurred relative to the reference period specified by a researcher. While there are no proven safeguards to prevent respondents from making these kinds of mistakes, the problem can be minimized through a technique called "bounding." Bounding is achieved by comparing incidents reported in an interview with incidents reported in a previous interview and deleting duplicate incidents. However, for this technique to be successful, it is necessary to interview each respondent twice over a given period of time. Since this practice is expensive, in Canada the GSS interviews each respondent only once. In the United States, however, the National Crime Victimization Survey (NCVS) does practise this technique (NAJCD, n.d.). In that survey

each visit to a household is used to bound the next one by comparing reports in the current interview with those given six months prior. When a report appears to be a duplicate, the respondent is reminded of the earlier report and asked if the new report represents the incident previously mentioned or if it is different. The first interview at a household entering the sample is unbounded, and data collected at these interviews are not included in NCS and NCVS estimates. However, if a household in sample moves and another [respondent] moves into that address, the first interview with the replacement household is unbounded but is included in NCS and NCVS estimates.

Victimization surveys face other limitations. For obvious reasons, these surveys exclude data such as homicide. They are also unable to collect information about crimes where there are arguably no clear-cut offenders. This would include circumstances related to prostitution, drug use, and illegal gambling. Finally, for ethical reasons, victimization surveys normally stay clear of including those who are under the age of 15. For this reason, victimization surveys are unable to measure levels of crime that take place within many teenaged populations.

Observational Accounts

The fourth method criminologists use to study and sometimes even to measure crime are **observational accounts**. Here, the researcher actually interacts with individuals on a face-to-face basis in a natural setting to gather information about crime within the context where crime or victimization occur. However, unlike UCR data, self-report, and victimization techniques, observational accounts are not undertaken to gather information about crime so that estimates can be made about the volume or character of crime in the general population. These techniques are simply not applicable to the collection of this type of information. Observational research normally takes place on a relatively small scale so that a deeper understanding and appreciation of crime and victimization can be achieved. While there are some examples of research conducted from direct observation—where the activities of a group are observed but the presence of the researcher is unknown to the group (Humphries, 1970)—most observational research in the field of criminology takes the form of what is called "participant observation." Participant observation generally involves a researcher interacting with a group while observing their behaviour. This method is a research practice that was first developed by anthropologists. However, criminological research early in the twentieth century also relied on the ethnographic approach to study crime. Research on gangs in Chicago in the 1920s conducted by Thrasher (1927), for example, used observational methods to understand how gangs were organized and the social function that gangs served. In fact, recent studies of gangs continue to favour this research method because of the difficulties inherent in gathering information about criminal subcultures using police statistics or surveys. Examples of this recent research include studies of male gangs by Huff (2002) and of female gangs by Campbell (1990) and by Chesney-Lind and Hagedorn (1999). Today, the ethnographic approach is used in many social science disciplines focusing on a wide range of research topics.

Quite a few criminological observational studies have taken place in Canada. A study by Wolf (1991), for example, examined an outlaw biker gang in western Canada. The technique has also been used to study punk rock subcultures in British Columbia (Baron, 1989) and in Ontario (Dumas, 2003), and "squeegee kids" in Toronto (O'Grady & Bright, 2002). In addition, Visano (1987) studied male prostitutes in Toronto by interacting with them and observing the work of male street hustlers.

Participant observation also has been used to study the people who make and enforce our laws. While such a technique is less popular today, participant observers have examined policing practices by actually accompanying one or more police officers on patrol duty. One of the first studies of this kind carried out in the United States by Black and Reiss (1970) involved the policing of juveniles. Similar research has taken place in Canada by Ericson (1981, 1982) who observed detectives while they were on the job.

More recently, observation for research purposes of practitioners involved in other areas in the administration of justice in Canada has been undertaken using the ethnographic approach. One such study by Parnaby (2006) involves research on practitioners whose job is **Crime Prevention through Environmental Design** (CPTED). The basic premise behind CPTED is that proper design of the physical environment can be effective in preventing crime. Examples of CPTED practices would include the installation of lighting in outdoor areas that are frequented by women during hours of darkness. Not only did Parnaby observe the work of CPTED practitioners, but he fully immersed himself in that role by enrolling in and successfully completing the training required to become a certified CPTED practitioner. Other observational research in Canada by criminologists has studied the private security industry (Rigakos, 1999) and bylaw informant officers responsible for enforcing Ontario's Tobacco Control Act (O'Grady et al., 2000). Work such as this does not only focus on lawbreakers; it carefully examines the processes and structures that are involved in the enforcement of criminal laws and other regulatory practices in society.

The strengths of the observational method clearly relates to the issue of validity. According to Neuman et al. (2004, p. 406), "Validity in field research is the confidence placed in a researcher's analysis and data as accurately representing the social world in the field." Thus, if the researcher's description of the social world that he or she is examining corresponds to the world of its members, then the work is valid. Given that the field researcher is observing first-hand the events that take place within the natural setting, observational techniques are more valid than UCR data, self-report, or victimization surveys. Good ethnographic accounts produce information that is impossible to gather using the other techniques. For example, while a self-report survey may be a useful method for collecting information about how often a group of youth may have committed a set number of crimes over a specified period of time, surveys are not able to reveal very much about the details surrounding the contexts within which criminal activity takes place, or about the lifestyle of those who are involved in crime. Besides, ethnographic accounts are useful for collecting information from individuals in marginalized groups—like outlaw bikers—who would likely be suspicious of the motives of survey researchers. Gaining the acceptance from such a group can take time. And until a level of trust can be developed and nurtured between the researcher and participant(s), little useful information can be gleaned from the research experience.

As with the other methods criminologists use to study crime, observational research has some limitations. First, it is not a very useful technique if one wishes to make generalizations or inferences about the level and character of crime in a larger population. In other words, even data collected from a thorough and systematic investigation of the illegal activities of a motorcycle gang would be insufficient for making inferences about the activities of other biker gangs in Canada. To be sure, there would likely be a number of factors influencing the nature of gang activities of a biker gang in Quebec, for example, that may be different from biker gangs in western or Atlantic Canada. Another limitation with field research concerns the fact that the researcher may be putting him or herself in dangerous situations. Since criminological field researchers can find themselves interacting with groups and individuals who may engage in risky lifestyles, before researchers take to the field their projects must be granted ethical approval. Within the university environment, researchers must have work involving human subjects vetted by university research committees. Not only do ethical reviews demand that every possible step be taken to ensure the safety of researchers, but researchers must ensure that those who are the subjects of their research will also be protected as much as possible from any deleterious physical or psychological events.

There is no getting around the fact that no ideal method exists to measure crime. Depending on the questions that are being asked, and the definition of crime being used, criminologists must decide to use one or more methods systematically and effectively to study the wide lexicon of crime and criminal justice.

Is Crime in Canada on the Rise?

After reading the preceding discussion, we know it is not feasible to definitively answer whether crime in Canada is on the rise. This is especially the case if one is interested in tracking changes in all types of police-reported crime, or in types of crime collected by methods other than UCR statistics. This difficulty is due, of course, to the limitations associated with the four primary data sources that are used to measure crime in Canada that have just been reviewed. However, there are two ways in which changes over time in levels of certain types of crime in Canada can be systematically analyzed. The first is by using victimization data from GSS surveys. It is possible to determine whether or not there have been changes, over the short term, in certain types of crime, such as sexual assault, robbery, and physical assault. The second method of analysis, which is appropriate for longer-term trends, is to rely on UCR data, specifically, the statistics that measure homicide. In fact, these are the only data regarded by the criminological community as providing a satisfactory (albeit imperfect) means of addressing the question of whether or not changes in levels of serious violent crime have occurred in Canada since 1962.

Beginning with GSS victimization data displayed in Table 2.3, rates per 1,000 of population for the years 1999, 2004, and 2009 indicate small increases in sexual assault and robbery, while levels of physical assault have

Table 2.3 Self-Reported Violent Victimization by Offence, 1999, 2004, 2009

Year	Sexual assault number (thousands)	rate[1]	Robbery number (thousands)	rate[1]	Physical assault number (thousands)	rate[1]
1999	502	21	228	9*	1,961	81
2004	546	21	274	11	1,931	75
2009†	677	24	368	13	2,222	80

† reference category
* significantly different from reference category (p < 0.05)
1. Rates are calculated per 1,000 population age 15 years and older.

Note: Excludes data from the Northwest Territories, Yukon, and Nunavut, which will be published at a later date.

Source: Statistics Canada, General Social Survey, 1999, 2004 and 2009.

fluctuated. In terms of property victimization, Table 2.4 shows that household victimization has also fluctuated, but theft of personal property has steadily risen from 1999 to 2009. Since victimization surveys have been carried out for only a relatively short period of time in Canada and because they are limited by measuring only a few types of crime, another information source must be found to learn the extent to which crime in Canada—in particular lethally violent crime—has been changing.

Not only have homicide statistics been systematically collected in Canada since 1962, these data also are regarded for a number of reasons to be reasonably valid and reliable measures of deadly interpersonal violence. First, homicide is one type of violent behaviour that is very likely to come to the attention of the police; virtually all homicides are reported to the police, partly because dead bodies are difficult to conceal. Second, unlike other police-reported crime, officials collect considerably more information about homicide than about any other crime because homicide investigations are much more thorough and rigorous than most other criminal investigations.

Table 2.4 Self-Reported Victimization 1999, 2004, 2009

Year	Total violent victimization[1] number (thousands)	rate[3]	Total household victimization[2] number (thousands)	rate[4]	Theft of personal property number (thousands)	rate[3]
1999	2,691	111	2,656	218*	1,831	75*
2004	2,751	106	3,206	248	2,408	93*
2009†	3,267	118	3,184	237	2,981	108

† reference category
* significantly different from reference category (p < 0.05)
1. Total violent victimization includes: sexual assault, robbery, and physical assault.
2. Total household victimization includes: break and enter, motor vehicle theft/parts, theft of household property and vandalism.
3. Rates are calculated per 1,000 population age 15 years and older.
4. Rates are calculated per 1,000 households.

Note: Excludes data from the Northwest Territories, Yukon and Nunavut which will be published at a later date.

Source: Statistics Canada, General Social Survey, 1999, 2004 and 2009.

As a result, more information is collected on homicide by the Canadian Centre for Justice Statistics than on any other crime in Canada. Finally, because homicide is similarly defined in most countries around the world, it is possible to compare levels of homicide in Canada with levels of homicide reported in other countries.

The Criminal Code of Canada classifies **homicide** as first-degree murder, second-degree murder, manslaughter, or infanticide. In Canada, **first-degree murder** refers to homicide that is planned and deliberate. A person may also be convicted of first-degree murder if he or she is found guilty of killing an on-duty police officer or correctional officer. The final criterion for first-degree murder is a murder that is committed during the course of other criminal acts, such as hijacking, kidnapping, forcible confinement, and sexual assault. The definition of **second-degree murder** is straightforward: It refers to all murder that is not first-degree murder. Most often the issue that would shift a first-degree murder charge to a second-degree murder charge or conviction would be the lower degree of intent legally attached to second-degree murder.

The punishment for both first-degree and second-degree murder is life imprisonment. There are important differences, however, between these two types of murder convictions in regard to the possibility of release on parole. For those convicted of second-degree murder, it is possible for the parole boards to grant early supervised release of the prisoner after he or she has served a designated period of time behind bars. Today, in Canada, parole boards are permitted to grant parole to second-degree murderers after their having served 10 years of their sentence. However, for first-degree murder the convict must serve the full 25 years before being allowed the possibility of parole, but may apply for a judicial review after 15 years (Goff, 2004). Although a rare occurrence, the court may designate certain inmates "violent offenders." Doing so would mean there is a strong possibility the offender would remain in jail until his or her natural death. The notorious Canadian serial rapist and murderer Paul Bernardo was designated a dangerous offender in 1995 and will likely never be released from prison. Interestingly, in 2010 when Russell Williams, the Canadian Armed Forces colonel who was the commanding officer at CFB Trenton, was convicted of dozens of crimes, including two for first-degree murder, the Crown attorney in that case did not seek a dangerous offender status for Williams because he felt that ". . . it would be redundant" since the Crown's record against Williams was believed to be so strong that "the parole board will be satisfied that he will pose a danger for the rest of his life. A dangerous offender request is superfluous" according to Crown attorney Lee Burgess (CBC, 2010). Data from the Correctional Service of Canada indicated that there 486 inmates were designated as dangerous offenders as of April 2012.

A person guilty of **manslaughter** would have killed another human in the heat of passion or by sudden provocation. A person legally guilty of **infanticide** in Canada would be a female who by willful act or by omission causes the death of her newly born child. The child must be under the age of 12 months, and the mother must not have fully recovered from the effects of childbirth. Psychiatrists are usually given the responsibility of making this determination.

Punishments for convictions of manslaughter and infanticide normally involve shorter jail terms than convictions for murder. The maximum penalty for manslaughter is 25 years of imprisonment. However, those convicted by the courts of manslaughter are usually given sentences that are shorter than the maximum, and parole eligibility occurs after an offender serves one-third of his or her sentence. The median prison sentence/time served for men convicted of manslaughter in 1999–2000 was five years (Belanger, 2001, p. 16). Mothers convicted of infanticide are liable to imprisonment for a maximum of five years.

Before turning to an analysis of the trends and correlates of Canadian homicide, it is important to place homicide within the broader context of how violent crime is defined in Canada. While homicide is conventionally taken to represent the most serious form of violent crime in Canada, and elicits the most attention in the mass media, according to Figure 2.3, homicides and attempted murders represented 0.4 per cent of all violent crime in 2004. In fact, over 77 per cent of all violent crime in Canada that comes to the attention of the police involves assault—the vast majority of which are "Assault level 1," or common assault. Thus, while homicide is certainly the most serious violent crime in Canada and receives the largest spotlight in the mass

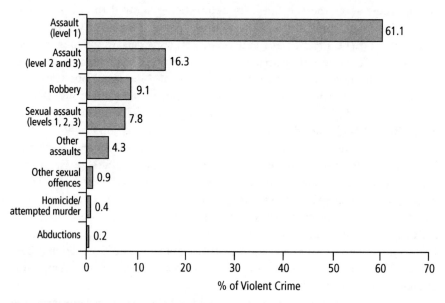

Figure 2.3 Categories of Violent Crime, 2004
Source: Statistics Canada

media, this offence represents a small fraction of all police-reported violence in the country (Gannon & Mihorean, 2005).

Trends and Correlates of Canadian Homicide

Homicide rates in Canada for the period 1981–2011 are presented in Figure 2.4. The overall trend in the Canadian homicide rate per 100,000 population has been one of slow but constant decline.

For the past several years the highest provincial homicide rates have been reported in Saskatchewan and Manitoba, followed by Alberta and British Columbia. Quebec's and Ontario's rates are below the national average, while the lowest rates are registered in Prince Edward Island and Newfoundland and Labrador. It is important not to overlook the fact that the homicide rates in Canada's three northern territories are higher than the rates in any province. The pattern whereby levels of homicide increase in Canada from east to west has been apparent for some time. Data showing these provincial differences in 2011 are displayed in Figure 2.5.

While several hypotheses have been generated by criminologists to explain this phenomenon, one reason that has been suggested for levels of homicide being higher in western Canada and in the North than is the case in other provinces (particularly in Manitoba and Saskatchewan) is the greater proportion of Aboriginal people who live in these areas of the country. Homicide is especially frequent on some First Nations reserves and communities that experience severe economic strain and cultural instability (LaPrairie, 1987).

rate per 100,000 population

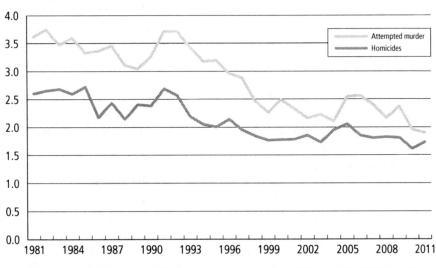

Figure 2.4 Attempted Murder and Homicide Rates Canada: 1981–2011, per 100,000 Population
Source: Statistics Canada, Canadian Centre for Justice Statistics, Uniform Crime Reporting Survey, 2011.

rate per 100,000 population

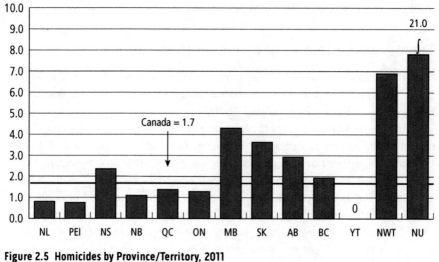

Figure 2.5 Homicides by Province/Territory, 2011
Source: Statistics Canada, Canadian Centre for Justice Statistics, Uniform Crime Reporting Survey.

Not only is there provincial variation in levels of homicide across Canada, but as is evident in Table 2.5, homicide rates vary considerably in Canada's Census Metropolitan Areas (CMAs). Consistent with patterns of provincial homicide rates identified in earlier, CMAs with populations over 500,000 in western Canada (e.g., Regina, Winnipeg, and Edmonton) have the greatest homicide rates in the country that were recorded between 2000 and 2009.

Table 2.6 on page 60 presents homicide rates from 2006–10 on the basis of the age and sex of homicide victims. The most notable pattern displayed is that males are more likely to be victims of homicide in Canada than are females. In fact, males were, on average over this five-year period, victims of 73.6 per cent of all homicides. Also evident in these figures is that there has been a rise in the total percentage of males who were victims of homicide: in 2006 males comprised 66 per cent of all victims while in the following four years males averaged 73.6 per cent of all victims. Table 2.6 also presents data for those who have been victims of homicide on the basis of age. For males, those aged 18–24 had the greatest number of homicide victims. For females, those in the 30–39 age groupings are where numbers are the highest.

The Canadian Centre for Justice Statistics also collects information on the numbers of homicides that involve firearms. While the overall rate of firearm homicides have fallen from 1979 to 2009, it is interesting to note that handgun homicides, as can be seen in Figure 2.6 on page 60, have generally risen over this 20-year period. Commencing in the early 1990s, handguns have consistently accounted for about two-thirds of all firearm-related homicides in Canada.

Table 2.5 Homicides by Census Metropolitan Areas (CMA), 2009–10

	2009		2010		2000 to 2009	
Census metropolitan area	number	rate[1]	number	rate[1]	average number	rate[1]
Thunder Bay	6	5.0	5	4.2	2	1.5
Saskatoon	6	2.3	10	3.7	7	2.8
Regina	4	1.9	8	3.7	7	3.7
Winnipeg	32	4.2	22	2.8	25	3.5
Halifax	12	3.0	11	2.7	7	1.9
Edmonton	30	2.6	32	2.7	32	3.0
Greater Sudbury	4	2.4	4	2.4	2	1.4
Abbotsford–Mission [2]	9	5.2	4	2.3	5	3.1
Moncton [3]	2	1.5	3	2.2	1	1.0
Saint John	0	0.0	2	1.9	1	0.8
Kingston [2]	4	2.5	3	1.9	3	1.7
London	3	0.6	9	1.8	6	1.2
Kelowna [3]	3	1.7	3	1.7	4	2.2
Hamilton	9	1.3	12	1.7	10	1.4
Peterborough [3]	1	0.8	2	1.6	1	0.6
Oshawa	3	0.8	6	1.5	3	0.8
Vancouver	61	2.6	36	1.5	54	2.5
Toronto	90	1.6	80	1.4	95	1.8
Victoria	3	0.9	5	1.4	4	1.3
Ottawa [4]	10	1.1	13	1.4	10	1.2
Montreal	44	1.2	49	1.3	59	1.6
Calgary	24	2.0	15	1.2	22	2.1
St John's	0	0.0	2	1.1	1	0.7
Barrie [3]	1	0.5	2	1.0	2	1.0
St Catharines–Niagara	5	1.1	4	0.9	6	1.4
Quebec	2	0.3	6	0.8	5	0.7
Kitchener–Cambridge–Waterloo	4	0.8	4	0.8	5	1.0
Brantford [3]	2	1.4	1	0.7	2	1.3
Sherbrooke	1	0.5	1	0.5	1	0.6
Gatineau [5]	2	0.7	1	0.3	3	1.2
Saguenay	5	3.5	0	0.0	2	1.0
Windsor	5	1.5	0	0.0	6	1.7
Trois-Rivières	3	2.0	0	0.0	2	1.1
Guelph [3]	1	0.8	0	0.0	1	0.8

1. Rates are calculated per 100,000 population.
2. Abbotsford–Mission and Kingston became census metropolitan areas (CMAs) in 2001. Average number and rate are calculated from 2001 to 2009.
3. Moncton, Kelowna, Peterborough, Barrie, Brantford, and Guelph became CMAs in 2006. Average number and rate are calculated from 2006 to 2009.
4. Ottawa refers to the Ontario part of the Ottawa–Gatineau CMA.
5. Gatineau refers to the Quebec part of the Ottawa–Gatineau CMA.

Source: Statistics Canada

Table 2.6 Victims of Homicide, by Age and Sex 2006–10					
Victims	**2006**	**2007**	**2008**	**2009**	**2010**
Males	444	431	465	450	400
0 to 11 years	16	13	17	21	21
12 to 17 years	12	23	22	30	20
18 to 24 years	110	119	128	122	89
25 to 29 years	69	60	67	61	64
30 to 39 years	91	78	73	83	62
40 to 49 years	70	62	86	63	67
50 to 59 years	39	39	37	39	47
60 years and over	36	37	35	31	30
Age not known	1	0	0	0	0
Females	162	163	146	160	152
0 to 11 years	16	11	12	13	9
12 to 17 years	16	8	8	12	11
18 to 24 years	24	22	20	17	21
25 to 29 years	16	16	21	16	20
30 to 39 years	32	33	22	38	24
40 to 49 years	23	36	28	27	31
50 to 59 years	20	18	16	17	12
60 years and over	14	19	19	20	24
Age not known	1	0	0	0	0

Note: Homicide includes Criminal Code offences of murder, manslaughter and infanticide.
Source: Statistics Canada

rate per 100,000 population

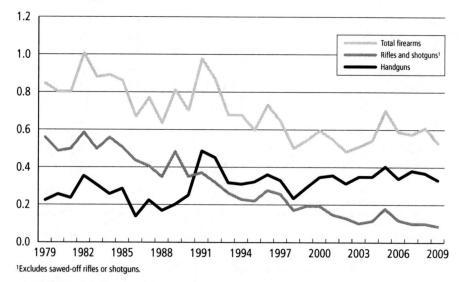

[1]Excludes sawed-off rifles or shotguns.

Figure 2.6 Firearm Related Homicides, 1979–2009
Sources: Statistics Canada, Canadian Centre for Justice Statistics, Homicide Survey.

Compared to many other industrialized nations, levels of homicide in Canada are quite high. For instance, the Canadian homicide rate is about three times the rate recorded in Japan. This may come as a surprise if, as is often the case, homicide rates in Canada are compared only with homicide rates in the United States—which are just under three times as high as they are in Canada. But when a wide range of other industrialized countries are used for comparison, as is shown in Figure 2.7 , homicide rates in Canada are by no means low. In fact, rates of homicide in economically developed countries such as Northern Ireland, France, Denmark, England and Wales, Australia, Sweden, Germany, Switzerland, Hong Kong, and Japan are all lower than rates recorded in Canada.

Conclusion

Compared to the media messages about crime that were presented in Chapter 1, the methods that criminologists rely on to study crime paint a different picture about the level and character of crime. Even though there are important limitations associated with UCR, self-report, victimization, and observational accounts, there is no getting around the fact that any intelligent explanation or discussion about crime—its causes or how best to react to crime—cannot

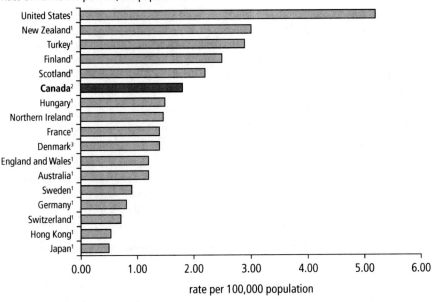

Rate of homicides per 100,000 population

1. Figures reflect 2008 data.
2. Figures reflect 2009 data.
3. Figures reflect 2007 data.

Figure 2.7 Homicide Rates for Selected Countries
Sources: Statistics Canada, Interpol Ottawa and National Statistical Office website.

be arrived at unless crime is defined and measured in a systematic, yet critical, fashion. Even for those who take the position that scientific knowledge has no more claim to the "truth" than taken-for-granted or common-sense understandings, such a viewpoint demands an awareness of the strengths and weaknesses of all forms of information. Only a broad and open-minded approach to the study of crime can foster the sort of intellectual climate that will be effective in confronting crime.

Critical Thinking Questions

1. What are the similarities and differences between UCR data and victimization surveys such as the General Social Survey?

2. Why is the crime severity index a more valid measure of crime severity than traditional UCR statistics that count different types of violent crime?

3. How would you respond to a friend who asked you to describe the level and character of homicide in Canada?

4. Why do you think crime rates in Canada are greatest in the West and in the North?

5. What reasons do you think explain why the homicide rate in Canada is greater than it is in many other economically developed societies?

Suggested Readings

Kaplan Bell, Elaine. (2013). "We live in the shadow": Inner-city kids tell their stories through photographs. Philadelphia, PA: Temple University Press. A unique qualitative study where the author gives cameras to a group of at-risk youth to show how they see life in a crime-ridden neighbourhood in South Central Los Angeles. This approach a good example of a recent observational methodology that was discussed in this chapter.

Kraska, Peter, and Lawrence Neuman. (2011). *Criminal justice and criminology research methods*, 2nd ed. Toronto, ON: Pearson. This comprehensive book explains, with relevant examples, the main methods used in criminal justice research.

Statistics Canada, *Juristat* series. This series of statistical reports deals with various dimensions of crime. The reports are regularly published by Statistics Canada and are available online through most Canadian university library collections. The *Juristat* series is written in a user-friendly and accessible manner. Excellent charts and graphs clarify the many patterns and trends within the field of crime and criminal justice in Canada.

Websites and Films

Statistics Canada
www.publicsafety.gc.ca/cnt/rsrcs/pblctns/2012-ccrs/#e3

This Statistics Canada website contains information on correctional services, courts, crimes and offences, legal aid, offenders, and police services in Canada.

Federal Bureau of Investigation

www.fbi.gov

>   The American Federal Bureau of Investigation website includes a special resource feature for students seeking information about crime in the United States.

The British Home Office

www.homeoffice.gov.uk

>   The British Home Office collects a wide range of statistics about crime in the United Kingdom, in addition to undertaking research projects that focus on crime, victims, security, drugs, immigration, and more.

CBC News: Counting Crime Statistics

www.cbc.ca/news/canada/counting-crime-in-canada-1.939285

>   This link provides a systematic examination of how crime is counted in Canada, placed within a political context.

The Man Who Studies Murder. (2003). National Film Board of Canada. This is an intriguing two-episode study of Elliott Leyton, a Canadian professor of anthropology who is an expert on murder, particularly serial murder.

3   Non-Sociological Explanations of Crime

Learning Objectives

After completing this chapter students will be able to:

◎   Appreciate the importance of Enlightenment thinking on crime and punishment.

◎   Understand the ideas proposed by the classical school of criminology.

◎   Recognize how criminality is understood according to biological explanations.

◎   Understand the logic of psychological models of crime and aggression.

Introduction

The aim of Chapter 3 is to introduce the reader to non-sociological explanations of crime. It begins with a brief discussion of pre-scientific accounts of crime, followed by an introduction to the classical school of thought, nineteenth-century biological accounts, and more recent individualistic explanations, including psychological social learning theory, ideas proposed by Sigmund Freud, and psychopathy. The chapter will conclude with a brief commentary addressing the types of questions about crime that individual accounts are unable to answer effectively.

Prior to presenting the major ideas of scientific criminology, it is important to consider briefly an explanation about crime that informed humankind for many centuries. In fact, most "scientific" ideas about crime encompass only a brief period of human history. Beginning with the demonic era and then moving on to the Enlightenment, this chapter will review how crime and criminals were understood in the Western world prior to the seventeenth century.

The Demonic Era

For thousands of years prior to the latter half of the 1600s, abnormal behaviour, including many forms of behaviour now called "criminal," were understood to be caused by demons, evil spirits, or simply by an indeterminate "force of evil." A mix of ideas, many of which were connected to religious doctrine, was used to account for the prevalence of crime. For instance, spirit possessions were seen to be a primary cause of much anti-social behaviour. Archaeologists have unearthed skeletal remains bearing indications that some early human societies believed "abnormal" behaviour could be eradicated by cranial surgery. Trepanation—holes drilled into the skull—of those who were thought to be in possession of these evil spirits was performed with the hope that the demons would be released and the inflicted soul would return to a "normal" state. However, given the primitive state of surgery during this period, it is unlikely many social deviants would have survived such torture. The notion of crime being caused by evil spirits is not an influence on public policy in Canada today.

Magna Carta

An understanding of the definitions of crime that criminologists work with today needs to consider definitions of criminal law in earlier periods. The **Magna Carta** is an important historical document because it is the foundation of modern laws and procedures in English law and in places such as Canada that were colonized by Britain. In 1215, British barons took advantage of King John's military defeats to demand that the king respect their traditional rights as landowners. Not only did the Magna Carta guarantee land rights to the barons, it also made guarantees under the law to freemen and protected religious rights and local customs. Four centuries later, in 1613, the impact of the Magna Carta became even more influential when it was interpreted by Edward Coke, an English chief justice, as the precedent that guaranteed individual rights and liberties to all British citizens. What this meant in practical terms for citizens relating to the judicial process was that a person could not be imprisoned or extradited by Britain unless he or she was lawfully judged to be guilty of an offence. The Magna Carta became, thus, the foundation of civil liberties in many countries around the world (Boyd, 1995).

Not long after, a powerful intellectual movement took place in Western Europe in the late 1600s and early 1700s. The Enlightenment marked a significant intellectual shift in Western European thought and had a direct impact on how crime came to be understood in society. During the Enlightenment (also known as the Age of Reason) changes were gradually built into the judiciary based on the ideas of certain philosophers. Notable among them, Thomas Hobbes (1651) wrote in his famous book *Leviathan* about a "natural state" of humanity where life in a pre-social state of nature was "nasty, brutish, and short." Hobbes argued that fear of violent death forces human beings into a **social contract** with each other that leads to the formation of the state. In Hobbes's view, the first principle of human behaviour is egoism, or self-interest, and this egoism is the root of all social conflict. The state, then, serves a protective function, but the trade-off for members of society is that they must give up their natural rights and give absolute authority to the state in return for its protection. Hobbes's implicit view of human nature is that without this social contract, chaos would be the order of the day (Dawe, 1978).

His theory is that if people were fully aware of their chances in states either with or without government, they would choose the state with a government as opposed to a state without one. This is because an individual is better off in a state where only the government can, in certain prescribed situations, legitimately exercise aggression. Even though Hobbes believed that it is *unnatural* for people to put themselves under the control of the state, it is *rational* for people to do so.

In 1690, another English philosopher, John Locke, challenged the conventional wisdom of the day that assumed people were born with a personality equipping them for the intellectual abilities required to navigate through life. Locke believed the natural human condition at birth was akin to a blank slate, on which social interaction and human experience wrote the principle contributions to the growth of the personality (Zeitlin, 1968). To update this notion using the metaphor of a personal computer, all children come into the world with a fully functional "operating system," one that equips the person to understand the basic concepts and ideas required to get through life. In essence, Locke was arguing that *nurture*, not *nature*, was the primary force that shaped the human personality.

Like Hobbes, Locke was concerned about the relationship between the individual and society. Through a social contract human beings compromise their natural state of freedom. But the compensation is that the state provides certain rights and protection to society's members. Thus, while the state does have power over the individual, the state is obligated to provide its citizenry with life, liberty, and health. This idea continues to inform modern ideas of citizenship.

The ideas proposed by Enlightenment philosophers are a natural point of departure for tracing the roots of criminological theory, for it was during this period that a belief in the scientific method and in rational thinking was being hailed as an alternative approach for understanding the social world. Superstitious beliefs and religious dogma became seen only as barriers to the truth.

It should be noted that within the parameters of Enlightenment thought no special attention was given to sex or gender as important to understanding the nature of crime. While it may have been recognized during this time that males were more likely to be involved in criminal behaviour than females, the classical school provided no gendered analysis of crime.

While there is no denying that the Enlightenment had a powerful effect in challenging existing superstitions about crime, this is not to say that pre-Enlightenment beliefs have been eliminated from society. Take, for example, the Catholic Church and its belief in the practice of exorcism. Even though cases involving exorcism do not necessarily focus on criminal behaviour, according to an article that recently appeared on the CBC the practice may be resurging, at least in western Canada, for dealing with certain forms of deviant behaviour (CBC News Online, 2012).

Despite the prevalence of a generalized sense of evil in the Western world at the dawn of the twenty-first century, the Enlightenment philosophy had a profound effect on eighteenth-century thinking about crime and criminality. The idea that people were self-determining entities was called rationalism: Free will and rational thought were deemed the basic building blocks of human activity and social organization.

Box 3.1 · Debates and Controversies

Exorcism

Even though exorcism is most often associated with pre-Enlightenment thinking, according to a CBC news report, the practice still takes place.

***

A case of what is being called possible demonic possession has prompted Catholic Church officials in Saskatchewan to consider the need for an exorcist.

CBC News spoke with a Catholic priest involved in the case, which arose in March, and agreed not to identify participants in order to protect their privacy.

According to church officials, a priest was called to a Saskatoon home by a woman who said her uncle showed signs of being possessed by the devil. The woman believed a priest's blessing could help the distraught man.

At the home, the priest encountered a shirtless middle-aged man, slouched on a couch and holding his head in his hands.

The man had used a sharp instrument to carve the word Hell on his chest.

When the priest entered the room, the man spoke in the third person, saying "He belongs to me. Get out of here," using a strange voice.

The priest told CBC News that he had never seen anything like this and was concerned enough to call police, for safety reasons.

He said he then blessed the man, saying he belonged to the good side, to Jesus. With that, the man's voice returned to normal for a short time.

Not a formal exorcism

The unusual voice returned when police arrived, and the priest continued to bless the man until he resumed a more normal composure.

CBC News followed up on the incident to learn if an exorcism had been performed, but church officials said a formal exorcism did not happen.

Bishop Don Bolen explained that the ritual of exorcism is a very structured exercise. He said it was not clear if the Saskatoon man was possessed or experiencing a mental breakdown.

"I would think there are perhaps more stories about exorcisms in Hollywood than there are on the ground," Bolen said. "But the Catholic Church

Continued

teaches that there is a force of darkness, and that God is stronger than that darkness."

Church leaders in Saskatoon have been considering whether Saskatoon needs a trained exorcist.

The last person in the city with formal training, Rev. Joseph Bisztyo, retired in 2003.

Nor does the Regina archdiocese have an exorcist, so Bolen said they are looking to other locations.

"We're kind of looking at what the diocese of Calgary does—they have a special commission for spiritual discernment," Bolen said.

He explained that the commission meets with people connected to a possible possession, "to ask whether there's some kind of psychological or psychiatric explanation to a situation," he said, adding the commission is also "open to the possibility of demonic possession."

Catholics are not the only ones examining what to do when presented with possible cases of possession.

The "work of the devil"

Anglican priest Colin Clay, who has worked with Bisztyo, told CBC News the topic of exorcism touches on questions that go back centuries.

The issues revolve around the nature of evil and how to respond to people who claim they have the devil in them.

"The churches have to respond," Clay said. "And they'll either do it by saying—some churches will say—'Well that's the devil, and the devil is at work in the world and we've got to deal with it,' or the churches will say, 'Well there's certainly evil in the world, whether there's an actual Satan or devil, there's certainly evil in the world, and it has a terrible effect on people's lives,' and so we've got to respond to it."

Clay said he does not dismiss how evil can affect people.

"I take evil very, very seriously," Clay said. "I take the effect that it has on people very seriously, but I don't think that there's any quick fix. The word exorcism worries me a little bit, because it's been given a Hollywood sort of flavour to it, and it's not as simple as that. You don't just say you've got the devil, I'm going to drive it out."

Like the bishop, Clay advocates a measured approach to dealing with claims of possession.

Source: CBC News Online, 2012.

The Classical School of Criminology

A preoccupation with the human capacity for rational thinking informed the writings of an Englishman, Jeremy Bentham, and an Italian, Cesare Beccaria, scholars who today are credited with forming what we look back to as the **classical school of criminology**. In 1764, Beccaria published *Essay in Crime and Punishment* where he argued for a philosophy of punishment diametrically opposed to the prevailing practice of the day, where criminals were punished based on the Old Testament of the Bible's basis of retribution, or "an eye for an eye." Beccaria believed that punishment should be formulated for the purpose of **deterrence**, that is, should be imposed in such a way that further offending would not be committed by offenders themselves or by others of like mind. Today, these ideas are known respectively as *individual* and *general deterrence*.

Beccaria believed that to achieve this goal the punishment of criminals should be swift and certain. The more promptly and closely punishment follows the commission of a crime, the more just and useful it will be. The logic of why the punishment should be certain and swift is once again based on the Enlightenment principle that human beings are rational thinkers. If it were known that a punishment would be imposed immediately following a criminal act, any rationally thinking person would simply refrain from committing that crime.

Beccaria furthered his analysis of crime by suggesting that the punishment issued by the state should be only severe enough to outweigh the personal benefits derived from the commission of the crime, and that additional punishment would be unnecessary. In short, the punishment should fit the crime.

At the time, not only were Beccaria's ideas regarded to be progressive, they had wide impact. Features of this reasoning can be seen, for example, in the American Constitution, the penal codes of France, and pre-revolutionary Russia (Laqueur, 2000). His ideas about jury selection also resonate with contemporary practice. Over 200 years ago, Beccaria argued that efficient and fair juries should be made up of an equal combination of those who knew the victim and those who knew the accused. The idea of using juries sensitive to both the victim and the offender is a key component of restorative justice, a recent model of doing justice that seeks to bring more community involvement into court and sentencing processes.

Finally, Beccaria is best known for systematically expostulating his conviction that criminals are rational, free-willed decision makers who choose to commit crimes, yet who can be deterred by the threat of punishment. Indeed, it would be fair to say that this logic is the primary tenet of Canada's criminal justice system and also underlies popular beliefs about the causes of most types of crime.

The classical school of criminology also has its roots in the utilitarian movement spurred by the works of Jeremy Bentham, in particular. Simply put, **utilitarianism** is the belief that reason requires decisions to be made according to what will procure the greatest good for the greatest number. Born in 1748, Bentham is best known for *An Introduction to the Principles of Morals and Legislation*. Utilitarian thought takes it as given that humans are rational actors. Consistent with other classical thinkers, Bentham believed society is, or should be, based on a social contract whereby liberties are exchanged freedoms—an idea proposed by Hobbes. Within this social contract, all of society's members are free-willed decision makers. For Bentham, in order for punishments to be effective in the prevention of crime they need to be severe, certain, and swiftly applied. Of these three, Bentham argued that certainty was the most important. Thus, if a person contemplating a crime were sure of being caught and punished, then the crime would not be committed—a concept we have already mentioned is known today as general deterrence.

Bentham also believed that punishment could serve the function of individual deterrence, whereby a criminal who was punished would not recidivate, or commit a further offence. Finally, according to Bentham's view (and a topic that continues to receive attention today), judges should not have the power to exercise complete discretion in passing a sentence; sentences should be about equal to the crime—an idea also known as determinant sentencing. In practice, this would ensure a person convicted of an armed robbery in a St John's, Newfoundland, court would be given a sentence very similar to an individual convicted of the same crime in a Victoria, British Columbia, court.

To understand the appeal of Enlightenment thought, such thinking needs to be placed within the context of the period. In eighteenth-century Europe, by Canadian standards today, punishments issued to offenders were undertaken in an arbitrary and barbarous fashion. It was a common practice for autocratic ruling elites to punish offenders in public places where large numbers of people would gather to witness the hangings, floggings, or beheadings. For example, one of the last public executions that took place in France involved the dismemberment of Robert-François Damiens for the attempted assassination of King Louis XV in 1757. Damiens was tortured first with red-hot pincers; his hand, holding the knife used in the attempted assassination, was burned using sulphur, molten wax, lead, and boiling oil. Horses were then harnessed to his arms and legs for his dismemberment. Damiens's limbs and ligaments did not separate easily; after some hours, representatives of the Parliament ordered the executioner and his aides to cut Damiens's joints. Damiens was then dismembered, to the applause of the crowd. His trunk, apparently still living, was then burnt at the stake. Proceedings such as these were not abolished in France until 1772 (Maestro, 1976).

As France and the rest of Europe moved into the industrial and urban era of the eighteenth century, it still held to its medieval penal practices. Moreover, not long before the French Revolution of 1789, poverty and starvation were increasing among the people. In order to secure protection from growing numbers of desperate citizens, the upper classes continued to employ ruthless oppression on those who challenged their authority. As social unrest and crime grew, so did barbaric penal responses. By the middle of the 1700s social reformers had come to take note of this state of social turmoil and began to think of alternatives for shaping the social order.

Such were the conditions and context that shaped the thinking of Bentham and Beccaria. Not only did these conditions give rise to new ways of thinking about crime, they also stimulated practical reaction to the treatment of offenders. For example, in direct response to the squalid conditions that existed in European prisons, John Howard made it his goal to reform the prison system and make it more humane. Between 1775 and 1790 Howard made several trips across Western Europe in search of a more humane prison system. Almost a century later the **John Howard Society** was formed, dedicated to the humane treatment of prisoners. Today, in Canada, the John Howard Society is active in all of Canada's 10 provinces and in the Northwest Territories (John Howard Society of Canada, 2010).

The classical school of reformist thought also influenced the development of the asylum, which, at the time, was a slightly more humane way to treat the mentally ill. In Europe during the Middle Ages the mentally ill were outcasts and were often left to roam from town to town. They were basically left to "God's device." But with the rise of industrial capitalism the "insane" were herded together and incarcerated along with criminals, the destitute, and other undesired persons. Under the influence of Enlightenment philosophical assumptions, the mentally ill were "liberated" and were placed, at first, in small institutions and treated according to the principles of "moral treatment." This marked a move toward "normalization"; that is, treating mentally disordered people as capable of rational thinking, rather than just as bodies with illnesses or as people with minds possessed by demons. In England these initiatives were spearheaded by William Tuke, and in France by Philippe Pinel (Porter, 1989).

However influential it may be, the classical school of thinking has been the object of criticism. According to Taylor et al. (1973), a classical system of justice can operate only in a society where property is distributed equally. For example, if the poor steal from the rich because they are poor, then punishment involving the removal of the criminal's property can only worsen the problem in the long run (Taylor et al., 1973, p. 6).

Another quandary produced by classical reasoning pertains to the idea of criminal responsibility. Is it truly the case that all men (no distinction was made for women by classical theorists) are rational actors with an equal ability to exhibit free will (ibid, p. 8)? Are all criminals equally responsible for their actions because "all crime is committed by free-willed actors"? Can consideration be given in classical thought for what might be described as "mitigating circumstances" or for situations that could be associated with individual differences or social environment? In other words, utilitarian analysis does not pay heed to the possibility that biological, psychological, or sociological factors could play a role in explaining criminal behaviour.

As a response to such objections, a body of thought known as neoclassicism emerged that does consider, to some extent, the physical and social

Debates and Controversies

John Howard Society

Prison reformer, John Howard, among prisoners
Source: Photos.com/Thinkstock

While the Federal Government put into legislation the Safe Streets and Communities Act in March of 2012 as part of their electoral mandate to "get tough on crime," there are many organizations around the world which use the name John Howard as an alternative to punitive crime measures. According to the John Howard Society of Ontario:

> Most of them are associated with correctional reform and/or services to help offenders make positive changes in their lives. Although the organizations outside of Canada are not formally aligned, they share a common purpose and philosophy which reflects the life and work of the man John Howard.

In Ontario, The John Howard Society traces its roots back to religious classes taught in Toronto's Don Jail in the late 1800s. In a more formal way, the organization was founded in 1929 by Brigadier General Draper, then the Chief of Police in Toronto. Draper recognized the futility in much of the work being done by police, trying to solve crimes and apprehend offenders, when prisoners who were being released from jail were thrust into circumstances of unemployment, isolation and poverty—circumstances that escalate rather than decrease the chances of re-offending.

Source: www.johnhoward.on.ca/about/index.html

environment in which crime takes place (e.g., Wilson, 1985). Some allowance can be given to the offender's past record. For example, a career criminal's actions could be determined by external circumstances much more so than a first-time offender. Children are also deemed less capable of making accountable decisions than adults. Finally, what about issues of incompetence or mental illness where premeditation is not a factor in the commission of a crime? These considerations are recognized by the neoclassical approach in the sense that they could modify the ability of the individual to exercise his or her free will.

The contribution of the classical school of thought to how criminal justice systems operate today has been enormous and is the dominant model of human behaviour subscribed to by criminal justice systems around the world. Despite consideration being given to factors such as age (in Canada, the Youth Criminal Justice Act) and criminal insanity (not guilty by reason of insanity) in determining culpability, the notion of human volition remains paramount in terms of understanding what causes and what prevents crime, and this notion continues to be very important in shaping public policies about crime today.

From Lombrosian Atavism to Modern Biocriminology

During the nineteenth century a shift was taking place in Europe that challenged the view of humans as rational beings who are fully aware of the causes and consequences of their actions. The new perspective emerging conceived human behaviour to be determined by forces beyond the control of the individual. While these forces were not thought to be a generalized form of evil as had characterized thinking in the Middle Ages, crime nevertheless was behaviour that could not be prevented by sheer willpower or moral training. Adhering to methods employed in the physical and biological sciences, the positivist school of thought distanced itself from classical thinking primarily because the latter was considered unscientific for being based on unsystematic obser-vation. The positivist school was a reaction to the non-empirical way of think-ing that characterized moral philosophers like Beccaria and Bentham. Nowhere in the works of these classical philosophers were there any system-atic *data* that could *prove* that a *causal* relationship existed between crime and hedonism and that all (or most) human behaviour is guided by free will.

The positivist school believed in the unity of the scientific method. They believed that the method scientists use to study the physical world—whether through chemistry, physics, or biology—could be employed to understand the social world. The goal of science is to predict how events occur in uniform pat-terns, whether it be crime or the properties of physical matter. Positivism is the application of the scientific method to the study of the human condition.

In early positivist thinking the causes of crime were rooted in human biol-ogy; the work of Charles Darwin was influential in this direction. Context no doubt affected the early development of biological criminology, and Darwin's belief in the theory of natural selection was essential to **positivist criminol-ogy**. In his famous book *On the Origin of Species* (1859), Darwin developed a theory whereby human development was understood to be the result of evo-lutionary change. This theory proposes that evolution occurs because those individuals of a species whose characteristics best fit them for survival are also the ones that are most likely to procreate. Their offspring will tend to have the adaptive characteristics inherited by their parents; therefore, the species is constantly adapting to the environment and improving from one generation to the next. Indeed, it is generally accepted that natural selection acts to elim-inate mutations that are non-adaptive. This, for Darwin, is the primary cause of evolution.

Cesare Lombroso is recognized as the best-known early practitioner of biological positivism. Lombroso is particularly noteworthy for his contention that criminals were biological throwbacks, or "atavists." To place Lombroso in context, he was an Italian medical doctor who was writing at a time when Darwinism was gaining recognition. The influence of **social Darwinism** is clearly found in Lombroso's claim that the causes of criminal behaviour are rooted in biological makeup, and that those individuals who display visible primitive, ape-like characteristics are specifically predisposed to crime. Thus, the notion of atavism was introduced to criminological thinking. A clearly articulated statement of just what these atavistic characteristics were com-prised of can be found in Lombroso's book *Criminal Man* (1861). Criminals, according to Lombroso, are quite distinct from non-criminals. Compared to non-criminals, criminals have a small and sloping forehead with large and protruding ears. Criminals are also likely to have protuberances (bumps) on the head. Other indicators included large eye sockets, beady eyes, a strong jaw, bushy eyebrows, tattoos, and high cheekbones. For Lombroso, since criminals could be identified on the basis of these physiological characteristics, criminals were *born*, not *made*.

You may wonder how Lombroso came up with such a theory. The answer rests in the method Lombroso used to collect his evidence. While the classical school's ideas were based on a moral philosophy and not subject to systematic empirical observation or testing, Lombroso went to some lengths to collect data to support his theory that crime is caused by certain biological characteristics. Based on a crude experiment where he compared criminals in prison with a control group of Italian soldiers, he found significant differences in the incidence of these atavistic characteristics between the two groups. In other words, the incarcerated sample (experimental group) was more inclined to have beady eyes, sloping foreheads, and so on, while the soldiers (control group) were not. Lombroso came to the conclusion that criminals were atavists. Thus, the atavistic criminal was introduced to criminology; criminals were deemed to be lower on the evolutionary scale than non-criminals.

While Lombroso's theory of atavism is most often regarded as his major work, his theory pertaining to female criminality is equally interesting but often overlooked. Lombroso published a book with Ferrero, *The Female Criminal* (1895; trans. as *Criminal Woman*, Rafter and Gibson, 2004), in which the authors attempted to explain the lower incidence of female crime and why a small number of women were criminals. They argued that women criminals are essentially "super males." The female-born criminal was perceived to have the criminal qualities of men plus the worst characteristics of women. These traits included deceitfulness, cunning, and spite, among others—traits that supposedly were not apparent among males. Criminal women were said to be genetically more male-like than they were female, and thus were considered to be biologically abnormal. Lombroso characterized short, dark-haired women with moles and masculine features as good candidates for crime.

There are several problems with Lombroso's theory, many of which were pointed out not long after it was first published. For example, Goring (1913) noted that the statistical techniques Lombroso used were inadequate. This means that the differences in bodily characteristics that he thought existed between those he observed in the prison population and those found in the military control group could have happened randomly, that is, by chance. Second, advancements in genetic studies have ruled out the possibility of the existence of evolutionary throwbacks: The state of atavism simply does not exist. Third, there is a good possibility that many of the physical attributes that Lombroso found in the inmates he observed were caused by their being incarcerated in nineteenth-century Italian prisons. Inadequate nutrition and poor hygiene could have had an impact on the physical attributes of these inmates. Finally, as Taylor et al. (1973) pointed out and what remains the case today,

Debates and Controversies

The Legacy of Lombroso

The Museum of Criminal Anthropology, located in Turin, Italy, opened in the late-nineteenth century in the heyday of biological positivism. The museum, created by Lombroso, was once only open to the scientific community. Today it is open to public viewing. The museum contains an extensive collection of criminal artifacts, including a cabinet of preserved brains of criminals, as shown below. While the study of criminology for much of the twentieth century was predominantly dismissive of the ideas proposed by Lombroso, his legacy has remained strong because much of the public continues to be intrigued by the idea that physical characteristics can distinguish "criminals" from "non-criminals."

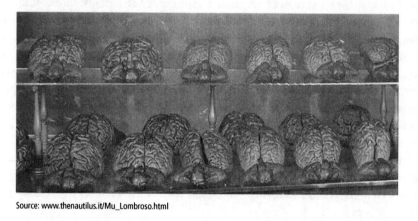

Source: www.thenautilus.it/Mu_Lombroso.html

no well-accepted studies have effectively explained variation in crime rates on the basis of biological variation alone.

Despite these criticisms, the idea that crime has a purely biological basis has resurfaced in well-known research by psychologist Phillippe Rushton (1995). While not explicitly formulating a theory of atavism, Rushton has proposed a theory accounting for racial differences in crime that is in keeping with Lombrosian logic. In his book *Race, Evolution and Behaviour* (1995), Rushton argues that blacks are much more prone to be violent, oversexed (because, according to Rushton, they have larger genitalia!), athletic, and less intelligent than the other races. Asians are prone to be more intelligent, undersexed, less violent, and less athletic than other races. Whites are more likely to be at a midpoint between blacks and Asians. Reasons for these differences are largely accounted for in differences in IQ between these three racial groupings, which is a direct function of differences in brain size. In evolutionary terms, using many different measures, blacks are at the bottom, whites are in the middle, while Asians are at the top.

However, like Lombroso's early biological formulations, Rushton's work is subject to significant criticism. First, simply categorizing racial groups into three categories (white, black, and Asian) is problematic because, according to theory and research in the anthropology of race, racial categories are rooted in history and have evolved culturally through laws, the media, and other social institutions (Graves, 2004). In other words, racial groupings are not "facts" that can be differentiated purely on the basis of biological characteristics. Second, crime rates vary *within* racial groups (Gabor & Roberts, 1990). As a result of such *intraracial* variation in crime, Rushton's contention that crime can be understood on the basis of race and evolutionary development is misguided.

Other research emerged over the course of the twentieth century that further developed the idea that criminality was associated with a particular set of body characteristics. William Sheldon (1940), for instance, developed a typology that differentiated three different body shapes with distinctive temperaments. First, there is the ectomorph. These are individuals who are thin, fragile, and imagined to be shy and introverted—not the kind of person who would be involved in crime. The second type, the endomorph, was characterized by Sheldon as being slow and comfort-loving, having a soft and round appearance. According to Sheldon, people with this body type also were not predisposed to crime. The mesomorph, however, with a hard, muscular body type and an active and aggressive personality, is prone to crime. Sheldon believed that bad blood or "germ plasm" that spread through breeding was responsible for such criminal body types.

The similarities between Sheldon's mesomorph and Lombroso's atavist are striking. Criminals are depicted by both as born with criminogenic traits. Like Lombrosian atavism, Sheldon's criminal typology has been subjected to academic scrutiny and the claim that body types determine crime is weak. First of all, Sheldon's criminal populations were inmates, most of whom were working-class males convicted of street crimes. This being the case, there is a strong possibility, as Gibbons (1968) has suggested, that delinquent subcultures are unlikely to recruit new members who are either fragile or obese. Rather, a premium is placed on agility and strength. This, of course, would suggest that admission to delinquent subcultures is dependent on body appearance that would be described as fitting the mesomorph typology. Another question emerging from this body of thought pertains to the definition of crime. For example, is the mesomorphic body type associated with white-collar or corporate crime? If the body types of the business executives (male or female) who have been accused of or sentenced to prison in the

United States for committing accounting fraud or obstructing justice are any indication, then Sheldon's model is clearly false.

While the work of Lombroso has been credited for its influence on many biological explanations of crime over the course of the twentieth century, an interesting and controversial field of research that is also linked to the ideas of Lombroso is that of sociobiology and the contemporary field of evolutionary psychology. **Sociobiological** explanations of crime suggest that human behaviour can be explained according to evolutionary principles. This body of thought claims that certain individuals have a predisposition towards criminality.

A version of this approach was put forward in the writings of Edward O. Wilson in *Sociobiology: The New Synthesis* (1975) and his more recent work, *Consilience: The Unity of Knowledge* (1998). The basic premise that forms the backdrop of Wilson's work can be boiled down to the idea that the primary determinant of human behaviour is the need to ensure the survival and continuity of genetic material from one generation to the next. An important aspect of this continued survival is territoriality. The "social" aspect of this theory holds the view that society acts as a civilizing, or controlling, force upon individuals. However, when human beings are placed in predicaments where their territory, or "turf," is challenged, then the civilizing forces of society can give way to aggression and violence. Seen in this way, the violence associated with street gangs would be a good example of the aggressiveness associated with territoriality.

Wilson, however, does not limit his analysis to violence that takes place between groups. His analysis also claims to explain violence that occurs within groups like the family. In fact, Wilson's analysis has informed the work of two Canadian evolutionary psychologists, Martin Daly and Margo Wilson. In a study of **domestic violence**, Daly, Singh, and Wilson (1993) found that stepchildren are at a significantly higher risk of being killed by adoptive parents than are children who live with their biological parents. The reasons for these differences were attributed to the notion that, because of evolutionary mechanisms, humans tend to act in a manner that ensures the continuance of their genetic material. Because killing biological offspring would jeopardize this genetic prolongation, biological parents are less prone to killing their children than are non-biological parents.

A more recent attempt to merge evolutionary principles with some social science to explain human behaviour can be found in the work of Pinker (2011). In the book *The Better Angels of our Nature: Why Violence has Declined*, a case is made that a variety of evolutionary forces are responsible for the declines that have taken place in levels of violence in Western societies. The modern era is less violent, less cruel, and more peaceful than any previous period of human history, contends Pinker. This decline in mayhem applies to many different types of violence, including: family violence; violence in communities; between tribes and between nation-states. People living today are less likely to die violently, or to suffer from violence or cruelty at the hands of others, than people living in any previous century. Pinker argues that declining levels of violence have been largely the result of evolution having re-shaped the basic design of the human brain, and hence our cognitive and emotional faculties. This biologically driven civilizing process has led, over time, to a more a more reasonable and responsible populace which has therefore created better governments, economic prosperity, an improvement in the status of women, gay and civil rights—all of which have made Western societies less violent. While this thesis has been prone to some important criticisms (Whitehead, 2011), it is a good example of how evolutionary thinking has been used to explain violence.

Chromosomal abnormalities have also been linked to criminal behaviour. The possession of an extra Y chromosome, although rare, is considered by some researchers to cause abnormal and uncontrollable aggressiveness in "super males." The normal chromosomal structure for males is XY, and for females a normal configuration is XX. To support the argument that an extra Y chromosome was a cause of criminal violence, some research revealed that a disproportionate number of XYY males were found within prison populations (Jacobs et al., 1965). As a result of this research the XYY defence was attempted in five court cases in the United States—an effort parallel to the McNaughton ruling in Canada of not being guilty by reason of insanity. However, in no case did the XYY defence succeed. In fact, with few exceptions, criminal courts and judges have been reluctant to trade their ideas regarding moral responsibility and culpability for biological, psychological, or sociological explanations of criminal behaviour (Rose, 2000). In fact, not long after these theories were proposed, flaws in this explanation of crime were revealed. For instance, even though those with XYY chromosome compositions may be more likely to be found within prison populations, the fact remains that over 95 per cent of prison inmates are of the XY type. In 1976, a paper was published which concluded that XYY males were more likely to be imprisoned, but that this was due to their low intelligence and low socioeconomic status, which placed them at higher risk of being caught (Witkin et al., 1976). Furthermore, when closer attention is given to the types of crimes that XYY males have committed, research has revealed that correlations exist only between "super males" and property crime, not crimes of violence (Saulitis, 1979).

In more recent years, abnormalities in levels of serotonin—a neural transmitter—in spinal fluid has been linked to offenders who have committed violent crimes. For example, research by Unis et al. (1997) found a link between abnormal levels of serotonin in adolescents and conduct disorders. Recent research in genetics has found that young men who carry a particular variation of the enzyme monoamine oxidase (MAO) are more likely to join gangs and use weapons in fights. Using data collected in the United States, Beaver et al. (2009) found that male gang members who carried low MAO levels were 4.37 times more likely to use a weapon than gang members who carried high MAO levels. Although the authors of the study were unable to identify the precise mechanisms that link low MAO to gang membership, they did suggest that male carriers of low MAO are attracted to violence and thus seek to join gangs. It was also suggested that violent adolescents are more likely to be recruited to join gangs.

In a review of this type of research, Rose (2000) notes that, unlike the situation where XYY research was being called on to defend the accused from criminal responsibility, the new "biocriminology" is being used to protect society from these violent criminals. Implicit in biocriminology, and linked to policy concerns, is the view that proper testing and diagnostics can help those afflicted with these physiological aberrations. But if effective treatment is not possible, then what are the available options for dealing with dangerous and unpredictable individuals? What is emerging in society, according to Rose (2000), is a new problem requiring regulation of the genetically at-risk individual. What was at one time a crime control issue is shifting into the realm of public health. While there are several possible policy interventions to reduce the risk of crime posed by such individuals, the possibility of selective incapacitation is one possible option: incarcerating people before they commit a serious crime. This very important policy issue will be picked up again later in the text when a more detailed discussion will focus on criminal justice policy.

The Psychology of Crime

Similar to biological explanations of crime, **psychological theories** of criminal behaviour also focus on the individual. Unlike some biologists, who would support the view that criminals are born, modern psychological explanations about crime contend that criminals are made. Individuals—especially children and adolescents— interacting within their social environments are key for understanding aggression and violence.

Psychoanalytic Theory

An early and well-known psychological theory of criminal behaviour was developed in Europe by Sigmund Freud in the latter part of the nineteenth and early twentieth centuries. The founder of **psychoanalytic theory**, Freud believed that a person's psychological well-being was dependent on a functional relationship among the three fundamental components of the human psyche: the id, ego, and superego. According to Freud, the id consists of primal urges that produce unconscious biological drives for things like food and sex. The ego, guided by what Freud called the *reality principle*, develops early in childhood and acts as a mechanism that keeps the urges of the id in check, so to speak. The third component of the human psyche, the superego, acts as a person's social conscience—a type of moral code. The superego develops according to the moral standards stemming from values associated with the family—especially one's parents—and the broader community. The superego is the moral component of a person's personality. The id, ego, and superego operate to control behaviour. For Freud, criminal behaviour and other forms of social deviance come about as the result of unresolved psychological conflicts.

To give an example of how this theory works, consider Mr Newman, who is walking down a busy street when a very attractive young woman winks at him. Mr Newman's id thinks, "I'd like to go and ask that woman if she wants to make love in that alley way." His ego kicks in by responding, "Wait, you can't do that in front of all these people, let's go to her house and do it there." The superego then says, "Stop, you can't do that at all, you're married."

While the psychoanalytic approach is an interesting and unique theory for understanding social deviance (especially sexual deviance), and Freud's technique of psychoanalysis continues to be practised, modern-day criminologists are hesitant to embrace the theory because the concepts are difficult, if not impossible, to operationalize and measure. For example, how can one scientifically prove that the id, ego, and superego actually exist? Indeed, there are no reliable tests to measure the presence or absence of these parts of the human psyche. Theories that cannot be tested are not very useful beyond the ideas they express.

Social Learning Theory

One of the first studies to make the connection between what children learn in their immediate environment and how that can affect levels of aggression was carried out by Sears, Maccoby, and Levin (1957). Based on interviews that focused on the disciplinary measures used by parents of kindergarten students, the researchers discovered that the use of parental physical punishment for disciplining children was positively associated with children's aggression. Hence, aggressive children were much more likely to come from homes in which parents relied on physical punishments as a disciplinary measure in addition to being highly permissive. That physical punishment carried out by parents is linked with children's aggression supports the familiar saying that "children do what they see, not what they are told." According to social learning theory, then, aggressive behaviour is learned through a series of psychological thought processes and perceptions.

The results of this study were later supported and further developed by Albert Bandura's (1973) version of social learning theory. Based on an experiment where one group of children watched a film of adults hitting an inflatable Bobo doll, while the other group of similarly aged children watched a non-violent film, Bandura discovered significant differences between the two groups when the film-watching concluded. The group that watched the aggressive film was much more likely to hit a Bobo doll with more intensity and frequency than the group who were not exposed to the violent media. In short, observing aggressive acts leads to aggression.

The policy implications of findings such as these are twofold. First, they have raised considerable debate in society about the appropriateness of parental physical disciplinary action administered to children and subsequent aggressive behaviour exhibited by children. Second, it raises the possibility that the violent messages children may view on television (i.e., watching violent cartoons) may be associated with hostility in children. However, since social learning theory tends to focus on factors that operate on individuals within their immediate environments, it has been criticized on that basis— that is, people do not operate within a social vacuum. While research and experimentation informed by social learning theory tends to concentrate on individual characteristics and the immediate environments in which they are socialized, it is difficult to explain criminal behaviour without taking into account influences of the community, the broader social environment, and the particular circumstances surrounding the criminal event itself. For reasons such as these, social learning theory is unable to account for changes in levels of crime over time, or differences in the spatial distribution of crime (e.g., difference in levels of crime between cities or between provinces).

While not necessarily using Bandura's social learning theory as a reference point, the logic that violent behaviour is learned from watching violence on television or by listening to music or watching music videos that contain violent subject matter has been the subject of much controversy in recent years. Groups in the United States such as the Parents Music Resource Center (PMRC) have lobbied governments to censure violence and sexually graphic content contained in musical recordings. Led by Tipper Gore, the wife of former vice-president Al Gore, from 1985–92 the PMRC contended that popular music, primarily hard rock, was responsible for what they believed to be an upsurge in youth violence, drug use, and teen suicide in the United States. The music community banded together to oppose the censorship on the basis of its being an infringement of civil liberties. Not long after several American musicians and the PMRC debated the effects of popular music on teen violence, an event at a high school in Littleton, Colorado, in 1999 served immediately to resurrect questions about the impact of popular culture on youth violence. Because the two youth who were responsible for killing 12 students, a teacher, and later themselves at Columbine High School were involved in what was believed to be the "Goth" subculture (black clothing, pale makeup, odd hair styles, body piercing, and occult involvement), links were made between the Goth subculture—including some forms of popular music—and violence. Indeed, some members of the media made similar connections between violence, the Goth subculture, and the viewing of violent video games such as *Postal* when Kimveer Gill went on a deadly shooting spree at Dawson

College in Montreal in September 2006. In that same year, a 12-year-old girl and her 23-year-old boyfriend were convicted of killing the girl's parents and brother in Medicine Hat, Alberta. While the precise motive of Richardson murders is not clear, Allan Steinke, the boyfriend who was convicted on three counts of first-degree murder, allegedly was a fan of the movie *Natural Born Killers*, had interest in vampires, and dressed like a "Goth."

But just what does the research literature reveal when the relationship between viewing violent images/material and actually engaging in aggression and violence is examined? Well, the relationship is complex, and the issue is very difficult to study. For instance, due to ethical and logistical reasons it would be virtually impossible to carry out an experiment where one group of young people were made to play violent video games for a prolonged period and then comparing their levels of violence to a second group who were not permitted to play violent video games. While experimental research such as this is lacking, non-experimental studies that have asked groups of youth to report their exposure to violent video games, "gangsta rap" music, and so on, along with their self-reported aggressive and violent behaviour, often find that those who are fond of violent video games tend to be more aggressive than those who do not like them. While these findings may suggest that playing video games may be associated with increased levels of aggression, it is also quite possible that those youth who enjoy playing violent video games or enjoy listening to certain types of hip-hop music and who may be aggressive share a common personality type (Anderson & Bushman, 2001). In other words, "aggressive" personalities may have a preference for certain forms of entertainment that contain violent images and messages in addition to relying on aggression to deal with problems that they encounter in "real life."

Psychopathy

Psychologists and psychiatrists interested in personality development have explained violence and aggression on the basis of **psychopathy**. A psychopath is a term used to describe a compulsive person who lacks guilt, remorse, and is unable to hold lasting bonds with others. During the Second World War, the specific traits of psychopathology were first catalogued by Cleckley in the book *The Mask of Sanity* and contained 16 traits. Over time, however, the psychological community has trimmed the number of traits down to 7, but to be diagnosed as a psychopath one has to possess only 3 of the following 7 traits:

1. Failure to conform to social norms
2. Deceitfulness, repeated lying, use of aliases, or conning others for personal profit or pleasure
3. Impulsivity or failure to plan ahead
4. Irritability and aggressiveness; fights/assaults

5. Reckless disregard for the safety of self or others
6. Consistent irresponsibility, failure of consistent employment
7. Lack of remorse, as indicated by being indifferent to or rationalizing having hurt, mistreated, or stolen from another

The connection between psychopathology and criminal behaviour is longstanding in this field of psychology. One Canadian study showed that the criminal histories of a sample of male inmates who were diagnosed as psychopathic had significantly more convictions for assault, robbery, fraud, possession of weapons, and escapes from custody (Hare et al., 1988). Psychopathy has alone been shown to be a predictor of recidivism. Serin and Amos (1995) found different rates for recidivism (committing another crime after being released from prison) between psychopathic offenders and non-psychopathic offenders. In this study, the overall base rate of violent recidivism was 17 per cent for the entire sample. The rate of violent recidivism among psychopathic offenders was 25 per cent, while for non-psychopathic offenders it was 5 per cent. In other words, 1 in 4 psychopathic individuals will engage in some form of violence when released from prison, compared to 1 in 20 non-psychopathic offenders (Andrade, 2008).

Research linking psychopathy and crime has been subject to two main criticisms. First, research has shown that there are many people in the general population who possess at least three of the traits to signal psychopathy that do not commit crime. Conversely, there are many inmates in prison who, according to psychological personality inventories, do not possess psychopathological traits. Second, there is no consensus in the research literature as to what causes psychopathy. While childhood abuse and poor parenting have been linked to personality defects in youth, an extensive review of the studies on the developmental correlates of juvenile psychopathy reveals that there are no decisive links between family history and psychopathy in adulthood (Howard et al., 2004). Incidentally, there are few studies that examine effective treatment for those given this diagnosis. According to Howard et al., this may "reflect the therapeutic pessimism that has accompanied the diagnosis of psychopathy" (2004, p. 483).

Conclusion

This chapter has presented an overview of a selection of explanations about crime, beginning with the demonic era, when criminal behaviour was believed to arise from a generalized force of evil. The school of thought now considered classical saw criminal behaviour as the deliberate choice of rational persons who could be controlled through swift and certain punishments. As an outcome of the Enlightenment's form of rationality, crime and punishment became understood as a function of evolution and natural selection. The classical idea that the proper use of state-sanctioned punishment can deter crime forms the basis of modern legal systems around the world, including Canada's.

With the rise of the positivist school in the twentieth century, rationality (in the classical understanding) was no longer considered relevant as an explanation of criminality. Instead, biological explanations were put forth contending that crime stems from individual pathology and abnormality. Whether evolutionary retardation, germ plasma, or chromosomal abnormalities, essential to this viewpoint is that notion that criminals are **born, not made**. Even though this line of reasoning had its origins in the late nineteenth and early twentieth centuries, we have shown that this way of thinking about crime still exists in certain recent sociobiological initiatives. We concluded by outlining ideas stemming from the psychology of crime. This included social learning theory, a psychological theory of aggression, Freud's theory about the unconscious mind, and psychopathy. While not as individualistic in its logic, this explanation of anti-social behaviour also focuses a great deal on individual attributes, albeit within the context of their immediate social environment.

While the weaknesses in these theories have been pointed out, it is important to consider these explanations of crime because they imply that criminal patterns—like those identified in Chapter 2 that examined homicide—can be changed by changing individuals who show these tendencies to crime. However, if such individualistic explanations about crime are reliable, then how do they explain why homicide rates in Canada increased from the 1960s to the 1980s and have been declining or levelling off since then? Can it be that the population contained more atavists 30 years ago than today? Similarly, are we able to explain why homicide rates are higher in the western provinces than they are in eastern Canada on the basis that there are more endomorphs, or that those with extra Y chromosomes are more likely to inhabit provinces like Manitoba and Saskatchewan than they are to reside in Newfoundland or Prince Edward Island? Given the fact that individualistic accounts are unable to offer reasonable explanations for these trends, many criminologists have turned to sociological theories as an alternative viewpoint to understand crime, which will be introduced in the next chapter.

Critical Thinking Questions

1. In what important ways do the theories of crime developed during the classical school of thinking about criminology differ from explanations of crime proposed by the positivist school of thought?

2. How does social learning theory understand the nature of aggressive behaviour? What influence does listening to certain types of aggressive music or playing violent video games have on criminal behaviour?

3. A critique of Freud's theory of psychoanalysis is that the id, ego, and superego are impossible to measure. Do you agree with the assumption that concepts which cannot be measured have little value in the social sciences?

Suggested Readings

Lombroso, Cesare, & Ferrero, Guglielmo. (2004 [1895]). *Criminal woman, the prostitute, and the normal woman*, trans. and intro. by Nicole Hahn Rafter and Mary Gibson. Durham, NC: Duke University Press. This classic in the field of criminology has been supplemented in this new edition with a new introduction that introduces the reader to some early ideas on the nature of female offending. Students will note that the explanation of female crime offered by Lombroso and Ferrero is quite different from how feminists today explain female criminality.

Zeitlin, Irving. (2001). *Ideology and the development of sociological theory*, 7th ed. Upper Saddle, NJ: Prentice Hall. A sociology textbook that covers the ideas of many classical theorists, including those of the Enlightenment who had a profound impact on the classical school of criminology.

Websites and Films

The New Sciences of Detection
http://chnm.gmu.edu/courses/magic/police/policework.html
> This website contains a number of photographs of "criminals" that are categorized on the basis of Lombroso's typology. It also contains early police mug shots.

Florida State University College of Criminology and Criminal Justice
www.criminology.fsu.edu/crimtheory/bandura.htm
> This website reviews the main ideas of social learning theory. The site also contains photographs of the famous Bobo doll experiment discussed in this chapter.

Natural Born Killers (1994). A film directed by Oliver Stone about a pair of serial killers, starring Woody Harrelson and Juliette Lewis. This movie is a satire about America's fascination with violent criminals. In fact, when the two killers are arrested for their murderous spree, the police treat them more as celebrities than criminals. The personalities of the two killers, while exaggerated, are depicted in a fashion very similar to the traits psychologists assign to psychopaths.

Madness: Out of Sight (1991). A documentary, narrated by Jonathan Miller, which examines the rise of the asylum and the conditions and treatments that were found there between the eighteenth century to the latter part of the twentieth century. The film explores the realities and often brutal treatment practices in such institutions, which was often at odds with their original purpose as a place for the care and safety of "lunatics."

4

Classical Sociological Explanations of Crime

Learning Objectives

After completing this chapter students will be able to:

◎ Understand how explanations of crime and its control offered by sociologists differ from non-sociological theories of crime.

◎ Identify the full range of classical sociological theories that attempt to explain crime and its control.

Introduction

The biological and psychological theories of crime we have been exploring make the individual criminal the object of study; sociological theories for explaining crime focus on the group. This does not mean that **sociological criminologists** are not interested in understanding the types of behaviours that characterize individuals; rather, they are more interested in understanding group action. For example, a sociological criminologist would like to know why the majority of prison inmates in Canada are from lower-class social backgrounds. Or why homicide rates in Canada generally increase by province from the eastern to western provinces. Even though levels of police-reported violent crime are higher in the United States than they are in Canada, why, after three decades of rising levels of crime, did crime rates in both countries begin to decrease in the 1990s? What is the reason that far more males than females are involved in most types of crime? Why do age levels of people involved in street crime tend to peak in the late teen years, then decrease rather steadily afterwards?

While different sociological theories address these questions in their own unique ways, they share the approach of trying to answer these questions by examining group characteristics—social class, gender, age, culture—rather than individual distinctiveness.

Durkheim

The origins of sociological thinking can be traced to the work of Émile Durkheim (1858–1917). While Durkheim's work extends much beyond the study of crime, his work in *Suicide* (1897), *The Rules of Sociological Method* (1895), and *The Division of Labour in Society* (1893) had a major impact on criminological theory over much of the twentieth century and into the twenty-first century. Durkheim took a sociological approach to the phenomenon of suicide. Using official statistics from several European countries in the mid-to-late 1800s, he noted that suicide rates were lower for Catholics than they were for Protestants. Moreover, people in larger cities were more likely to commit suicide than people in small towns, and suicide rates were higher among people who lived alone than among people who lived in families. What could explain such variation? For Durkheim, the explanation was not accounted for on the basis of individual attributes in the population (e.g., rates of mental illness). Rather, Durkheim explained these differences on the basis of varying degrees of social integration and social cohesion. Simply put, people with weak links to their communities are more likely to take their lives than people who have strong social ties.

Since the publication of *Suicide*, his argument has been tested substantially and has been met with some opposition. For example, Douglas (1967) noted that Durkheim did not pay enough attention to how suicide statistics were collected, particularly by not addressing the problems surrounding how coroners interpret causes of death and produce inaccurate statistics.

Despite this and other criticisms, the fact remains that Durkheim was remarkable for proposing an explanation of behaviour that challenged biological and psychological assumptions. He showed that society was not simply the result of individual action. He also believed, unlike the classical school, that society was not a direct reflection of the characteristics of its individual members. Society, somehow, was more than the sum of its parts.

The Chicago School

Durkheim's ideas and approach quickly spread to North America. One of the earliest adherents to this new way of thinking can be found in the writings of the **Chicago School**. Early in the twentieth century, a group of sociologists at the University of Chicago began to examine crime in this midwestern American city on the basis of its spatial distribution. Among the adherents of what was to become known as the *ecological school of criminology*, members argued that crime was not randomly distributed across the population. Similar to Durkheim's earlier findings pertaining to the distribution of suicide, Robert Park and Ernest Burgess (1967) provided evidence that levels of crime in Chicago were not distributed evenly throughout the city. Instead, crime was geographically patterned. Believing that cities naturally grow like a tree, with concentric circles growing around the central business district, Park and Burgess proposed that crime was concentrated in the "zone of transition" (see Figure 4.1). This was an area of the city that surrounded the central business district and contained the oldest housing in the city. Due to the affordability of its housing, the area tended to attract people who had little money, such as new immigrants and racial minorities. The zone was seen as being in transition because the people who lived there were transient, and the housing was soon to be torn down to make way for business expansion (Driedger, 1991, p. 85). The other zones they conceived are displayed in Figure 4.1.

Even though the applicability of this model to other cities is debatable, especially in more recent years as older, inner-city housing has been gentrified (i.e., renovated for richer residents) in many North American cities, the model is important because it associates criminal activity with areas in cities that are in turmoil or are otherwise socially disorganized. The logic of this argument runs counter to individualistic explanations of crime that suggest criminals have a tendency to gravitate to certain areas of the city. In contrast, ecological explanations of crime suggest that rates of crime rise for people who are displaced—such as new immigrants—because of their inability to successfully integrate into a foreign city and a strange culture.

Crime and Social Disorganization

Shaw and McKay (1942) followed this ecological line of thinking in their study of delinquency in Chicago when they plotted the spatial distribution of crime on maps of Chicago and other American cities. In keeping with early sociological theories of crime, Shaw and McKay argued that crime and juvenile delinquency were not randomly distributed in the population. Rather, they discovered that police-reported crime was concentrated in the area of Chicago identified by Park and Burgess as the zone of transition, an area characterized

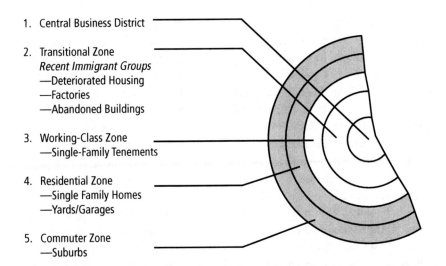

1. Central Business District

2. Transitional Zone
   Recent Immigrant Groups
   —Deteriorated Housing
   —Factories
   —Abandoned Buildings

3. Working-Class Zone
   —Single-Family Tenements

4. Residential Zone
   —Single Family Homes
   —Yards/Garages

5. Commuter Zone
   —Suburbs

Figure 4.1 The Concentric Zone Model

by substandard housing, low incomes, and a concentration of visible minorities. Shaw and McKay argued that high delinquency rates were caused by the types of neighbourhoods in which youth grew up. **Social disorganization**, not biological or psychological pathology, was responsible for crime. In such neighbourhoods as the zone of transition, social controls had broken down as a result of the immigrants who populated these areas having few social ties and at the same time being disadvantaged (especially economically) in the means of effective parental control over their children.

The social disorganization perspective can also be found in the work of Thrasher (1927), the pioneer of American gang research. The sociological merit in Thrasher's work, which also took place in Chicago, is obvious. Like Shaw and McKay, Thrasher argued that gangs emerge in environments where conventional controls on youth are either absent or lacking. It was no surprise to Thrasher that the youth gangs of Chicago during the early part of the twentieth century were found in socially unstable neighbourhoods. For Thrasher,

> The gang is an interstitial group originally formed spontaneously, and then integrated through conflict. It is characterized by the following types of behavior: meeting face to face, milling, movement through space as a unit, conflict, and planning. The result of this collective behavior is the development of tradition, unreflective internal structure, esprit de corps, solidarity, morale, group awareness, and attachment to a local territory. (1963 [1927], p. 46)

While the social disorganization perspective has been influential on the sociological study of crime, it has been subject to some important criticism. The idea that cities naturally grow according to the concentric zone model proposed by Park and Burgess has been shown not to apply to all cities. In fact, since its original formulation in 1916, several other models of urban growth have been proposed that take into account variations in ecological growth patterns, such as the multiple nuclei and sector theories. In fact, research in Canada has shown that while cities like Montreal, Toronto, and Vancouver in some ways follow these zonal patterns, other Canadian cities, such as Calgary and Ottawa, do not (Balakrishnan & Jarvis, 1991). Even for those cities that do follow this model of urban growth, street crime is not necessarily concentrated in transitional zones that border the central business district.

The idea that high-crime areas, like the zone of transition, are socially disorganized has also been subject to criticism. For example, not long after these ideas were first proposed, Whyte (1943) conducted a study of crime in an American slum and found that, far from being socially disorganized, much crime in "Cornerville" was in fact well organized. At the same time, research on corporate wrongdoing has clearly shown that crime is not limited to the powerless and the disenfranchised and that juvenile delinquency is not restricted to the inner city.

Despite its shortcomings, the ecological/social disorganization approaches remain important examples of research and theory, demonstrating that society, in the form of community and its controls, exert a powerful influence on human behaviour. The idea that most street crime is committed by "normal" people living in "abnormal" environments means that efforts to control crime need to focus on reorganizing disorganized communities.

A recent effort aimed at reorganizing a community that had a reputation for being socially disorganized, is the rebuilding of Regent Park, Canada's oldest and largest social housing project that was built in the late 1940s. However, as the material in Box 4.1 shows, social engineering projects can have unintended consequences.

Box 4.1

Debates and Controversies
Sara Thompson and Sandra Bucerius

Regent Park Revitalization: Has It Created an "Us Versus Them"—

The news that a spate of downtown shootings stems in part from "a war over the new Regent Park" was, sadly, not a surprise to us.

Our research strongly suggests that the ambitious program to rebuild Regent Park with an influx of higher-income newcomers has had unintended and even negative effects on community networks and, consequently, on crime and violence in the neighbourhood.

The social order that governed the old neighbourhood, despite its well-known problems, has been washed away with the relocation of so many residents to other locales and the disruption of existing networks. Regent Park youth find themselves more adrift, both those left facing an "us and them" tension with newcomers and those attempting to fit in to new neighbourhoods while bearing the stigma of being Regent Park kids.

"Before the revitalization, there were certain rules, like no shootings at daytimes, no shootings in certain places and so on," says one of our interview subjects. "Now, things have just become random."

The revitalization is based on a policy trend to "deconcentrate" poverty and other forms of disadvantage by engineering more socially and economically mixed residential environments. The core action is to create a new, broader mix of market-value, affordable and social-housing stock. The "new" Regent Park will shift from what was once a neighbourhood comprised entirely of social-housing units to a mixed-income, mixed-use community that is zoned for residential and retail purposes.

Harvard sociologist William Julius Wilson popularized this approach through what's come to be known as his social isolation thesis. Wilson argues that residents of high-poverty neighbourhoods are isolated from informal job

Continued

networks and opportunities, positive role models, mainstream institutions and patterns of behaviour. Such "underclass behaviours" as teenage pregnancy, delinquent and criminal actions and high dropout rates emerge and are transmitted across generations.

According to Wilson, the lack of positive role models who could transmit more mainstream standards of behaviour keeps residents in these neighbourhoods from becoming successful members of society. By introducing "social mix" and encouraging middle-class people to buy units in these neighbourhoods, it is hoped that networks will form between the original and new residents, creating a "middle-class buffer." That will create stricter standards of behaviour and socialize children with "proper" mainstream values.

Wilson's theory is predicated on an assumption that residents in high-poverty neighbourhoods do not share common, mainstream values, making it harder to mobilize and intervene on behalf of the common good (what we academics like to call "collective efficacy.") It also assumes that the influx of working- and middle-class residents, with the social ties and resources they carry, will create safer, healthier neighbourhoods.

The Regent Park project is an example of a distinctly Canadian application of the social-mix model. Existing residents are supposed to be displaced only until a new unit becomes available in Regent Park.

Our findings mirror research on American applications of the social-mix model, which found that despite many sustained improvements, positive effects do not seem to extend to all residents, particularly young males. Young men in social-mix programs in the U.S. are more likely to report marijuana use, more likely to be arrested for property crime and tend to score higher on an index of behavioural problems, including aggressive behaviours.

If one of the main goals of the social-mix model is to make the community safer and thus produce lower crime rates—the notion central to the discourse on the revitalization of Regent Park—our findings seem rather counterproductive and should give us pause.

Our research also challenges the assumption that disadvantaged neighbourhoods lack common values and the willingness to mobilize and intervene on behalf of the common good—that "collective efficacy." All of our study participants report that social bonds and networks among residents in Regent Park were dense and strong prior to the revitalization process.

In addition to providing much-needed services, involved organizations also forged interactions and connections among residents, facilitating the building of trust and collective efficacy. So, contrary to the social-mix model's assumption, that sense of a common good was already high in many segments of Regent Park.

The revitalization project thus appears to be disrupting and/or destroying supportive social networks among residents. Many of the young adults we interviewed indicate that they can no longer rely on the social networks that once kept them from engaging in criminal activity. Many told us that older family friends and neighbours used to act not only as positive role models, but also as an important means of social control: "I could never get involved in anything bad, people would tell my mom the same day, I swear."

Young people are also concerned about being victims of violence in the new neighbourhoods to which their families are displaced. "Whether you have been involved (in crime) or not, you still have the stigma of being from Regent Park. People know," one interviewee said.

Very little cross-class interaction is actually occurring in the revitalized areas of Regent Park, our research suggests. All of the youth we interviewed claim that linkages between old and new residents are non-existent. There appears to be very little expectation that a new, melded community will emerge.

Among the comments we heard from youth toward their new, higher-income neighbours:

- "They look at us as if we're animals."
- "There's a division there, like there's a clear division in terms of us and them."
- "Do I like them? . . . That's a good question. I have no clue. I haven't seen them."

Such comments raise concern that not only are the intended benefits of social mix unseen to date, returning residents may find themselves in an even more isolated position.

The displacement of so many residents also appears to be upsetting long-established codes of conduct in Regent Park. The physical demolition of the old neighbourhood has altered the drug dealers' territorial claims and hierarchies. The recent violence in and around Regent Park does not reflect the social order that used to keep things under relative control, our young interview subjects claim.

We need to think more carefully about the ways disruption of social networks may affect levels of crime and violence. More has to be done build networks between old and new residents, particularly to avoid "us versus them" tensions.

Source: Thompson and Bucerius, 2012.

Strain/Anomie Theory

Durkheim's influence is found in another well-known and influential sociological theory of crime: anomie or strain theory. Not long after the Chicago School made its mark, Robert Merton published "Social Structure and Anomie" in the *American Sociological Review* (1938). The concept of **anomie**— a French word meaning *normlessness*—was adapted from Durkheim's writings on suicide. According to Durkheim, anomic suicide is characterized by a social condition causing the individual to feel lost or in a predicament of normlessness. This sense in an individual of social norms having lost their meaning can be triggered when the equilibrium of society is radically altered.

For example, following the stock market crash of 1929 there was a sharp rise in the American suicide rate. For Durkheim, this rise in suicide could have been predicted because many investors had nowhere to turn for emotional or financial support when they lost great sums of money in a very short period of time.

However, Merton used the term *anomie* in a slightly different way. Merton sets his theory within the context of American capitalism and the social inequality generated by it. He maintains that anomie is a situation where societies inadvertently bring to bear pressure, or strain, on individuals that can lead to rule-breaking behaviour. This strain is caused by the discrepancy between culturally defined goals and the institutionalized means available to achieve these goals. Merton argued that the dominant cultural goal in the United States is the acquisition of wealth. The message that happiness is equated with material success is transmitted through a variety of social institutions, including the mass media, family, and the educational system. This idea, coupled with the belief that hard work and education are what is required to achieve these material goals, means that everyone thinks that those who apply themselves to study and work will succeed financially. And those who do not succeed are labelled as either lazy or defective.

According to Merton, the problem with American society is that the legitimate means for achieving material success are *not* uniformly distributed. In other words, those from wealthier backgrounds have considerably more access to the legitimate means than do those who are economically disadvantaged. As a consequence, anomie, or social strain, is generated and produces certain "modes of adaptation," or coping strategies, that the disadvantaged people use to deal with the pressures that are brought to bear on them. While there are five modes of adaptation in Merton's model—conformity, innovation, retreatism, ritualism, and rebellion—the one most often used to explain crime is innovation. The innovator is one who believes in the culturally defined goals in society but rejects the legitimate means to achieve these goals. Such individuals use the proceeds from crimes such as theft, fraud, and illegal drug-dealing to access the so-called American Dream. By and large, then, the main predictor of crime according to Merton's theory of anomie is low socioeconomic status.

Merton's theory continues to play a role in contemporary sociological theorizing about crime today (e.g., Young, 2003). Yet limitations to this classical sociological explanation of crime have been identified. The first systematic criticism of Merton's theory was the focus of *Delinquent Boys: The Culture of the Gang* written by Albert Cohen in 1955. Cohen was interested in the fact that much delinquent behaviour was "non-utilitarian, malicious and negativistic' (Cohen, 1955, p. 25) and, therefore, not explained by Merton's model. That is, while Merton could explain crimes such as theft on the basis of innovation, nowhere in his formulation was there an account of why youth engage in behaviours such as vandalism or, as Cohen writes, "stealing for the hell of it" (ibid., p. 26). In keeping with the strain tradition, Cohen agreed with Merton that much crime is likely to be found within the ranks of the working class. However, the reasons why lower-class youth are overrepresented in official crime statistics had more to do with the restricted opportunities accessible to working-class boys to attain social status on the basis of a middle-class value system. The process of working-class exclusion, according to Cohen, took place within the educational system. Here working-class boys are continually evaluated according to what he calls a "middle-class measuring rod." Since working-class children share the status of their parents, the working-class child starts off with a handicap; and if a working-class youth cares what middle-class people think of him, or has internalized the dominant "middle-class attitudes towards social class position," then the youth feels shame (ibid., p. 110). For Cohen, much of this shame occurs within the context of the school, where working-class youth do not fit into a system where they are judged mostly by teachers with middle-class backgrounds and have to perform according to curricula also set by those with middle-class backgrounds. Youth from socially deprived backgrounds who are unable to compete within the context of this educational system react by turning to delinquency. Cohen theorizes that those alienated youth whose self-esteem is damaged turn to a delinquent **subculture** where they are able to achieve an alternative source of status. The process of rejecting the dominant value system and endorsing the values of the delinquent subculture value system is described by Cohen as "reaction formation." The delinquent subculture is a way of dealing with problems of adjustment. When working-class youth fail to measure up to the criteria set by the dominant value system, they collectively turn to an alternative value system, one that can provide status-granting criteria that they *can* meet. Failing to gain status by getting good grades, for example, the alienated working-class youth turns the middle-class values upside down and achieves another source of self-worth by engaging in delinquent activities such as stealing and fighting.

Strain theory—both Merton's and Cohen's versions—was very influential until about the 1960s. You will recall from Chapter 2 that at this time criminologists began to question the reliability and validity of official police statistics, which consistently had shown crime to be mainly a lower-class phenomenon. More and more studies of crime that used self-report techniques failed to detect a social class connection to crime. Particularly in self-report research that was undertaken in high schools, evidence was no longer found to indicate that working- or lower-class youth were any more likely to engage in delinquency than middle-class youth. For this reason, the idea that low social status leads to crime, the main assumption of strain theory, was seriously questioned. Moreover, when definitions of crime are broadened to include activities such as corporate wrongdoing, the class–crime connection proposed by strain theory is further put into question. In short, if crime is simply caused by the strain associated with low social status, then why do educated and financially successful business executives engage in criminal activity? Perhaps the most obvious inadequacy of strain theory pertains to its failure to account for the fact that most crime in society is committed by males. If economically induced strain is the major cause of crime, then why are so few women involved in illegal activities? Do they not feel the pressure of economic strain as much as men? Even though the status of women has improved in North America over the years, the fact remains that women continue to be at an economic disadvantage relative to men. In Canada, for example, women who work full time, on average, earn approximately three-quarters of what similarly employed men earn (Shalla, 2011). Interestingly, women's marginal economic standing both in the past and at present is not directly associated with rates of female crime.

The ideas in strain theory have been used to develop crime control strategies in communities where residents—particularly young people—have few legitimate means of reaching their goals. In Toronto, for example, the city has identified 13 "priority neighbourhoods" historically recognizable for high levels of poverty, gun violence, and gang activity. By building partnerships with business and labour, the city is working on providing thousands of youth from vulnerable communities with access to education, training, and apprenticeship opportunities. Programs like the one recently introduced in Toronto have been used to address crime in many other North American cities, too (see Box 4.1 page 91).

Control Theory

Another theory that purports to explain the causes of crime, most notably youth deviance, is control theory. Before reviewing the essential components of control theory, it is useful first to contrast its major assumption about human nature with that of strain theory.

Hirschi (1969), the modern originator of control theory, agrees with strain theorists that an understanding of the causes of crime includes the awareness that society plays a fundamental role in shaping the criminal. While control and strain theories are both sociological, the role that society plays, according to each theory, is quite different. For strain theorists like Merton and Cohen, social pressure is the key to understanding criminality. Society exerts a criminogenic influence on those people who accept certain societal goals but reject the legitimate means of achieving these goals. **Control theory**, on the other hand, views society as a set of institutions that acts to *control* and *regulate* rule-breaking behaviour. This theory is based on the assumption that humans, by nature, are risk-takers—even to the point of being egocentric. Consequently, humans seek to satisfy their desires by the easiest—at times criminal—means possible. However, if an individual is properly bonded to society, then he or she will not engage in crime. But if social bonds are broken or weak, then an individual could be open to their egocentric impulses and, therefore, engage in crime.

But just what are these bonds, and what function do they play? According to Hirschi, there are four types of social bonds. The first two, often referred to as "inner controls," are *commitments* and *beliefs*. The other two "outer controls" are *involvements* and *attachments*. Commitments refer to the idea that a person has an investment or stake in conforming behaviour. For example, if a high school student is doing well academically and is committed to attending university, engaging in illegal behaviour could put this goal into jeopardy and she will try to control her behaviour toward that end. The second inner control is beliefs. This control essentially refers to a person's loyalty to a dominant value system. Since beliefs often take the form of "moral imperatives," committing an act that violates these beliefs causes a person to experience a deep sense of guilt or remorse. For example, if a Jew accepts the Ten Commandments, he likely believes that stealing, a violation of the eighth commandment "Thou shall not steal," is a moral wrong. If such a person were to steal, then he would have to come to terms with his having violated a moral imperative.

Attachment, one of two outer controls, refers to the extent to which individuals are emotionally tied to and respect the opinions of the group to which they are members (e.g., family and school). A young person who is close to his family would tend not to violate a social norm if that violation would hurt or embarrass his parents. However, if the bond that a young person has with her parents is weak or non-existent, then that individual feels she has less to lose and would be more inclined to commit an illegal act. Involvement is the final bond in Hirschi's theory, and generally refers to physical activities, such as organized sports, that are of a non-deviant nature. The claim here is that if youth are highly involved in organized hockey, for example, then they will have less time and inclination to engage in illegal activities.

While control theory has been shown to be a rather effective explanation of non-serious forms of youthful delinquency, it has not been proven to be as effective for explaining more serious youth crime or crime that is committed by adults. Moreover, control theory has been challenged for its adherence to a rather conservative view of the broader social order. Control theory predicts that children who are properly bonded, or attached, to their parents would be involved in less crime than children who have weak parental bonds. This assumption, of course, is that the family is a naturally law-abiding institution and if children are attached to law-abiding parents then they too will be law-abiding. What about children who are attached to parents who are not law-abiding? Jenson and Brownfield (1983), for instance, found that close attachments to drug-abusing parents does not serve to control drug use among youth. Furthermore, just because youth become involved in pro-social activities such as after-school sports programs is no guarantee that illegal or socially injurious behaviour are not also being engaged in. Indeed, control theory assumes that involvement in a sport like high school football or track and field would occupy young people's time so that they would not have the opportunity to become involved in other after-school activities, such as illegal drug use. While this may be the case for some forms of deviance, by no means is it true that such involvement in conventional and normative activities guarantee protection from all forms of deviance. An obvious example is athletes who use performance-enhancing drugs, or hazing rituals common in many different types of organized sports that have led to degradation and physical injuries (Nuwer, 2009).

Despite these limitations, efforts to prevent crime have been informed by social control theory, like policies that attempt to strengthen the social institutions that socialize young people such as the family and the school. Parenting programs that attempt to improve parenting skills are designed so that children's bonds to parents are strengthened. Within the school setting, programs that are designed to reduce delinquency by strengthening pupils' commitment to school and their attachment to conforming members of the community are examples of control theory in action. Such programs may include guest appearances in schools by professional athletes who encourage youth to stay in school and keep out of trouble, helping to bond youths to the conventional system.

Differential Association Theory

The last of the classical causal theories of crime to be reviewed is differential association theory. Originally proposed by Edwin Sutherland in 1939, **differential association theory**, like the other sociological theories that have been reviewed thus far, is rooted in the idea that human beings act in reference to their environment. More specifically, Sutherland suggests that criminal behaviour is learned behaviour. This means that criminal behaviour is not caused by brain damage or by abnormal biological traits but is learned in interaction with other people in a socialization process that normally occurs within the context of a small group. What is involved in this learning process, according to Sutherland, pertains to the techniques of crime, which can be simple (e.g., how to smoke crack cocaine) or more complex (e.g., learning how to rob an armoured truck). This process also involves learning the motivations and rationalizations for criminal behaviour. Indeed, this is a key point for Sutherland because it means that for an individual to internalize criminogenic motives they must be learned in a context where the commission of crime is viewed in favourable terms. In fact, a person is more likely to become embedded in criminal activity if surrounded by an excess of socializing definitions favourable toward norm-violation over definitions that are unfavourable to the violation of social norms. Conversely, an individual becomes non-deviant as the result of an excess of socializing definitions that are unfavourable to the commission of deviant acts.

Another important quality of differential association theory concerns the frequency and intensity of interaction. In other words, the amount of time that a person is exposed to particular definitions and at what point the interaction began are both crucial for explaining criminal activity. In general, the process of learning criminal behaviour is really not any different from the process involved in learning any other type of behaviour. Sutherland maintains that there is no unique learning process associated with acquiring non-normative ways of behaving.

Compared to other classical sociological theories of crime, Sutherland's theory is unique in that it purports to explain more than just juvenile delinquency and crime committed by the lower classes. Since crime is understood as learned behaviour, the theory is also applicable to white-collar, corporate, and organized crime.

The most common critique of differential association theory was first raised in the early 1960s, and it pertained to the notion of oversocialization. Dennis Wrong (1961) argued that it is common for socialization theory—not only Sutherland's theory—to fail to factor in the idea that people can be independent, rational actors and individually motivated. Wrong questions the idea that the environment in which one is placed is *the* determinant of human behaviour. In other words, are *all* deviant acts the result of learning? Likely not.

The practical implications of differential association theory would include practices that endeavour to keep young people away from the "wrong types of people" and instead expose them to peers who hold viewpoints that endorse conventional behaviour. Parents who try to steer their children away from hanging around with those they consider to be "bad influences" is a position that is in keeping with one of the key assumptions of differential association theory.

Labelling Theory

The origins of **labelling theory** can be traced back to the symbolic interactionist tradition. **Symbolic interactionism** understands human behaviour by examining the interaction that takes place between people through symbols. A basic premise of this perspective is that people do not respond to the world directly, but do so by attaching symbolic meanings to themselves in relation to the physical and social world. Based on the early work of Charles Cooley (1902) and George Herbert Mead (1934), social life involves a continuous process of interpreting meanings of our own actions and those of others.

The first time that the symbolic interactionist perspective was directly applied to the study of crime can be found in the writings of Frank Tannenbaum (1938). A key concept introduced by Tannenbaum, who was a great influence on subsequent labelling theorists, is the notion of "tagging." From research he was conducting with delinquent youth, Tannenbaum saw that the stigma that accompanies the deviant tag or label could cause a person to fall deeper into non-conformity (Pfohl, 1985). Being identified as an outsider, or social deviant, can cause a person to start thinking about him or herself as "a bad person," which can lead to the formation of a deviant persona. Tannenbaum's basic argument is that the more attention society directs toward a person who has been in trouble with the law, the greater the likelihood that the tagged person will come to identify himself or herself as a criminal.

Even though the roots of labelling theory can be traced back to the late 1930s, it really was not until the 1960s that the impact of this approach became dominant within sociological criminology. One of the most important points to grasp about labelling and other social-reaction theories, including conflict theories, is that no attempt is made to explain *why* particular individuals *initially* engage in crime. Rather, labelling theorists are more interested in explaining how crime and deviance are defined (see the discussion of labelling theory in Chapter 1) as well as understanding how rule-breaking is reacted to by those with power in society. Unlike strain, control, and differential association theories, for example, labelling theory is more concerned with examining the processes involved in defining deviant behaviour, how social deviants are reacted to, and how those who have been labelled respond and react to such labels.

The ideas of Edwin Lemert (1969) illustrate the logic of the labelling approach. Two concepts are central to Lemert's theory: primary and secondary deviation. Primary deviation is ubiquitous in society: We all do it. Norm violation is very common and the causes are multifaceted—psychological, biological, sociological—but have an inconsequential impact on the rule-breaker. However, if the primary deviant act is "tagged" then it is very possible that secondary deviation will emerge.

Take the hypothetical example of a teenaged girl who takes a bottle of vodka from her parent's liquor cabinet prior to a party at a classmate's house. She may have taken the liquor because one of her friends asked her to bring some alcohol to the party. Or, since she was attending a party where older youth were going to be present, she may have taken the vodka simply to "fit in" and appear to be more adult. Regardless of the reason why she stole the vodka, it is quite possible that this event would be a one-time experience and that her relations with peers and family would be unaffected. However, suppose that she drank too much of the vodka too quickly and became so intoxicated that she passed out in front of her friends, causing the host of the party to call for paramedics who take her to the hospital where she is treated for alcohol poisoning. On returning home, her parents punish her both for stealing the liquor and for her irresponsible drinking, and subsequently her classmates taunt and tease her because of her inability to "hold her liquor" and for being grounded by her parents. The young woman, feeling angry because of the way she has been treated by her peers and parents, decides to take another bottle of alcohol from her parents. But this time she drinks it on her way to school. The teacher recognizes signs of drunkenness in the girl and reports her to the principal. As a result of a "zero-tolerance policy" adopted by the school board, the girl is suspended from school for a week. Continuing to comply with board policy, the principal reports the incident to the police, who subsequently charge her for being drunk in a public place and for being under the legal drinking age. In youth court, the young woman is found guilty of these charges and is placed on probation for one year. One of the conditions of her probation is to refrain from the use of drugs, including alcohol. Feeling that she has been treated unfairly in comparison with how adults, such as her parents, are treated for *their* drinking, she breaks her parental and legal curfews by sneaking out of the house and attempts to steal a bottle of wine. Spotted by store personnel, she is detained in the store and once again arrested by the police. Her parents have scheduled a tropical vacation and have decided this behaviour is the culmination of many problems for which they blame their daughter. They decide that "tough love" means abandoning her in this predicament so that she can "shape up and act like an adult"; they do not help her find an attorney and instead leave for Tahiti, so that no one accompanies her to court. The young woman wears the most extreme outfit she can contrive from her closet to court. Seeing the young woman appear in court for the second time—charged for theft under $5,000 and for breaching probation—the judge decides to place her in an open-custody facility. While in custody she encounters several other girls who have experimented with a wide range of illicit substances and risky behaviours. Soon after her release, she finds she is no longer welcome in her former social circle and starts to hang around with a group of substance-abusing people who are older—and soon she is arrested for a third time, for being in possession of crystal meth.

According to Lemert's formulation, the young woman in this story has become a secondary deviant. While her deviant behaviour was not caused by a single event, she has internalized the negative labels that have been imposed on her by her family, peers, and most importantly, the criminal justice system. She now views herself as a problem drug-user and young offender. In the idiom of labelling theory, her self-concept was altered and she has assumed a deviant identity.

What makes labelling theory unique is that, unlike most other criminological theories that assume the crime leads to social control (labelling), the line of causal relationship is reversed: social control (labelling) leads to crime. In the case described above, if the girl had not experienced the social controls that resulted from her drinking at the party, she would not have internalized the deviant self-concept and would have continued to occupy the role of a conformist. Thus, the basic idea behind labelling theory is that those who are labelled as deviant are likely to take on a deviant identity, which can then lead to further offending. Delinquents, or criminals, through a process of social interaction, conform to the labels that have been conferred on them by society.

There is no denying that labelling is provocative in that it raises the point that efforts by society to control social deviants can have unintended consequences. But there are some key problems with this perspective. First, labelling theory does not consider the possibility that punishment and labelling for wrongdoing can be effective in deterring offenders from future offending. According to Akers (1993), the application of criminal labels in "reintegrative shaming"—a form of punishment that is thought to reinforce the moral bond between the lawbreaker and society—tends to deter crime. Second, this perspective does not consider that illegal activity can take place over a prolonged period of time, even when the perpetrator's actions never come to the attention of the criminal justice system. A good example of this last point would be the Scarborough rapist and serial killer Paul Bernardo. During the time when Bernardo was sexually assaulting dozens of women in Scarborough, an inner suburb of Toronto, he had no criminal record. The same pattern is also evident with other serial killers. For example, Denis Rader, also known as the BTK (bind, torture, kill) killer, was responsible for at least 10 murders that took place in Wichita, Kansas, between 1974 and 1991. He had no criminal record when he was arrested in 2005. More recently, in October 2010, Colonel Russell Williams, who also had no previous criminal record and was the commander of one of Canada's largest military bases, pleaded guilty to two counts of first-degree murder, two counts of sexual assault and forcible confinement, and numerous break-ins and attempted break-ins.

Applications of labelling theory can be found within several domains. Within the school system, opponents to "streaming," or placing weak students in non-academic courses, believe that the practice lowers student aspirations, motivation, and achievement. This is because students in the lower streams who are "looked down upon," or labelled by teachers and students as underachievers, come to view themselves in this negative light and hence internalize this "deviant identity." There is also good reason to believe that the law prohibiting the publication of information that identifies young people charged under the Youth Criminal Justice Act is based on labelling theory. Keeping the names of young offenders out of the news media serves the purpose of not publicly labelling the young person as a social deviant, which lessens the stigma associated with breaking the law.

Critical Criminology

Critical criminology emerged not long after labelling theory appeared in the 1960s. The roots of the critical perspective are based in conflict theory and Marxism, and can be traced back to the writings of Karl Marx in the nineteenth century and to the work of Bonger (1916) in the early twentieth century. But it was not until the late 1960s and early 1970s that the critical perspective made its mark on sociological criminology. Early examples of **critical criminology** include the works of Turk (1969), Quinney (1970), Chambliss and Seidman (1971), Platt (1969), and Taylor et al. (1973). This body of work concurs that, as an economic and social system, capitalism is not characterized by a consensus concerning shared values. On the contrary, societies like the United States are best characterized, according to this critical perspective, by the struggle and conflict that take place between the powerful and less powerful classes. The meaning of crime for critical theorists, then, is not to be taken for granted. Critical theorists would insist that it is a mistake to assume that laws merely reflect socially agreed-on norms and values. Moreover, and in keeping with what was brought to light by the labelling perspective, the critical perspective believes that the focus of criminology should be directed not only to the rule-breakers, but also to the rule-makers.

Where critical theory differs noticeably from the labelling perspective concerns the way in which power is distributed in society. In general terms, labelling theory views society as having a plurality of interests. This means that power is something that individuals and groups strive for to maximize their own opportunities and rewards. For pluralists, the state functions as a neutral arbitrator that sets rules so that access to power is not unfairly attained by greedy individuals or by unscrupulous organizations.

Informed by Marxist political economy, the critical perspective rejects the claim that society is based on a pluralistic model. Social relations do not operate on a basis where different individuals and social groups can lobby the state and compete for a "bigger slice of the pie." For critical criminologists, gaining and maintaining power in society is an issue of social class position and privilege. Such a position is determined by membership in one of the two fundamental social classes: the bourgeoisie (economic elites) and the proletariat (working class). The bourgeoisie own the means of production in society and have access to capital and property, while members of the proletariat are without these means and are forced to sell their labour power to the bourgeoisie to survive. Unlike the pluralistic viewpoint, the state is not neutral according to critical criminologists. Rather, the state secures and maintains the interests of the economic elites because of the close ties that exist between those with political power and those with economic control and influence. In fact, research has shown for some time just how close-knit the political elites are with the economic elites in Canada (Clement, 1975).

Without going into the details of Marxist political economic theory here, it is sufficient to say that the critical model of criminology views the social conflict created by the class struggle between the elites and the working class to be closely related to how crime is defined and how criminals are reacted to. Since law-making and enforcement activities are engaged in by a state that supports the interests of the capitalist class, the working class bears the brunt of this power imbalance. For this reason, the illegal activities that take place within the working class are subject to criminalization, while the socially injurious activities of the economic and political elites are engaged in with impunity. Thus, it comes as no surprise that officially recorded crime is higher in the working class than in the elite class. Law, for conflict theorists, is a powerful tool for maintaining class power and privilege.

To support these claims critical theorists point out that laws relating to theft, for example, were enacted originally by people in positions of power who had more to lose from theft. Critical criminologists often cite the work of Jerome Hall (1952), who argued that the emergence of theft and property laws in England can be traced to the early days of industrial capitalism. As the capitalist class grew more prominent, laws were created to protect the material interests of merchants and traders. These laws were not created on the basis of a "value consensus" but instead to protect the propertied class (bourgeoisie) from the working class. According to this viewpoint, property laws are rooted in the perceived threat that the working class posed to the bourgeoisie.

Early critical thinking was extremely effective in pointing out that many criminal laws do not reflect the interests of society at large. More than this, critical criminologists also contended that most sociological thinking tended to be dominated by the idea that the majority of crime was committed by the lower classes, since much law-breaking was seen to be the result of the strain and disorganization experienced by the poor and those discriminated against for their racial origins. As a corrective, the critical perspective put a spotlight on corporate and organized crime. In Canada some of this early work included analyses of occupational health and safety violations (Reasons et al., 1981) and anti-combines legislation (Goff & Reasons, 1978). More recently, critical criminological research has focused on analyses of the disposal of toxic waste in Canadian harbours and oceans (McMullan & Smith, 1997) and the Westray coal mine disaster in Nova Scotia (McMullan, 2006).

While critical criminology is rooted in an analysis of crime within the context of capitalism, more recent schools of thought that can be classified as "critical" extend beyond this class-based focus. Newer critical approaches such as feminist criminology, left realism, peace-making criminology, and postmodern criminology remain critical of the social organization of society, but by no means are these analyses driven solely by a class analysis.

Left Realism

The left-realist perspective can be traced back to an essay written by Jock Young in 1975 entitled "Working Class Criminology," in which Young introduced the notion that with a unidirectional focus on the crime committed by the powerful—such as corporate crime—most critical criminologists ignored the crime and victimization that was being experienced by the working class. This was deemed problematic by many socialist criminologists because it opened the doors for conservative law-and-order approaches that viewed working-class crime as a phenomenon caused by a lack of discipline, so that more policing and stricter punishments were necessary to control it.

A more detailed pronouncement of the left-realist perspective can be found in Young's collaborative writings with John Lea. Similar to the point raised by Young almost a decade earlier, the left-realist position was critical of what it termed the left-idealists' position on crime because it did not take seriously the crime and victimization within the working class. Written in the context of the conservative Thatcher government in Britain from 1979 to 1990 and with a practical approach to crime in mind, Lea and Young (1984) wanted to refocus the agenda on how to better understand and deal with the causes and consequences of working-class street crime. With a focus on the victims of street crime, left realists highlighted the fact that most victims of street crime were people with working-class backgrounds. Much of the information about working-class victimization was revealed through local crime victimization surveys, drawing samples from households in impoverished working-class neighbourhoods such as in Islington, an East London neighbourhood (Jones et al., 1986).

Besides wanting to take crime seriously from a left-leaning, progressive position, **left realism** was based on the following basic assumptions that have been nicely summarized by White and Haines (2004). They note that crime for left realists is defined, for the most part, as what is contained in the *Criminal Code*; most crime of concern to the working class falls in the category of street crimes, such as muggings and break and entering. The main causes of working-class street crime are twofold. The first, "relative deprivation," means that it is not necessarily abject poverty that causes crime—homeless people stealing food for survival, for example—so much as a desire for something that others have but the thief does not. The origins of the concept can be traced by to Peter Townsend's research on poverty in the 1950s in England and to the work of Stouffer in the United States in the late 1940s. The notion of relative deprivation is based on the assumption that people's attitudes, aspirations, and grievances depend largely on their frame of reference. For example, if one community observes another community or reference group to be relatively prosperous, a feeling of deprivation will arise. For Lea and

Young, this type of situation gives rise to feelings of powerlessness, exclusion, and social breakdown and incites criminal behaviour. The second cause of crime is the police's antagonistic and ineffective response to this situation. Poor policing creates a distrusting public and an unwillingness to co-operate with police investigations of crime, which only exacerbate the social malaise.

The majority of crime in this context in intraclass based—crime that takes place within groups, not between different groups. Unlike left idealists who understood the essence of working-class crime in a Robin Hood fashion where the poor steal from the rich, left realists argue that most working-class criminals prey on victims from within their own communities. Also worthy of note is the left realists' focus on "practical" responses to crime. This includes the development of more effective police–community relations and greater community control and involvement with the criminal justice system in general. Crime prevention methods and meeting the needs of victims are also on the agenda for left realists (White & Haines, 2004, p. 158).

The work of Walter DeKeseredy is a good example of a researcher who has been influential in popularizing left realism in Canada. A study by DeKeseredy et al. (2003) of poverty and crime in an Ontario public housing complex is a good example of the left-realist analysis. Using a small-scale victimization survey, the authors show that the residents of "West Town" live amid chronic socioeconomic disadvantage, crime, and fear. Over half of the respondents were victimized by predatory crime, and a disproportionate number of females experienced partner and stranger violence in public settings. For DeKeseredy et al., the residents of West Town are exposed to levels of risk above and beyond those experienced by the general Canadian population. In this study, there was no doubt that the victims of crime were poor, disenfranchised people who were victimized by criminals from similar backgrounds. This study is a good example of a left-realist analysis because it also offered several "practical" crime-prevention strategies beyond the realm of the criminal justice system, such as improving housing conditions, bettering labour-market opportunities (jobs that pay more than minimum wage), and enhancing public transportation.

Like any other criminological theory, left realism is not without its detractors. A common criticism questions the claim that left realism is in fact a criminological theory in its own right. Left realism is best described more or less as a political rather than as a theoretical perspective on the grounds that it simply argues that crime and crime control should be taken seriously—not a whole lot more is offered. Indeed, the major cause of crime for left realists is relative deprivation, a concept that was first developed shortly after the Second World War. Moreover, left realism has also been chastised for not sufficiently addressing issues pertaining to women violence (DeKeseredy & Schwartz, 1991). Another criticism has arisen from those who left realists would label *left idealists*. Concerns have been raised about the assumption that disenfranchised communities can work with the *criminal* justice system to overcome the problems associated with crime. The concern here is that if the conditions that give rise to crime are about community breakdown and lack of social justice, how could the crime problem be ameliorated by the criminal justice system? Some critics have gone so far as to say that left realists have gone dangerously close to adopting a "radical law and order program" for curbing such behaviour (Beirne & Messerschmidt, 1991).

Since the main idea of critical criminology is to be critical of the criminal justice system, in addition to focusing attention on the lawmakers in society (as opposed to the lawbreakers) as far as public policies to control crime are concerned, the impact of this radical perspective has been limited. Society would have to undergo a major reorganization, which may entail a social revolution, for the "practice" of this perspective to be put into action. However, the left-realist version of this perspective would be generally supportive of the crime control strategies offered by the more mainstream theories (e.g., strain and social disorganization) that have been introduced in this chapter.

Feminism and Criminology

Feminist contributions to the study of crime tend to centre on two areas. One is victimology—mainly men's violence against women. The other is concerned with the causes of female crime and deviance. The discussion of feminism and criminology involves the following concepts used in feminist analyses: *feminism, patriarchy, gender,* and *sex.* Before exploring victimology and the causes of female offending, these three concepts will be introduced first.

Feminism is the "advocacy of the rights and equality of women in social, political, and economic spheres, and . . . a commitment to the fundamental alteration of women's role in society" (Leuner, 1977, p. 231). Feminism is closely tied to the women's liberation movement and was most publicly visible in what is often referred to as the second wave of feminism that emerged in the late 1960s and 1970s when women took to the streets to protest for the rights of women. The first wave of feminism usually refers to the early twentieth-century movement of women who, among other things, successfully lobbied governments for the right to vote. In Canada, the efforts of Nellie McClung exemplify the first wave of feminism.

Patriarchy refers to any social system of male dominance and power, not simply family headship, as it formerly connoted. Males continue to dominate in several sectors of society, including the economic organization of the household and the family, in the world of paid employment, in governments and educational systems, and in most cultural spheres, whether public (such as advertising), private (sexuality), or anti-social (such as violence and crime) (Charles, 2002). Feminist analysis makes a clear distinction between the concepts of "sex" and "gender." *Sex* is a biological trait indicative of genital differences between males and females, whereas *gender* is a social construct pertaining to what it means in a culture to be masculine or feminine. In other words, gender is not a natural fact simply derived from biological difference and reproductive capacities. While several variants of feminism can be identified (e.g., liberal, radical, Marxist, socialist, postmodern), feminists generally are in agreement that behaviour considered by society to be *masculine* and *feminine* is not defined simply on the basis of the biological differences that exist between males and females. Rather, gender relations and constructs of masculinity and femininity need to be understood on the basis of men's social, political, and economic power over women.

Male Violence Against Women

Feminist analyses of crime point out that traditional, legal definitions of behaviours such as prostitution, pornography, sexual assault, and domestic violence have been defined according to a male perspective, and not according to the experiences of women. Moreover, prior to the late 1960s and early 1970s there was a "virtual conspiracy of silence" around issues such as rape and domestic violence in Canada and elsewhere (Clark & Lewis, 1977, p. 26). **Feminist criminology** was part of a social movement that helped change social attitudes and criminal justice system responses to these issues. In fact, changes that were made to Canadian rape laws and changes that took place in how the criminal justice system responds to domestic violence were initiated in part by feminist criminologists such as Lorenne Clark and Debra Lewis (1977). In 1983, rape laws in Canada were renamed and redefined so that under the new sexual assault statutes it became illegal for a man to rape his wife. Under the former rape provisions, a man could not be charged for raping his wife.

Also during this period, changes were undertaken with the criminal justice system's approach to domestic or intimate violence. Even though men and women are both victims of domestic violence in Canada, research has shown that the consequences of assaults inflicted on women by their partners are more brutal than female spousal assaults against men. Female victims are more likely to be injured, to need medical and shelter services, or to be killed (Johnson & Pottie Bunge, 2001). Prior to the mid-1980s, police who responded to "domestic disturbances" often did not lay charges. If charges were made, the perpetrator (in most cases a male) would likely be charged with "being drunk and disorderly in the home" (not a *Criminal Code* violation), not with assault (O'Grady et al., 2000). As the result of feminist lobbying efforts, between 1983 and 1986 federal and provincial attorneys general and solicitors general in Canada adopted policy directives requiring police and Crown prosecutors to charge and prosecute all incidents of spousal abuse where there were reasonable and probable grounds to believe that an offence had been committed. This is just one example of how a feminist approach has had a direct influence on criminal justice policy.

Feminist criminology continues to pursue victimology: the study of crime victims. For example, in 1995 a study of selected economic costs of three forms of violence—sexual assault, woman abuse in intimate partnerships, and incest or child sexual abuse—estimated the partial annual costs of violence against women in the areas of social services/education, criminal justice, employment, and medical/health costs. The study estimated that $4,225,954,322 per year is spent as the result of such violence. The authors of this study estimated that 87.5 per cent of these costs were borne by the state, 11.5 per cent by the individual, and 0.9 per cent by third parties (Greaves et al., 1995).

Not only are the financial costs associated with this violence high, but support services for victims of spousal violence are not well funded or are non-existent. A study in the United Kingdom, for example, found that over one-third of local authorities provide no services whatsoever for victims of domestic violence (Coy et al., 2007).

Box 4.2 | **Debates and Controversies**

Preventing Male Violence against Women

Domestic violence prevention programs have recently been directed at male athletes who play organized, physically aggressive sports. Research shows, for example, that contact sports team players are more likely to engage in sexual assault activities where they are either part of or know that the behaviour is happening (Flood & Dyson, 2007.)

In order to prevent such violence programs like **Mentors in Violence Prevention (MVP)** have worked with thousands of student-athletes and other student leaders at hundreds of colleges and universities in the Unites States. In fact, since the late 1990s, MVP programs have trained the coaches and players of the NFL's New England Patriots football team. The Patriots were the first professional football team to adopt MVP. Today a quarter of the teams in the NFL have since participated.

According to Katz, these are ten things men can do to prevent gender violence:

1. Approach gender violence as a MEN'S issue involving men of all ages and socioeconomic, racial, and ethnic backgrounds. View men not only as perpetrators or possible offenders, but as empowered bystanders who can confront abusive peers.

Continued

2. If a brother, friend, classmate, or teammate is abusing his female partner—or is disrespectful or abusive to girls and women in general—don't look the other way. If you feel comfortable doing so, try to talk to him about it. Urge him to seek help. Or if you don't know what to do, consult a friend, a parent, a professor, or a counselor. DON'T REMAIN SILENT.

3. Have the courage to look inward. Question your own attitudes. Don't be defensive when something you do or say ends up hurting someone else. Try hard to understand how your own attitudes and actions might inadvertently perpetuate sexism and violence, and work toward changing them.

4. If you suspect that a woman close to you is being abused or has been sexually assaulted, gently ask if you can help.

5. If you are emotionally, psychologically, physically, or sexually abusive to women, or have been in the past, seek professional help NOW.

6. Be an ally to women who are working to end all forms of gender violence. Support the work of campus-based women's centres. Attend "Take Back the Night" rallies and other public events. Raise money for community-based rape-crisis centres and battered-women's shelters. If you belong to a team or fraternity, or another student group, organize a fundraiser.

7. Recognize and speak out against homophobia and gay-bashing. Discrimination and violence against lesbians and gays are wrong in and of themselves. This abuse also has direct links to sexism (e.g., the sexual orientation of men who speak out against sexism is often questioned, a conscious or unconscious strategy intended to silence them. This is a key reason few men do so).

8. Attend programs, take courses, watch films, and read articles and books about multicultural masculinities, gender inequality, and the root causes of gender violence. Educate yourself and others about how larger social forces affect the conflicts between individual men and women.

9. Don't fund sexism. Refuse to purchase any magazine, rent any video, subscribe to any website, or buy any music that portrays girls or women in a sexually degrading or abusive manner. Protest sexism in the media.

10. Mentor and teach young boys about how to be men in ways that don't involve degrading or abusing girls and women. Volunteer to work with gender violence prevention programs, including anti-sexist men's programs. Lead by example.

Source: Katz, 1999. Copyright Jackson Katz, www.jacksonkatz.com.

Besides undertaking research and developing theory in the field of victimology, feminist criminology has also been active in trying to understand the nature of female offending.

Explaining Female Crime

Prior to the late 1960s and early 1970s, criminologists tended to ignore women in seeking explanations of criminal behaviour. Women who were involved in crime were most often considered to be more masculine than non-criminal women (Lilly et al., 1995) and, therefore, not deserving of a category apart from men. Such an explanation clearly is rooted in biological assumptions. If women or girls were mentioned in sociological accounts of crime, they were usually discussed in terms of what Albert Cohen calls "sexual delinquency" (1955, p. 144). According to the explanation that Cohen developed around subcultures, male and female delinquency was different. And the most notable difference "is that male delinquency, particularly the subcultural kind, is versatile, whereas female delinquency is relatively specialized. It consists overwhelmingly of sexual delinquency or of involvement in situations that are likely to 'spill over' into over sexuality" (ibid.).

The idea of female criminality being restricted only to the sexual realm is also evident in W.I. Thomas's *The Unadjusted Girl* (1923). Reviewing the case records of juvenile girls in Chicago, Thomas discovered that the majority of these young women were placed in custody for prostitution and related offences. Working within the perspective of social disorganization theory, Thomas dismissed biological reasoning for why these females were involved in these illegal activities. Rather, he argued that these young women worked as prostitutes because they were a product of the times. By this Thomas meant that the crime that these young women were engaging in was a product of social disorganization, since these young women came from a part of the city characterized by a lack of social cohesion. A lack of familial social controls and the strain that was brought to bear by the social pressures to acquire consumer goods—most notably female fashion items—forced these young women to sell their bodies to make money.

Criminological explanations of female roles in crime and delinquency continued for the next 30 years to focus on the "non-normative" sexual behaviour of women that was understood primarily in terms of personal pathology due to biological factors or from inappropriate socialization.

Origins of the feminist perspective can be found in the writings of Carol Smart (1976) in Britain, and Freda Adler (1975) and Rita Simon (1975) in the United States. The major contribution offered by Smart centred on the observation that females were either completely ignored or only offhandedly attended to by just about all sociological theories of crime. Because men and women were seen to experience the world in different ways, Smart thought that it was important for criminologists to explain female crime with a conceptual framework that was not so male-centred. In fact, Smart suggested that since the field of criminology was historically dominated by males, interpretations of female crime were seen to rest largely on biased, sexist assumptions.

In response to the belief that female crime rates were rising in the United States during the 1960s, Adler (1975) and Simon (1975) embarked on a more empirical exercise and proposed that rising levels of female crime were the result of growing levels of educational attainment and increases in women's involvement in what traditionally had been male-dominated occupations. This argument, commonly referred to as the liberation/emancipation hypothesis, suggested that a "new female criminal" was emerging. As gender equality increased, so would the numbers of women involved in male types of crime, such as violent, organized, and business crimes. Simon (1975) also noted that as occupational opportunities for women expand, the criminal justice system would display less chivalrous attitudes toward women, hence augmenting the number of recorded female crimes. Evidence used by Simon to support the contention that the quality and quantity of female crime was changing was largely drawn from the correlations made between female labour force participation rates and official female crime rates.

This work was welcomed because it moved beyond biological explanations of female criminal behaviour. It also took the step of attempting to locate the causes of female crime within the broader social and economic order. Nevertheless, Adler's and Simon's work has not been without some disparagement. Critical assessment has largely been based on the evidence used by Adler and Simon when they suggest that the emancipation of women is responsible for rising crime rates. According to UCR data collected in the 1970s and 1980s, many women who were involved in crime did not fit the image of the modern woman who was reaping the benefits from post-secondary education and lucrative employment. In fact, the kinds of crime that women were committing were common property offences such as shoplifting and fraud—writing bad cheques and welfare deception. These were not women receiving the benefits of this second wave of feminism. Rather, they were women engaging in traditional types of female crime, and most shared backgrounds of economic and social marginalization (Faith, 1993).

Not long after this, Adler's (1975) and Simon's (1975) work appeared, and research by Hagan, Gillis, and Simpson (1979) showed that the link between sex and crime can be found within the stratification system. That is, the lower crime rates for women, relative to men, could be explained by women's restricted access to the reward structure of the labour market within the public realm and at the same time, their isolation to the private realm of the household (Hagan et al., 1979, p. 25). This idea grew into what became known as power control theory.

Unlike the work of Adler and Simon, which had relied on aggregate data (official crime rates and labour force statistics), **power control theory** was developed through a series of self-report surveys administered to high school students and their parents in suburban Toronto. Hagan and his colleagues contended that gender and the social class of the students' parents had an impact on how much freedom these students had. Coming of age as a female, they argued, was a more limiting experience than growing up as a male. While this seems obvious, they found that the amount of power a parent had in the workplace was related to the control displayed in the household over their teenaged children. Interestingly, parents who had the types of jobs where they must supervise the activities of subordinates also tended to be relatively tolerant of the trouble-making behaviour of their children, particularly of their sons. This meant that teenaged boys are freer to deviate than teenaged girls. This study also found, focusing on relatively minor forms of deviance such as shoplifting and breaking street lights, that middle-class youth actually were freer to deviate than working-class youth.

Like other control theories (e.g., Hirschi, 1969), power control theory did not view crime as caused by low social status. By comparing the gender roles and parental control mechanisms in two different types of families, patriarchal and egalitarian, these researchers were able to explain differences in self-reported male and female misconduct. More specifically, in the more traditional or patriarchal families, it was typical for fathers to work outside of the home while mothers would remain in the household and were responsible for day-to-day child-rearing. In egalitarian families, work roles and household roles were shared on a more equitable basis between mothers and fathers. In fact, in many egalitarian families both mothers and fathers worked outside of the home and held positions of authority. In such households, girls and boys were given similar amounts of supervision. This theory was attempting to examine an issue that was absent in previous research: the linking of authority relations in the workplace with authority relations in the household. With further research Hagan et al. (1979) found that the delinquency rates of girls from patriarchal families were considerably lower than those of boys in similar types of families. In egalitarian households, however, self-reported delinquency was more similar for boys and girls.

Over the years this theory has been refined (McCarthy et al., 1999) and tested with non-traditional family formations, such as single-parent and step families (Bates et al., 2003; Mack & Leiber, 2005). Early attempts to test this theory in the United States by Singer and Levine (1988) found mixed support for the theory. While mothers were seen to be more controlling over their daughters than their sons—supporting power control theory—the authors also found this to be more so with egalitarian than patriarchal families, which is a finding opposite to what power control theory would predict. Not only are researchers continuing to test this theory, but the implications of this approach on public policy have been suggested. For example, intervention programs that target high-risk children and high-risk families have been associated with this theory:

> Formal policies that support *all* families through parenting classes to explain the importance of consistent monitoring or recourses designed to increase the ease of monitoring (for example, policies that subsidize daycare for those families that cannot afford it) would be consistent with this theory and these findings. (Bates et al., 2003, p. 184)

In a review of power control theory, Tanner offers two interesting critical comments. First, the theory is intended to explain the "common delinquencies of ordinary adolescents" not serious or repetitive delinquency (Tanner, 2001, p. 206). The theory is not likely to predict, therefore, the overly aggressive and violent behaviour among some youth. Second, by suggesting that egalitarian households contribute to female delinquency, power control theory implicitly blames increases in female crime on mothers who are in the labour force. In a way, then, this theory is similar to the "liberation" hypotheses whereby women's liberation is associated with rises in female crime. This, of course, is counter to UCR data that show an inverse relationship between female labour force participation and official levels of female criminality.

The study of crime and gender has also evolved into a controversy about the adequacy of theories of crime that originally were developed by males and tested, for the most part, on male populations. The question raised by some feminist criminologists is whether these "malestream" theories are effective for explaining female crime. The reason why the applicability of traditional theories of deviance has been questioned for explaining female deviance pertains to the assumption that female and male delinquency result from different processes. For example, males report significantly more involvement in just about every type of crime. Moreover, for those females who come into contact with the criminal justice system, most are arrested for relatively minor property crimes. Because the level and character of female crime is so different from the patterns of male crime, it is believed that traditional sociological explanations of crime are inconsistent with the lives of females and that a specific explanation of female crime needs to be developed. To date, however, there has not been a fully developed feminist theory of crime that has effectively accounted for the uniqueness of female criminality.

Conclusion

Sociological accounts of crime, in contrast to individualistic theories of crime, focus on the group and the social patterning of crime. In its early stages, North American sociological theorizing was based on ecological and social disorganization approaches. Inspired by Durkheim, the Chicago School set out to show the ways in which crime is socially patterned and that these patterns are the result of poverty and social disintegration, not of individual pathology. The notion that crime was associated with lower-class standing is also a major theme evident in strain theory. Whether it is the strain produced by a society that does not provide equal access for its citizenry to the legitimate means and resources necessary to achieve cultural goals, or a protest against the norms and values of middle-class culture, crime was regarded as a lower-class phenomenon.

Control theory links the onset of criminality to the weakening of ties that bind people to society. Unlike strain theory, which assumes society creates social pressures that lead to crime, control theory as formulated by Hirschi assumes that all individuals are potential law-violators otherwise kept under control because they fear that illegal behaviour would jeopardize established bonds with parents, teachers, and friends.

Differential association theory suggests that people learn criminal behaviour much as they learn conventional behaviour. As formulated by Edwin Sutherland, differential association theory considers criminal behaviour to arise when people perceive an excess of definitions in favour of crime over the cumulative force of perceived definitions that support non-criminal values. The assumptions of this theory can apply either to street or to corporate crime.

Labelling theory holds that criminality is promoted when people become negatively labelled or tagged, especially by the criminal justice system. According to Lemert, once an individual is labelled as "criminal," expectations are created so that the labelled individual takes on a deviant identity, which locks him or her further into a lifestyle of crime and deviance.

Critical, left-realist, and feminist theories, although a diverse body of thought, suggest that crime in any society is caused by class and gender conflict. Rather than focusing on why individuals break the law, critical approaches examine law-making processes and law enforcement practices. Laws, according to this approach, are created by those who hold power in society for self-interest. For this reason, the powerful commit crimes with relative impunity, while crime committed by the lower classes is diligently enforced and punished or, to use one conflict theorist's phrase, "the rich get richer and the poor get prison" (Reiman, 2004). Because conflict theory fails to take into consideration the fact that most street criminals prey upon the poor and disenfranchised, left realism emerged as a compromise between radical approaches to crime and more traditional sociological explanations, like strain theory. Because theories of crime historically have not explained the differences between male and female criminal behaviour, feminist analyses of crime have focused on issues surrounding violence against women and on approaches, such as power control theory, that make an effort to explain female criminality.

Critical Thinking Questions

1. Name some categories of criminal offending that would *not* be explained adequately by Lemert's labelling theory. Identify the theories of criminology that have been developed to explain these categories of crime.

2. How has feminism challenged what has been referred to as "malestream" criminology? Has this critique resulted in a feminist theory of female offending remarkably different from the more traditional sociological explanations of crime?

3. At the beginning of this chapter it was suggested that sociological theories attempt to explain crime *and* its control. Which theories presented in this chapter are better suited for explaining the causes of crime, as opposed to its control?

Suggested Reading

Rafter, Nicole. (2006). *Shots in the mirror: Crime films and society*, 2nd ed. New York, NY: Oxford University Press. This book provides an analysis of the theory embedded in crime films in society. Several of the explanations offered in this book relate to many of the theories reviewed in this and the previous chapter.

Sampson, Robert. (2012). *Great American city: Chicago and the enduring neighborhood Effect*. Chicago, IL: University of Chicago Press. This detailed study shows that neighbourhoods greatly influence levels of crime. In many ways, this book is an update of the Chicago School of Sociology that was discussed earlier in this chapter. The book is a testimony of the longstanding legacy of this approach for understanding crime.

Taylor, Ian, Walton, Paul, & Young, Jock. (1973). *The new criminology: For a social theory of deviance*. London, UK: Routledge. This book offers a thorough critique of many of the theories of crime introduced in this chapter. The authors conclude with a conflict view of criminology that had an important influence on the field of critical criminology.

Websites and Films

The Criminology Mega-Site
www.drtomoconnor.com/criminology.htm
This website has dozens of links related to criminology, including criminological theory.

Jason Katz
www.jacksonkatz.com
This website provides more information on the Mentors in Violence Prevention Program which was introduced in this chapter.

Roger and Me. (1989). A documentary directed by and featuring Michael Moore (*Capitalism, Fahrenheit 9/11, SiCKO, Bowling for Columbine*). Many scenes of this film can be applied to the ideas contained in social disorganization theory and the Chicago School in addition to some of the general assumptions of the conflict approach.

The Informant. (2009). A satirical film by Steven Soderbergh, starring Matt Damon, deals with the topic of corporate price-fixing in the United States.

5 Recent Sociological Approaches to Crime

Learning Objectives

After completing this chapter students will be able to:

◎ Understand how *A General Theory of Crime* and general strain theory differ from their earlier formulations, presented in the previous chapter.

◎ Recognize the different types of research studies that have relied on the life course perspective.

◎ Be able to explain why routine activities theory is not interested in examining motivations to offend.

◎ Understand research that supports rational choice theory.

◎ Be able to discuss the main points of Crime Prevention through Environmental Design (CPTED).

◎ Know what is meant by "actuarial" criminology.

Introduction

This chapter reviews a selection of contemporary theoretical explanations of crime, many of which build on the previously introduced theories. Gottfredson and Hirschi's ***A General Theory of Crime*** will be examined first, along with relevant empirical research that has assessed this causal explanation of offending. This will be followed by a review of the life course perspective; an assessment of Agnew's updated version of strain theory; and rational choice and routine activity theories, both of which have roots in the classical tradition. Then, we discuss a theoretical approach where the built environment is suggested to have a direct bearing on crime and its control. Chapter 5 concludes with a brief review of ideas that explore crime within the context of a risk society.

A General Theory of Crime

In 1990, Michael Gottfredson and Travis Hirschi published *A General Theory of Crime*. The book soon became an academic bestseller, and its theory is now one of the most widely tested among all criminological theories. Unlike Hirschi's 1969 version of control theory, which centred on four social bonds (beliefs, attachments, involvements, and commitments), the contention behind *A General Theory of Crime* is that crime and other analogous behaviours such as smoking, drinking, gambling, irresponsible sex, and careless driving are all the result of low self-control. For Gottfredson and Hirschi, these sorts of behaviours provide short-term gratification and are caused by the inability of some people to exercise self-control (1990, p. 91). Individuals who lack self-control are believed to be self-centred, impulsive, lacking in perseverance, and likely to exhibit involvement in risk-taking behaviour, including criminal activity. Gottfredson and Hirschi claim that self-control is internalized early in life and determines who will be likely to commit crime (Grasmick et al., 1993, p. 7). Children with behavioural problems will tend to grow into juvenile delinquents and, in due course, into adult offenders (Gottfredson & Hirschi, 1990, p. 155). Because the path toward or away from crime begins early in life, the level of self-control in a person depends on the quality of parenting received in the child's formative years.

The theory purports that parenting is the most important factor determining the level of self-control that children learn. For instance, if a child has an abusive or neglectful upbringing, he or she will tend to be impulsive, insensitive, physical (as opposed to mental), a risk-taker, short-sighted, non-verbal, and will also tend to engage in the analogous criminal acts outlined above (ibid., p. 90). Conversely, children whose parents care about them and supervise and discipline their misconduct will develop the self-control needed to resist the simple temptations that are offered by crime. This theory contends that developing self-control will help people in the future with school, work, and relationships.

A fairly large body of research has been amassed that has tested Gottfredson and Hirschi's theory (Pratt & Cullen, 2000), and *A General Theory of Crime* has had mixed results when put to the empirical test. A study of drunk driving by Keene (1993) confirmed that drunk drivers have low levels of self-control. Other research by Brownfield and Sorenson (1993), using data Hirschi collected in the 1960s, also argued juvenile delinquency is associated with low levels of self-control. And while these two studies are generally supportive of the theory, other research has not been as supportive. For example, an assessment of the theory by Grasmick et al. (1993) found that **crime opportunity** was just as strong a predictor of fraud and aggression as was low self-control. Moreover, low self-control was a better predictor of drinking and gambling than it was for explaining smoking. Some researchers believe that the idea that low self-control leads to crime does not explain enough variance in criminal behaviour (Longshore et al., 1998). More specifically, the theory was not that successful in predicting serious forms of violent behaviour, like homicide. More recent Canadian research that has tested self-control has been carried out by Baron (2003). His research on homeless youth found that low self-control predicted several criminal behaviours. However, Baron's results also found that factors besides self-control predicted certain types of criminal behaviour, including drug use.

A General Theory of Crime, at least in its original formulation, according to Akers (1993), is tautological. In social science, a tautological explanation refers to circular reasoning, and a tautology gives the appearance of a causal relationship where one does not exist. *A General Theory of Crime* is considered to be tautological because it does not define self-control independent from the tendency to commit crimes and related behaviours (Akers, 1993, p. 123). In other words, the terms *criminality* and *lack of self-control* are used synonymously, which is equivalent to saying low self-control causes low self-control, or criminality causes criminality.

A longitudinal study showed that adult social bonds, like stable employment and a cohesive marriage, can redirect offenders into a lifestyle of conformity even though they are far beyond the childhood years of socialization (Lilly et al., 1995, p. 104). These findings run counter to the idea that levels of self-control and crime are constant over the life course—a major contention of *A General Theory of Crime*. Moreover, white-collar crime does not seem to be adequately explained by this theory. Individuals who rise to positions of power in the work world have already proven that they can endure delayed gratification during the time it took to achieve the educational credentials required to assume corporate positions (Benson & Moore, 1992, p. 270).

Notwithstanding the empirical assessments of *A General Theory of Crime*, the theory carries certain paternalistic and conservative undertones. Gottfredson and Hirschi, for example, find the traditional roles of women and men to be crucial to the development of children. Their theory implies that if society could regain traditional American values, with mothers staying at home, fathers working during the day, and the children disciplined by both parents, criminality would decrease. They do not seriously consider the outcomes of their theory for single parents, either divorced or unwed, but such family configurations are a reality in contemporary society. The logical extension of self-control theory could be policies calling for limits on the number of children "at-risk" women may have, and mandating enforced birth control: both extremely paternalistic and impractical ideas. Also, suggesting that men or women stay committed to unhappy marriages so that children might learn self-control is unrealistic. The theory makes it appear that society can do nothing about crime except rise to the challenges of early identification and selective incapacitation. In other words, if children with low self-control can be identified early in life, control efforts could be implemented so that these risk-seeking youth could be monitored, controlled, or even removed from the public. However, putting efforts such as these into practice would be complicated and would undermine the civil rights and liberties for those targeted as possessing the criminogenic trait of low self-control.

One of the main assumptions of this self-control explanation of crime, as stated previously, is that criminality is an attribute that is constant throughout life. If a child does *not* learn self-control early in life, Gottfredson and Hirschi predict that the motivation to commit crime and participate in deviant behaviour will persist well into adulthood. Recent research has shown, however, that levels of self-control may in fact change from childhood into adolescence. A longitudinal study by Na and Pasternoster (2012) discovered that efforts made to improve the childrearing behaviours of caregivers of at-risk children led to higher levels of self-control when the youth were teenagers. The findings of this study suggest that self-control is malleable if youth are properly attended to when they are young.

In terms of the policy implications associated with this theory, the most obvious would be improving the parenting skills for the mothers and fathers of

---

Box 5.1   Debates and Controversies

Are Programs that are Directed for "At Risk" Youth Effective?

In the aftermath of a shooting in Toronto that killed two people in 2012 at an outdoor block party, Toronto mayor Rob Ford stated to the media that more police and stiffer penalties is needed to deal with gang related crime.

"I don't believe in these programs. I call them 'hug a thug' programs, and they haven't been very productive in the past, and I don't know why we're continuing with them" (Armstrong, 2012).

However, according to the information below from the University of Wisconsin, research shows that such programs can be effective if they follow these points:

Program Design and Content

- Interventions are most effective when they are theory-driven and use active learning methods. Many effective juvenile offender programs are based on social learning theory. These programs achieve behavior change through social interaction, role modeling, and roleplaying positive new behaviors with people the offender can relate to. Cognitive-behavioral treatments are also quite effective. These interventions help offenders to replace their negative thought patterns with more positive ones. These programs or therapies also offer opportunities for participants to practice their new skills and positive behaviors.
- Effective programs target dynamic criminogenic needs or risk factors. Programs address current issues in a given offender's life that are correlated with criminal activity, more so than they target non-criminogenic needs. One study found that programs targeting four or more criminogenic needs reduced recidivism, while programs targeting three or fewer actually increased recidivism among participants.

young children throughout the entire society, especially for those living in "high-risk" communities. As difficult as this parenting policy would be to implement, the assumption that those children who lack self-control stand a really good chance of becoming criminals in adulthood is directly contradicted by the next perspective, crime and life course theory, to which we now turn.

The Life Course Perspective

In recent years, the life course perspective has been gaining the attention of criminologists who are interested in knowing more about the long-term effects

Program Relevance
- High-risk and low-risk offenders should never be in the same program. Putting low-risk offenders in overly restrictive programs with higher-risk peers increases recidivism for the low risk offenders. The more resource-intensive, high-supervision programs should be reserved for medium- and high-risk offenders, with lesser sanctions available for low-risk offenders.
- Using a validated risk assessment tool is the best way to ensure that offenders' risk of recidivism is fairly measured and taken into account.
- Effective juvenile justice systems are responsive to offenders' individual characteristics and readiness for treatment. Offenders who have substance abuse issues, for example, need Alcohol and Other Drug Abuse (AODA) treatment before they will be able to take responsibility for their actions or make lasting changes in their behavior. Courts and juvenile justice officials also need to be responsive to offenders' individual characteristics such as learning style and motivation to change, in order to assign offenders to the most appropriate programs. Consistency of staffing over time is important to program success.
- Effective programs are mindful of the risks of peer influence. Studies comparing group and individual administration of similar programs have found that the grouping of deviant youth can reduce positive effects of interventions and even cause adverse effects. Younger youth who are modestly deviant are the most susceptible to negative peer influence and should not be aggregated in groups. These youth should especially not be grouped with slightly older youth who have committed similar crimes. When offenders are grouped, staff should actively create and maintain a prosocial peer culture, and provide a high level of structure to group interactions.
- Staying true to the program design is critical to program effectiveness. When implementing a program that has been successful in the past or in other settings, it is important to closely replicate the program model. This means maintaining core program components such as caseload limits, frequency of contact with offenders, and total hours of program contact.

Source: Small, 2008; O'Connor, 2008; http://whatworks.uwex.edu/

of offending and victimization. The basic premise of the **life course theory** is that problem behaviours—as well as their termination—are age-related, caused by certain events that take place in the developmental process. Unlike the hypothesis proposed by Gottfredson and Hirschi, the premise of the life course perspective is that individuals will refrain from crime and deviance as they enter stages of life where adult roles such as marriage and employment can act as "turning points" that consequently put a stop to criminal careers.

To understand the influence that these turning points can have on crime, life course research often relies on longitudinal research designs that track the activities of groups of individuals over time. Normally, these surveys begin when subjects are children, adolescents, or teens, and then track these youth until they reach various stages of adulthood. Until recently, longitudinal surveys focusing on crime were found primarily in the United States (i.e., the National Longitudinal Survey of Youth) or in Britain (i.e., the Cambridge Study in Delinquent Development). The first effort to carry out this type of research in Canada has been the development of the National Longitudinal Survey of Children and Youth that began in 1994 when data were first collected on a sample of 25,000 Canadian children aged 0–11. The children in the sample were subsequently followed up with every two years. This Canadian study, like life course research in general, collects data when respondents are young because it is generally recognized that criminogenic influences have the largest impact early in life.

Research on criminal careers draws attention to the observation that criminal behaviour tends to follow predictable patterns over the life course. During childhood, serious criminal behaviour is not very common, but crime does tend to increase during adolescence and early adulthood, and then declines thereafter. In fact, the observation that street crime peaks in the late teens and then diminishes afterwards is one of the more well-known and conclusive correlates of crime that has been identified by criminologists (Hirschi & Gottfredson, 1983).

Research in this field dates back to the 1930s when Sheldon and Eleanor Glueck examined the criminal careers of 500 boys from Massachusetts. Information about these boys—in addition to a control group of 500 non-delinquent boys—was gathered from interviews with the boys, their parents, their teachers, and from official criminal justice records. These subjects were interviewed several years later and the general finding of the study was that the more disturbed the children had been, the more likely that they would have problems, including criminality, in adulthood (Sampson & Laub, 1993).

Data from the original Glueck study were reanalyzed by Robert Sampson and John Laub several years later. The original raw data were transferred to an electronic database and then analyzed using modern statistical techniques. Sampson and Laub identified certain turning points in the criminal careers of those sampled in the original study. Informed by control theory (i.e., Hirschi, 1969), Sampson and Laub discovered that a certain number of these research subjects—those who continued to be involved in crime in early adulthood—had stopped their criminal involvements after they became employed or when they got married. In other words, when these men established legitimate social ties with conventional social institutions—family and the labour market—their involvement in crime desisted. A clear policy response to these findings would ensure that inmates released from prisons would receive an adequate discharge plan that would include secure housing, help reconnecting to supportive families, and finding employment.

More recently, Laub and Sampson (2003) have analyzed newly collected data on crime and social development up to age 70 from a group of men who were in the original Glueck study. This research is probably the longest study of age, crime, and the life course that has been carried out to date. By analyzing these long-term data, combined with in-depth interviews, Laub and Sampson show that individual traits such as poor verbal skills, limited self-control, and difficult temperament do not actually account for long-term trajectories of offending. By connecting variability in behaviour to social context, they find that men who desisted from crime were rooted to strong social ties with family and community. As a result of these findings, Laub and Sampson specifically reject the notion that personality characteristics or experiences in childhood or adolescence—like not learning self-control—mark criminality in offenders. They infer from their study that these turning points cannot be predicted in advance because meeting the right woman, finding the right job, or fitting into a rewarding military role may depend on luck and personal agency—or simply being in the right place at the right time. Thus, Laub and Sampson avoid a deterministic approach to crime causation because they emphasize the choices (human agency) that their research subjects made at various points in their lives.

As interesting as this research is, one element missing—as it is from most longitudinal research on crime—the impact that gender plays on offending over the life course. Unfortunately, the original data collected by the Gluecks that Laub and Sampson have analyzed extensively did not contain any females. One longitudinal study that has included girls compared the effects of parental psychiatric problems and supportive parent–child communications and found that low parental support had a greater impact on boys' deviance than on girls' (Johnson, 1995). Another longitudinal study that asked boys questions about their sisters was carried out by Farrington and Painter (2004). These researchers found that although risk factors for criminal involvement were similar for brothers and sisters, low family income, a low standard of housing, and poor parental supervision were more important for sisters, while parental characteristics (e.g., educational levels) were more effective for predicting crime among brothers. Although it was not clear why these differences existed, it does point to the fact that much more life course research needs to be done to properly address the long-term implications of female offending.

Rather than examining criminal careers over the life course, other longitud-inal research has explored the impact that getting into trouble as a teen has on adult labour market achievements. A study by Tanner et al. (1999) examined a wide range of delinquent activities reported in a sample of American teens (males and females) who were first interviewed in 1979. Twelve years later, when the sample was aged 25–30 years, those same individuals were asked questions about their jobs, income, and whether or not they had experienced unemploy-ment. The study found, not surprisingly, that those who had gotten into trouble when they were young had lower-status adult jobs and earned less money than the youth in the sample who were not involved in delinquency. The major reason for these differences had to do with the fact that their delinquency adversely affected their educational outcomes for those who did less well career-wise in adulthood. In other words, getting into trouble as a teen negatively affects school performance, which then adversely affects employment prospects in adulthood.

One of the more interesting findings of the study was the impact played by gender. The effects that delinquency had on employment status in adult-hood were more pronounced for males than they were for females. While the authors of the study were not able to definitively explain why this was the case, they hypothesized that delinquency has a smaller impact on female occupa-tional outcomes because of the lesser amount of variation in women's occu-pational prospects. That is to say, because the range of labour market opportunities are more limited and generally less lucrative for women than they are for men, the effects of delinquency on labour market outcomes are less pronounced for females. More research is required to systematically address these gender differences, but the study was nevertheless one of the first to include both males and females in an examination of the long-term impact of delinquency on occupational achievements.

Not only does this style of research focus on the consequences of youthful offending in adulthood, but it has also addressed the question of what hap-pens in adulthood to those who have been a *victim* of crime during their youth. Does the experience of victimization during the teen years carry nega-tive repercussions later in life? To address this question, Macmillan (2000) used data from a longitudinal survey and a cross-sectional survey (a survey done at only one point it time with no follow up). First of all, Macmillan's findings show that, yes, there is indeed a link between experiencing victimiza-tion as a youth and problems later in life. He found that adolescent victimiza-tion has a negative impact on adult earnings. Using three measures of violent victimization, he found that earnings per hour were $1 lower for those that were victims of crime. More specifically, Macmillan found that sexual assault victims suffered an income deficit of about $6,000 per year. A major reason for these deficits had to do with the fact that sexual assault victims were not as successful with school as were non-victims. Indeed, he showed that an additional year of education was associated with an increase in income of

$1,500 per year. Macmillan further tested to see whether there was an impact of age of the victim at the time of abuse, and his findings revealed that when the victim was in adolescence during the victimization, annual income was decreased by $6,000. This is compared to an annual decrease of $3,700 when the victim was aged 18–19 at the time of the violence. Macmillan's findings are consistent with the life course model because he showed that not only does being victimized by crime affect adult income, but that the timing of victimization is important as well. The obvious policy option here would be to ensure that social supports are provided to those who have been victimized by crime so that these long-term disadvantages may be prevented.

General Strain Theory

Not only has control theory been revised and reformulated, so too has strain theory. Robert Agnew recognized that strain theory as originally put forward by Merton (see Chapter 4) was limited in terms of fully conceptualizing the range of possible sources of strain in society, especially among youth. For Merton, innovation (the mode of adaptation used to explain most crime) occurs when society emphasizes socially desirable and approved goals but, at the same time, provides inadequate opportunity to achieve these goals with the legitimate institutionalized means. In other words, those members of society who find themselves in a position of financial strain, yet wish to achieve material success, resort to crime to achieve socially desirable goals. Agnew supports this assumption, yet he also believes that, especially when dealing with youth, other sources of strain are evident in society and that they, too, can incite criminal behaviour.

Agnew's revision of general strain theory begins by suggesting that several types of negative experiences can lead to stress, not only those that are economically induced and do not allow individuals to achieve socially valued goals. For Agnew—and keep in mind that he is referring mainly to youth—the stresses associated with the inability to achieve such immediate goals as good grades, popularity, and athletic achievement can be linked with strain. The three types of strain that comprise Agnew's model are (a) the inability to achieve positively valued goals (similar to Merton's innovators); (b) the removal or the threat to remove positively valued stimuli; and (c) to present a threat to one with noxious or negatively valued stimuli. The first source of strain is clearly macro, as society is unable to regulate social behaviour because of the imbalance between institutional goals and means. However, the other two forms of strain are micro, in that Agnew draws from the psychological literature on aggression and stress and contends that strain can involve more than the pursuit of positively valued goals. Strain can also be caused by the *loss* of positively valued stimuli. For example, the loss of a boyfriend or girlfriend, the divorce or separation of one's parents, or getting suspended from school can all lead to strain. Attention to alternative forms of strain—again, informed by literature on aggression by psychologists—probes the impact that the actual or anticipated presentation of negative or harmful stimuli might have. The logic is that the exposure to noxious stimuli can lead to delinquency for adolescents just as it may be a mechanism to escape or avoid negative experiences, or as a means to stop them. Revenge against the source of the stimuli provides another possibility for inciting a criminal response, according to Agnew (1992). The basic idea for this theory is that these stressful experiences are anger-producing, and that anger and frustration may lead to crime and aggression. Since his theory was first proposed in 1985, it continues to be updated on a regular basis (see Agnew, 2012).

One of the more appealing aspects of the generalized strain theory concerns the way in which it deals with gender. Indeed, a major failing of Merton's original strain theory was its inability to deal with the question of why there are profound differences in levels of male crime compared to female crime, although females in society face as many sources of strain as males, if not more. Yet female involvement in most forms of crime and delinquency are far lower than are rates for males.

In an attempt to explain the high rate of male delinquency as compared to female delinquency, Agnew and Broidy (1997, p. 275) analyzed the gender differences between the awareness of strain and responses to it. The first part of the explanation explored the *quantity* of strain experienced by males and females. According to stress research reviewed by Agnew and Broidy, females tend to experience at least as much strain as males. That females experience as much or more strain does not explain the higher rate of male delinquency, at least not according to the general strain theory. In order to explain this seeming paradox, Agnew and Broidy explore further the differences in male and female experiences of strain, as shown in Table 5.1.

These different types of strain experienced by males and females explain the gender differences in the types of crimes that are committed (ibid., p. 281). Agnew and Broidy then put forward the idea that there may be differences not only in the types of strain, but also in the emotional *responses* to strain. These differences are summarized in Table 5.2.

Table 5.1 Differences in Types of Strain

Females	Males
Concerned with creating and maintaining close bonds and relationships with others—thus lower rates of property and violent crime	Concerned with material success—thus higher rates of property and violent crime
Face negative treatment, such as discrimination, high demands from family, and restricted behaviour	Face more conflict with peers and are more likely to be the victims of crime
Failure to achieve goals may lead to self-destructive behaviour	Failure to achieve goals may lead to property and violent crime

Source: Agnew and Broidy, 1997, pp. 278–81.

Table 5.2 Gender Differences in Emotional Response to Strain

Females	Males
More likely to respond with depression and anger	More likely to respond with anger
Anger is accompanied by fear, guilt, and shame	Anger is followed by moral outrage
More likely to blame themselves and worry about the effects of their anger	Quick to blame others and are less concerned about hurting others
Depression and guilt may lead to self-destructive behaviours (i.e., eating disorders)	Moral outrage may lead to property and violent crime

Source: Agnew and Broidy, 1997, pp. 281–3.

Agnew and Broidy found that there were differences in the emotional responses to strain and that these explain gender differences in crime participation. Males and females have been found to experience different types of strain and different emotions according to the general strain theory. Agnew and Broidy also investigated why males may respond to strain with crime, and their research indicated that females might lack the confidence and forms of self-esteem that may be conducive to committing crime and instead employ escape and avoidance methods to relieve their strain. Females may, however, have stronger relational ties that might help to reduce strain. Male participation in crime has been studied from the standpoint of several different theories such as control theory and differential association theory. Males are said to be lower in **social control** and to socialize in large, hierarchical peer groups. Females, on the other hand, form close social bonds in small groups that help to alleviate strain. Because of this, males are more likely to respond to strain with crime (ibid., pp. 283–287).

Agnew and Broidy mention that much research remains to be done in this area and note that most of the data used to support their formulation came from previous studies that focused on stress (ibid., p. 279), and not from studies that were conducted specifically to test this theory.

It is one task to explain why there are higher rates of male than female crime; it is something quite different to explain why females commit crime in the first place. To answer this question Agnew and Broidy return to the types of strain that females face, and focus on goal blockage, breaks in interpersonal bonds, and the unfairness females experience in attempts to achieve their financial goals. In addition, as an example of a loss of positive stimuli, females may face barriers to particular social settings because of discrimination. Females also are the targets of sexual, emotional, and physical abuse, which are examples of negative stimuli. These types of strain may pave the way to female criminality; however, female criminals seem to differ from female non-criminals in that they have an increased opportunity to commit crime, are lower in social control, and have delinquent peers. Agnew and Broidy found that not only can general strain theory explain the higher rate of male crime, but it can also explain why females would participate in crime (ibid., pp. 288–294). The empirical support for this theory appears rather impressive, as several studies have provided empirical support for the propositions Agnew has set forth in general strain theory. A significant positive relationship between various strain measures and delinquency has been reported in studies (e.g., Agnew, 2002; Agnew and Brezina, 1997). However, research examining forms of individual coping strategies, thought to directly affect how the individual adapts to strain, have been mixed.

Most tests of general strain theory have followed Agnew's (1992) initial micro-level account of the theory where he focuses on individual differences in levels of strain to see if these are associated with criminal involvement. More recently, however, Agnew (1999) elaborated the general strain theoretical model so that it now provides a macro-social approach. In other words, in this newer version of his theory Agnew has put together a model that attempts to explain differences in crime rates between communities. Agnew suggests that differences in the inclination to commit crime within underprivileged communities depend on the "strainful" experiences of individuals in these communities (Agnew, 1999, p. 125). The variation in community crime rates depends on the levels of aggregate strain. For example, economically disadvantaged communities create strain and anger by blocking community members' abilities to achieve positive goals, creating a loss of positive stimuli, exposing members to negative stimuli, and increasing overall relative deprivation (ibid., pp. 126–30). Moreover, Agnew suggests that disadvantaged communities are more likely to select and retain strained individuals and have higher levels of angry individual interaction than more advantaged communities.

There have been very few tests of macro general strain theory. Warner and Fowler (2003) and Wareham et al. (2005) attempted to test this theory. Both studies, however, produced findings that showed mixed support for the model. As is the case with new theoretical formulations, there is a need for more research. It remains unclear how capable macro general strain theory is for further understanding how much and what types of strain are present in communities. Moreover, more information is needed regarding how and why some groups are able to cope with strain more effectively than others (Agnew and Broidy, 1997, p. 296).

The policy implications that stem from general strain theory echo those proposed by Merton's initial version of strain theory. However, besides providing disadvantaged youth with legitimate means (i.e., employment and educational opportunities) that are required to gain access to conventional goals, proponents of general strain theory also advocate for programs that would deal with non-economic strains that young people face, such as anti-bullying programs in schools. Moreover, the generalized version of strain theory would also find great value in policies that would provide social supports, such as bereavement counselling and support for youth who experience sexual or physical abuse. Box 5.2 focuses on **cyber bullying** and illustrates the intense strain that some youth can experience who are victims of this new form of bullying.

Rational Choice Theory

The roots of rational choice theory can be traced back to the field of economics and the classical school of criminology. The basic assumption of **rational choice theory** is that human behaviour, including criminal behaviour, is the result of conscious decision making. Based on the "expected utility" principle in economic theory, crime is assumed to be calculated and deliberate—that criminals are rational actors. Individuals are seen to make rational decisions based on the extent to which they expect the choice to make the most of their profits or benefits and reduce costs or losses. According to this perspective, crime is understood to be influenced by variations in opportunity, environment, target, and risk of detection—each of which change depending on situational context and type of offence (McCarthy, 2002). This way of thinking bridges the gap between structural theories of crime—such as strain theory—with event-based explanations, in an effort to understand why an individual at a particular point in time makes the choice to participate in an unlawful act.

One of the key points raised by rational choice theorists is that criminology has been too preoccupied with explaining individual criminality while neglecting explanations of the criminal event (Cornish & Clarke, 1986). Attempts are made to merge explanations of crime, which focus on the impacts of outside social and economic factors over which individuals have little or no control (e.g., population density, the business cycle, geographic locale), with the situational context, which places emphasis on the factors specific to the criminal event. Hence, the decision to commit a crime is influenced by people's estimates of an illegal opportunity's availability, costs, and benefits versus a lawful opportunity's availability, costs, and potential for realizing similar returns (McCarthy, 2002). However, it is incompatible with explanations that argue that structural conditions or socialization produce character defects that make an offender's decision making distinct from that of non-offenders (e.g., Gottfredson and Hirschi, 1990).

The rational choice model has been used to explain a wide range of offences, including tax evasion (Varma & Doob, 1998); traffic violations (Corbett & Simon, 1992); corporate crime (Paternoster & Simpson, 1996); drunk driving; larceny; and sexual assault (Nagin & Paternoster, 1994). The approach has also been used in a study undertaken in Ontario that examined illegal sales of tobacco products to underage youth. O'Grady et al. (2000) found that merchants/clerks working mainly in convenience stores, gas bars, and grocery stores make a deliberate assessment of the costs and benefits that are involved in selling cigarettes to minors. The study found that a risk assessment occurs at the point when a merchant is confronted with the opportunity to sell tobacco to a young person, and also explains why the age (older youth) and gender (females, who generally mature earlier than males) were the groups most likely to be sold tobacco. The study also found that merchants were

Debates and Controversies

Is Cyber Bullying on the Rise?

For years in most elementary school classrooms in Canada, you were bound to find children who bully, are victims of bullying, or are bystanders of bullying. In recent years bullying has taken on a new dimension: cyber bullying. Cyber bullying refers to the use of the Internet and other digital technology to threaten, humiliate, or embarrass another person. The term normally is used within the context of youth. But when the behaviour is engaged in by adults it goes by different names, such as cyberharassment or cyberstalking and can result in criminal prosecution. A well-known—and tragic—example of cyber bullying involved a British Columbia teen, Amanda Todd. The 15-year-old girl took her life in 2012 after suffering years of online torment. Before she died, Todd posted a YouTube video in which she used flash cards to tell of her experience of being blackmailed and humiliated. The video went "viral" after her death which resulted in widespread media attention.

While there is evidence to suggest that cyber bullying has become more prevalent with the growth in the use of social media such as Facebook, there is debate in the research literature about whether or not cyber bullying has reached or even exceeds levels of traditional verbal bullying. According to an article that appeared in the *National Post* newspaper, an interview with a Norwegian psychologist, Dan Olweus—an expert in the area—suggested that rates of cyber bullying were ". . . one-quarter to one-third those of traditional verbal bullying" (Hamilton, 2012, p. A10). In the same story, however, research by Wendy Craig, a psychologist from Queen's University in Ontario, noted that while there is no solid evidence to argue that cyber bullying has grown in recent years, Canadian research shows that 19 per cent of youth had been victims of cyber bullying (Hamilton, 2012, p. A10).

more likely to sell to underage youth during the evening. This was suggested to be the case because tobacco enforcement officers, who are responsible for enforcing tobacco youth access laws, generally work during the regular business hours of 9:00 a.m. to 5:00 p.m.

Rational choice theory also has been used in research that has examined policies relating to domestic violence and has had mixed results. Several years ago an American study supported the rational choice assumption that men make rational choices during domestic disputes, specifically because legal threats were shown to deter potential offenders (Sherman & Berk, 1984). In fact, the results of this Minneapolis study led to mandatory arrest laws that were implemented in 15 states. This was the same period when policy

directives were introduced in Canada that required police and Crown prosecutors to charge and prosecute incidents of domestic assault (see Chapter
2). However, the findings of a later US study challenged these earlier findings.
Research by Sherman (1992) found that arresting offenders had no crime
reduction effect in repeat domestic violence. In fact, arrests led to an *increase*
in re-offending for offenders who had a low stake in conformity: the unemployed and the unmarried.

Rational choice theory, like its predecessor the classical school, has been
criticized primarily for its assumption that everyone is capable of making rational
decisions. If this is the case, then it is difficult to explain why Canada—and every
other Western democracy—has young offender/delinquency laws whereby youth
are deemed to be less criminally responsible than adults. Similarly, legal codes
also "interpret" crimes committed by those deemed by the courts not fit to stand
trial due to reasons of insanity or mental incompetence. In the end, rational
choice theory tends to be a more effective explanation for crimes that are "instrumental" rather than those that are "expressive" (Chambliss, 1975). **Instrumental crimes** involve some planning and weighing of risks and include offences
such as break and enter, accounting fraud, and embezzlement. **Expressive
crimes** are often impulsive and emotional such that people who commit
these acts are not likely to be concerned at the time of their commission with the
future implications of these actions. Examples of expressive crimes would include
non-premeditated murder and assault. The idea behind rational choice theory is
that the deterrent impact of punishment would be greater on instrumental
crimes than on expressive ones. This perspective will be taken up again when we
focus on corporate crime (see Chapter 7). In any case, crime control policies that
would sufficiently fund the enforcement and regulation of corporate or white-
collar crime would be an example of a practical application of this theory.

Routine Activity Theory

Routine activity theory is an explanation of crime closely related to rational
choice theory. Originally proposed by Cohen and Felson (1979), this theory
suggests that changes in levels of crime in society are closely associated with
changing lifestyles. For example, rises in official levels of crime that occurred
in most Western societies during the 1960s and 1970s were seen to be caused
in large part by increased affluence and the greater number of activities that
took place outside of the home. Increased affluence meant that criminals had
more desirable targets for stealing, for example. And increased activity outside
of the home—for example, more women in the post-secondary educational
system and the labour market—brought about an increase in personal victimization by strangers.

Unlike strain and control theories, routine activity explanations of crime
do not focus on what motivates people either to engage in crime or to refrain

from illegal activities. Rather, this theory simply begins with the premise that crime is likely to occur when a motivated offender and suitable victim come together in an environment that does not provide protection to the potential victim. In this way, the risk of victimization varies significantly according to the situations and locations where people place themselves or their property (Cohen & Felson, 1979). Consider, for instance, the situation where an individual has been drinking at a bar all night and then decides to walk home alone at 3:00 a.m. The chances of this person being robbed or assaulted are far greater than for another individual who stayed home that same evening and did not go out drinking.

Felson (1994) has used the routine activity perspective to explain why there has been a general increase in youth crime over the course of the twentieth century, particularly since the 1950s. Due to changes in education, work roles, and technological advancements, Felson suggests that youth have increasingly become "out of sync." During much of the nineteenth century most working-class teens had left school by the age of 12 or earlier and were working with adults in the labour market. Since these youth were essentially being monitored by the older generation, it helped to keep them out of trouble. Also, since most of the work in this era took place close to or in the household, youth were less able to stray from family settings (Felson, 1994, p. 97). A final control that this earlier era placed on youth related to marriage and family responsibilities. During the nineteenth century in the United States the average age of marriage for females was 16 or 17 and about 18 for males. Given the fact that children arrived shortly thereafter, these young adults had little time for getting involved in the types of activities that would lead to trouble.

However, by the 1960s important changes were well underway in Canada and the United States in transitions to adulthood that, according to Felson, were responsible for giving rise to more opportunities for youthful involvement in crime. In fact, during the 1960s, crime rates in the United States had tripled. For Felson, one of the reasons for the rather sudden increase in crime had to do with the fact that the school day ended at around 3:00 p.m. and therefore freed up a period when parental supervision was absent. "Even if one teenager's parents were home in the afternoon, friends' parents might be gone, opening up a vast opportunity for teenagers to do whatever they wanted" (Felson, 1994, p. 98). This freedom from parental supervision resulted in greater opportunities for youth to get into trouble.

Changes that were underway in mass transit have also been identified by Felson in making it easier for young people to get into conflict with the law. Since youth can easily travel away from their neighbourhoods, not only do they escape parental supervision, but they also expose themselves to more trouble-making opportunities.

Rising levels of youth crime, according to the routine activity perspective, had little to do with increased motivations for youth wanting to commit crime.

Rather, these increases are best understood as a result of the rise in the number of temptations that became available for youth to commit crime, along with a decline in parental controls as it became more common for both parents to be working outside of the home.

Critics of rational choice theory have pointed out that opportunities to commit crime do not necessarily lead to crime even when controls are absent. Routine activity theory tends to ignore the research literature that associates crime with offender characteristics (social learning, strain, identity, self-esteem). To be fair, however, recent versions of the theory have corrected this in part by moving toward a more complex and realistic conceptualization of the "likely offender" that includes attention to the offender's available resources and to technological developments (Ekblom & Tilley, 2000).

Another criticism of routine activity theory centres on the issue of crime displacement. This occurs where increased guardianship in one area simply moves crime to another locale. Clarke (1997, p. 28) notes that much of the early literature on situational crime prevention reported some levels of crime displacement. In their experiment on the prevention of shoplifting, Farrington and Burrows (1993) found some evidence of increased theft in nearby stores that did not use electronic tags. In rational choice theory, the offender has to reconsider whether alternative courses of action, that is the commission of a comparable crime elsewhere or at another time, is worth the risk.

There are two obvious policy implications that would be informed by the rational choice perspective. On the one hand, homeowners, for example, would be encouraged to fortify their properties with alarm systems and other "target-hardening" devices and strategies. Greater police surveillance of evening entertainment areas in large cities where large groups of people congregate to drink and party would be another example of a crime prevention practice associated with the rational choice approach.

Reducing the Risk: Crime Prevention through Environmental Design

Crime Prevention through Environmental Design, commonly known as CPTED (pronounced *sep-ted*), was first introduced in the work of C. Ray Jeffery in 1971. The theoretical underpinnings of CPTED are based on the notion of "defensible space" (Newman, 1972). This means that crime can be prevented if the built environment is properly designed so that opportunities for motivated offenders to commit crime are removed. CPTED is, arguably, more a crime prevention strategy than a theory of criminal behaviour. Nevertheless, CPTED is based very closely on the classical notion that people make rational choices about engaging in crime according to the costs and benefits that are associated with the behaviour. Criminals are seen as rationally calculating actors, and the way to prevent crime is to design an environment so that any reasonable, thinking person would understand that the costs involved in committing a crime exceed the benefits. This perspective neither purports to explain why certain individuals would be more inclined to commit crime than other individuals, nor does it attempt to understand why society reacts to crime in the way that it does.

There are four main ideas associated with this perspective: natural surveillance, natural access control, territorial reinforcement, and maintenance. These points are outlined on the CPTED Ontario website (www.cpted ontario.ca).

The first of these concepts, natural surveillance, means that correct placement of the built environment—this can include objects or people—that maximizes natural visibility or observation can deter crime. For example, an employee lounge in a basement of a building that contains no windows for natural observation to the hallway would be construed as an unsafe environment. However, with the installation of a window, the lounge would be "crime-proofed" in the sense that there would now be increased visibility and a consequent reduction in the opportunity for crimes, such as theft or sexual assault.

Natural access control is meant to deter access to a crime target by creating an increased perception of risk to the offender. This could be achieved physically by guiding people coming and going from a space by means of the careful placement of entrances, fences, landscaping, and lighting. This principle helps deter access to a crime target or to a victim and creates a perception of risk to a perpetrator.

The third principle of CPTED is territorial reinforcement. This is the use of physical attributes that express ownership, such as fencing, pavement treatments, signage, and landscaping. An example of this would be a multi-family housing community that installed fencing to help control access to the site. A fence around the perimeter of the property defines the property lines and simultaneously provides access control. The sort of fence that could be seen through would also provide natural surveillance opportunities.

The final element of CPTED is maintenance. A well-maintained space allows for the continued use of a space for its intended purpose, as well as creating the appearance of diligent ownership. For example, uncut grass and weeds make a home or area look uninhabited. Such an unkempt environment sends a message to a rationally thinking criminal that no one cares about the property, thus making the property appear to be more inviting for invasion.

A Canadian study of CPTED has been carried out by Parnaby (2006), where he interviewed 25 professional practitioners and supporters of this crime prevention model. Many individuals who are trained and receive CPTED accreditation are ex-police officers and those working in the private security industry. His analysis suggests that some of the guiding principles of CPTED are questionable as they are based on rather simplistic assumptions. For example, Parnaby's research revealed that CPTED practitioners are guided by the notion of "foreseeable danger," meaning that if the flaws identified with unsafe built environments are not fixed, then it will only be a matter of time before a criminal event will occur. The problems inherent in this approach are that CPTED practitioners use the language of certainty, not probability, in predicting crime and view the causes of crime as one-dimensional—that is, crime is the result of poorly designed environments. Hence, the only solution to crime is the successful application of CPTED principles. Other crime prevention strategies, such as those that might be implemented in schools or in neighbourhood programs, are most often overlooked in the CPTED literature.

A second problem identified by Parnaby is that, according to this way of thinking about crime, society is seen to be composed of two groups of people: responsible citizens and criminals. In the words of one CPTED practitioner who Parnaby interviewed: "Deviants go shopping where they are going to get the most bang for their buck" and the "right kinds of people" should occupy and protect themselves by properly crime-proofing their property and the pri-vate and public spaces that they occupy (Parnaby, 2006, p. 9). This way of separating "good" people (bona fide users) with "bad" people (intruders), according to Parnaby, is likely to be based on social stereotypes grounded in preconceived notions about race, socioeconomic status, and gender, not according to an accurate risk assessment of who may pose a legitimate threat. This, of course, has implications in terms of excluding certain types of indi-viduals or groups from certain neighbourhoods.

A final issue that was revealed in Parnaby's research concerns the way in which CPTED practitioners rally their clients to become willing participants. This goal is achieved by framing risk management as though it were an indi-vidual's moral, ethical, and civic responsibility. The problem with such "responsibilization" is that governments were seen to not have the resources or the abilities to manage crime-related risks on their own, and thus it is claimed that individuals need to take more responsibility for their personal safety. An important issue here is that order maintenance and crime preven-tion are no longer seen to be the exclusive domain of a social consensus, not even through the means of the public police force. In other words, the approach can lead to a sort of vigilantism.

Like the highly debated two-tiered system of health care, where those who have access to financial resources can afford expedient and quality health care, the future of crime control also could become two-tiered. Those without finan-cial resources would have to rely on a deteriorating and poorly funded public policing system for protection from crime, whereas others, who could afford CPTED and other security measures, would be better protected and safer.

Defensible Space (before)

Defensible Space (after)

These two photos are a good illustration of how defensible space can be created by subdividing and assigning all the previously public grounds into space for individual families. Such a modification of the built environment removed it from the gangs and drug dealers. Source for both photos: Newman, Oscar (1972) *Creating Defensible Space*, US Department of Housing and Urban Development.

This perspective, perhaps more than any other that has been addressed thus far in this book, lends itself in the most direct way to policy. Indeed, the four basic premises of CPTED—altering the built environment, natural access control, territorial reinforcement, and property maintenance—are the cornerstones of this particular crime control strategy.

Risk and Actuarial Criminology

Parnaby's analytical approach to CPTED is in keeping with a recent body of literature in criminology that is known as **risk theory and actuarial criminology**. This body of thought is an offshoot of postmodernism; a perspective that, in simple terms, is skeptical about theories that claim to know the "truth" about anything, including crime, especially when it comes to explaining the causes of crime. The postmodern position sets forth the idea that reality is complex and that the social world is not easily knowable. In a manner similar to the critical perspective (discussed in Chapter 4), analyses of crime that focus on risk make no effort to explain the causes of rule-breaking behaviour. Rather, the focus is on understanding emerging forms of **social control**.

Rigakos (1999) has discussed the main points of a risk analysis of crime. The first point relates to the concept of *governmentality*. Drawing on the work of Michel Foucault (1991), governmentality refers to societies where power is decentralized and the citizenry plays an active role in their own self-governance. Analogous to Parnaby's research on CPTED, individual citizens are increasingly being controlled by non-invasive, routinized forms of surveillance. As the world globalizes, societies are moving to new forms of decentralized organization where the state no longer provides the dominant set of social institutions that exercise power and control over the population. Within this new context, corporate entities take on increasingly larger roles in classifying and organizing the population.

Decentralization runs counter to more traditional models of social control where "society," controlled by elites through institutions like the criminal justice system, exerts power and control over the masses (a view subscribed to by early conflict theory). Today, power stands for an interlocking set of networks where coercion can be found at many levels of society, not just with those holding economic and political power. Power is now localized in a wide array of institutions including the family, schools, and prisons, each of which has specialized techniques for discipline. For example, Donzelot (1979) in *The Policing of Families* introduced the notion that public intervention and regulation of the family has increasingly shifted away from the family into the public domain. This has been achieved through surveillance activities associated with social work, psychiatry, and mass education. Mass education, in particular, has played a pivotal role in increasing surveillance of the family in several ways. Take the example of a teacher who observes suspicious bruising on a student. In such a situation it is the teacher's responsibility to report the incident to Family and Children's Services if there is reason to believe that the child has been abused. Child welfare workers who investigate such reports have the power to remove children from their homes if it is deemed that a child is living in an unsafe environment and is being abused. Prior to mass education, knowledge of such abuse would have stayed within the confines of the household.

Another point raised by Rigakos is that the assembly of knowledge in a risk society is accelerated. Through the use of computer technology in both the private and public realms, bureaucratic managerial information systems are set up so that more and more information about the population is gathered and stored in electronic databases. Examples of this include health records, credit and banking information, even information that is provided by consumer reward or loyalty programs. In this last example, companies that offer these programs to consumers—where compensation or rewards are provided to "members" in terms of air travel and other "gifts"—have information about what types of products consumers buy, how often they buy them, and how much money consumers spend on certain goods and services. This development is like the concept of "Big Brother" introduced by George Orwell in his novel *1984*. However, in a risk society there is no one Big Brother, because the state does not have a monopoly on this surveillance technology nor the power to employ it; instead, corporations are now taking the lead in collecting such information.

Another component of the risk perspective concerns the way in which the different institutions of the criminal justice system are becoming more and more fragmented. Examples of this fragmentation are particularly pronounced in policing and corrections, where the boundaries between what is public and what is private have become increasingly blurred. With the rise of private security companies and the privatization of prisons, social control is increasingly being diffused among a wider array of public and private institutions. In Canada, for some years now, private security (mainly private investigators and security guards) have outnumbered public police officers. According to Statistics Canada there were 69,438 police officers in Canada and 140,000 private investigators and security guards in Canada in 2011 (Statistics Canada, 2011). The key difference between private security guards and public police is that the latter are paid from the public purse and the former are employed by corporations. Another important difference is that crime is not the focus of private security guards, since they are employed to deal with the security concerns of the companies for which they are employed. But some criminologists have pointed out that a blurring of boundaries is occurring whereby private security is involved in dealing with the public. Shearing (2005) considers the examples of private security guards who are in place in many shopping malls, entertainment facilities, and airports across Canada:

> When this happens, private security is concerned with managing what are essentially public spaces, but they are not doing so on behalf of the state, they are doing so on behalf of the companies whose job it is to manage those spaces. There are a variety of relationships which emerge between these companies and the people who are being managed in these public spaces. (Shearing, 2005, p. 1)

This blurring of social control is also evident in risk sociological analyses of insurance companies and their actuarial methods, particularly when corporate operatives are engaged in investigations of claimant allegations of fraud (Ericson & Doyle, 2004). Because "fraud" is defined and dealt with internally by insurance companies, "crime" is defined through private justice mechanisms where boundaries of what constitutes fraud, as opposed to exaggeration, are in flux. In fact, when asked to define "fraud," Ericson and Doyle argue that "insurance investigators do not refer to criminal code or legal definitions, and face difficulty defining fraud at all" (ibid., p. 121). Rather than trying to understand the underlying causes of crime, in a society that is preoccupied by risk, analysts contend that crime is often taken for granted. In the insurance business, for example, fraud is routinely tolerated. Ericson and Doyle have identified several reasons why companies do not very often accuse clients of fraud. One reason is that the evidence required to justify a claim as fraudulent is tough to ascertain or expensive to collect, especially in personal injury claims. Generally speaking, fraud is dealt with through "'private justice mechanisms' because moving such cases to the public realm is just not economically feasible" (ibid.). Contending with fraud, from the insurance companies' standpoint, is just another form of business loss. Since insurance companies need to remain profitable, economic imperatives prevent fraud from entering into the realm of the criminal justice system and premiums reflect the shortfall created by fraudulent claims. In short, the insurance industry is about business, not about enforcing society's laws.

The criminological realm of corrections, risk, and actuarial analyses point out that the criminal justice system is deemed by many groups and individuals to be incapable of rehabilitating offenders. Within this context, crime is most appropriately dealt with by effectively assessing the risks posed by offenders, classifying and deciding where prisoners are to be placed within institutions, and choosing when they are to be released. The correctional system is increasingly becoming involved in risk management so that dangerous groups that pose a threat to society can be effectively managed and controlled.

This assumption of control has occurred without the institution asking why some groups have become dangerous. The next question that arises, of course, is "a threat to what part of society?" If the profits of the insurance companies are too high, do those institutions not become part of the reason clients want to press for higher reimbursement through their claims? Those whose task it is to devise such systems have been called "administrative criminologists" (Young, 1999). Routine activity, rational choice, and environmental criminology (like CPTED) are examples of approaches to crime that suggest the most effective way to deal with crime is to reduce the opportunities to commit crime.

Since risk and actuarial analyses of crime are relatively recent theoretical developments in criminology, a systematic critique of this approach has yet to be developed. As yet, crime control policies cannot be associated with this perspective. However, like postmodern theory in general, this new approach to understanding crime and its control is often written in language that can be difficult to comprehend. Therefore, at this time, much of this subject matter is accessible only to a relatively small group of experts in the area.

Conclusion

This chapter has reviewed a select number of recent sociological theories of crime, many of which build on earlier theories that we reviewed in Chapter 4. The first three—self-control theory, life course theory, and general strain theory—assume that crime is caused by a lack of self-control, a lack of ties with conventional institutions, or by multiple sources of social strain where there is no support system in place to help the individual deal with such strain. While these three approaches were shown to differ in terms of how they explain the causes of crime, they all share the assumption that problematic social environments help to produce social deviants.

Routine activity theory and rational choice theory are also causal theories of crime. However, since both have their roots in the classical school, ideas about rationality, human agency, and choice-making continue to be viewed as the most important factor for explaining criminal events. The basic assumptions of CPTED also share the idea of offenders being rational actors and the belief that changes in the built environment will prevent criminal activity.

This chapter concluded with an introduction to risk and actuarial criminology. Unlike the other perspectives addressed, no attempt is made in this approach to uncover causal mechanisms, that is, the etiology of offending. Rather, the focus is on how new forms of social control are emerging in society. One of the more important issues addressed in this literature concerns what happens when institutions other than the state—such as private policing, private prisons, and insurance companies—become actively involved in monitoring, policing, and sanctioning the citizens of the state.

Critical Thinking Questions

1. Why are both *A General Theory of Crime* and general strain theory considered to be *general* theories of crime?

2. Have you ever changed your housing environment to protect yourself from crime? If so, which of the main assumptions of CPTED did this alteration relate to?

3. Which theory covered in this chapter is best for explaining why youth engage in bullying behaviour?

4. In what ways do risk and actuarial criminology differ from theories of crime that focus on the causes of criminal activity?

Suggested Readings

Agnew, Robert. (2011). *Toward a unified criminology: Integrating assumptions about crime, people and society*. New York, NY: NYU Press. This book centres on the core assumptions that criminologists make about the nature of crime, human beings, society, and reality. Agnew describes the assumptions made by different theories and perspectives and argues that they are often opposed and this opposition makes it difficult for theoretical integration to be successful. The book draws on recent work from a number of disciplines to evaluate these assumptions and proposes a new, integrated and uniform set of criminological insights.

Innes, Martin. (2003). *Understanding social control: Deviance, crime and social order*. Buckingham, UK: Open University Press. Readers are introduced to the concepts of social control within surveillance, risk management, audit, and architecture. Innes explores how and why the mechanisms and processes of social control are changing.

Laub, John, & Sampson, Robert. (2003). *Shared beginnings, divergent lives: Delinquent boys to age 70*. Cambridge, MA: Harvard University Press. Laub and Sampson interviewed men in their 70s who were in reform school in the 1940s. This book is the longest longitudinal study of crime to date. The authors argue that social context is extremely important for understanding why some people continue to commit crime over the life course while others stop.

Websites and Films

Crime Prevention through Environmental Design
www.cpted ontario.ca
A website for the public and for CPTED practitioners, this resource gives photographic examples of the principles of Crime Prevention through Environmental Design.

Risk Research Canada
www.riskresearch.ca
This website's perspective about "risk" is in keeping with the *social constructionist* viewpoint which was introduced in Chapter 1. Here risks are seen to be the products of "human interaction and are seen to reflect human values, desires, politics, institutions and relations of power."

The Up Series (Seven Up / 7 Plus Seven / 21 Up / 28 Up / 35 Up / 42 Up / 49Up /56 Up)
While not intended to be a scientific study, the premise behind the *Up* series is a
good example of the types of findings that can be collected from a longitudinal
study. A cross-section of children who were seven years old in Britain in 1964 was
asked about their hopes for the future. The filmmakers return every seven years to
note their progress. The results of these programs show that social class and background has an indelible effect on the kids for the rest of their lives; the upper-class
boys and girls seem confident to the point of boorishness, while the middle- and
working-class children seem resigned to a life of hard work or inevitable failure
because of their backgrounds.

6 Crime and Social Exclusion

Learning Objectives

After completing this chapter students will be able to:

◎ Define the concept of social exclusion.

◎ Identify the reasons why homeless youth may engage in crime.

◎ Understand why some youths join gangs.

◎ Recognize why Aboriginal people are overrepresented in the Canadian criminal justice system.

◎ Define *hate crime* and know which groups in Canada may be victims of hate crime.

◎ Recognize the types of violence women are more likely to be subjected to.

Introduction

This chapter surveys research on crime and victimization among certain socially excluded groups in Canadian society. The concept of social exclusion is introduced as an approach demonstrating how economic marginalization and other exclusionary mechanisms influence criminal offending and victimization. The following groups will be examined:

- homeless youth
- youth gangs
- Aboriginal Canadians (and their overrepresentation in the criminal justice system)
- hate crimes
- violence against women

Defining Social Exclusion

In recent years the concept of social exclusion has emerged and been used by politicians, government policy analysts, and social scientists as a better way to understand social inequality. For some, the term *social exclusion* has taken the place of *income inequality* or *poverty*. This is not to suggest, however, that all groups who may face social exclusion are necessarily poor. For example, even though individuals in gay and lesbian communities have been subjected to discrimination—sometimes violently—because of their sexual orientation, "gay bashing" and other hate crimes do not discriminate on the basis of income. Nevertheless, for many groups in Canada, the crime and victimization that they are involved in and experience is often the result of their marginalization and exclusion.

Historically, the term **social exclusion** originated with the French author Lenoir in the early 1970s to "refer to groups or persons not covered by the traditional social security system" (Vlemincx & Berghman, 2001). While the popularity of the phrase is most evident in Europe, it is being used increasingly in North America as a better way to understand a wide range of social problems, including street crime and victimization. Walker and Walker (1997, p. 8) define social exclusion as "the process of being shut out, fully or partially, from any of the social, economic, political, or cultural systems that determine the social integration of a person in society. Social exclusion may, therefore, be seen as the denial (or non-realization) of the civil, political, and social rights of citizenship." This definition clearly states dimensions along which individuals can become excluded.

A large part of what makes the concept of social exclusion so appealing to sociologists is its multi-dimensionality (Reimer, 2004). An aspect of analyzing social exclusion's multi-dimensionality is the consideration of the interconnectedness of people's positions on the different dimensions. Some individuals may be included within some parts of society, but may be excluded in other ways, which Muffels and Fouarge clarify:

> [P]overty leads to some sort of social exclusion whereas social exclusion does not always mean that somebody is living in poverty. For example, the elderly might be excluded from work and social participation because of the existence of "age discriminatory" practices [on] the side of employers giving precedence to young workers instead of older workers and/or societal institutions. (2001, pp. 104–5)

In other words, various causes facilitate social exclusion. Poverty, although a major cause of exclusion, does not imply that poor individuals are not being excluded in some other way, too. Nor does exclusion along a particular dimension (other than poverty) necessarily imply that the individual is also impoverished. Nevertheless, Whelan and Whelan state that "poverty is seen as being *attributable to lack of material resources* . . . even when social scientists use one of these other terms [*deprived, marginalized, socially excluded*], their main focus is still, in most cases, on those who are materially disadvantaged" (1995, p. 32). In nations possessing generally more material wealth, a lack of access among some of its citizens to material goods can escalate feelings of relative deprivation and create a sense of injustice. Anyone aware of the circumstances surrounding the French Revolution can make those connections. Social scientists may have noted the relationship between people being materially disadvantaged and crime; however, this unidimensional approach does not take into account other areas where individuals can also experience a sense of injustice. Unlike impoverishment, social exclusion refers to the overall inclusion (or exclusion) of individuals within society, not just within the economic sphere (Binns, 2005).

This chapter considers a number of groups in Canada through the prism of social exclusion. While each group experiences different forms of exclusion, they all represent people who have been subjected to disproportionate levels of crime or victimization.

Homeless Youth

In recent years the study of criminal activity among homeless youth has captured the attention of researchers in many countries throughout the world, including Canada. There are several reasons for this attention. The most obvious has to do with the fact that the numbers of homeless people, including many homeless youth, have risen or have become more publicly visible. Within a Canadian context, **homeless youth** means any male or female for whom the street (in the widest sense of the word, including unoccupied dwellings, parks, rooftops, shelters for homeless youth, etc.) has become his or her habitual abode or source of livelihood, and who is inadequately protected, supervised, or directed by responsible adults.

Within the Canadian context, it is estimated that there are more than 8,000 people who use shelters in Canada's nine largest metropolitan areas (Hwang, 2001). Many of these homeless people are youth, who range in age from 16 to 24. In Toronto it has been estimated that there are approximately 2,000 homeless youth out of doors on any given night (Gaetz et al., 1999). These numbers have drawn attention from the mass media, mostly focusing on issues such as child prostitution, drug use, and the perceived violence associated with so-called squeegee kids (Parnaby, 2003).

A second reason for this attention is more theoretically and methodologically based. From Chapter 2 you will recall that by the late 1960s, particularly in the United States, self-report surveys became the standard tool used by researchers to measure and attempt to explain the causes of crime and delinquency. In fact, social control theory (Hirschi, 1969) was developed on the basis of information collected from youth who participated in surveys within the school setting. While researchers learned much about how youths' failures to develop social bonds within family and school settings were associated with minor delinquency, these studies neglected to access youth who were not attending school. This included students who may have skipped school on the day when a self-report survey was administered, in addition to those who had dropped out of school. Thus, most self-report research on youth crime did not include marginalized and troubled youth who had been excluded from the educational system.

In an attempt to correct this problem, Hagan and McCarthy (1997) conducted an important study showing, perhaps not surprisingly, that street youth were much more likely to be involved in illegal activities such as serious theft, drug use, theft of food, and prostitution compared to youth who participated in school-based surveys. Not only did Hagan and McCarthy discover homeless youth to be more involved in street crime than youth who were not street involved but these researchers also suggested that the reasons why street youth engaged in these types of illegal activities had more to do with their current adverse situations than with their disadvantaged backgrounds. The experiences of contending with the adverse conditions of street life were very much related to criminal activity. When homeless youth are hungry, they often steal or commit other types of property crime to feed themselves. Being without a legitimate job, and not having any money or a place to sleep—especially for females—explained why a number of youth turned to prostitution.

Also essential to understanding homeless youth is the fact that the backgrounds of many homeless youth are marred by turmoil. For instance, many street youth come from homes where parents had frequently experienced unemployment. Not only did a large number of these youths share the experience of growing up in economically marginalized households, but several reported to have been physically and/or sexually abused while growing up. Moreover, many family settings of these youth were characterized by parental criminality and alcohol and drug abuse (Hagan & McCarthy, 1997, p. 24).

While other research that focused on the backgrounds of street youth is generally supportive of these findings—especially the data showing that many of these youth had been victims of abuse—a more recent study of street youth in Toronto has shown that while many of these youth do come from working-class families, many others do not. For example, a study carried out by Gaetz et al. (1999) found that a considerable number of homeless youth grew up in families where one or both parents were employed either as managers or as professionals. In fact, when this sample of street youth were asked about their families' financial situations while growing up, three-quarters of them reported that it was "average" or "above average" (Gaetz & O'Grady, 2002, p. 444). There is good reason to believe, then, that homeless youth face exclusion on several different fronts.

Other research exploring crime among homeless youth has raised an interesting point about why street life can lead to crime. Baron and Hartnagel (1997) mention that stressful situations, like not having a job, can cause homeless youth to resort to criminal activity. They show how important it is to understand the subjective interpretations, or attributions, that homeless youth use to describe why they find themselves in adverse predicaments. What they found was interesting. If unemployed street youth attributed their lack of employment to factors that had little to do with themselves (e.g., they blamed the government or employers) they were more involved in property crime than youth who attributed their inability to secure a job to their own personal inadequacies and shortcomings (e.g., that they had not looked hard enough for a job). These results can be interpreted that street youth who felt the most excluded by society in general were the ones at greatest risk of committing crime.

The theme of social exclusion can be found in other studies of Canadian street youth. In a study that compared the lives of two groups of Toronto homeless youth—those who made money by squeegee-cleaning drivers' windshields and those who used other means to make money—found that the group of squeegee cleaners were less involved in crime than the non-squeegee sample (O'Grady et al., 1998). The squeegee cleaners also reported themselves to be better housed (could afford rooming houses and motels from time to time) and were less engaged in serious drug use than the other group of homeless youth. Moreover, the squeegee cleaners were less depressed than their non-squeegee working peers.

As the study was relatively small scale (only about 100 youths were surveyed in total) and was unable to track the activities of these youths over time, it was not possible to know for certain if squeegee cleaners were less disposed to criminality than the youth from the comparison group. Nevertheless, it is not unreasonable to argue that the entrepreneurial activity of squeegee-cleaning, in a small way, does allow these youths to feel more valued than other groups of street youth. Squeegee cleaners felt that they were providing a service to the public—even though their roadway soliciting was not always welcomed. In fact, interviews with these youth did show that while squeegee-cleaning was not considered to be a long-term economic strategy and solution to their problems, it was an activity that kept these youth physically active and socially involved. Therefore, the differences that were recorded in levels of reported crime, drug use, housing quality, and psychological well-being can be interpreted from the viewpoint that these squeegee cleaners, in relative terms, were more socially included than their non-squeegee counterparts.

Additional research on street youth has shown just how diversified economic life is for these disadvantaged street youth. In other words, crime is but one of several economic activities engaged in by homeless youth. A study by Gaetz and O'Grady (2002) that surveyed homeless youth from Toronto found that money-making spanned a broad range of economic activities such as paid employment, social assistance, panhandling, squeegee-cleaning, sex-trade work, property crime, and drug-dealing. Even though the economy of the street is varied and diverse, with many youths citing involvement in several kinds of economic activities, patterns of street work were shown to be linked to their backgrounds and prior experiences in addition to their current situations. For instance, those youths who reported that their main money-making activities fell into the domain of paid employment were also very likely to have completed high school and reported that it was only relatively recently that they had become street-involved. Moreover, levels of drug use for this group were relatively low, as were reports of depression and other mental health problems. By contrast, for street youth who were working mainly in the sex trade, very few had completed high school. Sex-trade workers were more likely to have had foster-care experiences, and many of them as children or adolescents had been victims of sexual abuse. Furthermore, this was the group that was the most likely to be using drugs such as cocaine or heroin on a regular basis.

Females in the sample were found to be the most likely to be relying on social assistance for economic survival. In large part, these patterns were accounted for on the basis that many were young mothers and were unable to work in other areas. In general, this research shows that street youth with the most troubled backgrounds, and those who were currently facing adverse situations, were the ones who were the most likely to be making money by engaging in risky or illegal activities.

Not only are homeless youth subject to greater involvement in criminal behaviour than housed youth, but they are also overrepresented by experiences of criminal victimization. We know this to be the case because of the findings of two studies that were carried out, once again in Toronto. The first, by Tanner and Wortley (2002), surveyed 3,400 high school students and 400 street youth in the Toronto area and asked them questions about their experiences related to criminal victimization. The study examined experiences that ranged from minor property crimes and threats to serious assaults, robbery, and rape. Similar to Hagan and McCarthy's findings that were reported earlier, more street youth than high school students (69 per cent compared to 39 per cent) reported they had been physically assaulted in the past year. Street youth also tended to be prone to experiences that involved sexual assaults compared to their high school counterparts (29 per cent compared to 6 per cent). The streets are a dangerous environment, especially for youth who are without stable and secure housing.

A second study on street youth and victimization carried out by Gaetz (2004) revealed similar results. This study was different from the Tanner and Wortley study in that the experiences of victimization reported by homeless youth were compared with data about domiciled youth (aged 15–24) that were collected by the 1999 Canadian General Social Survey. Gaetz found that homeless youth were five times more likely to have been victims of assault and theft than youth who had homes. Even more alarmingly, homeless youth reported levels of robbery that were 10 times greater than the non-street youth sample. Finally, 51 per cent of females reported to have been sexually assaulted in the past year, compared to 6.6 per cent of females who were not homeless (Gaetz, 2004, p. 51).

Gaetz interprets these results as showing that homeless youth are much more vulnerable to exploitation than youth who are housed. Street youth are prone to victimization by petty criminals, sexual predators, and unscrupulous landlords or employers because potential perpetrators recognize that young people who are homeless have few resources to defend themselves and little recourse for challenging them (ibid., p. 55). In short, being young and homeless means increased exposure to dangerous situations and presents opportunities for involvement in risky behaviours within a context of heightened exposure to potential offenders. Gaetz concludes his study by stating, "The social exclusion of street youths puts them in the contradictory position of being at increased risk for criminal victimization, on the one hand, and the target of public efforts to control crime and deviance, on the other" (ibid., p. 57).

Research on street youth—whether it explores offending, income generation, or victimization—points to the fact that vulnerability and marginalization go a long way in accounting for the problems experienced by these young people. It is not surprising that many of the major theoretical approaches in criminology we have been examining—strain, social bonding, self-control, differential association, and rational choice—have been used to explain why crime plays a significant role in the lives of street youth. Box 6.1 demonstrates why a socially excluded individual must rely on "deviant" work to survive.

As research accumulates we now know more and more about the reasons why youth leave home and wind up on the streets. Research also tells us of the patterns and behaviours that these youth adopt to survive and cope with living on the streets. What is less understood, however, is research that addresses the question, "How do young people get off the street?" According to Karabanow (2009), who has been researching homeless youth in Canada for several years, the exiting process for many homeless youth involves a number of stages. While these steps are not necessarily mutually exclusive, they were mentioned by all the youth Karabanow interviewed who successfully exited street life. Figure 6.1 on page 151 illustrates the steps of this process.

Due to the many challenges noted in this figure, young people who did end up exiting the streets had often made several unsuccessful attempts before. For those who were finally able to become unengaged with street life, many still had problems related to "fitting in" with a mainstream lifestyle. Besides trying to maintain stable housing and keeping a job or being able to stay in school, many youth reported that, at times, it was difficult for them to build a new network of non-street friends and relatives. In the words of Roger, a 24-year-old male from Halifax:

> Successfully getting off the streets is getting your own apartment, having a very successful job, avoiding street life like not panning, not having to fly a sign or go squeegeeing or anything like that. (Karabanow, 2009)

Social Exclusion

Blacc's situation illustrates why a socially excluded individual (a young home-less male living in New York City) relies on "deviant" work to survive. Even though many street youth are often told by passers-by to "get a job" while engaging in activities such as panhandling, according to Teresa Gowan, it is not that simple: ". . . . with little education or job training, most street youth, at best, find only short-term, minimum wage work. . . . most street youth find that they can make more money in the illegal street economy. . . . Street kids have four main ways of making money while homeless: sex work (prostitution), drug trade, theft, and panhandling. While some also have jobs in the formal econ-omy, most are minimum wage and do not provide enough to rent an apartment in New York City. Blacc and his friends chose the third option (theft) by 'bending' subway cards. They would pick up spent Metro cards, bend them in a particular way so that they would work again and then charge people money to swipe them onto the subway."

"We would bend Metro cards and swipe. We would find them on the ground. We would bend them until they worked and then we would swipe people in with the Metro cards, onto the train . . . it would be really crazy . . . If it was a local, you'd make a dollar for a two dollar ride . . . because they know. But if it was a tourist, you'd get the whole two dollars. Or you'd say, 'I'll swipe all four of you on for six dollars.' So you'd be giving them a break, but you'd be getting them out of the way to get more customers."

Source: Gibson, 2011, p. 69.

Youth Gangs

Youth gangs are active in several communities across Canada today. Particu-larly in urban centres, relying mainly on information provided by the police, the mass media regularly depict gang activity as a growing and violent menace. Keeping in mind the theory discussed in Chapter 1 regarding moral panics, we must be careful that such reporting alone does not form our knowledge base about the "reality" of gang activity in Canada. However, the problem that we face in Canada today is that, besides mass media accounts, very little system-atic information is available about street gangs. While criminologists are no doubt interested in the topic of gangs, very little Canadian research exists in this area. Hence, we cannot affirm how many youth are involved in gangs in Canada, and it is not possible to state with any certainty if the numbers of youth who are mixed up in gangs today is greater than it was in the past.

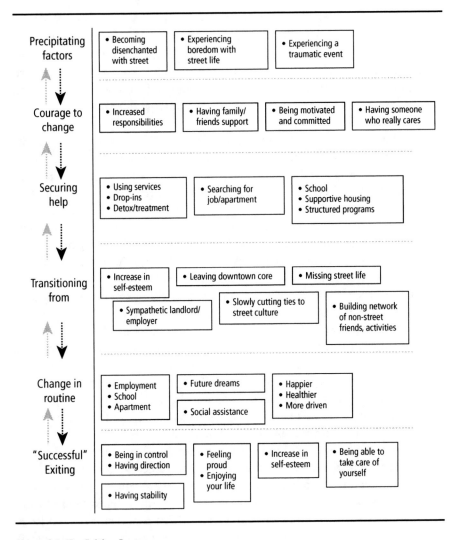

Figure 6.1 The Exiting Process
Source: Karabanow, 2009, p. 322.

In the United States, where the gang problem is more widely recognized, three main sources have been developed that address how prevalent gangs are and whether or not the numbers are changing. According to Tanner (2010), the first comes from the United States where the National Youth Gang Center collects data from a large sample of American police forces on gang activity; this survey is generally regarded as the official count of gang activity in the United States. This sort of information from the police is occasionally sought in Canada—especially by the media—but it is not collected on a regular basis. Second, surveys—normally school- and community-based—are used to ask youth about their own gang-related activities. Once again, national information such as this is not available in Canada. Third, gang behaviour can also be measured by case studies and observational research. Here researchers study small groups of youth who have been pre-identified as gangs. Based on all of this information it is estimated that there are more than 1,000 jurisdictions in the United States where the police believe gang activity is present, and this is five times greater than the number estimated in 1980 (Tanner, 2010, p. 166).

Yet if we were to rely solely on the information about gangs that appears in the mass media, which is most often generated from police reports and press conferences, answers to the above questions would generally paint a picture something like this: Yes, there is more youth gang activity today in Canada than was the case in the past. Moreover, gang activity is now more ruthless and violent than it once was. And one of the major reasons for this rise in gang-related violence has to do with the problem of more criminals using hand guns. Finally, gang membership is often associated with youth from certain ethnic, minority, or immigrant groups. In Toronto the "gang problem" is often depicted as a "black" problem, while in Vancouver and surrounding areas gang members are depicted in the media as being overrepresented by Asian and South Asian youth, and in the Prairie provinces by Aboriginal youth. According to a piece of investigative journalism carried out by Michelle Sheppard (1998) that appeared in the *Toronto Star*, it was claimed that there were more than 180 youth gangs operating in Toronto. The police estimate that over 2,000 youth are involved in gang activities (Mellor et al., 2005). More recently, police estimate that there are 340 known gangs in Canada wherein females make up 6 per cent of gang membership (*Toronto Star*, 2006).

Since rather broad definitions may have been used to generate these estimates, these statistics must be treated with extreme caution. Frankly, the information required to adequately address concerns about how many youth are members of gangs, and from what ethnic or racial backgrounds gang members come from, is unavailable in Canada. This is unfortunate. Statistics Canada does not collect data about crime in Canada on the basis of it specifically being "gang related." However, this is not to say that there is a total void of information about youth gangs in this country. We rely on existing Canadian research, in addition to a more developed body of research on gangs that has been developed since the 1920s in the United States, to present a systematic account of the nature of youth street gangs.

One of the greatest challenges that researchers face when trying to study gangs is the issue of how properly to define the term *youth gang*. Walter Miller, a sociologist who has spent a large part of his career studying gangs in the United States, has identified 20 different types of law-violating youth groups (Miller, 1975). However, only a small number from this group of 20 were actually considered to represent a gang. According to Miller, a **gang** is "a group of recurrently associating individuals with identifiable leadership and internal organization, identifying with or claiming control over territory in the community, and engaging either individually or collectively in violent or other forms of illegal behavior" (1975, p. 9).

International research literature on youth gangs is dominated by studies conducted in the United States. This research originated with the work of Frederick Thrasher (1927) who studied Chicago gangs during the 1920s. Based on interviews with more than 1,000 gang members, Thrasher found that gangs were most likely to flourish in neighbourhoods that were "socially disorganized." By this Thrasher meant that disadvantaged social conditions give rise to the formation of gangs, most of which were transitory, contained fewer than 30 members, and mainly fulfilled the function of sociability—in other words, most of the time gang members simply spent time hanging out with each other. In describing the structure and function of gangs, Thrasher found that the sometimes violent protection of neighbourhood "turf," that is, "discouraging other youth from occupying their neighbourhood," was a fundamental role that gangs played.

Besides economic disenfranchisement, another common feature of American gang membership is race. A common element found in post–Second World War research on this topic is that young men from racialized or ethnic minority groups (mainly black, Puerto Rican, and Chicano) are overrepresented in the ranks of youth gangs. According to Tanner's review of American youth gangs:

> Faced with few job prospects and limited non-criminal opportunities, they turn to both instrumental and expressive forms of gang delinquency as a means of relieving the pressures upon them and retaining their dignity. Subcultural membership is therefore an important source of income and identity in an urban wasteland. (2001, p. 136)

The development of the modern gang came about during a period of American history when the economic and social climate was changing rapidly. The 1960s gave rise to the "super gang." Compared with the gangs of Thrasher's day, which were mainly groups of juvenile males who were neighbourhood and kinship based, American gangs of the late 1960s became larger and more powerful. Two main explanations have been offered as to why gangs grew, became more sophisticated and more violent, and were not entirely composed of juveniles. The first factor pertains to economic restructuring and deindustrialization that eliminated many working-class jobs from many inner cities across America. Gang research carried out by Hagedorn (1998) in Milwaukee, for example, suggests that with the decline in the numbers of full-time manufacturing jobs there were fewer economic incentives available for inner-city, minority youth who had few educational qualifications. This decline in legitimate economic opportunities caused gang membership to become a more enduring condition.

A second reason for these changes in gang patterns concerns the role played by the drug trade. In response to the rise in demand for illegal street drugs, gangs rapidly became involved in the distribution of illegal drugs throughout the United States and elsewhere. However, not only can the drug trade be financially attractive for uneducated youth who possess few marketable skills, working in the drug trade can be dangerous and violent. For example, in 2011 Statistics Canada reported that of the 598 homicides that took place that year, 95 were considered by police to have been committed against individuals who were involved in drug-dealing, organized crime, or gang activity (Statistics Canada, 2012).

While the issue of urban gangs and gang violence is a constant and perhaps growing preoccupation of the Canadian mass media, as we pointed out earlier, systematic research on this topic is in relatively short supply in Canada. According to a survey of police agencies from across the country, 59 per cent of the Canadian population is served by police forces who acknowledge the presence of youth gangs in their jurisdictions. The provinces of Saskatchewan, Manitoba, and British Columbia are the regions of the country with the highest percentage of jurisdictions reporting active youth gangs (Mellor et al., 2005, p. 2). In fact, many of the gangs from the Prairie provinces are composed of Aboriginal youth. Like most assessments and analyses of gangs that rely exclusively on information supplied by the police, the information contained in the Canadian Police Survey on Youth Gangs is limited because the study did not systematically define the term *youth gang*, and the study was based only on police perceptions about the level and character of gang activity within their jurisdictions, not on systematic, empirical research.

Research on gang activity in Vancouver carried out by Gordon (2000) found, like much of American research, that gang activity in Vancouver does have a racialized dimension. A total of 85 per cent of those involved in street gangs were members of visible ethnic minorities according to Gordon. This West Coast study is interesting also because it revealed that even though the police and media often refer to much criminal activity as being "gang related," the types of groups who may appear to be gang members—according to their clothing and demeanour—are actually "wannabe groups." That is to say, these are groups of youth who spend large amounts of time hanging around together in public places such as shopping malls and who dress in clothing evocative of the style and attire of "gangsta rap" musicians. But, according to Gordon, members of these wannabe groups do not actually self-identify as gang members. Indeed, self-identification is a fundamental criterion in defining a gang. It is important that an individual actually believes that he or she is a member of a gang. However, groups such as "street gangs" and "criminal business organizations" who are involved in the kinds of criminal activities thought of as fitting with gang behaviour—especially the criminal business organizations—keep a low profile and are seldom seen associating with each other in public places because that would draw unwanted attention to their dubious methods of generating income.

More recently, Julian Tanner and Scot Wortley (2002) carried out a study of gangs in Toronto. Based on survey research conducted with 3,393 high schools, they found that 89 per cent of the student population had never been involved with a gang, 5 per cent were former gang members, and 6 per cent claimed current membership in a gang. The study also surveyed close to 400 street youth and found approximately one-quarter of those interviewed were either current or former gang members, while three-quarters reported that they had never been a member of a gang. Table 6.1 displays the range of activities in which these gang members were involved. It is interesting to note that for student gang members, the most popular activities were non-criminal, such as socializing with other gang members, followed by "protections" (defending turf and each other), going to parties, and playing sports. These conformist behaviours were followed by admitting to the deviant activities of drug use, fighting, property crime, and the selling of drugs. With the exception of sports, the street youth in the sample reported greater involvement in the assorted types of gang activities listed in Table 6.1.

Like much of the American research on gangs, this Toronto study found that gender (males), poor school performance, dysfunctional families, low socioeconomic status, and visible minority status all were associated with current or past gang involvement. This survey did not rely only on self-administered questionnaires; the research team also interviewed and spoke with 125 current or former gang members and asked these youths a number of questions about why they first became involved in a gang, why they stayed in a gang for so long, and the benefits of being a gang member. Their research revealed that power, money, respect, protection, and social support were the reasons that these youth identified with gangs. Below are the themes and

Table 6.1 Per Cent of Current and Former Gang Members Who Report That They Engaged in Various Activities within the Gang Context

Type of Activity	Students (%)	Street Youth (%)
Sold illegal drugs	39	76
Engaged in property crime	40	53
Fought against other gangs	57	65
Used alcohol and illegal drugs	57	76
Participated in sports	64	50
Went to parties or clubs	73	80
Protection	77	81
Socializing	83	85

Source: www.toronto.ca/metropolis/metropolistoronto2005/pdf/wortley_714b.pdf.

excerpts that were captured by Wortley and Tanner's research (Wortley & Tanner, 2005b):

Power and Respect

It's like people in my neighbourhood give you respect when you is in the gang. They know who you are and they don't mess. Nobody knew me before I got involved. Now I'm famous in my area. People know me now. (male, 22)

I like the respect. I like the power. You walk into a place with your boys and people notice you, ladies notice you. Ya got status, you can swagger. People know that you ain't no punk. (male, 19)

Money

I like it for the money. We made lots of money sellin' drugs and stealin' and ripping people off. I got to buy stuff that I could not get with no job at McDonald's. In this world you got to have some bling. (male, 21)

Obviously I do it for the cash. If there weren't no money in it I'd be gone. But the cash is good, man. Bought me a car, some clothes, gave me money for the club, got me money to get women, gave me money to help my moms. (male, 20)

Money and Respect

I'm not workin' at McDonald's or some place like that. That's slavery. They pay you shit and make you dress like a goof and have some punk manager order you around. Nobody respects some guy flippin' burgers or wearing some stupid ref shirt at Foot Locker. I make real cheddar in the gang, we are our own bosses, and we get plenty more respect from people cause of the money we got and because we never sell out. (male, 22)

Protection

In my area, man, if you ain't with a gang you're gonna get punked and jumped all the time. If ya can't beat 'em, join 'em. The gang got your back and people don't mess with you because they know you got backup. (female, 19)

Social Support and Companionship

The guys in my gang, we are all from the same neighbourhood: the projects. We grew up together from small. They are family. It's like us against the world. We respect each other, support each other. Nobody in the outside world helps or cares, so it's up to us. That's it man. Family. (male, 20)

What chance does a guy like me got in the real world? A poor black guy. Schools are shit; teachers don't think that you can do the work. Nobody's gonna give me a job. So I'll get paid and live in another way, in another world where I can get respect and nobody cares what I look like or where I come from. I know I'll probably die young or go to jail, but what other chance is there? (male, 22)

On the basis of such themes and excerpts, this research provides strong evidence that youth are initially attracted to gang life because of the protection it provides from an unsafe and intimidating neighbourhood environment. Moreover, having the perception that legal, well-paying, and respected employment opportunities are unavailable to them, these youth become involved in economic activities such as drug-dealing as an alternative means to attain a worthwhile "paycheque."

One aspect of research on youth gangs is that relatively little is known about the roles females play. Early research on gangs generally depicted females as playing an auxiliary role. Even though there has been a female presence in gang life since at least the latter part of the nineteenth century, females generally have been viewed as associating with gangs only in terms of their gendered relationships—mainly as the girlfriends—of male gang members. Partly as a result of public perceptions and beliefs that females were becoming more violent, criminologists began to turn their attention to the study of females in gangs in the late 1980s. In the United States, Anne Campbell (1990) carried out an important study that examined the gang-related activities of a group of Puerto Rican girls. According to Campbell, most females involved in gang activity do so within the context of a male gang. It was rare to find all-female gangs under the direction of a female.

The vast majority of females who were interviewed by Campbell had economically impoverished and socially disadvantaged backgrounds where there was not much hope for attaining the American Dream through legitimate means such as educational credentials and employment with high-demand occupational skill sets. On the contrary, the future for these girls was pretty bleak: sustained poverty, unemployment, and single parenthood. The appeal of joining a gang, according to Campbell, has to do with a perception that gang life would be the complete opposite of their current reality. Gang life represents power, control, material possessions, parties, and excitement—all aspects of life that they currently lack.

Of course, the reality of gang life is something quite different from these socially manufactured images. According to Campbell, a typical day in the life of a female gang member is fairly routine and much time is spent hanging around doing not much of anything. So even though there is a great deal of "tough talk" uttered among female gang members—about past fights and wild parties—Campbell contends that gang members are deliberately fooling themselves. Hence, for a short time they are able to make themselves believe that their lives are more exhilarating and consequential than they really are. But the more these young women become entrenched within the culture of the gang, the greater the likelihood that their lives will mirror those of their mothers—single parenthood with few educational or occupational opportunities.

<table>
<tr><td>Box 6.2</td><td></td></tr>
</table>

Box 6.2   Debates and Controversies

Mass Shootings

A shooting that occurred in Toronto during the summer of 2012 that killed 2 and injured 24 was noted by the Toronto Police Service to be one of the worst cases of gun violence in North America, and that gang conflict was behind the tragedy. However, as this story shows, there have been several other serious mass shootings in North America that did not involve rivalries between street gangs, including the shooting that took place in Newtown, Connecticut, in December 2012 that killed 22 children and 6 teachers.

Toronto shooting "a terrible case," but not the worst

Early Tuesday morning, after 2 people died and 24 were hurt in Monday night's shooting on Danzig Street in Scarborough at a community barbeque, an emotional Toronto Police Chief Bill Blair had this to say:

> "I've been a cop for 35 years and this is the worst incident of gun violence, in my memory, anywhere in North America."

It was said in the immediate aftermath of a shocking display of violence against largely innocent partygoers, but it was, nevertheless, inaccurate.

"It's a terrible case," agreed Scot Wortley, an associate professor of criminology at the University of Toronto's Centre for Criminology and Sociological Studies. "I don't know how you rank such cases but I think that you could probably find a large number of cases in North America where the death toll was significantly higher than the Scarborough shooting."

Toronto and Montreal have the lowest homicide rates of any major North American city of a similar size, said Worley. The risk of dying a violent death, he said, may be increasing for a young male living in an economically and socially disadvantaged community.

"The rest of us, the average citizen, particularly if you are over 30 and live in a middle-class community, you are safer in Canada than you have ever been."

From 1991 to 2010, the number of firearm-related incidents involving multiple victims in Canada peaked in 1991 with 25 such incidents, according to the Canadian Centre for Justice Statistics. It was at its lowest in 2010 at 12 shootings.

A look at a selection of the most violent mass shootings in the United States and Canada in the last 35 years.

UNITED STATES

Virginia Tech

Thirty-three dead, including killer Seung-Hui Cho, and at least 17 injured at Virginia Tech in Blacksburg on April 16, 2007. Cho, who had earlier been diagnosed with an anxiety disorder, shot himself in the head after the attack.

Luby's Cafeteria

Twenty-four dead, including killer George Hennard in Killeen Texas, on October 16, 1991. Hennard drove his pickup truck into the cafeteria, started firing at random and then killed himself after being wounded by police officers.

San Ysidro

Twenty-two dead, including killer James Oliver Huberty in San Ysidro, California, on July 18, 1984. Huberty was shot dead by a police officer.

University of Texas

Seventeen dead, including killer Charles Whitman, and 31 injured after Whitman opened fire from the university's clock tower on August 1, 1966.

Columbine High School

Fifteen dead, 26 injured when students Eric Harris, 18, and Dylan Klebold, 17, opened fire at the high school in Littleton, Colorado, before killing themselves on April 20, 1999.

Wah Mee club

Thirteen dead, one injured after three men opened gunfire in Seattle's Chinatown club in February 1983.

Fort Hood

Thirteen dead, 29 injured. US Army Major Nidal Hasan, who was paralyzed from the chest down after getting shot by two police officers, is accused in the November 5, 2009, shooting.

CANADA
École Polytechnique

Fourteen women dead, 13 injured at Université de Montréal's École Polytechnique on December 6, 1989. The killer, Marc Lepine, killed himself.

Concordia University

Four dead, one injured at the Montreal university on August 24, 1992. Valery Fabrikant, an associate professor of mechanical engineering at the time at Concordia, is serving a life sentence in prison.

Dawson College

Two dead, including shooter Kimveer Gill, and 19 injured in Montreal's Dawson College on September 13, 2006.

Source: Kauri, 2012. Material reprinted with the express permission of: National Post, a division of Postmedia Network Inc.

Other research on American gangs by Joe and Chesney-Lind (1998) generally supports Campbell's work. However, these authors add that while the majority of male and female gang members grow up in high-crime and economically poor neighbourhoods with high numbers of visible minorities, girl gang members are much more likely than their male counterparts to have experienced parental physical and/or sexual abuse. As such, joining a gang for a female is considered to be a refuge of sorts and a social support in the form of an alternative family.

Aboriginal People in Canada

Aboriginal people in Canada have experienced social exclusion since early European settlement. Indicators of continuing exclusion are manifested today in the high incidence of Aboriginal suicide, diabetes, heart disease, stroke, lower than average life expectancy, homelessness, substance abuse, and **overrepresentation** in the Canadian criminal justice system. According to data collected by Correctional Service of Canada, Aboriginal people represent 17 per cent of the federal inmate populations and 19 per cent of inmates in provincial institutions, yet stand for only 3 per cent of the total Canadian population (Roberts & Melchers, 2003). It is also important to point out that Canada is not alone in incarcerating Aboriginal people at rates far above national averages. For example, in Australia and New Zealand a similar problem is evident. In Australia, Aborigines represent just over 2 per cent of the population, but 20 per cent of the prison population. In New Zealand, 14 per cent of the population is Maori yet, in 1999, 38 per cent of all New Zealand inmates were of Maori descent (ibid.).

While Canadian research in this area has noted this overrepresentation for some time, and the Royal Commission on Aboriginal Peoples emphasized the issue in its 1996 report, the situation has not improved very much since that time. Aboriginal people continue to be overrepresented in inmate populations across the country, particularly in the Prairie provinces. In fact, research in Canada has done a reasonable job of describing the patterns and trends associated with Aboriginal overrepresentation, but attempts to explain and, more importantly, efforts to reduce these numbers have been less than successful.

Nevertheless, from what we do know, there are two general but interrelated reasons for this overrepresentation: discriminatory treatment and economic and social inequality. Some research has argued that discriminatory practices engaged in by the criminal justice system explain much of this overrepresentation. These types of findings are most often revealed in qualitative case studies where researchers reveal abuses and mistreatment that Aboriginal people have experienced by the police and the courts.

An acute example of such mistreatment concerns the case of Donald Marshall. A Mi'kmaq from Cape Breton, Nova Scotia, Marshall was wrongfully convicted for murder and spent 11 years in Dorchester Penitentiary for a crime he did not commit. A provincial Royal Commission investigating this case revealed in 1990 that the Nova Scotia justice system failed Marshall from his arrest, wrongful conviction, and beyond his acquittal in 1983. As a result of these findings, Marshall was given a financial compensation of $270,000 for his time spent in jail. While the Marshall case is perhaps the best known in Canada, by no means is it the only occasion when an Aboriginal person has been discriminated against within the purview of the criminal justice system (Burtch, 2003).

Undeniably, abuses such as this took place in the past, and racial profiling and selective enforcement likely continue to play a role today in accounting for some of this overrepresentation. Yet the deprived socioeconomic conditions faced by many Canadian Aboriginal people cannot be ignored as a key reason for why so many of Canada's Aboriginal people are serving time in Canadian penal institutions. In a study carried out by Carol LaPrairie (2002), who examined the living conditions of Aboriginal people surviving in cities throughout western Canada, she suggests that unemployment, substance abuse, low levels of formal education, homelessness, and lone-parent families cannot be overlooked as factors accounting for this overrepresentation. In theoretical terms, such reasoning is in keeping with the social exclusion perspective. LaPrairie suggests that because Aboriginal people often reside in areas of Canadian cities that are characterized by poverty and isolation, "criminogenic structures and cultures arise" (2002, p. 196). A more recent study by Yessine and Bonta (2009) found that Aboriginal youth offenders, compared to non-Aboriginal offenders, were more likely to come from an impoverished background characterized by an unstable familial environment, substance use, and negative peer associations. These criminogenic risks and needs contributed to their serious and persistent pattern of criminality.

Other research has suggested that many Aboriginal people serving relatively short periods of time in provincial institutions are being imprisoned for fine default (Hagan, 1974). In other words, because many Aboriginal people are unable to pay fines that are imposed on them by the courts, they end up serving time in jail. Research by McMahon (1995) has shown just how important the issue of fine non-payment is for explaining patterns and trends in levels of provincial inmate populations.

Roberts and Melchers (2003) have offered two remedies to alleviate the problem of Aboriginal overrepresentation in the correctional system. The first relates to efforts to educate criminal justice professionals—particularly judges—about the severity of the problem, and to have them adopt a broader range of sentencing alternatives. The second, a more ambitious project, is to reduce the numbers of Aboriginal people who are being brought into the criminal justice system in the first place. Meeting such a challenge would, of course, only be possible if the unacceptable social conditions that plague the communities of so many Aboriginal people in Canada are greatly improved.

Hate Crime

With the exception of research on victimized street youth, we have concentrated on how social exclusion can lead to overrepresentation in *offending* behaviour. But it is also the case that social exclusion can be linked to certain forms of criminal victimization experienced by selective groups in Canada.

Hate crime is crime motivated by antagonisms toward race, ethnicity, sexual orientation, or religion (Berk, 1990). Even though the Canadian government has recently enacted laws to protect vulnerable groups, hate crimes are not new. In the United States, for example, the lynching of African Americans by white racists exemplifies what today we call hate crime. Although it is not possible to present accurate statistics of the number of African Americans who have been victims of lynching, according to Hofstadter and Wallace (1970) there were more than 5,000 lynchings *after* slavery was abolished in the United States. One may also argue that hate-related violence has historical roots in Canada as well. During the 1920s and 1930s anti-Semitism was widespread in Canada, especially following the rise of the Nazi movement in Germany and the rise to power of Adolf Hitler. On 16 August 1933, a baseball game during an amateur tournament in Toronto involved one team made up largely of Jewish players. At the end of the game, a group of Nazi sympathizers unfurled a large swastika flag and shouted, "Heil Hitler." A riot soon erupted in which Jews and Italians pitted against Anglo-Canadians fought for hours. Due to the large size of the crowd, the police were unable to restore order. Some estimates put many as 10,000 people involved in the riot (Levitt & Shaffir, 1978). A recent Halloween party that took place at the Campbellford, Ontario, Canadian Legion shows us that insensitivity about the lynching of African Americans remains in some circles of society. At the party, two partygoers, one wearing a Ku Klux Klan costume draped with a Confederate flag led around the other wearing "blackface" with a noose around his neck, took the first place costume prize at the Legion that evening (Allen, 2010).

In Canada the legal definition of hate crime can be found in sections 318 and 319 of the *Criminal Code*. Hate propaganda refers to "advocating genocide, public incitement of hatred, or the willful promotion of hatred against an indefinable group including those distinguished by colour, race, religion, ethnic origin, or sexual orientation" (Silver et al., 2004, p. 4). In 1996, the federal government amended a section of the *Criminal Code* that pertains to sentencing. Specifically, section 718.2 was changed so that the courts could now take into consideration whether an offence was motivated by prejudice based on "race, national or ethnic origin, language, colour, religion, sex, age, mental or physical disability, sexual orientation, or other similar factor" (ibid.). In this way the criminal law is being used as an institutional mechanism designed to protect particular groups in society who have been socially excluded historically largely on the basis of certain ascribed characteristics.

Police reports and victimization surveys are the two primary methods used by researchers and policy analysts to collect information about hate crime in Canada. These techniques, in addition to their strengths and weaknesses, were reviewed in Chapter 2. According to the 1999 and 2004 General Social Survey (GSS), 4 per cent of criminal incidents were considered by victims to have been motivated by hate (Gannon & Mihorean, 2005). Race or ethnicity was cited by victims as the basis for 43 per cent of the reported offences in 1999 and 65 per cent in 2004. The remainder of reports included offences that involved categories such as religion, sex, and sexual orientation. One of the more disturbing aspects of hate crime concerns the level of violence that can occur. Not far from half (43 per cent) of hate crime incidents were assaults, compared to 18 per cent of all victimizations that were recorded in the 1999 GSS. Because it is not unusual for hate crimes to involve acts of physical violence, victims of hate crime often experience considerable physical and psychological trauma (Levin & McDevitt, 1993, cited in Silver et al., 2004). Unlike general crime statistics, which show that victims and offenders often know one another, in almost 50 per cent of incidents of hate crime the perpetrator was unknown to the victim; in other words, the antagonism toward the victim has a quality of abstraction: The victim might be anyone who bears indicators that "trigger" the hatred of the perpetrator. According to a police pilot project that monitored hate crime in several major urban centres across Canada, the largest single ethnic group targeted by hate crime was Jewish people or Jewish institutions such as cemeteries and synagogues. The second most targeted group were blacks, followed by Muslims, South Asians, and gays and lesbians (Silver et al., 2004).

The same police study also collected information about the "precipitating factors" that are involved in hate-related incidents. Racial slurs were the most common precipitating factor identified in the study, particularly in cases involving race or ethnicity, religion, and sexual orientation. Hate crimes based on sexual orientation were the most likely to be brought on by a fight (ibid.). An example of this sort of incident, commonly referred to as "gay bashing," occurs when one or more individuals suspected of being homosexuals are besieged by a group of males, taunted, and then assaulted.

The Internet has been used by those wishing to disseminate hateful messages. In 2006 Reni Sentana-Ries (also known as Reinhard Gustav Mueller) was given a 16-month jail sentence for being found guilty of inciting hatred against Jews on his website. The website contained material which denied the Holocaust and stated that Jews created diseases such as AIDS and Ebola (*Edmonton Journal*, 2006). Who commits hate crime in Canada? While it may seem reasonable to assume that hate crimes are committed by those involved with extremist groups, according to the record of those events that come to the attention of the police this is not necessarily the case. In fact, only 4 per cent of hate crimes were linked to an organized or extremist group (Silver et al., 2004). Based on information collected from 520 individuals accused or charged of hate crimes by police in 2001–2, the vast majority (84 per cent) were male, with an average age of just under 30. Less than 10 per cent of those accused had criminal records, and less that 5 per cent had previous hate crime involvement (ibid.).

While these statistics provide a basic profile of who is implicated in hate crime in Canada, at least of those who come to the attention of the authorities, the reasons why these acts are committed are not well understood, particularly in Canada. However, according to an analysis carried out in the United States by Levin and McDevitt (1993), through humour, religion, and politics a growing *culture of hate* is emerging whereby people who differ from the *in-group* are targeted. This growing culture provides a basis for degrading, insulting, and essentially excluding people on the basis of difference. Barbara Perry, a Canadian researcher who studied hate crime in the United States, has offered a similar explanation to account for this type of crime. She argues that hate groups mobilize in their efforts to emphasize a narrow, exclusive understanding of national identity by providing a belief system that presumes the dominance of white, heterosexual, "Christian" male power. Successful hate groups are able to form a collective identity within their community that seeks to "negate, exclude and repress those groups that fall outside of the norm, namely non-Whites, non-Christians, non-heterosexuals, and even non-males. And they do so by invoking ideological claims to superiority and power" (Perry, 1998, p. 32).

In Canada, Barrett (1987) has carried out an anthropological case study of racist skinheads. Even though Canada is a country that prides itself on tolerating racial and minority difference, Barrett's study of racist and anti-Semitic organizations shows that organized hate groups exist nevertheless in this country. While his ethnographic account supported many of the claims that have been raised above about who are involved in such groups, as well as their ideological fervour, Barrett also suggests, at least for one group that he was in contact with, that hate can transform into outright stupidity. For example, some of the people Barrett interviewed actually believe that the CN Tower, situated on Toronto's waterfront, is actually a communications beacon linking North American "Jew Communists" to co-conspirators in Russia (Barrett, 1987, p. 94)! Apart from revealing such foolishness, Barrett's work shows that most of the hate groups he studied are a milder form of the hate groups evident in the US extreme radical right, such as the Ku Klux Klan.

Ellen Faulkner, who has studied hate crime within the gay and lesbian communities in Canada, argues that insufficient data are available to estimate meaningfully the level and character of this kind of crime. Even though the GSS does ask questions about hate crime, because the sexual orientation of the victim is not always clear the survey is unable to provide an accurate picture of the nature of the problem in Canada. Yet smaller-scale survey research has shown some interesting differences in the experiences of victimization reported by lesbians and gay men. Members of the lesbian community are much more likely to report being victimized by heterosexual people whom they know, such as co-workers and family members, assaults that take place largely within the private realm. Conversely, gay men were more likely to be victimized by strangers, male youths in the public domain such as streets and parks (Faulkner, 2003). The finding that lesbian women are prone to victimization in private locations such as the home also applies to the situation faced by many heterosexual women, an issue that we will look at shortly.

Using data from Ottawa collected in the mid-1990s, Roberts (1995) speculates about the level of hate crime in Canada:

> In that year (1994), 211 . . . hate crimes were recorded by the Ottawa police. Assuming that only one-third of all incidents are ever reported to the police, this suggests that 633 incidents were actually committed. Since Ottawa accounts for 7 per cent of the total *Criminal Code* offences for the major urban centres in Canada, this implies that the total number of hate crimes committed in nine urban centres (Halifax, Montreal, Ottawa, Toronto, Winnipeg, Regina, Calgary, Edmonton, Vancouver) is approximately 60,000. This estimate is consistent with estimates of the incidence of hate crimes in other jurisdictions. For example, the British Home Office has estimated that there are approximately 100,000 hate crimes committed annually in England and Wales. This British estimate is based upon a single form of hate crime (racially motivated crimes), while the estimate for Canada's urban centres includes other forms of hate crime such as crimes motivated by hatred based on religion, ethnicity and ethnic orientation. (Roberts, 1995, p. viii)

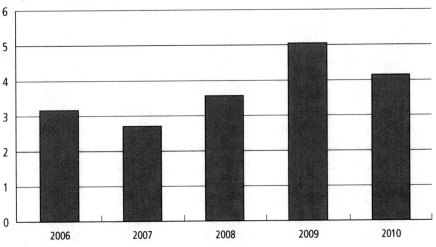

Figure 6.2 Police-Reported Hate Crimes, Canada, 2006–10
Source: Dowden and Brennan, 2012, p. 6.

However, until more systematic efforts are put into place to more accurately measure the incidence of hate crime in Canada, we must be very cautious about assuming the validity of these guesstimates. Roberts suggests that Canada lags behind other nations in collecting comprehensive statistics on hate crime (1995, p. ix).

Violence against Women

The social and economic status of women in Canada has improved over the course of the past 50 years. Yet contemporary research on women and violence indicates that social and economic exclusion continues to play a fundamental role in accounting for much of the violence that women experience, particularly within the context of intimate, domestic relationships. This section of the chapter will begin by discussing intimate-partner violence and then turn to other forms of male violence from which women are at risk. This will include a discussion of non-intimate-partner sexual assault and date rape.

Before exploring the issue of intimate violence against women, it is important to clarify that women in heterosexual relationships are not the only victims of abusive partners. Research has shown that men in heterosexual relationships, men in same-sex relationships, and women in same-sex relationships also experience violence that is perpetrated against them by their intimate partners (McClennen, 2005). However, research has also shown that women are most likely to experience the severest forms of violence and are more likely to be killed by men within the context of heterosexual relationships. According to Statistics Canada, in 2004 the spousal homicide rate against women was *five* times greater than it was for men (Dauvergne, 2005). But it is important to point out that the definition of "domestic violence" extends beyond homicide. In fact, there is considerable debate within the criminological community on the most effective way in which to define *domestic violence*. Spousal or domestic violence can be as broad as referring to any act or omission done or not done to a partner "that is perceived as psychologically, socially, economically, or physically harmful" (DeKeseredy & Schwartz, 1996, p. 321). Examples of such abuse would include the destruction of personal property, public humiliation and embarrassment, and not providing an economically dependent spouse with sufficient funds to adequately care for herself or her children. Given that combining such a wide array of acts makes it difficult to determine the reasons for such violence, it is more common for research on domestic violence to focus generally on what the *Criminal Code* would classify as **Physical Assault Level 1**—pushing, slapping, punching, and face-to-face threats (Sauvé, 2005). But, as DeKeseredy and Schwartz (1996, p. 322) point out, a focus only on physical assaults assumes that these acts, in both the short and long term, are more destructive than psychological, sexual, or economic harm.

Due in part to these sorts of definitional issues, it is difficult to estimate just how much spousal violence against women actually occurs in Canada on an annual basis. Most scholars who investigate this issue would agree that most data sources underestimate the true extent of this problem. But the most highly regarded method used to measure the extent of domestic violence in Canada is the General Social Survey (GSS). According to the 2009 GSS, women and men experienced similar levels of physical or sexual violence from their current partner in the previous five years: males 5 per cent; females 6 per cent. Females, however, reported higher levels of repeated violence and were more likely than men to experience serious injuries. More specifically:

> . . . women were more likely than men to state that the most serious form of violence they had experienced included being beaten, choked or being threatened with or having a gun or knife used against them (23 per cent versus 15 per cent for male victims). Women were also twice as likely as men to report experiencing more than 10 violent episodes (21 per cent versus 11 per cent), more than twice as likely to suffer an injury (44 per cent versus 18 per cent), and three times more likely to fear for their life because of the violence (34 per cent versus 10 per cent). (Gannon & Mihorean, 2005, p. 7)

A useful starting point for understanding domestic violence asks the question, "What keeps battered women from leaving home?" While many women do leave abusive partners (Johnson & Ferraro, 2000), it is the case that women can be confined to abusive relationships for a number of reasons. For instance, some women are simply too afraid to leave because they expect fallout or retaliation from the abusive partner. According to data collected by Statistics Canada, there is good reason for this trepidation. The police reported that in 63 per cent of spousal homicides there had been a history of prior violence (Dauvergne, 2005). In a good number of these cases the police had made previous calls to the residence where ultimately lethal violence took place. While this statistic refers to legally married women and women living in common-law relationships, women in common-law relationships are the most likely to be victims in spousal homicides. Even though there is no well-established answer for why married women appear to be more protected than women who live with male partners outside the conventional definition of marriage, one factor that may explain these differences is age. The relationship between marital status and homicide victimization exists not necessarily because marriage somehow protects women, or that people who are married are more law-abiding than people who are not. A more likely reason pertains to the fact that younger people tend to be more likely to co-habit without being married, and that age is a key predictor of intimate partner violence. Couples under 25 are at the greatest risk of spousal violence, while those over 45 pose the lowest risk (Johnson & Dawson, 2011:80). A good reason to doubt the protective function of marriage is that, according to the 2004 GSS, levels of domestic assault are lowest in the province of Quebec, which also has the highest per capita number of couples who are living in common-law relationships in Canada.

Largely informed by feminist analyses, which were introduced in Chapter 4, the context of women violence is most often within the boundaries of the family, since much of this violence takes place within the home. While this may be true, it is also important not to overlook the fact that violence between intimate partners can also spill over into the workplace. Lloyd (1997) suggests that women who are victimized by their spouses within the home are not protected from such abuse when they are in the workplace. Quite frequently abused women receive harassing phone calls from abusive partners while at work, and it is not unusual for the abusive partner to visit his spouse in the workplace, thus bringing the violence out of the home into the public realm.

Why, then, do women remain in abusive relationships? While each individual woman has her own motives for deciding to remain or leave an abusive relationship, research has identified a number of common reasons that battered women report for staying. However, note first that most female victims of domestic abuse do, in fact, leave batterers (Johnson & Ferraro, 2000). But for those who remain, one reason for doing so has to do with fear and uncertainty. Many female victims of intimate violence believe that the batterer will respond to their departure with extreme violence—particularly if children leave as well. And, unfortunately, there is good reason for a lot of women to believe this to be the case. According to data from the 2009 GSS, 20 per cent of women who had contact with a former spouse experienced physical or sexual violence by this person while still living together or after separation (Sinha, 2013: 24). Interestingly, this phenomenon does not apply to men. In other words, when men leave relationships because of spousal violence, very few report that the abuser's violence increased in severity (Gannon & Mihorean, 2005).

A second reason why many battered women remain in abusive relationships is related to economic exclusion. Due to the fact that many abused women are economically dependent on their spouses, and do not have marketable employment skills, leaving would result in financial ruin. Besides providing women with safe refuge, an awareness of the precarious economic circumstances that many battered women face is a key reason for the rise of the shelter movement. In fact, the vast majority of women who seek refuge in the shelter system were, or are, economically dependent on their partners.

Third, many women in abusive relationships do not leave because constant abuse essentially renders them inoperative and without the capability of leaving. This notion, which first came to be known as "learned helplessness," was proposed by Lenore Walker, an American psychologist, in the late 1970s.

The idea attempts to explain how the ability to manage control over the events in one's life becomes jeopardized with repeated abuse. Similar to research with animals in laboratory settings, repeated beatings, like electric shocks administered to lab rats, negatively affect a woman's ability to respond, resulting in a passive state. Over time, learned helplessness causes depression, anxiety, and low self-esteem, whereby any action needed to alleviate an abusive situation is considered to be futile (Walker, 1979, p. 50).

While this theory does make a plausible case for why some women remain in abusive relationships, especially over prolonged periods of time, the theory is rather limiting because most women who experience intimate violence do in fact leave their abusers and do not end up in a state of learned helplessness. In fact, one British study (Horley, 1991) estimates that over 85 per cent of beaten women do in fact leave violent relationships.

While most research on the abuse of women has been focused within the domain of the family, it is important to recognize that women are at risk from other forms of male violence, such as non-spousal sexual assault and date rape. In 1983 section 143 of the *Criminal Code* was amended whereby the "rape" statute was changed to **sexual assault**. This change in the wording of this section was not merely an issue of semantics. Rather, the amendment marked a fundamental shift in terms of how sexual offences were to be defined

---

Box 6.3   Debates and Controversies

Are Intimate Partner Femicides Typically "Crimes of Passion"?

Femicides (generally understood to mean the murder of women by men mainly because they are females) are often perceived to be "crimes of passion." However, according to research by Myrna Dawson a Canadian expert in the field of domestic violence, this is not often the case as 30 per cent of femicides in Ontario appeared to be pre-meditated. These included cases where:

- The offender intercepted the victim when leaving home or work.
- The offender broke into the victim's home.
- The victim was sleeping when she was killed.
- The offender previously threatened to kill the victim/himself.
- The offender brought a gun to the location of the killing.
- The offender purchased a gun prior to the killing.
- The offender wrote a suicide note before the killing.

Source: Johnson & Dawson, 2011, p. 135.

in Canada. Under the old version, for a person to be found guilty of rape, Goff (2004, p. 30) writes that the following five conditions had to be established:

1. The complainant had to be female.
2. The accused had to be male.
3. The complainant and accused were not married to each other.
4. Sexual intercourse occurred.
5. The act of intercourse occurred without the consent of the woman.

The current sexual assault legislation allows for husbands to be charged with sexual assault irrespective of whether penetration has occurred. Moreover, unlike the previous rape statute where the victim had to be female and the perpetrator male, both victims and those accused can be either male or female. Finally, the revamped sexual assault law contains three levels of assault that are based on the seriousness of the crime. Sexual Assault Level 1 pertains to acts involving the least amount of physical injury and can include acts short of sexual penetration such as unwanted sexual touching. For a sexual assault to be elevated to Level 2, the assault must involve a weapon, or the threat of a weapon, or result in bodily harm to the victim. Level 3 sexual assault, also known as aggravated sexual assault, results in the wounding, maiming, disfiguring, or endangering the life of the victim (Sauvé, 2005, p. 7).

Even though the sexual assault statute has been "de-gendered," meaning that victims and accused can be either male or female, it is important to point out that the vast majority of sexual assaults that come to the attention of the police in Canada involve female victims.

While not an official category listed in the *Criminal Code*, the recently popularized term *date rape* refers to sexual assault that occurs within the context of a dating relationship. In fact, an individual found guilty of committing date rape is liable to the same punishment as a person convicted of a sexual assault in a situation where the victim and offender were strangers. However, unlike the case of stranger rape, one of the key issues surrounding date rape is proving that a sexual act or unwanted touching occurred without the consent of the victim. Indeed, this is one of the key reasons why so few date rapes are ever reported to the police. Date rapes often occur when a male has expectations that his date will be sexually compliant if he spends enough money on food, entertainment (movies, concerts, etc.), or drinks at a nightclub. The expectation here is similar to a socially perceived bargain or exchange: money/food/gifts for sex. Due to the fact that some men feel that they are entitled to sex from their dates, campaigns have been spearheaded by women's groups to bring more attention to this issue. There have, however, been incidents in Canada where men defied and mocked such campaigns. An example of such defiance took place on the campus of Queen's University in the fall of 1989 in response to a "No means no" campaign against date rape that was sponsored by the student council. TV cameras and newspaper photographs showed male residences on campus displaying signs such as "No means kick her in the teeth" and "No means give her more beer." Even though the signs were ordered by the Dean of Women to be taken down, some reports indicate that some of the signs were still up a week later (Dickie, 1990).

Another context for date rape concerns the "spiking" of a woman's drink with drugs such as Rohypnol (commonly referred to as "roofies"). Once ingested, the victim becomes disorientated, submissive, and often is unable to recall events following the drug's having taken effect. While there is not much reliable information on the extent of this problem in Canada, and some researchers claim that the recent concern over date-rape drugs is actually akin to a moral panic (Moore & Valverde, 2003), these actions have taken place in Canada and women are overwhelmingly the victims of such events.

Conclusion

This chapter has presented research on a number of groups who experience particular forms of social exclusion. This exclusion was shown to impact certain offending behaviours or experiences of victimization. Beginning with a brief discussion of the meaning of social exclusion, we drew on research that has focused on homeless youth and the problems these young people face on the streets. Homeless youth were shown to be involved in crime largely as a result of their inability to survive from legitimate economic sources. Other groups of criminally involved youth who gather together and form gangs were also described as being excluded from society in several ways, most notably in terms of their social class and in some cases by their racial or ethnic associations. The reasons why females join gangs were also discussed.

The chapter then turned to the situation facing Aboriginal people in Canada and their overrepresentation in the criminal justice system. While Aboriginals in Canada comprise approximately 3 per cent of the population, they account for about 20 per cent of adults who are incarcerated. Reasons for this overrepresentation lie partly with discriminatory practices. However, as was pointed out by LaPrairie (2002), any attempt to fully understand the problems faced by many Aboriginal people in Canada is complex, where discriminatory practices—particularly in the past—and social and economic exclusion must be considered.

Hate crimes, incidents where groups of people are targeted simply on the basis of their religious affiliation or sexual orientation, have been taking place in Canada for some time, yet only recently has the issue garnered public attention, and insufficient data have been gathered on these serious forms of intolerance. Women were shown to be particularly vulnerable to intimate-partner violence and sexual assault. Some of their reasons for responding in

particular ways to this violence were explored. The laws in Canada for pros-
ecuting violence against women or men who have been sexually assaulted
were outlined.

Critical Thinking Questions

1. Why in recent years has the study of homeless youth gained the attention of researchers?
2. Why don't most youth in socially excluded communities join street gangs?
3. Explain why Aboriginal people are overrepresented in Canada's criminal justice system.
4. What steps need to be taken in Canadian society so that hates crime can be eliminated?
5. Can you think of any other examples of murders that could fall under the category of femicide?

Suggested Readings

Decker, Scott H. (2008). *A guidebook for local law enforcement strategies to address gang crime*. Office of Community Oriented Policing Services. US Department of Justice. Washington, DC. This report was written for policy makers and practitioners to prevent and control gang violence in the United States.

Perry, Barbara. (2001). *In the name of hate: Understanding hate crimes*. New York, NY: Routledge. This book defines hate crime and explores which groups in society are victimized by this type of crime. Perry also examines hate groups and their ideologies.

Websites and Films

Raising the Roof
http://raisingtheroof.org
A site that contains information about research, programming, and fundraising on homelessness in Canada, including work on homeless youth.

Reading Hate
http://criminologyandjustice.uoit.ca/hatecrime/index.html
This website contains information about hate crime in Canada, including data on hatecrime legislation, notable Canadian hate crime cases, and more.

Heaven on Earth. (2008). The universal shame of domestic violence provides the context of director Deepa Mehta's drama. Preity Zinta plays Chand, a vibrant young
woman who travels from India to Canada to join her new husband Rocky (Vansh
Bhardwaj) and his traditional family. Meeting for the first time at the airport, Chand
walks into her new life with optimism. That hopefulness passes quickly when Rocky,
a man burdened with familial obligations, unleashes his frustrations on her with his
fists. To save her marriage Chand accepts a magical root from a co-worker, one that
promises to snag her husband's love. Soon magical events mirroring an old Indian
fable occur and blur the lines of their true relationship.

Hate Crime. (2005). Directed by Tommy Stovall, *Hate Crime* is a testament to the power of love and the damaging consequences of intolerance. Robbie and Trey live peacefully in a quiet neighbourhood until an unexpected conflict arises in the form of a hostile new neighbour, Chris, a preacher's kid. Blindsided by a brutal attack, Trey winds up in a hospital bed fighting for his life. Chris becomes the prime suspect, but he has a solid alibi. After he himself becomes a suspect, Robbie desperately attempts to carry out a complex and dangerous plan that will uncover shocking secrets and turn many lives upside down (www.hatecrimemovie.com/synopsis.html).

The Break. (2012). This is a documentary where viewers are introduced to three diverse young people: Ava, Nancy, and Rob. All are currently homeless. The world is shown through their eyes—the looming dangers, the struggles for food and shelter, and the overwhelming obstacles holding them back. The documentary film is hosted by Anne Mahlum.

7

Crime in the Context of Organizations and Institutions

Learning Objectives

After completing this chapter students will be able to:

◎ Define white-collar crime and provide Canadian examples of it.

◎ Identify the social groups who are victims of white-collar crime.

◎ Know how criminologists explain corporate offending.

◎ Be able to describe various types of political crime.

◎ Understand the nature of police deviance.

◎ Be aware that crime is committed within institutions regarded with trust: religious organizations, the medical profession, education, the law.

◎ Understand transnational crime.

Introduction

To this point in our study, it might appear that most crime is generated by lower-class males who are not properly bonded to society, have bleak futures, or else face insupportable emotional strains. In fact, a number of criminological theories were developed to explain male street crime. But how do criminologists explain why a group of people who appear to have a great stake in conformity commit more crime than impoverished inner-city youth? These individuals may have homes in more than one country, may hold positions as CEOs of large business enterprises, or may even have their own airlines, television shows, clothing lines, or very profitable home-decorating chains of stores. It is unlikely that these individuals suffer from atavism, low intelligence, or are economically disenfranchised, but they break the law nonetheless. This chapter will focus on white-collar or corporate, transnational, environmental, and political crime before turning to an analysis of wrongdoing committed by police, religious leaders, and others in positions of trust. The point of addressing crimes that are committed by these groups is to demonstrate that sometimes citizens presumed responsible are involved in crime. The protective immunity of their affiliations—from which such people benefited in the past—has begun to weaken only relatively recently.

White-Collar and Corporate Crime

American sociologist Edwin Sutherland was the first scholar to draw attention to crime committed by groups in society who occupied positions of power and influence. In 1939, Sutherland introduced the term **white-collar crime** to the American Sociological Association. In drawing attention to "crime that is committed by a person of respectability and high social status in the course of his [*sic*] occupation" (Sutherland, 1939, p. 2) Sutherland was calling for criminologists to bring an end to the practice of exclusively focusing on crimes committed by the socially disadvantaged. Not only was Sutherland interested in broadening the definition of crime, but he also wanted to draw attention to the issue because of the respectable social status and power held by white-collar criminals. Because these types of rule-breakers lived in prosperous neighbourhoods and were held in high regard, society in general—even criminology—was turning a blind eye to massive harm being inflicted on society by such individuals. What sorts of harm was Sutherland speaking of? Consider the following list that he compiled on the brink of the Second World War:

- Misrepresentation in financial statements of corporations
- Manipulation in the stock exchange
- Commercial bribery
- Bribery of public officials directly or indirectly to secure favourable contracts and legislation
- Misrepresentation in advertising and salesmanship
- Embezzlement and misappropriation of funds
- Misapplication of funds in receiverships and bankruptcies

Anyone who follows the news could be under the impression that this inventory was put together only recently. For example, the first item, the "misrepresentation in financial statements of a corporation," might refer to the scandal surrounding WorldCom, the large American telecommunications company that filed for bankruptcy protection in 2002 because it was $41 billion in debt and had to lay off 17,000 employees. Due to a series of "accounting irregularities" (i.e., by inflating profits in financial statements, the company appeared to be more profitable than it really was), the CEO of the company, Bernie Ebbers, was found guilty of fraud and for filing false documents to regulators and was sent to prison for 25 years (CBC News Online, 2006).

Another well-publicized example of corporate fraud involves the once huge American energy company Enron. Like WorldCom, Enron Corporation was billions of dollars in debt, and to conceal the corporation's financial problems from shareholders, earnings reports were exaggerated. After Enron filed for bankruptcy, numerous Enron employees lost billions of dollars in retirement savings invested in Enron stock. Even though they knew that Enron stocks were losing value, Enron executives prohibited employees from withdrawing their retirement funds while at the same time, allegedly, selling their overvalued stocks at enormous profit. Kenneth Lay, one of the central figures of the scandal, was reported to have made $146 million from options trades (Beirne & Messerschmitt, 2006, p. 210). Both Lay and Jeffrey Skilling, another Enron executive implicated in the corporate swindle, were convicted of multiple counts of conspiracy and fraud.

While Sutherland focused almost exclusively on one type of white-collar crime—corporate crime—not all white-collar criminals are corporate criminals. The two types of activity are similar in the sense that both white-collar crime and corporate crime take place within the context of the business world. However, the difference between the two comes down, in part, to who benefits from the illegal activity. If the beneficiary is an individual, then we are talking about white-collar crime. On the other hand, if the offences benefit the corporation, than it is a corporate crime. Of course, the two types of offences are not always mutually exclusive because individual and corporate gain can occur simultaneously. For example, if a corporate executive "cooks the books" so that his or her company appears to investors to be worth more than it actually is, then, if the accounting fabrications are not detected, in the short term at least, the individual may make money from profit-sharing or from stock price increases. This appears to be what occurred in both the Enron and the WorldCom cases.

Crime committed within the context of the workplace is not confined to white-collar and corporate wrongdoing. Individuals who commit crime within the course of their employment roles are engaging in **occupational crime**. The two most common forms of occupational crime are theft and fraud. Examples of occupational thefts are the removal by employees of job-related items from the workplace. While there are obviously various degrees of employee theft—from stealing a pencil to stealing furnishings or a car—most employees do steal, and if such costs are multiplied by the numbers who do, the expense is high. In the United States, "inventory shrinkage," which not only includes employee theft but also shoplifting, is estimated to add 15 per cent to the cost that consumers pay for goods and services (Coleman, 2002).

An example of occupational fraud is insider trading. This illegal activity occurs when an employee uses information not available to the public to gain personal advantage over others in the buying and selling of stock. Such information is obtained simply because a person's job happens to have given her or him access to privileged information. But stocks are supposed to be open to the public with equal opportunities for those with money to access their purchase through the stock market.

The profile of insider trading in the United States and elsewhere was raised in the public view by the misfortune of Martha Stewart, the well-known American entrepreneur and "lifestyle diva" who has amassed considerable wealth from her work in the mass media and in the retail sector. In 2001 Stewart sold shares she had invested in ImClone—a pharmaceutical company that manufactured a cancer drug—earning about $40,000 from the sale. Regulatory officials were concerned about Stewart's profit, and possible insider trading, because she was a friend of Sam Waksal, founder of ImClone. Stewart was initially charged with insider trading, but was later convicted only of lying to investigators and was sentenced to five months in prison and fined $4,000—the maximum fine for this offence. Even though Martha Stewart's profit was minuscule in the financial world she inhabited, and a case might be made for her having been pursued for her "misdemeanor" because she is a successful woman with an abrasive personality in what is essentially a man's world, her case is nevertheless an example of a situation where a powerful person was found guilty of breaking the law.

More recently, in 2009, Bernie Madoff, a New York investor who reportedly enjoyed a lavish lifestyle, was sentenced to prison for 150 years after pleading guilty to 11 charges for bilking investors worldwide of more than $60 billion dollars (MacDonald, 2009). Madoff had organized a wide-reaching **Ponzi scheme**, which is a form of fraudulent investment. Named after Charles Ponzi, who was notorious for using the technique in the United States during the 1920s, the illegal scheme pays returns to investors from their own money or money from other investors rather than from profits earned. The Ponzi scheme attracts new investors by offering returns far higher and more consistent than other—normally legal—investments. The perpetuation of the returns that a Ponzi scheme advertises and pays requires an ever-increasing flow of money from investors to keep the scheme going. Similar to a Ponzi scheme is a pyramid scheme. The difference between the two is that Ponzi schemes actually appear to investors as a real investment opportunity, whereas pyramid schemes normally require that participants make a payment for the right to recruit other people into the scheme, at which point they will receive money.

Canadians are not immune to these types of illegal financial activities, of course. In 2009, after a long and well-publicized trial, Canadians Garth Drabinsky and Myron Gottlieb were found guilty of fraud and forgery and were later sentenced to prison for seven and six years, respectively. Drabinsky and Gottlieb were the founders of Livent, a company from Toronto that produced elaborate musical theatre shows such as *Phantom of the Opera* and *Ragtime*. Their scheme consisted of altering the accounting books to inflate the profits of the public company, thus artificially rising share prices and asset values. The end result was that banks and other investors were deceived into paying more than $500 million to Livent in the form of stock purchases and loans.

Ex-Canadian Conrad Black, who rescinded his Canadian citizenship to become a British Lord (Lord of Crossharbour), was sentenced in 2007 to six-and-a-half years in a Florida prison for his role in the misappropriation of millions of dollars from the Hollinger newspaper empire he once headed. He was released from prison in 2012 and returned to his home in Toronto. Interestingly, Black once was on the board of Livent.

Limited Data on White-Collar and Corporate Crime

It is important to be aware that the information criminologists use to study corporate crime is rather limited. By and large, the data used to study corporate offending are produced by the criminal justice system or other regulatory bodies. In other words, only "official" information is available about those who are charged or convicted of corporate wrongdoing to researchers or anybody else interested in studying this phenomenon. There are no reliable, large-scale, self-report surveys, for instance, that contain information about the prevalence of this type of crime throughout society. So there is really no way of knowing if the types of offences that come to the attention of the authorities, and the people who are identified in this type of law-breaking, are actually representative of corporate offending more generally.

The Public as Victim

A common misconception about corporate crime is that its effects are mainly financial. This idea cannot be further from the truth. The harm that comes to the general public, workers, and consumers from illegal corporate activity is significant. The public is exposed to the noxious effects of corporate anti-social behaviour in a number of ways.

Corporations are deemed persons under the law, but they are not subject to laws pertaining to persons, a circumstance that gives them great power with few controls regarding responsibility to the societies in which they flourish. The legal status of corporations has allowed them to wreak havoc on some people's lives (e.g., mistakes or false claims made by some pharmaceutical companies about their products, the dumping of toxic wastes by mining and chemical companies) and on the planet (engineering travesties on the environment through mining, drilling, and open-pit mineral extraction, etc.). Persons as individuals and through class action suits make attempts to sue companies for criminal sorts of activities to bring their behaviours under some kind of control. For years the odds weighed heavily on the side of the corporations, not only because of their wealth but because of their status under the law. It has therefore been difficult for the courts to successfully prosecute corporations for breaking the criminal law because it was difficult to prove that a corporation was of a requisite guilty state of mind. However, with the changes made to Canada's corporate criminal liability laws in 2012, the law now makes reference to *organizations* rather than corporations. While the motivation for these changes was arguably made to make it easier for authorities to prosecute terrorist organizations, they do have implications for making it less onerous on the Crown to prosecute white collar criminals. Only time will tell if these changes will lead to more prosecutions for while collar offenders.

One infamous example of corporate irresponsibility is the Love Canal tragedy. For years the Hooker Chemical Company dumped tons of toxic waste into the abandoned Love Canal, located at Niagara Falls, New York. In the mid-1950s a school board purchased this dump site for a nominal fee and then sold it to a private housing developer. The canal had been covered with landfill so that houses could be built on top of this toxic storage container. In the 1970s many families who had moved to this housing development were experiencing major health problems, including miscarriages and birth defects in their infants. According to Simon, "There is evidence that Hooker Chemical knew of the problem as far back as 1958 but chose not to warn local health officials of any potential problems because the cleanup costs would have increased from $4 million to $50 million" (1996, p. 9).

A toxic waste site of an even larger scale can be found in a city on Canada's east coast. For nearly a century, the operation of a steel plant in Sydney, Nova Scotia, has created what has been called "the largest toxic waste site in eastern Canada" (McMullan & Smith, 1997, p. 61). Several thousand tons of poisonous by-products from the coking operation lie in an area known as the "tar ponds." According to McMullan and Smith, scientists from Environment Canada have reported that the contaminants contained in the tar ponds pose a serious threat to the workers and families who live near the site.

Corporate pollution is a problem not limited to the Canadian steel industry. For years, pulp and paper manufacturers have been dumping toxic waste into Canadian waterways at levels far above government standards. For example, in 2004 Irving Pulp and Paper pleaded guilty to a violation of Canada's Fisheries Act and was fined $30,000. The company had dumped untreated paper mill effluent into a river near Saint John, New Brunswick (Environment Canada, 2004).

In May of 2000, 7 people died and 2,300 became ill after drinking E. coli contaminated water in Walkerton, Ontario, a town of just under 5,000 people about 250 kilometres northwest of Toronto (Snider, 2004). The tragedy in this small Ontario town made front-page news across the country, and after a public inquiry and nine months of hearings, the O'Connor Report was released, which was highly critical of the provincial government's role in the deregulation of municipal drinking water. According to an analysis of the tragedy undertaken by Snider, the privatization of water-testing, along with the closure of public laboratories in 1996, played an important role in why the E. coli in the Walkerton drinking water was not detected until it was too late. In fact, this line of thinking was clearly expressed in the report prepared by

Dennis O'Connor, an Ontario Court of Appeal judge who was appointed to lead the public inquiry. Snider views the incident at Walkerton as the "culmination of a series of deliberate decisions that put business, and business interests, ahead of people" (ibid., p. 283).

Crime against Consumers

Consumers are also subject to victimization from corporations. A primary concern pertains to consumers who have been harmed by using unsafe products. While figures are difficult to assemble for Canada, in the United States it is estimated that some 20 million people have been injured as the result of using unsafe products (Simon, 2001). Over the years a countless number of products have been found to be injurious to consumers. An appalling example of an unsafe product that killed as many as 900 people (Dowie, 1977) during the 1970s was the Ford Pinto, an economy-sized vehicle that was also popular on Canadian roads at that time. Because the Ford Pinto was manufactured with a defective fuel system, the gas tank had a tendency to rupture upon rear impact (Simon, 1996, p. 124). Even though the Ford Motor Company was aware of the problem, executives decided against a recall or to retool assembly line machinery because of the unwanted costs that would be incurred. During his detailed analysis of the case, Simon learned that Ford carried out a cost–benefit analysis that estimated that 180 burn deaths, 180 burn injuries, and 2,100 burned vehicles would cost $49.5 million (each death was estimated at $200,000). Ford also estimated that it would cost $11 per vehicle to remedy the problem, but undertaking a recall of all Pintos and doing the $11 repair would cost the company $137 million. Simon describes such a decision as a "profits-over-human consideration" (ibid., p. 125). In 1978, nearly a decade after the federal government first investigated the carnage caused by the Pinto, and despite Ford Motor Company's lobbying efforts to keep the cars on the road, tests undertaken by the Department of Transportation deemed the car to be unsafe and ordered a recall on all 1971–6 models (ibid., p. 126).

An example of a case that has been considered to have negatively affected the health of thousands of Canadian women concerns silicone gel breast implants that were on the market in the early 1990s. Many women reported ill health after having breast implant surgery. A class action suit was filed against Dow Corning, one of the largest manufacturers of breast implants at that time. A civil settlement was reached in 1999 where $25 million was awarded to those women who survived who had received implants (Schwartz et al., 2005).

Another realm where consumers are affected by corporate wrongdoing concerns a practice known as **price-fixing**. This term refers to a situation where companies get together and agree to set or fix prices on goods or services, which they then sell on the open market. In Canada in the latter part of the nineteenth century, formal rules and regulations were first put in place designed to protect competition in the marketplace. In 1889 the Combines Investigation Act was introduced to regulate business activities. Today the Competition Bureau is responsible for the administration and enforcement of the

- Competition Act;
- Consumer Packaging and Labelling Act;
- Textile Labelling Act; and
- Precious Metals Marketing Act

A recent example of a case of price-fixing involved a graphite electrodes cartel that lessened competition for the product on the world market. In 2005, Nippon Carbon Co., Ltd pleaded guilty and was fined $100,000 by the Federal Court of Canada for aiding and abetting an international conspiracy to fix the price of graphite electrodes used in steel production. The company was the seventh party to be convicted in Canada for being involved in the cartel. Two former executives of UCAR, another company involved in the price-fixing scheme, were fined $25 million for their roles in the worldwide conspiracy.

While consumers of products are the ultimate victims of such illegal business practices, corporations can also be adversely affected by the unscrupulous practices of other corporations. Take, for example, a case that occurred in the Canadian airline industry when Air Canada waged a $220 million lawsuit against rival WestJet Airlines. WestJet agreed to settle with Air Canada by offering to pay $5.5 million of Air Canada's legal expenses and promised to donate "$10 million in the name of both airlines to children's charities across Canada" (Westhead, 2006). A statement released jointly by WestJet and Air Canada declared that "in 2003–4, certain members of WestJet management engaged in an extensive practice of covertly accessing a password protected proprietary website to download detailed and commercially sensitive information without authorization or consent from Air Canada" (ibid.). Moreover, WestJet admitted that the activity took place "with the knowledge and direction of the highest management levels of WestJet and was not halted until discovered by Air Canada" (ibid.). Air Canada alleged that WestJet used the information to schedule its own flights on Air Canada's most profitable routes and times.

Workers as Victims

Since Canada first began to industrialize in the middle of the nineteenth century, countless numbers of workers have lost their lives while on the job. Conventional wisdom might have us believe that workers who die or who get injured on the job do so as a result of their own fault (worker carelessness or accident proneness). But some criminologists—most notably critical criminologists—suggest otherwise. Reiman (2004), for one, believes that the conditions under which many workers must labour cannot be overlooked as a key factor in accounting for "accidents" that take place within the workplace.

In Canada, researchers who share Reiman's perspective suggest that the organization of the workplace plays a fundamental role in understanding the mayhem that occurs in the lives of many Canadian workers and their families. Considering statistics measuring the major causes of Canadian death rates, it is not surprising that heart disease and cancer are at the top of the list. However, what would be surprising to most Canadians is that **occupational death** is the third leading cause of death in Canada—even greater than motor vehicle accidents and considerably greater than homicide (Reasons et al., 1981). In fact, in 2003 there were 6.1 work-related deaths per 100,000 workers in Canada. In that same year the homicide rate in Canada was 1.72 per 100,000 population (Krahn et al., 2007). Since that time the work-related death rate has remained about the same and the work-related death rate in Canada continues to be much greater than the homicide rate.

A case study that meticulously documented the anguish experienced by a group of fluorspar miners from a small community in rural Newfoundland has been carried out by Elliott Leyton (1975). Fluorspar is a mineral used in the manufacture of products such as aluminum, gasoline, and insulating foam. Leyton's study vividly describes the slow and agonizing deaths of miners whose lungs had been contaminated by high levels of radon gas. Moreover, the study also points a finger at both the company and the government for its knowledge that these miners were working in an extremely dangerous environment, yet little action was taken to protect these workers. In total, approximately 200 workers lost their lives as the result of industrial disease between the 1930s and the 1970s (Rennie, 2005). An analysis of the period from 1933 to 1945 reveals that well before it was confirmed that radon gas was a health hazard, the alleged conditions in the mines in St Lawrence, Newfoundland, were having a severe impact on miners' health, and the miners fought to have those fears recognized and addressed. During this period, workers continually demanded that action be taken about their health concerns. However, according to Rennie,

> In all instances, however, their concerns were ignored or downplayed by government and corporate interests who did not wish to have the issue placed on the labour relations agenda. The actions of the Trade Dispute Board stand out as an especially striking instance among a series of neglected opportunities to curtail somewhat the impending disaster. Perhaps most importantly, a study of the origins of this industrial disaster demonstrates that while workers at St Lawrence were victims, they were neither passive nor unknowing. Rather, their knowledge was ignored and devalued and their actions undermined by corporate and political interests whose goals were widely divergent from and even contradictory to those of the workers. (2005, p. 3)

This idea that harm to workers that occurs during the process of resource extraction, which are the collective result of the interplay between the federal and provincial government agencies and the private sector who own and operate the mining of the resource, has been captured in a phrase coined by Kramer and Michalowski as **state–corporate crime**. They define this term as "illegal or socially injurious actions that occur when one or more institutions of political governance pursue a goal in direct co-operation with one or more institutions of economic production and distribution" (cited in McMullan & Smith, 1997, p. 63). This position has also been applied to the situation in Sydney, Nova Scotia, where the health both of workers and of the community at large was jeopardized as the result of being exposed to large quantities of industrial pollution.

Causes of White-Collar Crime

Understanding the nature of white-collar crime and white-collar criminality is complex, and over the years a number of different theoretical approaches have been used to explain "elite deviance," ranging from differential association theory to conflict theory. Generally speaking, the literature on the causes of corporate crime can be broken down into two perspectives: macro and micro explanations. Macro explanations (structural/large scale) tend to focus on the sorts of issues that were addressed in Chapter 4 when the critical perspective was introduced where it was argued that the criminal law reflects the concerns and interests of the dominant class. And since in a capitalist society it is mainly economic and business elites which are the dominant class, they control the state and subsequently the legal system will primarily reflect their interests. Therefore, laws which regulate corporate malfeasance remain weak and their enforcement ineffective. While this macro explanation, conflict perspective, is useful for drawing attention to the class based nature of law-making, the fact remains that some laws do exist which are meant to control corporate crime, and people have been sent to jail in Canada for violating such laws. Moreover, it is also true that not all "capitalists" engage in corporate wrongdoing. Partly in response to these issues, more micro explanations of corporate offending have emerged which focus on the kinds of people and the more immediate environments in which corporate offending occurs. A useful framework for understanding this type of offending at a micro level (where individual opportunities and behaviour is explored) has been put forward by Shover and Wright (2001), who have approached this issue by considering three sets of factors: (1) white-collar criminal opportunities; (2) white-collar decision making; and (3) the characteristics of white-collar offenders.

Opportunity plays a role in corporate crime. With the use of high-speed electronic information networks, money from banks and business accounts can now be controlled almost instantaneously and over long distances. This technology, along with the developments in finance capitalism—a relatively new form of economic activity where profits are made possible through the management of financial accounts—is a feature of the new economy and of globalization, which also enhances opportunities to make money illegally. This, of course, is very much unlike the old, non-digital economy that was dominated by the manufacturing of goods and the production of services. The emergence of new communication technologies has basically changed the ways people relate to one another in organizations. An unintended consequence of these developments has been an increase in the availability of white-collar criminal opportunities.

The second factor that criminologists examine in attempting to explain corporate crime involves decision making. Many opportunities to offend present themselves within the corporate world, but this does not mean that all individuals or organizations do so. One perspective explains the particularities of decisions around offending as rational choice theory. Introduced in Chapter 5, rational choice theory alerts us to the observation that organizational crimes are the result of real-life decisions made by managers and executives. Decisions to commit accounting fraud, for example, are seen to be based, in part, on the actor's ability to weigh and calculate the potential consequences of rule-breaking. Paternoster and Simpson (2001, p. 205), rational choice proponents, have proposed a social psychology model of corporate offending based on the costs and benefits of illegal behaviour. They contend that it's important to consider the following factors when attempting to understand the choices that managers and executives make:

- Perceived certainty/severity of formal legal sanctions (external legal system: criminal, civil, or regulatory);
- Perceived certainty/severity of informal sanctions (loss of job, demotion, loss of status);
- Perceived certainty/severity of loss of self-respect (self-image of a "respectable person" could be jeopardized);
- Perceived cost of rule compliance (loss of profits and competitiveness);
- Perceived benefits of non-compliance (promotion);
- Moral inhibitions (how wrong is it, for example, to price-fix?);
- Perceived sense of legitimacy/fairness (reasonableness of rules, evaluation of experience of judicial or regulatory process);
- Characteristics of criminal event (cultural conduciveness, environmental factors); and
- Prior offending by person.

The final set of factors that criminologists examine when attempting to understand corporate crime are the characteristics of those who have been implicated and identified by the authorities. Like street crime, gender is by far the best predictor of white-collar criminal activity. While there are certainly exceptions to this general tendency (such as the case involving Martha Stewart), males continue to fill the roles of corporate criminals. These gender differences reflect the number of males who continue to dominate positions of power in large corporations in North America. Even though almost as many women as men participate in today's labour market, and women now outnumber men in Canadian universities, women continue to lack access to positions of power and authority in the corporate work world, so they lack the opportunities that would be necessary for them to engage in corporate crime.

This is not to say that women are uninvolved in crime in the workplace. According to Daly (1989), there is such a thing as "his and her white-collar crime." While the numbers of females who are involved in crimes such as anti-trust violations, bribery, and security fraud are very low (less than 5 per cent of the total), it is not unusual for women to be involved in credit card and postal frauds, and women comprise 45 per cent of convicted bank embezzlers. However, according to Daly (1989), most women who are implicated in embezzlement in the banking industry are tellers, while males involved in this crime tend to occupy more senior positions, such as financial officers. Women's motives for occupational theft are more likely than men's to be based on financial need for themselves or their families. Men, on the other hand, were more likely to report that they were influenced by others, and some steal because they want to advance their careers or obtain desired status symbols— that is, money to buy a sports car (Bartol, 2001).

While corporate crime has likely been around since the dawn of the corporation, more and more of these types of wrongdoings—especially more serious violations—are making their way to the courts and drawing the attention of the mass media. However, given the difficulties involved in collecting information on white-collar crime that does not come to the attention of authorities, there is really no way of knowing the true extent of such crime. If recent incidents that have appeared in the media represent a shift in enforcement practices aimed at such offending, such crime is likely to continue to increase.

Criminologists are increasingly expressing an interest in a field that is closely related to the study of corporate crime. This is an area known as green (or environmental/conservation) criminology. **Green criminology** is the study of environmental damage, caused by human activity, viewed through a criminological lens. A growing number of criminologists have come to recognize that a wide range of crime and criminal justice activity takes place that is directly related to environmental issues. In sync with the social-reaction perspective introduced earlier in Chapter 1, the study of environmental harm is part of a tradition that critically questions the definition and meaning of crime in society. Until recently a great deal of human-made environmental damage that took place on the planet went unquestioned in society. However, in the aftermath of the Exxon Valdez oil spill off the coast of Alaska, the Union Carbide gas tragedy in Bhopal, India, and the BP fire and massive oil spill in the Gulf of Mexico in 2010 where 11 men died, more and more attention is being given to such human-made damage. Not only does green criminology draw attention to the human costs associated with such damage but it also attempts to understand these events within the context of corporate power and political influence. Green criminology draws attention to environmental issues such as the illegal disposal of hazardous waste (e.g., E-waste), wildlife violations (e.g., trade in endangered species or animal parts such as elephant and rhinoceros tusks), the illegal extraction of natural resources (e.g., illegal logging, fishing, mining, and plant removal), and illegal land management (e.g., illegal filling of wetlands, endangered species habitat removal) (Gibbs et al., 2010, p. 133). Similar to the general field of criminology, in theoretical and methodological terms, green criminology is very much a multi-disciplinary framework integrating insights acquired from the social and natural resource sciences.

Political Crime

Another area of wrongful activity among revered people is political crime. Historically, like corporate crime, these types of crimes often were not recognized by society. Even within the criminological community, until recently, the study of political crime has not been paid much attention. **Political crime** has two principal dimensions: crimes committed against the state and crimes committed by the state.

One example of a crime committed against the state is when a social group resorts to violence in an effort to transform the social order. There are several examples of this type of violence throughout Canadian history, beginning in the 1830s with the Upper and Lower Canada rebellions led in what today is Ontario by William Lyon Mackenzie and in what today is Quebec by Louis-Joseph Papineau. These violent conflicts were fought against the established order of the time to gain "responsible government." A more recent series of incidents marked by such violence occurred during the 1970 October Crisis, which involved the activities of a small group of Quebec terrorists known as the Front de Libération du Québec (FLQ), who were devoted to bringing about a sovereign, socialist Quebec. In their quest for recognition, members of the FLQ kidnapped the British Trade Commissioner, James Cross, and later kidnapped and killed a Quebec cabinet minister, Pierre Laporte. Prime Minister Pierre Trudeau responded to these terrorist tactics by invoking the War Measures Act. This was a controversial piece of legislation in its own right as it allowed the police to arrest and detain people without a warrant. In fact, more than 400 people were arrested and detained in Quebec at that time merely for being sympathetic to the cause of Quebec separation.

Today in Quebec there is a provincial party (Parti Québécois) and a federal party (Bloc Québécois) both committed to the cause of Quebec independence. While most Canadians were relieved that the FLQ crisis was over, many wondered if Trudeau's use of the War Measures Act was an overreaction to the political situation in Quebec.

Activities of groups labelled as "terrorists" have been in the spotlight in many countries throughout world, especially since the destruction of the World Trade Center in New York on 11 September 2001. In Canada, for example, in May 2006 a group of 18 young men, mainly from the Greater Toronto Area, were accused by Canadian authorities of plotting to storm the House of Commons and take hostage several members of Parliament. The investigators found evidence that the group of Islamic fundamentalists was intending to behead the prime minister, blow up the Toronto Stock Exchange, and destroy with a homemade bomb the Toronto facility of the Canadian Broadcasting Corporation. Of the 18 males who were charged by the police, 7 had their charges dropped or stayed, 4 were found guilty, and 7 pleaded guilty (Gazze, 2013).

Not all protest activity committed against the state is violent, however. In fact, most political crime directed against the state is deliberately non-violent. Protestors usually commit acts like blocking roads or highways, carrying placards and singing or chanting, pasting advertisements of their opinions on public property, or setting small fires to keep themselves warm in winter but also using them to burn effigies of opponents, slogans, or other symbolic items. The environmental movement has been involved in such actions in British Columbia. Aboriginal protestors have also blocked roads (Caledonia, Ontario) and occupied parks (Ipperwash, Ontario) to express discontent over issues of disputed land rights. On the east coast, groups of people from fishing communities have blocked highways to protest government mismanagement of the cod fishery.

Political crimes also can be committed by the state in conjunction with the private sector. The sponsorship scandal that played a prominent role in the 2005–6 Canadian federal election campaign, and likely was a key factor for the Canadian electorate's ousting of the Liberals and electing a minority Conservative government led by Stephen Harper, can be seen as an example of such activity. The sponsorship program was initially set up by the federal government to oppose the separatist movement in Quebec after the 1995 Quebec referendum was narrowly won by federalists. Allegations were made that a fraudulent scheme was linked to the program. More specifically, $155 million in federal funding allegedly was given to Liberal-friendly advertising agencies in Quebec where little or no work was done for the money. Moreover, "part of the money was siphoned back to the Quebec wing of the federal Liberal Party, with $800,000 in official donations and more than $1 million in kick-backs" (CTV News, 2006). A public inquiry was struck to investigate

Box 7.1   Debates and Controversies

Terrorism

Following the terrorist attacks of 11 September 2001, the United States enacted "homeland security" legislation such as the Patriot Act and the Maritime Security Act. These laws have extended the powers of government to surveillance of public transportation facilities such as airports, bus and train stations, and ferry terminals.

Shortly after these anti-terrorist laws were enacted in the United States, similar legislation was introduced in Canada. In December 2001, Canada's Anti-Terrorism Act became law. This legislation provided measures to identify, prosecute, convict, and punish terrorists by

- defining and designating terrorist groups and activities to make it easier to prosecute terrorists and those who support them;
- making it an offence to knowingly participate in, contribute to, or facilitate the activities of a terrorist group or to instruct anyone to carry out a terrorist activity or an activity on behalf of a terrorist group;
- making it an offence to knowingly harbour a terrorist;
- creating tougher sentences and parole provisions for terrorist offences;
- cutting off financial support for terrorists by making it a crime to knowingly collect or give funds, either directly or indirectly, to carry out terrorism, denying or removing charitable status from those who support terrorist groups, and by making it easier to freeze and seize their assets.

The police have also been granted new powers so that it is easier to use electronic surveillance to monitor suspected terrorist groups. The Anti-Terrorism Act allows the police to arrest and detain suspected terrorists without actually having to press charges. As long as the authorities suspect that an individual is a terrorist, he or she can be detained indefinitely.

This Act however, has not been without its critics. This legislation gives police the right to incarcerate people merely on the suspicion they may be a terrorist and are believed to be about to commit a crime. The authorities also have the power to force testimony from anyone they believe has information associated with a terrorism investigation. The act also allows for closed trials and can deny an accused and his/her counsel full knowledge of the evidence against them (Department of Justice Canada, 2003).

This website has more information about this issue: http://ccla.org/2011/04/04/op-ed-anti-terror-laws-must-uphold-canadian-values/.

matters, and after a lengthy series of hearings that included the testimony of former prime minister Jean Chrétien, the Gomery Commission determined that there had indeed been a misappropriation of public funds, which later resulted in fraud charges being laid against Chuck Guité, a senior bureaucrat closely involved with the sponsorship program, along with Jean Brault and Paul Coffin, two senior advertising executives from Montreal who had been given contracts by the federal government. Coffin, the first person to be charged with fraud, originally received a conditional sentence of two years less a day, which was to be served in the community. Later, however, as a result of the case being appealed to the Quebec Court of Appeal, Coffin was given an 18-month prison term for defrauding the federal government of $1.5 million in sponsorship funds. Brault was also found guilty of five fraud-connected charges and was sentenced to 30 months in prison (ibid.). Chuck Guité, the federal bureaucrat who ran the sponsorship program, was also found guilty in the case.

As with corporate crime, there are not many examples that have implicated women in political corruption cases in Canada. This fact is no doubt associated with the same reasons that were given in the earlier discussion regarding gender and corporate crime. Only relatively recently have women become actively involved in institutional politics in Canada. Men continue to outnumber women in the House of Commons and in provincial legislatures.

State political repression occurs when the state uses its power to remove or suspend the rights and liberties of targeted groups within the population for fear that these groups represent a threat to the social order. While some may regard the use of the War Measures Act in 1970 as an example of state repression, others felt the invocation of that measure was reasonable. In the past in Canada, state police and the military have been used violently on numerous occasions in support of corporate Canada to break up strikes, worker movements, and Aboriginal protests—the Winnipeg General Strike (1919), the On-to-Ottawa Trek (1935), the Asbestos, Quebec, strike (1949), and the Oka, Quebec (1990), and Ipperwash, Ontario (1995), confrontations are only a few of many such instances.

The internment of the Japanese community in British Columbia during the Second World War is also an example of state repression. Not long after the bombing of Pearl Harbor and the declaration of war on Japan in 1941, persons of Japanese descent were rounded up by government authorities and taken away from their homes and livelihoods. Approximately 22,000 members of the British Columbia Japanese community—many of whom were born in Canada—were relocated away from coastal areas of the province because they were regarded by the government as posing a threat to national security. Many families were not kept together. Men were usually sent to camps in the interior of British Columbia, or ended up in camps in Ontario and Saskatchewan, while most women and children were relocated to inland areas of British Columbia. There is evidence to suggest that the living conditions for the Japanese were so harsh in these camps that the Red Cross responded by providing the evacuees with additional food. It was not until four years after the war that the Japanese were permitted to return to their homes. By that time, however, many decided not to return as they had established roots elsewhere. Those who did try to return found most of their property had been confiscated by the government and sold for only a fraction of its worth. In 1988 the Canadian government formally apologized for the internment and offered all surviving evacuees $21,000 in compensation. Canadian scientist and award-winning environmentalist David Suzuki was, with his family, among those interned during that period in a British Columbia internment camp.

Given the broad set of circumstances that can be involved in political crime, there is no one explanation that has been developed to account for these activities. However, in situations where politicians misappropriate public money using fraudulent means, the motivations and rewards suggested in the previous section to explain corporate crime would also be appropriate to political wrongdoing.

Organized Transnational Crime

Organized transnational crime is organized criminal activity that takes place across national jurisdictions. With advances in transportation and information technology, law enforcement officials and policy-makers have needed to respond to this form of crime on a global scale. There are several different types of organized transnational crime. These include **human trafficking**, money laundering, drug smuggling, illegal arms dealing, cybercrime, and terrorism. While it is impossible to precisely measure the extent of this type of criminal activity, in 2009 the Millennium Project, an international think tank, assembled statistics on several aspects of transnational crime. Below is a summary of this information (all on an annual basis):

- World illicit trade of almost $730 billion
- Counterfeiting and piracy of $300 billion to $1 trillion
- Global drug trade of $321 billion
- Trade in environmental goods of $69 billion
- Human trafficking of $44 billion
- Weapons trade of $10 billion
- McAfee estimates that theft and breaches from cybercrime may have cost businesses as much as $1 trillion in 2008.

For more information on the Millennium Project, visit www.unmillennium project.org.

It has only been relatively recently that criminologists have begun to study this phenomenon. For example, the Australian Institute of Criminology has released a series of policy papers that have taken some important steps in defining and providing case studies of transnational crime within an Australian context.

<table>
<tr><td>

Box 7.2

</td><td>

Debates and Controversies

</td></tr>
</table>

Can Law Enforcement Alone Control Human Trafficking?

Most countries in the world, including Canada, attempt to control human trafficking—"the recruitment, transportation or harbouring of persons for the purpose of exploitation—typically in the sex industry or for forced labour" (RCMP, 2013) mainly by increased police enforcement and harsher penalties for those convicted of these crimes. However, according the blog below, supply-side issues also need to be considered.

"This $32 billion-per-year 'industry' is driven by the basic market laws of demand and supply and will not stop so long as the risk of being caught is low, and the profits remain high. More elements should be brought into the picture than just law enforcement. Certainly, punishing perpetrators and seeking justice for victims needs to be part of the response to human trafficking, but more emphasis needs to be placed on strengthening prevention measures.

There are difficulties in trying to accurately estimate the number of victims that suffer from human trafficking. The sordid business often involves sophisticated networks, even transnational networks, and cover-ups by authorities that make it difficult to keep track of every case. Identifying at-risk groups is less difficult. Allocating resources to raise awareness among vulnerable groups, and reducing their exposure, should be a greater priority rather than attempting to repair the damage after the fact, with law enforcement efforts that usually amount to too little too late.

Preventive actions must create, or strengthen, safety nets in which vulnerable groups develop. Prevention includes coordination and collaboration from the immediate community that surrounds them all the way up to the international sphere; it includes spreading information and fighting myths; it includes a 24/7 surveillance and creating incentives and the infrastructure to report any crime. Law enforcement best serves to attack the demand side and the illegal supply of human trafficking. Prevention will help to reduce the pool of possible victims that fuel the supply."

Reducing human trafficking is a sum of law enforcement and prevention actions and not a choice between both.

Source: Alcántara, 2012. Permission granted by Columbia University.

While criminologists have made advances in defining and measuring transnational organized crime, the discipline is still far from developing a parsimonious explanation of transnational crime. This is largely because of the wide range of crimes that fall under this rather broad umbrella term and the lack of information about opportunities and motives of those involved in such activities. However, since transnational crime is organized illegal activity, the phenomenon logically lends itself to explanations offered earlier about corporate crime (opportunities, decision making, and backgrounds of offenders). In addition, questions asked about transnational crime have generally been informed by issues related to policing. For example, Beare (2003) notes that countries are expected to react to and police organized crime and corruption in a uniform manner based upon international agreements, conventions, and accords. Yet until more empirical research is carried out in this area, Beare contends that the costs and effectiveness of these enforcement measures remain clear.

Police Misconduct

Like politicians, the police are a public institution whose mandate is not only to serve the public but to offer protection as well. Yet police officers become involved in wrongdoing from time to time. **Police misconduct** is defined as situations when the actions of police officers are "inconsistent with the officer's legal authority, organizational authority, and standards of ethical conduct" (Barker & Carter, 1986, cited by Goff, 2004, p. 144). This may include acts such as tampering with evidence or raiding a suspect's home without a valid search warrant, or abuses of authority that involve intimidation—physical or verbal—when apprehending or interrogating suspects.

The United States has a well-documented history of police corruption and provides criminologists with a range of examples of what can go wrong in that social group. The issue of police wrongdoing came to a head in the United States after a report was released by the Knapp Commission in 1970. The Commission looked into allegations of police corruption in New York City, and the findings were attention-catching. The Commission found that police corruption was extensive. It ranged from officers collecting small gratuities (e.g., accepting free meals at restaurants) to more serious actions, such as receiving payoffs from construction companies, illegal gambling outlets, and drug dealers (Knapp Commission, 1973). As a result of the Commission's findings, police departments throughout the country were placed under greater public scrutiny and efforts were made to ensure more accountability from the police.

However, police wrongdoing in the United States continues to flourish. For example, in the late 1990s an investigation discovered several corrupt acts had been committed by officers of the Los Angeles Police Department (LAPD). Several officers of the anti-gang unit were caught up in bribery, making false arrests, and framing innocent people (Coleman, 2002). Besides the fact that dozens of criminal convictions were overturned as a result of these findings, the federal government was given responsibility to reform the LAPD. This is the same police force that was in the spotlight in 1991 over the Rodney King beating. Commonly referred to as the best-known case of abuse of force by the police in American history, four members of the LAPD were caught on amateur videotape as they beat and Tasered (an electronic shocking device used by police to subdue suspects) King after he had been asked to pull his vehicle over to the side of the road. Portions of the incident that were captured on the tape were telecast by major news networks across the United States and around the world. Since King was a black man, and because the LAPD had a reputation for being tolerant to rough treatment of suspects, especially when dealing with blacks and Hispanics, millions of viewers were watching when the four police officers who were involved in the incident were facing charges in a jury trial (Martin, 2005). Not long after the officers were acquitted on all charges, a massive three-day riot broke out on the streets of south central Los Angeles that killed several people and caused extensive damage to property. Subsequent to a successful appeal by the state, two of the four officers were later found guilty of charges related to the King incident and were sent to jail (ibid.).

As one might suspect, Canada is not immune from police corruption. One instance related to the FLQ crisis in Quebec, mentioned above, and involved an RCMP plot to steal Parti Québécois membership files in 1973. The intent of accessing this information was to determine whether any members of the federal civil service were separatist supporters. If civil servants' names did appear on the list, then these individuals could be monitored by the RCMP Security Service—which was later disbanded when the Canadian Security Intelligence Service (CSIS) was formed in 1984.

Not only was the RCMP implicated in the theft of Parti Québécois membership lists but they were also found to be involved in an illegal barn-burning incident in Quebec. This time federal civil servants were not the target, but two alleged terrorist groups were: the FLQ and the Black Panthers—a revolutionary group from the United States that was committed to ethnic and working-class emancipation. On a tip from the FBI, the RCMP Security Service burned a barn near Montreal that was thought to be the clandestine meeting place for the two groups. While no one was injured in the incident, an act of arson was nevertheless committed (Mann & Lee, 1979). No arrests, or even reprimands, were given to the officers involved in the incident. Quite a different outcome, however, happened in 2010 to Sheldon Cook, a 19-year veteran of the Peel Regional Police Service. After being convicted for stealing what he believed were packages of cocaine (they were in fact bags of flour) from a botched RCMP drug sting, Cook was sentenced to five years in prison.

A number of explanations have been offered to explain police wrongdoing. The most popular but least accepted by the criminological community is the **bad-apple theory**. The adage is "one rotten apple spoils the whole barrel." The theory is that a little police corruption spreads like rot among apples. The counterclaim by the police is that one rotten apple can be removed and the rest of the organization protected. The underlying assumption of this view is that police wrongdoing is due to individual shortcomings in a small number of "bad-apple" police officers who break the law while on the job. While senior police officials will agree that there may be a few rotten apples within any police force, they claim that these can be monitored and removed and that, overall, the barrel (i.e., the organization as a whole) remains trustworthy.

Explanations such as this are regularly used by police departments to account for wrongdoing within their rank and file. In fact, this was the reasoning used by the LAPD when allegations were made about corruption within that particular police force (Martin, 2005). Claims are made to suggest that the actions of a small number of officers are not to be seen as indicative of the standards and behaviour within the broader organization. This perspective, however, was not used to account for police wrongdoing in the Knapp investigation noted earlier. According to Knapp's thorough and systematic investigation of the New York Police Department (NYPD), individual corruption was found to be a symptom of organizational pathology. Because Knapp found that corruption within the New York City police force at that time was so extensive, and senior staff did so little to deal with these problems, he could not accept the proposition that wrongdoing could be understood simply on an individual basis. Indeed, corruption was found in every plainclothes gambling enforcement squad, in addition to squads that enforced drugs and criminal investigations. Moreover, according to Henry (1994), "a system of internal corruption was revealed where managerial discretion and favour were bought and sold in a marketplace of payoffs" (cited in Newburn, 1999, p. 15).

Partly in recognition of the findings of the Knapp Commission, sociological accounts of police wrongdoing that focused on systemic and organization factors became much more prevalent during the 1970s and afterwards. A new centre of attention on police corruption steered away from looking simply at the characteristics of deviant officers and examined more broadly how policing is organized and how subcultures emerge that foster a corrupt environment.

An excellent model of police corruption has been put together by Sherman (1974). He draws attention to two sets of causes of police wrongdoing: constant and variable. Constant factors begin by identifying the role played by discretion. The reason why police discretion is linked to wrongdoing relates very much to material gain, as opposed to professional judgment. Consider a hypothetical situation where a police officer stops a person who has been speeding. When the officer asks the occupant of the speeding vehicle for her licence and insurance, a $100 bill is put into the hand of the officer. While taking bribes is a criminal offence, there is no doubt that there are occasions when an event such as this would invoke some degree of temptation in the mind of the officer to take the monetary bribe and simply let the speeder go without charging her.

Another organizational factor in police wrongdoing relates to police officers' actions taking place in situations of low visibility to their supervisors. Returning to the above example, it would be very unlikely that the police officer who took the bribe in such a situation would actually be seen doing this by one or more of his or her supervisors. Similarly, there are also very low levels of public visibility for police officers in such situations.

A constant factor in much police work concerns the high levels of police secrecy; police culture is characterized by solidarity and secrecy. For instance, if an officer observes an impropriety of another officer, it would be unlikely that such an event would come to the attention of superior authorities. Even if the event did come to the attention of police management, since most police officers in management positions have worked their way up through the rank and file, they share many of the same values as those they manage and supervise.

Sherman had also identified, as noted above, a second set of variable factors that play an important role in predicting police wrongdoing. This set of factors pertains to both the culture of the police organization and to the culture of the community being policed. One of the more important of these variable factors is the level of moral cynicism in a community. In short, if the citizenry who are being policed are cynical of the legal system, then the police may also adopt similar attitudes, especially if there is close and daily contact with lawbreakers. A second feature of variability concerns the opportunities for corruption—the greater the number of opportunities for corruption, the greater the likelihood that corruption will occur. For example, vice-squad work can often provide police with temptations to break the law. Consider a supposed situation when officers who are working in a drug enforcement squad happen to confiscate two kilos of cocaine in a raid of a drug dealer's home. Who would ever know if the officer(s) involved in the raid were to keep half of the amount of the drug that was originally confiscated for his or her personal use? As the street saying suggests, "Cops always have the best drugs."

While these are just a few of the causal factors that have been identified by Sherman as affecting the development of corrupt police practices, the point has been made through his model that to effectively understand police wrongdoing one must move beyond the study of bad apples and study the environment in which policing occurs.

Crime in Trusted Social Organizations

Several examples could be given illustrating cases where individuals have betrayed public trust within their occupational roles. Teachers, lawyers, university professors, medical doctors, and clergy—from several different religious denominations—have been implicated in various forms of wrongdoing.

For example, during the late 1980s and early 1990s several cases came to media attention in the United States that involved the dubious activities of several high-profile religious figures. Jim Bakker, a **fundamentalist evangelist** known through his PTL (Praise the Lord) Club television program, was convicted in 1989 of fraud and conspiring to commit fraud. Bakker was later sentenced to 45 years in federal prison for diverting donations from his followers' organization for his own personal use. There have been several more recent cases where Roman Catholic clergy have been prosecuted for sexual abuse. There is, of course, a terrible irony in spokespersons for the conversion from a life of wrongdoing to a life of holiness being found guilty of criminal behaviour.

In Canada, there have also been cases where clergy have been prosecuted for sexual assault. One case that drew national attention and led to a public inquiry involved Mount Cashel, an orphanage in St John's, Newfoundland, that was operated by the Roman Catholic Christian Brothers from 1898 to 1991. Investigations of child sexual abuse in the orphanage had been reported to the police as far back as the mid-1970s. Two police investigations, one in 1975 and a second in 1982, resulted in one charge of a sexual offence where one Christian Brother was sentenced to four months in jail and three years probation (Harris, 1990). However, as a result of a 1989 open-line radio show in St John's to which a caller had suggested that a government cover-up of abuse had occurred at Mount Cashel, a judge who heard the allegation was successful in opening the case again. This time, after a more thorough investigation and a number of victims who had grown up at the orphanage had come forward, 14 people (nine brothers and five civilians) were arrested on 88 counts of physical and sexual abuse (ibid.). Furthermore, the Department of Justice was found to have indeed interfered with earlier police investigations. The authorities were well aware that abuse was taking place at the orphanage, but nothing was done to protect the young boys from further neglect and assault. Not long after the report of the Hughes Commission was released to the public, the Mount Cashel Orphanage was destroyed, the property sold, and the proceeds were used to compensate victims who took civil action against the Christian Brothers.

In Ontario, 25 ex-employees from St Joseph's Training School for Boys, a reform school that was also run by the Christian Brothers from 1933 to 1974, were charged with a total of 182 offences of physical and sexual abuse (Native Women's Association of Canada, 1992). The charges stemmed from incidents alleged by approximately 400 former students of the training school. Although criminal charges were not laid in this case, a $16-million compensation package was agreed on by the Ontario government and the Roman Catholic Church for the victims of said abuse in 1999. Another parallel to the Mount Cashel case was that cabinet ministers, cardinals, and archbishops had been made aware of the abuse that was taking place in St Joseph's yet had failed to act (ibid.).

In recent years information has been uncovered, mostly in western Canada, concerning the experiences of Aboriginal youth within the residential school system. The residential school system dates back to 1874 when, under the Indian Act, the federal government began to provide educational services for Aboriginal children. The residential school system was composed of a variety of institutions (i.e., industrial, boarding, and residential schools) that were located in most Canadian provinces and were run mainly by religious organizations, such as the Anglican Church. According to the federal government, approximately 100,000 children attended these schools between the latter part of the nineteenth century and most of the twentieth century. The original idea behind the schools was to assimilate Aboriginal children into mainstream Canadian society, thereby "solving" the Aboriginal problem by phasing out Aboriginal culture altogether. Given the large Aboriginal presence in western Canada, many of these schools were located in Saskatchewan and British Columbia. Mainly during the 1990s, many Aboriginal people who had attended these schools came forward with agonizing stories of sexual and physical abuse that occurred while they attended these schools. In fact, in 1996 the Royal Commission on Aboriginal Peoples revealed many such accounts of abuse. As a result of the abuses that took place over the years at these residential schools, in 1998 the federal government committed $350 million for a community-based healing strategy to assist Aboriginal communities where physical abuse, sexual abuse, and drug and alcohol problems remain problematic.

There is no specific, agreed-on theory to explain situations in which members of the clergy become involved in sexual or physical wrongdoing. Explanations similar to those that have been presented to explain wrongdoing by those who hold positions of power or privilege in society (e.g., police deviance) may have some relevance. The fact that some religious bodies require sexual abstinence from their members may create interior pressures beyond the ability of some individuals to contain within their vows. No doubt individual and psychological factors are involved in such offending, but these behaviours need to be understood within the context of the broader social organizations in which they occur. Belonging to an authoritative organization where one is granted a high level of trust opens up opportunities to offend that are unavailable to those who do not hold such positions. Moreover, historically, society has associated these positions of power with behaviour that has been beyond reproach, which indeed some of the individuals holding these offices have demonstrated. However, when expectations become rigid and human abilities to meet these expectations falter, there need to be fail-safe measures in place in institutions. Children are always vulnerable—a fact that was not recognized by most social institutions until the mid-twentieth century.

Some institutions have addressed the problem. The Anglican Church of Canada publicly apologized on behalf of its former representatives to those of the residential schools who had been hurt, not only by sexual assaults but by the traumatic removal from their homes and societies. The Roman Catholic and Anglican churches in negotiations with Aboriginal peoples and the federal government, have made substantial monetary reparations as signs of their regret for the abuses that had occurred (Anglican Church of Canada, 2008). In the Anglican Church, every individual congregation shared proportionally in that monetary expression of regret.

In November 2002, the government and the Anglican Church of Canada reached an agreement that detailed the payment of compensation to residential school survivors. Under the agreement, the federal government agreed to pay 70 per cent of the compensation and the Anglican Church committed to pay 30 per cent, to a maximum of $25 million. In March 2003, the agreement was ratified. In November 2005, the federal government and legal counsel for former students, legal counsel for churches, the Assembly of First Nations, and other Aboriginal organizations signed an agreement-in-principle to all outstanding residential schools issues. The agreement stipulates five major issues to be addressed:

- a "common experience payment" to be made to all former students;
- an "independent assessment process" (IAP);
- a "truth and reconciliation process";
- commemoration; and
- ongoing healing.

Accusing members of the clergy of misconduct takes courage, especially if one is a committed follower and believer of a religious faith. Since the legitimacy of the organization would be seriously undermined if the public were to lose confidence in its members, it is not surprising that church officials, having been made aware of wrongdoing, are reticent to take action against clerics. Like police deviance, wrongdoing within religious organizations tends to be accounted for on the basis of the bad-apple theory. The religious institution, however, considers that it provides an opportunity for change (through confession, repentance, forgiveness, and reformation) and may be prone not to reject or prosecute the perpetrator of a crime but to offer that opportunity for reformation as an alternative to prosecution under the law. Prosecutions, such as those we have descri bed, may have the effect in the future of bringing crimes committed within the context of the religious institutions into the public judicial system.

Conclusion

The crimes discussed in this chapter take place among people who occupy positions of power or privilege. Sutherland's (1939) initial work on defining white-collar crime and raising the profile of corporate wrongdoing within the criminological community was introduced. Recent examples of corporate crime were presented that drew on cases from the United States and Canada. Contrasting the types of crime that have been discussed earlier, information about crime committed by those with high social standing is usually only revealed when it comes to the attention of the authorities. There are not any large-scale self-report surveys available that measure these types of rule-breaking.

The harms resulting from "elite deviance" were acknowledged, beginning with those felt by the public, which include environmental pollution. This was followed by examples of corporate wrongdoing that adversely affect consumers and workers. There is no doubt that the damage caused to society by white-collar crime is massive. Explanations for the causes of these types of crime were also suggested.

Political crime, police deviance, and crime committed by religious leaders were also introduced to show how those in society who hold positions of power and have public trust are not immune from criminal behaviour, but may be provided with unique opportunities to commit crime in addition to organizational protection from criminal prosecution.

Critical Thinking Questions

1. Besides sex-industry crime, what other illegal activities would fall under the banner of human trafficking?

2. What are the main points proposed in the model of corporate offending offered by Sherman?

3. Discuss the differences between "macro" and "micro" explanations of white-collar crime.

4. What are the similarities in the crimes committed by some members of religious organizations with other forms of "elite deviance"?

Suggested Readings

Bales, Kevin. (2004). *Disposable people: New slavery in the global economy*. Berkeley, CA: University of California Press. This is a book about human trafficking written in the global context.

Farrell, Fred. (2006). *Corporate crooks: How rogue executives ripped off Americans and Congress helped them do it*. New York, NY: Prometheus Books. An investigative journalist explains what happened in a recent number of American cases of white-collar crime. Farrell also explains ho w government efforts to control what were believed to be runaway executive salaries in the early 1990s were circumvented by corporate lawyers and accountants.

Harris, Michael. (1990). *Unholy orders: Tragedy at Mount Cashel*. Markham, ON: Viking. Written by an investigative journalist, this book examines the sexual abuse that took place at the Mount Cashel Orphanage in St John's, Newfoundland.

Simpson, Sally. (2002). *Corporate crime, law and social control*. Cambridge, UK: Cambridge University Press. This book reviews criminal, civil, and regulatory systems and how they attempt to control corporate offending. The author contends that deterrence-based approaches to controlling corporate crimes are limited.

Websites and Films

Canadian Centre for Occupational Health and Safety
www.ccohs.ca
   The Canadian Centre for Occupational Health and Safety offers publications and other information about workplace health and safety in Canada.

Corporate Crime Reporter
www.corporatecrimereporter.com
   Corporate Crime Reporter is an American legal print newsletter featuring a wide range of stories relating to corporate crime.

Human Trafficking. (2005). This film, starring Donald Sutherland, depicts women from various countries around the world who are victims of international sex-slave traffickers.

The Boys of St Vincent. (1992). A two-part docudrama based on the events involving what took place at the Mount Cashel Orphanage in St John's, Newfoundland, which was one of Canada's most well-known sex abuse scandals (National Film Board).

8 Responding to Crime

Learning Objectives

After completing this chapter students will be able to:

◎ Understand the law-and-order approach to crime control.

◎ Know the stages in the Canadian criminal justice process that involve policing, the courts, and corrections.

◎ Understand the origins and nature of the youth criminal justice system.

◎ Define the term *racial profiling*.

◎ Know the "broken-windows" theory.

◎ Understand the meaning of *conditional sentences*.

◎ Assess the impact of boot camps on recidivism.

◎ Explain evidence-based crime prevention practices.

◎ Describe restorative justice and harm reduction.

◎ Be able to understand the difference between drugs being legalized versus drugs being decriminalized.

Introduction

A plan for reducing crime in Canada that is espoused by many politicians and social commentators is putting more police officers on the streets; mandating the courts to impose stricter, mandatory minimum sentences; and building more prisons. The following are three recent examples of where the federal government has planned to introduce "law-and-order" legislation in Canada. The first example took place in 2010 when the government introduced Bill C-13, which would impose an absolute ban on pardons for those convicted of a sexual offence involving a child. The introduction of this Bill followed an announcement in the press that Graham James, the hockey coach who abused Sheldon Kennedy and Theoren Fleury (both former NHL players) in addition to many other young players, was given a pardon after serving a three-and-a-half year prison term in 1997. A second example is Bill C-25, the "tough-on-crime" legislation that will end two-for-one credit for time served in pre-custody (the time served in jail before an accused goes to trial). A final example of legislation that aims to "get tough" on criminals pertains to a federal government proposal to impose mandatory minimum sentences on people convicted of growing a small number of marijuana plants. Actions such as these may be appealing to an anxious citizenry who believe crime and violence is on the upswing, but, as this chapter will explain, this line of thinking does not find much support from criminological research on criminal behaviour and on crime prevention.

This chapter will begin by reviewing the basic elements of a law-and-order approach to crime and its philosophical underpinnings. Afterwards, selected issues and debates related to policing, sentencing, and corrections will be presented, in addition to a review of the youth justice system. This discussion will not only inform readers about the stages in the criminal justice process in Canada, but it should also raise doubts about the effectiveness of quick-fix law-and-order policies to control crime. The chapter will conclude with crime control initiatives that do not necessarily view the police, the courts, or prisons at the forefront of effective crime control.

Crime, Law, and Order

Law-and-order approaches to crime control are not unique to Canada. In fact, many criminologists would argue that the way in which crime is reacted to in this country is more progressive than policies employed in some other Western societies. Take, for example, the situation in the United States. This is a country where a "war on drugs" has been waged since the mid-1980s, and incarceration rates are now among the highest in the Western world. The United States is also the only Western country that has not abolished capital punishment; the death penalty is permitted in many American states. In simple terms, a **law-and-order** platform supports a *strict* criminal justice system. This tough-on-crime logic extends to all three major elements of the criminal justice system—the police, the courts, and the prisons. In philosophical terms, a tough-on-crime approach is in keeping with the deterrent theory that the fear of harsh punishment is the most effective way to deter crime. Even though there is some empirical support for the idea that the *fear of getting caught* may prevent some types of criminal behaviour, long prison sentences, mandatory minimum sentences, and even capital punishment are not particularly effective policies for reducing crime, even though they do serve the retributive function of punishing criminals and reducing the risk to society posed by violent offenders—only while they are incarcerated.

At times, victims of crime and, especially, their advocates play important roles in terms of promoting a more punitive criminal justice system. In this regard, the mass media often features stories about innocent bystanders who have been severely injured or killed by gun-toting criminals because they were in the wrong place at the wrong time. There is no question that society currently fails adequately to support crime victims and their families. However, in the American context, "victims' rights" does not mean that things are done to help the victim, but that things are done to the offender (Clear, 1994).

Box
8.1

Debates and Controversies

The Safe Streets and Communities Act

On 13 March 2012 the Safe Streets and Communities Act received Royal Assent. This law, according to many of its critics, is a good example of a law-and-order approach to crime control. According to the Canadian Bar Association, an organization which represents over 37,000 lawyers in Canada, there are 10 reasons why the passage of this controversial law was a mistake.

1. Ignoring reality. Decades of research and experience have shown what actually reduces crime: (a) addressing child poverty, (b) providing services for the mentally ill and those afflicted with fetal alcohol spectrum disorder, (c) diverting young offenders from the adult justice system, and (d) rehabilitating prisoners, and helping them to reintegrate into society. Bill C-10 ignores these proven facts.
2. Rush job. Instead of receiving a thorough review, Bill C-10 is being rushed through Parliament purely to meet the "100-day passage" promise from the last election. Expert witnesses attempting to comment on more than 150 pages of legislation in committee hearings are cut off mid-sentence after just five minutes.
3. Spin triumphs over substance. The federal government has chosen to take a "marketing" approach to Bill C-10, rather than explaining the facts to Canadians. This campaign misrepresents the bill's actual content and ensures that its public support is based heavily on inaccuracies.
4. No proper inspection. Contrary to government claims, some parts of Bill C-10 have received no previous study by parliamentary committee. Other sections have been studied before and were changed—but, in Bill C-10, they're back in their original form.
5. Wasted youth. More young Canadians will spend months in custodial centres before trial, thanks to Bill C-10. Experience has shown that at-risk youth learn or reinforce criminal behaviour in custodial centres; only when diverted to community options are they more likely to be reformed.
6. Punishments eclipse the crime. The slogan for one proposal was Ending House Arrest for Serious and Violent Criminals Act, but Bill C-10 will actually also eliminate conditional sentences for minor and property offenders and instead send those people to jail. Is roughly $100,000 per year to incarcerate someone unnecessarily a good use of taxpayers' money?
7. Training predators. Bill C-10 would force judges to incarcerate people whose offences and circumstances clearly do not warrant time in custody. Prison officials will have more latitude to disregard prisoners' human rights, bypassing the least restrictive means to discipline and

Continued

control inmates. Almost every inmate will re-enter society someday. Do we want them to come out as neighbours, or as predators hardened by their prison experience?

8. Justice system overload. Longer and harsher sentences will increase the strains on a justice system already at the breaking point. Courts and Crown prosecutors' offices are overwhelmed as is, legal aid plans are at the breaking point, and police forces don't have the resources to do their jobs properly. Bill C-10 addresses none of these problems and will make them much worse.

9. Victimizing the most vulnerable. With mandatory minimums replacing conditional sentences, people in remote, rural and northern communities will be shipped far from their families to serve time. Canada's aboriginal people already represent up to 80 per cent of inmates in institutions in the Prairies, a national embarrassment that Bill C-10 will make worse.

10. How much money? With no reliable price tag for its recommendations, there is no way to responsibly decide the bill's financial implications. What will Canadians sacrifice to pay for these initiatives? Will they be worth the cost?

Source: Ernst, 2011. Reprinted with permission of the Canadian Bar Association.

Nevertheless, law-and-order remedies to crime, which often gain support when the disturbing plight of crime victims and their families is brought to public attention, do not, as one might expect, reduce or prevent crime. Unless we are prepared to live in the type of society where the government has an iron grip on just about every aspect of civilian life and where human rights are kept at a bare minimum, common forms of crime are impossible to curtail through rigid state control. However, since the Canadian public is not interested in living under an authoritarian regime, the society must be prepared to consider alternatives to crime control that fall outside the historic or traditional boundaries of a punitive criminal justice system. According to Doob and Cesaroni (2004), who are experts in the field of youth criminal justice, changes in the criminal justice system will do little to solve the youth crime problem. In fact, they argue that the amount of youth crime, and the severity of official measures that are aimed at controlling it, are quite unrelated.

Policing

Not long ago, when Canadian beauty pageant contestants would compete at international competitions, they often would be attired in replicas of the ceremonial red uniform worn by the **Royal Canadian Mounted Police (RCMP)**, complete with wide-brimmed hats. The image of the tall, white, male RCMP officer persists as an icon of Canadian identity. National symbolism aside, policing in Canada has undergone significant change since the North-West Mounted Police (precursor to the RCMP) was formed in 1873 to aid in the non-Aboriginal settlement of the Canadian Prairies. Not only have the numbers of police grown in Canada—in 2012 there were almost 70,000 police officers in Canada—but today many women and members of visible minorities can be found within the ranks of police departments across the country. It is quite common today for police officers to be university graduates. In addition to changes that have taken place in police hiring practices, the structure and purpose of policing is now much more complex than it was following Confederation.

Policing in Canada is carried out at four levels: federal, provincial, municipal, and First Nations. At the federal level, RCMP detachments are found in all of Canada's provinces and territories. The RCMP is responsible for enforcing all federal statutes, including the Controlled Drugs and Substances Act. It should also be pointed out, however, that in many communities throughout Canada, under contract from provincial governments, RCMP detachments are engaged in the day-to-day policing of small communities. In Newfoundland and Labrador, for example, the Royal Newfoundland Constabulary is responsible for policing urban centres of the province, while the RCMP provides service in hundreds of smaller communities on the island and in Labrador.

Few people realize that the mandate of the RCMP extends beyond Canada's borders. In recent years, mainly acting in a peacekeeping and advisory capacity, members of the RCMP have served in several African countries, in the Middle East, and in the Caribbean. Another little-known fact about the RCMP is that its members are prohibited by federal legislation from joining a trade union. In contrast, all of Canada's other provincial and municipal forces are allowed to join police associations and unions (Griffiths, 2007).

Despite there being 10 provinces and three territories in Canada, there are only three **provincial police forces**: the Ontario Provincial Police, the Sûreté du Québec, and the Royal Newfoundland Constabulary. Enforcing provincial laws, in addition to the *Criminal Code*, provincial police generally serve smaller communities. The Ontario Provincial Police, for example, have been given the responsibility of policing rural areas in the province in addition to waterways, highways, and trails (e.g., snowmobile trails in the winter).

Most police work in Canada is carried out by metropolitan, regional, and municipal services. Besides enforcing the *Criminal Code* and the Controlled Drugs and Substances Act, municipal police departments also enforce local bylaws. The largest municipal police force in Canada is the Toronto Police Service, which employs approximately 5,000 officers. The Toronto Police Service has one of the most powerful and active police associations in Canada.

A fairly recent development in Canadian policing concerns services that are provided for First Nations communities. Due in part to the overrepresentation of Aboriginal people in Canada's criminal justice system, in addition to conflicts that have taken place between Aboriginal people and the police over land claims and other disputes, Aboriginal communities have the option of establishing their own police forces. Independent Aboriginal police services can be found in areas of the country where there are substantial numbers of Aboriginal people residing on reserves. These police services are distinguished from other police services in Canada in that their constables are of Aboriginal descent and are often recruited from the communities they police. Since the pool of on-reserve recruits is not large, some First Nations police services have had difficulty attracting qualified recruits (Cardinal, 1998).

Another issue related to policing that has arisen in Canada in recent years and in keeping with a law-and-order approach to crime is the "broken-windows" model, originally proposed by Kelling and Wilson (1982) in the United States. Their view is that social incivilities such as loitering, public drinking, urinating in public spaces, and property incivilities like vacant lots and abandoned, boarded-up buildings produce a set of behaviours and environments that, if left to further deteriorate, will cause serious anti-social behaviour, even violence. This model suggests that poor, rundown neighbourhoods, appearing as though residents are not concerned about the quality of life in them, are a lure for the criminal element in society. This perspective suggests that there is an inevitable association between public "disorder" and crime. The style of policing that accompanies a broken-windows model is known as **zero tolerance policing**. The primary goal of zero tolerance policing is "the maintenance of order," where the police target those individuals who are perceived as the most important causes of disorder. Goff describes zero tolerance policing in this way:

> To eliminate disorder, the police decide to pursue an aggressive policy throughout designated neighbourhoods with disorder problems. This means a confrontive [sic] style of policing, as the police target those individuals they feel are responsible for disorder and incivility within the community. (2004, p. 121)

The broken-windows model and zero tolerance policing have been adopted in some large American cities, for instance, in New York during the 1990s when Rudolph Giuliani was mayor. Aspects of this law-and-order approach to policing, however, can also be found in Canada. The Ontario Safe Streets Act, referred to in Chapter 1, that outlawed squeegee-cleaning and "aggressive panhandling" in Ontario is a good example of a law that targeted "disorderly" people. The following is an excerpt taken from a young Toronto homeless woman's account of the situation on the street just prior to the enactment of the legislation when a zero tolerance police crackdown on squeegee cleaners was underway. This account demonstrates the acrimony this style of policing can invoke from those who are targeted.

I don't think that it's fair at all, you know. It's basically a hate crime, you know—cops are doing this "target policing" thing, and looking at people who look weird or have squeegees in their hands and then immediately going to them like they're causing all the trouble. I don't think it's fair at all . . . we are just trying to live; they're looking at us like we're animals or something, like we're not human beings, and I just don't think that it's fair at all. Like, cops will come and hassle you and they really know how to intimidate you—scare you into doing things, like, confusing stuff. They're just big bullies. Uh, the police were a lot nicer when I first started. Now they're just rude and come up to you and they'll shove you around and swear at you and stuff. They're, like, really rough. They won't listen to reason and they're just a lot more violent and stuff. (O'Grady & Bright, 2002, p. 26)

Research from the United States suggests that there is limited support for the argument that a broken-windows model/zero tolerance policing are effective ways to reduce violent crime. In New York, where this model was vigorously applied, there were substantial reductions in murders, robberies, and burglaries. But, at the time when crime rates were decreasing, civil rights complaints against the NYPD were increasing, particularly in visible minority neighbourhoods. In fact, according to Amnesty International, zero tolerance policing in New York was accompanied by a growth in police brutality and strained police–community relations (Goff, 2004). Moreover, at the time when crime rates were declining in New York, crime rates were also declining in many other large American cities that did *not* adopt zero tolerance policing. In San Diego, California, a city that implemented a community-oriented policing style, crime rates decreased substantially with only a small increase in police recourses (Greene, 1999).

A second aspect of policing that has generated a sizable amount of controversy in recent years, particularly in culturally diverse communities, is **racial profiling**. The term *racial profiling* refers to members of the police force systematically targeting members of racial groups on the basis of a perceived criminal proclivity of the whole group. Racial profiling is most commonly associated with police contact with visible minority groups.

Recent controversies over racial profiling in Canada have mainly focused on two groups: Muslims and other people of Middle Eastern origin (post-9/11) and black people. The Muslim community has complained that they are unfairly stopped, searched, and interrogated by police—in addition to customs officers and airport security guards—because they are suspected of being terrorists (Turenne, 2005). While there has been little systematic research on racial profiling in Canada focused exclusively on Muslim and Middle Eastern communities, racial profiling research in Canada has focused on black communities, who also feel that they are unfairly treated by the police. From their survey of Toronto high school youth, Wortley and Tanner

(2005a) suggest that racial profiling does occur in Toronto. Their research shows that black youth are much more likely to report being stopped and searched by the police than youth from other racial backgrounds.

Some commentators have suggested that the reasons why black youth are more likely to be stopped by police may be warranted. Are black youth more involved in criminal activity than other youth, hence their being stopped by police is justified? Or could it be that black youth, compared to other youth, tend to be more involved in leisure activities that take place in public places, thus explaining why they draw more attention from police (Gabor, 2004)? Wortley and Tanner's research shows that these two possibilities do not provide an adequate explanation for why black youth are stopped by the police more often than youth from other racial backgrounds. When taking into account factors such as deviant behaviour, drug and alcohol use, social class, and various public leisure activities, black students *still* are much more likely to be stopped and searched by the police than students from other racial backgrounds. For example, 34 per cent of black students who self-reported that they were not involved in illegal behaviour also reported that they had been stopped by the police, compared to only 5 per cent of white students who were not involved in deviant activity. At the same time, black drug dealers were almost twice as likely to report that they had been arrested as were white drug dealers (Wortley & Tanner, 2005a). These findings were interpreted as being consistent with the concept of racial profiling.

The provocative nature of these findings needs to be placed within the correct context. Since the study took place in Toronto, and collected data only from high school students, the results cannot be generalized for policing practices across the country, nor can they be construed to apply to all age groups in the population. Also, the data that were collected did not include official police stop-and-search activities. While the police in some areas of the United States and Britain are required to record the racial background of the people who they stop and search, police in Canada are not subject to these types of regulations. Wortley and Tanner believe that if a recording practice such as the ones used in the United States and Britain were systematically put into place in Canada, supported and endorsed by all police services across the country, a larger pool of reliable and valid information would be available to researchers who study racial profiling. It might also have the effect of reducing racial profiling that appears to be in effect in some places. Despite these limitations, the results of their study do suggest that the stopping and searching of black citizens can contribute to the tendency of the black community to perceive that they are subject to more police discrimination than are other racial groups in Canadian society (ibid.). More recent research by Wortley and Owusu-Bempah (2011) in Toronto found survey black respondents were more likely to view racial profiling as a major problem compared to whites or Asians. Their study revealed that the black community's concern with racial profiling may be warranted, as black respondents were a lot more likely to report being stopped and searched by the police over the past two years than respondents from other racial backgrounds, even after controlling for other relevant factors. When confronted with accusations of racial profiling, the police—particularly police officials—normally adamantly deny such claims. Yet, according to a study on racial profiling undertaken by Satzewich and Shaffir (2009), what police refer to as *criminal profiling*, and view as necessary for efficient and professional policing, their critics identify as *racial profiling*. In the words of one officer interviewed in the study,

> Some people seem to think that race is a dominating factor in the way the police do their job; that is, there's a black guy walking down the street. I'm going to stop him, maybe he's a drug dealer or something. [Right.] Whereas race is really one of several factors that the police will look at. Like, for instance, you might see a black guy walking down the street. He might be wearing a certain style of clothes, baggy clothes, hip-hop type clothes. [Right.] He might have a red bandana which is often worn by gang members. He might meet up with another guy. You might see them kind of make a hand slide to each other . . . You might see the one guy reach out, they quickly exchange something hand-to-hand. You look at all those factors. The conclusion the police officer is going to come to is a drug deal just went down. Looking at all those factors employed, the hand-to-hand, the hand slides, but when you approach that person, well [he will claim], "they're just busting my ass 'cause I'm black." (Satzewich & Shaffir, 2009, p. 211)

Satzewich and Shaffir contend that the key to understanding the police's reliance on racial profiling relates this issue to professionalism and police work. The job of policing, according to the police, requires a level of conduct that cannot be undermined by concerns that minorities or interest groups may cry foul or be identified as victims of unfair targeting. From the perspective of the police, "while particular groups may garner attention, this is hardly the outcome of racialized police practices; they engage in criminal profiling, not racial profiling" (ibid., p. 220). This research shows us that there is a fine line between what the police regard as criminal profiling and what some critics of the police would view as racial profiling.

While police racial profiling is an issue that is not specifically related to a law-and-order approach to crime, racial profiling is connected to order *within* policing. Who polices the police? Law-and-order proponents of crime control are very seldom critical of the police. The efforts of the police are generally deemed to be beyond reproach, perhaps allowing the possibility that, from time to time, a small number of "bad-apple" officers do break the rules. Hence, while it may be accepted that racial profiling may occur, the practice is certainly not seen by proponents of the law-and-order approach to be indicative of broader problems that lurk in the organization or structure of policing. Yet, it might be good to bear in mind what we have learned of the effects of power and privilege and the abuses thereof in other segments of the society.

Courts and Sentencing

The next step in the criminal justice system for those who have been arrested for committing a crime is the court process. The court system in Canada has several jurisdictions. The **criminal division** of provincial courts hears all summary convictions. These refer to less serious offences that carry a maximum of $2,000 fine or six months of incarceration. The court also hears all indictable offences that fall under section 533 of the *Criminal Code*. Examples of such indictable offences include keeping a common bawdy house (a prostitution-related offence) and driving while disqualified. Provincial courts also are responsible for processing cases that fall under the jurisdiction of the provinces, such as liquor licensing and motor vehicle acts (Boyd, 2007). Youth courts also fall under provincial jurisdiction. These courts hear cases that fall under the Youth Criminal Justice Act.

The **trial division** of the provincial superior courts hears more serious indictable offences, such as murder. On rare occasions, the **Supreme Court of Canada**, which hears federal cases on civil, criminal, and constitutional matters and is the last court of appeal, is applied to in criminal cases when there has been disagreement on a subject of law from provincial courts of appeal (ibid.). One example of an out-of-the-ordinary criminal case heard by the Supreme Court of Canada concerns Robert Latimer, a Saskatchewan man who was charged with the murder of his 12-year-old, severely disabled daughter in 1993. Latimer argued that his actions (a "mercy" killing) were the result of his wishes to spare his daughter the pain that she was expected to experience throughout the rest of her life. After several years in the Saskatchewan courts and much media coverage, the Latimer case eventually was heard by the Supreme Court of Canada, which found him guilty of second-degree murder. Latimer was given the mandatory 10-year minimum sentence. While the Latimer case touched on a number of significant issues of law and punishment, the point being made here is that exceptional criminal cases, like that of Latimer, can find their way to Canada's court of last resort.

Sentencing

The ultimate role that courts play in Canada relates to sentencing. Sentencing has been a longstanding and controversial issue. Some people, such as those who promote a law-and-order position, argue that the sentences issued by the courts are too lenient, while others believe that judgments are too severe. **Sentencing** is a process whereby judges make reasoned decisions on how to punish convicted criminals. While the punishments available to judges depend a great deal on the offence committed, the judiciary in Canada has a wide range of punishments from which to choose. And there are four fundamental philosophical reasons that lie behind the sentencing process: deterrence, incapacitation, justice, and rehabilitation.

Deterrence

The concept of **deterrence** plays a key role in judicial sentencing. Within the context of the courts, deterrence simply refers to the idea that society can be protected from crime through the prevention of criminal acts. There are two forms of deterrence: general and specific. Specific deterrence refers to the notion that punishing law violators will deter their future offending. In other words, punishing a criminal discourages him or her from committing further crime. General deterrence signifies that if a sentence is severe enough it will deter others of "like mind" from committing similar criminal acts. For example, when the sentences of corporate offenders are made public and appear in the mass media, according to the logic of general deterrence, this will have the effect of dissuading other executives from engaging in corporate crime.

There is a vast amount of literature in criminology that tests to see if deterrence actually works. Briefly, the results are mixed. According to Hagan (1985, p. 305), "it is still impossible to specify with clarity and certainty the precise conditions under which sanctions are likely to be important influences on behaviour . . . we can only conclude that the burden of evidence at least supports the hypothesis that *certainty* of criminal sanctioning is causally related to criminal behaviour." What this suggests, then, is that it is not the harshness of punishment that deters offending, but it is the expectation of *getting caught* that deters offending behaviour. This logic, of course, supports the position that increasing levels of surveillance in society is more likely to lead to a reduction in crime, but *not* more lengthy prison terms or the reinstatement of the death penalty. However, this deterrence-based argument also assumes that criminals are rationally thinking actors who have the capacity to understand when they are likely to get caught and when they are not, an assumption that is not necessarily true.

Incapacity

Selective incapacitation is a second philosophical operative that affects the sentencing process. This refers to the idea that individuals with lengthy criminal records should be removed from society for extended periods of time. Issuing long prison sentences to chronic or career offenders is considered to be a wise action according to this perspective, because it is believed to decrease the overall crime rate in society. While some research exists that indicates that this may be true to some extent (e.g., Ehrlich, 1975), it still raises one important issue: approximately 90 per cent of prisoners are eventually released back into society.

Rehabilitation

Rehabilitation is yet another rationale used by the courts to pass judgment on criminals. This approach is based on the idea that offenders, if treated properly, can actually stand to gain by being incarcerated. Given the brutal and violent manner in which prison life is depicted in the mass media, such an idea sounds incomprehensible. But supporters of rehabilitative sentences contend that it is more advantageous for both the inmate and society in general to take care of people when they are in prison. Supporters of the rehabilitative approach point out that the vast majority of inmates in Canada are disadvantaged in a wide number of ways, including high levels of illiteracy, mental illness, and drug dependency. If inmates can learn to read and write properly, or overcome other personal challenges while under sentence, then when these individuals are released into the community they will have more opportunities to integrate effectively into society and will be less likely to re-offend.

Justice

The justice model of punishment refers to the idea of retribution, that is, offenders should be punished so that they "pay" for their offences. This view is essentially based on the "eye for an eye" principle, whereby the severity of the punishment is on par with the seriousness of the offence or with the harm that was inflicted on the victim(s). The retributive goals of the justice model, unlike deterrence and incapacitation, focus on past events, not future ones. People are punished for the harm they caused in the past. This means that the focal point of determining an appropriate sentence should be on the nature of the offence that was committed, not on who the offender is or whether or not he or she may offend again in the future.

In Canada, the judiciary relies on all four of these rationales when decisions are made to punish offenders. Furthermore, it is quite common for judges to pass sentence on the basis of more than one of these grounds. For example, a person may be sent to jail for 25 years because the judge feels not only that the offender is a risk to society (incapacitation), but that the passing of such a long sentence would also act as a general deterrent.

Capital Punishment

Capital punishment, that is, the state taking the life of a criminal, is the ultimate penalty that a person can pay for breaking the law, usually by committing murder. Although Canada abolished capital punishment in 1976, some Canadians would like to see this penalty reinstated. For example, in 1997 the Canadian Police Association lobbied the federal Minister of Justice at the time, Anne McLellan, for the reinstatement of the death penalty in

Canada for certain offences, particularly those involving the death of a police officer. Those who advocate bringing back the death penalty usually cite the following perceived benefits:

- The death penalty is the only proportionate punishment for first-degree murder. This is based on the retributive logic of "an eye for an eye" based on the Old Testament of the Bible.
- The death penalty acts as a deterrent to murder—people would think twice about killing other people if they knew that they would face the death penalty.
- The death penalty is deemed to be more humane than imprisoning an individual for the rest of his or her life.
- The death penalty is cost-effective. The government spends up to $70,000 a year to keep an adult male in prison in Canada.
- The death penalty protects against re-offending.

Arguments commonly used against reinstating the death penalty cite the following points:

- Human life is revered in a civilized society. Allowing the state to take the life of a person convicted of murder lowers society to the same moral (or immoral) level as the murderer.
- The majority of empirical research on this subject fails to find support for the notion that the death penalty acts as a general deterrent. In the United States, where the death penalty is used in the majority of states, there is no difference in the rate of homicides in states that have capital punishment and those that do not (Vago, 2000).
- To suggest that the death penalty is more humane than life imprisonment is impossible to verify empirically. To do so, research would have to compare the experiences of those who have been executed to those who have served life sentences. This, of course, is a logically impossible research design.
- To suggest that the death penalty is a cost-effective measure overlooks research, once again from the United States, showing that the costs involved in trials and appeals of capital cases are estimated to range between $3 million and $5 million. In fact, in the state of Missouri the cost of imprisoning an inmate for 50 years is approximately $1 million (ibid.).
- While it is true that a person who is executed will not get an opportunity to re-offend, it is also true that the death penalty can cause innocent people to be killed by the state.

Prisons

Sending a convicted criminal to prison—or to a "correctional institution," as they are referred to by the federal Ministry of Correctional Services—is usually considered to be the harshest punishment that judges can issue to offenders in Canada today. Prisons have existed in Canada since 1835, when Kingston Penitentiary was first opened. While jails existed prior to this time, they were typically used to lock people up before trial or while the guilty were waiting to be sentenced. In pre-Confederation Canada, those found guilty of breaking the law were sometimes hanged, but criminals were normally fined, whipped, or transported to other jurisdictions in the Dominion.

Today, in Canada, there are 45 federal institutions for men and 7 for women. To be incarcerated in a **federal penitentiary**, an offender must be sentenced to a term of two years or greater. Those sentenced to terms of two years less a day are incarcerated in institutions that are managed by the provinces. Even though the numbers of offenders admitted to federal and provincial institutions has been slightly declining in recent years—no doubt, in part, a reflection of the declining crime rate that was pointed out in Chapter 2— compared to other economically advanced nations, Canada's incarceration rate is quite high. In fact, the number of inmates incarcerated in Canada ranks fifth highest out of 16 leading industrialized countries, with 117 inmates per 100,000 population in 2010–11. The country with the highest rate was the United States with an astonishing 743 inmates per 100,000. At the other end of the scale is Finland, which has an incarceration rate of 59 inmates per 100,000 population (Walmsley, 2012).

One of the most striking shifts to have taken place in Canada over this period is the growth in **remand custody,** which continues as a trend from the mid-1980s. Remand custody refers to holding those who await further court appearances in custody in corrections facilities. According to Statistics Canada:

> In more recent years, the increase in the remand population has coincided with a gradual decrease in the number of adults in sentenced custody. Specifically, the number of adults in remand has increased 84% since 2000/2001 while the number in sentenced custody has declined 9%. As a result, there has been a shift in the composition of the custodial population from a predominantly sentenced population to a predominantly remand population. In 2009/2010, adults in remand accounted for 58% of the custodial population while those in sentenced custody comprised the remaining 42%. Ten years ago, the proportions were reversed, at 40% and 60%, respectively. (Porter & Calverley, 2011)

Figure 8.1 clearly demonstrates declines recorded for sentenced offenders (particularly at the provincial level) and the rises in the number of remands from 2000–01 to 2009–10.

number of adults in custody

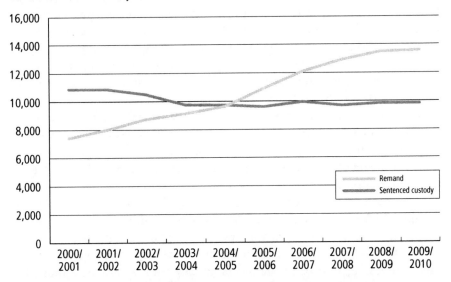

Figure 8.1 Average Counts of Adults on Any Given Day in Provincial and Territorial Correctional Facilities, by Type of Custody, Selected Provinces and Territories, 2000/2001 to 2009/2010.
Notes: Excludes Prince Edward Island and Nunavut due to the unavailability of data for the full 10-year period. Data for 2009/2010 do not match information presented elsewhere due to differences in survey coverage.
Source: Statistics Canada, Canadian Centre for Justice Statistics, Adult Key Indicator Report.

Several factors, suggests Statistics Canada, may explain the increasing use of remand and the decreasing use of sentenced custody. First, the drop in police-reported crime during the 1990s and the decline in the number of adults charged have reduced the number of individuals in court and sentenced to prison. Second, the implementation of conditional sentences—these alternatives will be discussed in more detail later in the chapter—in 1996 provided the courts with a community-based alternative to imprisonment, which likely had an impact on the drop in the number of sentenced prison admissions. A third factor is the crediting, during sentencing, of time served on remand. Judges may, at their discretion, give an offender credit for the time spent on remand when issuing a sentence. Consequently, the number of offenders in sentenced custody relative to those individuals serving time in remand may be lessened (Statistics Canada, 2005a). However, in 2009 the law was changed so that the amount of credit for time served was capped at a ratio of 1-to-1. Only in exceptional circumstances may judges give credit to a ratio of 1.5-to-1. Under the previous law, judges normally gave 2 for 1 credit.

People who are incarcerated in Canada do not represent a cross-section of the population. Two dimensions stand out most: gender and race. First, males outnumber women by a ratio of about 10:1. Second, Aboriginal people comprise 20 per cent of the prison population, even though this population represents just 3 per cent of all Canadians. Black Canadians, who comprise 2 per cent of the population, comprise 6 per cent of the prison population. Canadians who are white, Asian, or South Asian are underrepresented (Trevethan & Rastin, 2004). And according to more recent statistics from Ontario, while black males made up approximately 5.2 per cent of the population in Ontario between 2005–11, 22 percent of Ontario inmates over that same period were black (Rankin et al., 2013). Moreover, people who are incarcerated in Canadian prisons generally lack formal educational credentials, have poor employment histories, suffer from substance abuse, suffer from fetal alcohol syndrome (CTV National News, 2001) and other mental health problems, and are more likely than the general population to have experienced homelessness.

The costs involved in paying for prisons in Canada are formidable. For example, in 2010–11 adult correctional service expenditures totaled $2.373 billion, the majority of which was spent paying for prisons. It costs about $113,000 a year to keep a federal inmate locked up (MacCharles, 2012). Since the vast majority of inmates are eventually released into the community, a great challenge that society faces is the successful reintegration of inmates into its midst. It is clearly in the interests both of offenders and of the community that re-offending not occur. But, at times, it does. This is what is referred to as **recidivism**. The recidivism rate is calculated by counting the number of offenders who are released from correctional institutions that re-offend and are subsequently returned to confinement. While it may be tempting to use the recidivism rate as a measure of program effectiveness (treatment programs that inmates may receive while incarcerated), to do so is unwise. For example, if a person was initially incarcerated for a serious, violent crime and is then returned to confinement for a relatively minor offence (e.g., shoplifting food) this could be viewed, in relative terms, as a case of success, not of failure. A second reason why standard measures of recidivism are not ideal for determining program effectiveness is the possibility that ex-inmates may commit crimes upon release that go undetected by authorities. Just because these individuals are able to stay clear of the police certainly does not mean that offences are not occurring.

The philosophical rationales that were identified with the sentencing process overlap with the purposes of prisons. The traditional approach to imprisonment is based on the idea that criminals are to be incarcerated for the reasons of incapacitation and deterrence. This is also referred to as the "custodial" model, where inmates are placed in a secure environment and subjected to strict discipline. Concerns about security and control are fundamental in a prison environment. In many respects, this model is in keeping with the justice model identified earlier.

The rehabilitation–reintegration approach to imprisonment emphasizes the role of treatment and programming for inmates so that they can successfully reintegrate into society. Correctional facilities help inmates work on their specific needs and problems with the expectation that they will not re-offend once released back into the community. Some contend that this risk-reduction model is the most influential approach in corrections in Canada today (Goff, 2004), and it probably is.

Essential to successful offender reintegration are well-informed discharge policies and programs. According to research from the United States, without adequate housing, employment opportunities, and familial and other social supports, inmates who are released into the community face major challenges, and many are likely to re-offend (Petersilia, 2003).

Youth Justice in Canada

Prior to 1908, if a Canadian youth broke the law and was caught by the authorities he or she would have likely received the same (or similar) punishment as an adult offender would have. Youth were not treated any more leniently than adults, nor were they placed in separate correctional institutions. According to Canadian law at that time, no distinction was made in dealing with offenders on the basis of how old a person was. With the onset of the Juvenile Delinquents Act, however, the way in which youth were treated under the law changed. While the reasons for this change are complex, and are normally discussed in more thorough detail in courses that specifically focus on young offenders, according to Tanner (2010, p. 28), Canada and other Western societies were increasingly becoming age-differentiated as the result of the industrial revolution. As Canada was becoming more urban and more industrialized, work shifted from the household (e.g., family farms) to factories in cities. During this period (mid- to late-1800s) many Canadian men, women, and children worked in factories. However, as technology advanced and more and more workers were being replaced by machines, youth labour was no longer in such high demand. As a result, the streets in major Canadian cities were being increasingly occupied by unemployed youth, and levels of property crime began to rise. While compulsory education was introduced in part as a way to control young people, and some reformers were concerned over the plight of many of these street urchins, the federal government reacted to this situation by eventually deciding to intervene in the hope of protecting or controlling these beggars, waifs, and orphans (Tanner, 2010, p. 31). Such intervention came in the form of the Juvenile Delinquents Act of 1908.

Unlike the law-and-order rhetoric that often characterizes how young offenders are reacted to today, 100 years ago a social welfare philosophy was the back drop for treating juvenile delinquents in Canada. Since many young delinquents were believed to be involved in crime for reasons not of their own making, youth who broke the law were treated more humanely than adult criminals. In fact, these youths were seen to be in a "state of delinquency" and not considered to be "criminals." Moreover, unlike adult criminals, juveniles who broke the law were considered to be more amenable to reform and thus required specific treatment. Such action took two forms: A separate court system was established just for juveniles, and a correctional system was put into place that separated youths from adults. The minimal age of criminal responsibility was seven in the country at this time, with the upper age varying from 16 to19, depending on the province.

Today, rules and procedures for young people (aged 12–17) who come into conflict with the law are dealt with by the Youth Criminal Justice Act (YCJA). The Act became effective in 2003, replacing the Young Offenders Act that had been in place since 1984. The YCJA does not apply to children under the age of 12. Experts who study child behaviour believe that children under the age of 12 are too young to fully understand and appreciate the consequences of their behaviour. Children who are involved in serious criminal acts (which are very rare in Canada) are normally dealt with by the medical or social service communities, not the criminal justice system.

Crime prevention, rehabilitation of the young person, and the determination of important consequences for criminal actions are the focus of the Act, which states that the criminal justice system for young people must

- be separate from that for adults;
- emphasize rehabilitation and reintegration;
- provide fair and proportionate accountability that reflects the reduced level of maturity of young persons;
- encourage [the youth] to repair the harm done to victims and communities;
- provide intervention in a timely fashion; and
- provide enhanced procedural safeguards to ensure that young persons are treated fairly.

Parents, extended families, the community, and social agencies may also have an opportunity to be involved in the young person's case. Much more so than the adult criminal justice system, a young person's gender, ethnic, cultural and linguistic background, special needs, and Aboriginal heritage may be taken into consideration.

Another important difference between the Canadian youth and adult justice systems relates to the issue of incarceration. While the maximum prison sentence for an adult in Canada is 25 to life (possibly longer if one is deemed by the courts to be a dangerous offender), the maximum amount of time that a youth can be placed in a closed custody facility is 3 years. However, if the young person is tried in youth court as an adult, he or she can receive an adult sentence. Normally, these are cases that involve repeat offenders who are charged with serious crimes, and are likely to be 16 or 17 years of age.

"Extra-judicial measures" are a final and unique aspect of the Canadian youth justice system. Normally applied to first-time, non-violent offenders, these measures are designed to respond to offending behaviour outside the bounds of the justice system. In effect, youth are diverted away from the youth criminal justice system. The law provides the police in Canada with three options when dealing with young offenders. They can issue the youth a warning, a charge, or can invoke an extra-judicial measure. If a police officer were to opt for one of these measures, a young person facing a drug possession charge, for example, would essentially have to admit to committing the offence, but would not be charged or need to appear in court. However, in exchange, the youth would be required to attend a drug/alcohol counselling program. If the program is regularly attended, the youth will not have a criminal record.

A comprehensive study by Bala et al. (2009) evaluated various aspects of the Youth Criminal Justice Act. They found that the YCJA succeeded, at a national level, in significantly reducing the rates in the use of court and custody without increasing recorded youth crime. However, the Act was not as successful in reducing various types of regional variation in the youth justice system. There continues, for instance, to be significant regional variations in rates of custody, as the Prairie provinces continue to have the highest rates of youth who were issued custodial sentences (Bala et al., 2009, p. 156).

It is also worthy to note, and keeping in mind the issue of regional variation pointed out above, that for many years Quebec has pursued youth justice policies that prioritize rehabilitation over punishment. The reasons for this approach are likely socio-historical, as the juvenile justice system in France operates under similar principles.

Alternatives to Incarceration

Prior to the 1950s, the Canadian judiciary had a limited range of punishment options available for making sentencing decisions. Offenders could be sent to prison, issued a fine, placed on probation, or given a discharge. Largely as the result of growing crime rates and rising prison populations that occurred during the 1960s and 1970s, governments were looking for ways to curb the costs associated with confining large numbers of inmates. There was also growing concern that incarcerating offenders was not terribly effective in terms of deterring crime or reducing recidivism. As a result, additional alternatives to incarceration were sought.

Conditional Sentences

Two recent alternatives to incarceration that have stimulated some debate within the adult and youth justice systems will now be addressed: conditional sentences and boot camps. Some organizations in Canada, such as Mothers

Against Drunk Driving (MADD), are opposed to the use of conditional sentences for those convicted of causing death or injury as the result of being impaired while driving a motor vehicle. The reason for this opposition stems from the fact that offenders who are given conditional sentences by the courts serve time in the community, not in a prison. Some people believe that not only are conditional sentences less punitive than incarceration, but they also have a weaker deterrent effect than incarceration. **Conditional sentences,** sometimes referred to as intermediate sentences, are sentences that fall somewhere between incarceration and probation. Conditional sentences were first introduced in Canada in 1996, with the goal of trying to reduce the prison populations. Similar to probation orders, conditions set for those serving conditional sentences would include requirements such as attending drug or alcohol treatment programs in addition to curfews, house arrest, and electronic monitoring. The general principles behind conditional sentences are threefold: denunciation, individual deterrence, and rehabilitation.

Home confinement and electronic monitoring are forms of conditional sentences designed to put a check on offenders while they are serving time in the community, and at the same time provide offenders with the opportunity to maintain family ties and employment while under sentence. To ensure that the offender abides by the conditions of house arrest, electronic monitoring systems are often employed. Although there are several types of electronic monitoring systems, what they all share in common is the ability to determine if the offender is confined to his or her residence for the court-imposed designated time. Normally, a person under house arrest is allowed to attend school or go to work, but must remain in the home at other times—taking into account medical appointments and some time to run errands. The most recent technological development in electronic monitoring relies on global positioning system (GPS) technology, where satellites are able to determine the precise location of the offender. If those under home confinement are found to be away from their residence when they are not supposed to be, then they are in breach of this intermediate sanction.

For the most part, low-risk offenders are normally selected by the courts for home confinement. In the United States, where these programs are fairly popular, they are most often used for those convicted of non-deadly impaired driving. In Canada the first electronic monitoring program took place in British Columbia in 1987. Similar to program participants in the United States, the majority of offenders in the Vancouver pilot project were serving sentences for impaired driving. While several provinces in Canada use home confinement, only Newfoundland, British Columbia, and Saskatchewan use electronic monitoring (Maidment, 2002).

There has not been a great deal of Canadian research to assess the success of home confinement and electronic monitoring. What has been done generally shows that electronic monitoring is no more effective for lowering recidivism than probation (Bonta et al., 2000). However, contrary to law-and-order critiques of conditional sanctions, research in the United States indicates that most offenders who are placed under house arrest were not prison-bound offenders. For Petersilia (2003) many offenders who are under home confinement would have been given regular probationary sentences if these new community confinement initiatives were unavailable.

In addition to this concern, a study that examined a group of offenders who had been placed on electronic monitoring in Newfoundland found that women generally face many more restrictions while under community confinement than men (Maidment, 2002). These gender differences were linked to the fact that women with children found it virtually impossible to fulfill their parenting responsibilities while they were under house arrest. For instance, when a child was ill and had to be taken to a doctor, mothers who would leave home to attend to the needs of their children would jeopardize breaching the terms of their sentence. Problems such as these were most pronounced for single mothers. On the other hand, since the majority of men who are under house arrest live with female partners or parents, these offenders had more available social supports. For example, in keeping with traditional societal gender roles, the partners and mothers supporting males under house arrest would normally provide groceries and other essentials. Since females under house arrest were given the same sort of time restrictions by the courts as were men—in terms of the amount of time that one was allowed to be away from the home (usually for work or school)—house arrest was more a restrictive experience for females than it was for male offenders. Maidment's research urged policy-makers to take these gender differences into account when decisions are made to place women under house arrest so that their conditions of detainment are not more restrictive than those of men.

Boot Camps

A second example of a relatively recent alternative to incarceration is boot camp. **Boot camps** are correctional institutions where inmates are treated like army cadets. Usually oriented to youth who have been in conflict with the law, the general philosophy behind boot camps falls under the rubric of punishment that is consistent with deterrence theory and with the law-and-order approach to crime. Boot camps are designed so that inmates learn discipline. In fact, according to those who advocate boot camps, troubled youth get into conflict with the law in the first place because they lack discipline. The role of the boot camp is, therefore, to instill the kind of respect and discipline that is thought to be lacking in the lives of delinquent youth. In short, offenders are deemed to have bad attitudes, and the simple role of boot camps is to turn bad attitudes into positive, pro-social attitudes. The resocializing experience of the boot camp is hoped to have long-lasting positive behavioural effects so that once youth are released back into the community they will not re-offend. Not surprisingly, law-and-order advocates have been long-time supporters of boot camps.

Boot camps were first established in the United States in the mid-1980s. While boot camps do remove offenders from the community, they are considered to be alternatives to incarceration because the facilities are generally smaller than traditional correctional institutions and lengths of confinement are shorter. In the United States, boot camps gained initial popularity because of the large growth in prison populations that occurred in the 1980s, in addition to the overextended probation system.

During the 1990s, images of boot camps were regularly featured on television programs that appeared on mainstream American networks. Programs such as the *Jenny Jones Show* (which ran from 1991 to 2003) would regularly feature, on stage, parents—usually single mothers—with an incorrigible child by their side. Having tried just about every known parenting technique to control the delinquent child, all to no avail, it was now time to send the child to boot camp. In from the side of the stage would appear a "boot camp sergeant" who would march up and proceed to demean and humiliate the delinquent adolescent and then usher him or her off to boot camp. Normally, at the end of the program, after an undisclosed period of time had elapsed, the once-delinquent child would reappear on stage, embrace the parent, and apologize profusely for all the past anguish that he or she had caused. The message of these shows was that the boot camp had done its job in terms of instilling discipline and respect for authority into the youth. The happy parent then leaves the stage, and life is now good, thanks to the boot camp.

Television programs such as *Jenny Jones* obviously provided American broadcasters with the level of viewer ratings necessary to attract and sustain advertisers year after year. Even though the success of the boot camp experience is unquestioned in the context of daytime television, empirical assessments of boot camps paint a more complicated story. For example, a study by Wright and Mays (1998) compared recidivism rates for first-time offenders who had been sent to boot camps with those placed on probation and with offenders who were sent to more traditional penal institutions. Unlike the scenario of boot camps commonly portrayed on American daytime television, Wright and Mays found that the offenders who had been placed in boot camps actually had higher rates of re-offending than the other two groups of youths. While this study does not support the contention that boot camps are effective tools to reduce offending, other research in the United States has shown that *some* boot camps are more effective than others in terms of reducing recidivism. The types of boot camps that had the most positive outcomes, however, were not because of the military training and strict discipline. Rather, the lower levels of recidivism associated with the successful boot camps were accounted for on the basis of the community *aftercare* that these programs provided (Mackenzie & Souryal, 1995). In other words, systematic and thorough community intervention following the boot camp experience appeared to keep youth from getting into further conflict with the law, and not the boot camp experience itself.

Not long ago, Ontario had a boot camp for young offenders. "Operation Turnaround" was open from 1997 to 2004 in Moonstone, a community located an hour north of Toronto. Modelled after American boot camps, Operation Turnaround was managed by the American private company Encourage Youth Corporation. An evaluation of the boot camp revealed that the program surpassed all expectations. According to a review of the program undertaken by T-3 Associates (2001), the rate of recidivism for boot camp graduates was considerably lower than it was for a comparison group of young offenders who did not attend the boot camp. However, after these results were analyzed more critically, Doob and Cesaroni concluded that

> a very thorough examination of the data found . . . no significant differences on recidivism between boot camp participants (or boot camp completers) and a comparison group. It did not matter whether one looked at recidivism at six months, one year, or whatever length of time the youth had been in the community. There was also no evidence of any overall beneficial psychological or academic impact of the boot camp experience over a standard correctional institution . . . the generalized failure of Ontario's boot camp to show statistically significant positive effects on youth is consistent with evaluations elsewhere. (2004, p. 258)

Operation Turnaround closed its doors in 2004. Details about why the Ontario government decided to close the boot camp for young offenders remain unclear. Yet it may not be a coincidence that the boot camp closed its doors soon after the Conservatives in Ontario were defeated by Dalton McGuinty and the Liberals. Interestingly, however, in the United States, the boot camp movement has been waning in recent years. Some commentators have speculated that the closing of several boot camps in states such as Florida are because of their unconvincing records for reducing recidivism, in addition to their rising costs. Moreover, several civil suits have been filed in the United States by families whose children have died while serving time in boot camps. A recent example of such a case in Florida in 2006 involved the death of a 14-year-old boy.

What Works for Children and Youth?

This chapter has raised some questions about the effectiveness of law-and-order approaches for preventing crime and reducing recidivism. Quick "get-tough" fixes simply are not the answer for preventing crime from occurring in Western democratic societies like Canada. If the traditional arms of the criminal justice system—policing, courts, and corrections—are not effective responses to crime, then what are? The remainder of this chapter will present findings from evidence-based research on crime prevention initiatives in addition to crime control initiatives that fall outside of the traditional boundaries of the criminal justice system. These initiatives have shown some potential for meeting the needs and challenges of criminals and their victims. According to a systematic review of the crime prevention literature, Welsh and Farrington (2005) suggest the following measures of what works for children, offenders, victims, and places.

Social skills training programs directed at youth who are 13 years of age and older who exhibit some problem behaviours have been shown to be effective in terms of reducing anti-social behaviour. Programs that employed what psychologists refer to as a **cognitive behaviour approach** were shown to be the most effective. This type of approach includes programs that teach at-risk children social skills such as starting a conversation, giving a compliment, entering an ongoing play group, and establishing and maintaining friendships. According to Doob and Cesaroni (2004, p. 261), initiatives such as these are particularly important for targeting youth who live in at-risk (disadvantaged) neighbourhoods. Interventions for older youth who have already been in conflict with the criminal justice system and are serious or violent offenders are best addressed by "multi-modal" approaches that deal with issues such as anger management, substance use and abuse, and academic programs. Within a Canadian context, the management of multi-modal programs requires the integration of the youth criminal justice system, mental health system, schools, and child welfare agencies.

What Works for Offenders?

Cognitive behaviour therapy (CBT) has also been shown to be an effective strategy for reducing recidivism in adult offenders. In general terms, CBT is an approach where clients and therapists work together to identify and understand problems that may have led to offending. Goals and strategies are then offered so that the lives of offenders can be improved. Moreover, drug-treatment programs offered to incarcerated inmates were found to be associated with an 11 per cent reduction in recidivism. Furthermore, the more intensive the program, the more effective it was for reducing both recidivism and drug use. Finally, sex offender treatment programs in prisons have been shown to be effective for reducing recidivism.

What Works for High-Crime Places?

Areas in cities such as parks, shopping malls, and parking garages are often "hot spots" for certain types of offending to occur. A review of research in this field shows that two practices led to a decline in crime: hot-spot problem-oriented policing and electronic video surveillance. Problem-oriented policing is a preventive style of policing that is not totally dependent on the use of the criminal justice system. Here, the police encourage community group involvement such as by social service agencies and by the business community in efforts to prevent crime. In fact, according to this model of policing, community problems that are not simply criminal in nature are collaboratively dealt with. Police officers gain the experience and insight that is needed to address a wide range of community problems that extend beyond crime. In effect, the community shows that it values police involvement in non-criminal problems and appreciates the broader input that the police can play in the community, while the police see people as multi-dimensional persons and not just as criminals.

The second strategy that Welsh and Farrington found effective for reducing crime in high-crime areas is the use of electronic surveillance cameras and better lighting. A combination of these two techniques was shown to have a positive impact on reducing crime in underground parking garages, places where women feel particularly vulnerable to sexual assault.

What Works for Victims?

Welsh and Farrington show that research on court-mandated intervention programs for batterers (counselling and education for male batterers) are an effective mechanism for reducing domestic violence. For victims of residential burglaries, not surprisingly, upgrades in security were shown to be associated with lower levels of home burglary. Finally, participating in restorative justice programs has been linked to victims who felt less likely to anticipate re-victimization. The next section provides a more detailed description of the concept of restorative justice.

Restorative Justice

A comparatively recent response to crime is **restorative justice**. While not falling completely outside of the realm of the conventional criminal justice system, restorative justice looks for effective ways of dealing with crime that are based on a consensus, rather than on traditional adversarial models of justice that stem from retribution and punishment. Adherents of restorative justice point out the ineffectiveness and costliness of the punishment model of crime control. In other words, not only are prisons an expensive system to contain and manage people who have been judged by the courts to have broken the law, but incarceration has also been found to have few constructive outcomes for those being punished. Proponents of restorative justice also point out that a system primarily geared toward punishing offenders offers next to nothing for those who have been victimized by crime. Excepting that a stiff prison sentence may provide crime victims with some sense of vindication or revenge, the punishment model does little to compensate or even to assist victims who may have had their lives severely altered as the result of one or more criminal events. Another appeal of this alternative crime control model is that, like the left-realist approach introduced in Chapter 4, it takes crime seriously without increasing repression and exclusion (McEvoy & Mika, 2002, p. 469).

Zehr and Mika (1998) have noted three key ideas that lie behind restorative justice. The first is the notion that the victim and community have been harmed by the actions of an offender(s) and some sort of restoration is needed. Unlike the situation in traditional criminal courts, victims, offenders, and community members all have a stake in the successful outcome of the process. Second, those who have broken the law have an obligation both to the victim and to the community to make up or compensate them in some way for the harm they have caused. The third proposition of restorative justice identified by Zehr and Mika (1998) is the idea of healing. This healing occurs on at least two levels. It is imperative that the victim be provided with information, restitution, safety, and social support. On the other hand, the offender's needs and competencies also need to be addressed. For example, if an offender broke into the victim's house and stole goods that were then used to purchase drugs to support a heroin addiction, then the addiction problem needs to be addressed so that the offender can be offered support to overcome his or her addiction. According to this principal of restorative justice, offering community support to the offender benefits all those involved in the process of fairly administering justice.

One special model of restorative justice can be traced back to the practice of Aboriginal sentencing circles, a traditional system of justice where a much broader cross-section of the community is involved in the judicial process. Unlike the traditional Western adversarial process of law that holds responsible and punishes offenders in a court of law and prison, sentencing circles are designed for problem solving and making efforts to reintegrate the offender into the community. It is important to note, however, that sentencing circles are available only to those people who have pleaded guilty to their offences.

In the actual process of a sentencing circle, all participants sit facing each other in a circle. Normally, a judge, Crown prosecutor, defence lawyer, the victim(s) with family, the offender, a police officer, and a small number of community residents—often including a small number of elders—participate in the sentencing circle. Compared to the traditional adversarial criminal court process where the sentence determines the outcome, sentencing circles are designed to help find a solution to the original conflict and to repair the relationships damaged by the criminal act. An appeal of restorative justice is that it offers the prospect of escaping the "zero sum," whereby what "benefits" victims must be hurtful for offenders (McEvoy & Mika, 2002). In other words, in the case of sentencing circles, the offender, the victim, and the community all stand to gain.

While sentencing circles have been in place in Canada for several years and the general idea of restorative justice appears to be gaining more and more popularity, such initiatives have drawn some important criticisms. Due process advocates, for example, suggest that sentencing circles lack proportionality. In other words, two cases that may appear similar in terms of the nature of the offence and harm inflicted on the victim could be resolved with considerably different outcomes, depending on how consensus was reached in the two processes. This could be unfair to the offender who receives a more punitive sentence for committing a similar crime.

A second concern about restorative justice relates to the idea that not all crime can successfully be resolved in such a close, interpersonal context. For example, it is understandable that female victims of sexual assault might be extremely uncomfortable and reticent to face their offenders in a sentencing circle. Finally, for sentencing circles to be successful, all participants must be committed to the general principles of restorative justice (Dickson-Gilmore & LaPrairie, 2005).

Despite these possible drawbacks, according to a review of empirical research on restorative justice, lower rates of re-offending were recorded for offenders who participated in restorative programs compared to those involved in the traditional adversarial process.

Research has shown, too, that all of those who have been involved in restorative justice programs are generally more satisfied with the outcomes relative to participants in traditional correctional approaches. Moreover, the costs associated with restorative justice are lower than those incurred in the traditional court system (Rugge et al., 2005).

Harm Reduction

Another approach to crime control having an arm's length relationship to the traditional criminal justice system is **harm reduction**. Harm reduction is both a public health approach and community practice that is designed to reduce the harm associated with risky behaviours, such as intravenous drug use. The harm reduction model maintains that abstinence from all forms of risky behaviour is an untenable goal for society. A more realistic approach to drug use, for example, is to control and reduce the use, not necessarily to stop the behaviour completely. For example, if somebody is going to use heroin, it is beneficial for both the user and for the community that the drug be consumed in a safer fashion. In the case of a behaviour like heroin addiction, the community might be willing to provide certain health measures so the addict would not contract HIV from sharing contaminated needles, nor die from an overdose, and so residents living in neighbourhoods where injection drug use is widespread would be less concerned about having to avoid contaminated needles in parks and in alleyways. Examples of harm reduction practices in these instances could include

---

Box 8.2   Debates and Controversies

Harm Reduction Practices Targeted at Illegal Drug Users

While harm reduction programs have been in place in Canada since the late 1980s, they have and continue to be the subject of some controversy. For those who hold a law-and-order viewpoint toward crime control, providing safe injection sites for heroin users and distributing clean pipes to crack cocaine users only serves to encourage the use of illegal drugs. However, research has shown that these practices are in fact effective means of reducing the harm associated with illegal substance use, and do not promote and encourage the use of illegal substances (Fischer et al., 2007).

Needle Exchange Programs

These programs provide clean needles and syringes for injection drug users, free of charge. Because hypodermic needles can be a haven for diseases such as HIV and hepatitis B and C, clean needles can prevent the spread of such diseases among users. The first official needle exchange program began in Vancouver in 1989. Today, similar programs are common in many large Canadian cities such as Toronto and Montreal. Users of these programs normally obtain clean needles and syringes from public health departments or from public health outreach programs that target communities where there is a high incidence of intravenous drug use. There are more than 100 needle exchange programs in Canada (CBC News, 2004).

Safe Injection Sites

North America's first legal supervised safe injection site opened in 2003 and is located in Vancouver, BC. Insite is a health-focused facility where injection drug users can be in the presence of health-care professionals and addiction services while they actually inject drugs such as heroin. The site does not provide users with illegal drugs. The goals of the program are to decrease public injection, reduce needle sharing, reduce the number of fatal overdoses, reduce the spread of diseases such as HIV and hepatitis, and increase addiction treatment.

---

needle exchange programs, safe injection sites, and the provision for crack users with kits designed to stop the spread of hepatitis from users sharing pipes and other drug paraphernalia. The details surrounding a harm reduction policy adopted by the Toronto Public Health on safer crack cocaine use is shown in Box 8.2. Similarly, the provision of methadone to heroin addicts serves as a strategy of crime reduction as well as harm reduction.

Thinking about drug use in terms of harm reduction principles has led to two alternative legislative perspectives for dealing with drugs: **legalization** and decriminalization. Both focus on drug-use treatment and prevention

Inhalation Rooms

While legal inhalation rooms have yet to receive government approval, the Rock Users Group, formed through the Vancouver Area Network of Drug Users, has held rallies insisting on the inclusion of an inhalation room within the supervised safe injection site. Such a facility would help public order by shifting crack-smoking away from the streets to a supervised facility. The Rock Users Group also suggests that since smoking drugs such as cocaine is safer than intravenous injection, the practice should not be discouraged by pushing users who smoke into alleys and other public places.

Methadone Maintenance

Methadone is a medication used for the treatment of narcotic withdrawal and dependence. The drug is a synthetic narcotic used to treat opium addiction. Taken orally once a day—normally at drug-dispensing counters located in many Canadian pharmacies across the country—methadone functions on brain chemistry by occupying opioid receptors in much the same way as heroin. The key difference between methadone and heroin is that methadone does not produce the "high" obtained from heroin, but it is effective in terms of eliminating withdrawal symptoms. Thus, the user is still "hooked" to an opiate, but since methadone is available free of charge, the user does not need to resort to crime to support his or her habit.

Crack Kits

In December 2005, Toronto Public Health began to distribute "crack kits" in the city through its needle exchange program. The distribution of the kits to high-risk user groups is designed to control the spread of hepatitis C. Since chronic crack use can cause bleeding and chapped lips (many users smoke crack in crude pipes made from aluminum soft drink cans), the kits include supplies such as clean glass stems for smoking crack, alcohol swabs (to clean the pipe when shared with more than one user), lip balm (to help prevent chapped, bleeding lips), condoms, and pamphlets on disease prevention. For more information on the program go to www.toronto.ca/health/professionals/communicable_diseases/harm_reduction_access.htm.

instead of punishing users. The following points are generally used to support these alternative approaches:

- The legal status of drugs has no substantial effect on drug consumption.
- Criminalization unnecessarily puts a lucrative trade in the hands of organized crime.
- The impossibility of stopping drug use leads to drastic measures that corrode civil liberties.
- Those who are convicted of drug offences carry with them the stigma of a criminal record.

• The costs associated with the enforcement of drug laws (police, courts, and prisons) are exorbitant.

In practical terms, there are some key differences between decriminalizing versus legalizing drugs. To **legalize** a drug would make its use legal (under certain conditions, e.g., minimum age regulations). This would lead to the development of a legally controlled market for the sale of drugs, such as marijuana, where users could purchase the drug from a safe, legal, and regulated source. This approach would be similar to how beer, wine, and spirits are regulated in Canada at the provincial level (e.g., the Liquor Control Board of Ontario [LCBO]), and obviously the government would collect tax revenues from such a system. **Decriminalization**, on the other hand, would reduce or end criminal penalties for certain acts. Decriminalized acts are no longer crimes, but they may still be the subject of regulation. In addition, drug production and distribution would not be the responsibility of the state.

Research shows that the impact that non-criminal intervention can have on drug use can be positive. For instance, in 2001, Portugal officially abolished all criminal sanctions for the personal possession of drugs, including marijuana, cocaine, heroin, and methamphetamine. A report that evaluated the impact of the Portuguese legislation found that drug use rates in the population remained relatively stable since the law changed, but deaths caused by drug overdoses declined as did rates of HIV (Greenwald, 2009).

Since the early 1970s, the Canadian federal government has toyed, from time to time, with the idea of decriminalizing small amounts of cannabis. The most recent musings came about in 2003 when Canada's Justice Minister at the time, Martin Cauchon, commented to the media that Canadian laws relating to marijuana could do with "modernization." Although the Justice Minister did not plan to go so far as to make marijuana legal, he did discuss the possibility of introducing legislation to parliament that would decriminalize the use and possession of small amounts of marijuana for personal use. In other words, the use and possession of small amounts of marijuana would remain illegal, but jail sentences and criminal records would be replaced with fines (Canada Online, 2003).

Conclusion

This chapter introduced the reader to the "get-tough," law-and-order approach to crime control. The major philosophical assumption behind this popular viewpoint was shown to rest on the idea of deterrence. Strict punishments, such as extensive jail time, are believed to prevent re-offending while deterring others from committing similar offences. The three main institutions that comprise the Canadian criminal justice system are the police, the courts, and corrections. The major goals of sentencing and punishment were outlined, in addition to a discussion about youth criminal justice in Canada. Research was presented on the broken-windows theory, racial profiling, and capital punishment. Alternatives to incarceration were considered, including conditional sentences and boot camps. Crime prevention practices that pertain to children and youth, adult offenders, high-crime places, and victims of crime were also discussed. The chapter concluded with an introduction to recent innovative approaches to crime control: restorative justice and harm reduction.

Critical Thinking Questions

1. Outline the law-and-order approach to crime control using examples that focus on policing, the courts, and corrections. Would the federal government's Safe Streets and Communities Act fall under a law-and-order approach to crime control? If so, why?
2. Discuss the jurisdictional matters involved in providing police services to Canadians.
3. How do incarceration rates in Canada compare to those in other Western democratic societies? Why do you imagine this to be the case?
4. Outline the pros and cons of capital punishment. Which position do you feel is the most logical? Why?
5. In what ways do restorative justice and harm reduction approaches differ from the law-and-order model of crime control?
6. Do you believe that the age range for youth offenders in Canada (12–17) is appropriate? If not, do you think the age should be lowered or raised?

Suggested Readings

Boyd, Neil. (2007). *Canadian law: An introduction*. Toronto, ON: Thompson. This text introduces the reader to Canadian public law. Boyd describes the principles and powers conveyed by the Canadian legal system. While the book does deal with criminal law, Boyd also reviews tort, family, and administrative law.

Doob, Anthony, & Cesaroni, Carla. (2004). *Responding to youth crime in Canada*. Toronto, ON: University of Toronto Press. This book, which focuses on the youth criminal justice system in Canada, challenges many myths that surround the social reaction to young offenders. The authors also raise several issues concerning policies aimed at controlling youth crime in Canada.

Manza, Jeff, & Uggen, Christopher. (2006). *Locked out: Felon disenfranchisement and American democracy (Studies in Crime and Public Policy Series) / Edition 1*. New York, NY: Oxford University Press. In the United States, 1 in every 40 voting-age adults is denied the right to vote in elections because of a past or current felony conviction. Manza and Uggen write about the consequences of large-scale disenfranchisement— both for election outcomes, and for public policy more generally.

Websites and Films

Correctional Service of Canada
www.csc-scc.gc.ca/index-eng.shtml
> This site provides a comprehensive overview of the mandate of the Correctional Service of Canada. Moreover, the site lists a number of careers within corrections in Canada.

RCMP
www.rcmp-grc.gc.ca/index-eng.htm
> The Royal Canadian Mounted Police site provides a description of the roles and priorities of the RCMP in addition to news and updates about the force.

The Canadian Harm Reduction Network
http://canadianharmreduction.com
> The Canadian Harm Reduction Network offers numerous forums, news items, and articles that relate to harm reduction in Canada.

Global News
www.youtube.com/watch?v=ASRRNnBNUYQ
> A news clip from Global News dealing with the debate about whether or not the Toronto Police Service should release data on race in the crime statistics that they collect.

The Nature of Things: Dealing with Drugs, New Options. (1997). This video examines the issue of harm reduction. David Suzuki interviews Bruce Alexander, author of *Peaceful Measures: Canada's Way Out of the War on Drugs*, in British Columbia. In Vancouver, the Portland Hotel is showcased as an alternative to criminal prosecution for drug offences. This is an attempt to break the welfare hotel cycle by providing safe accommodation and health care together in a tolerant setting. This includes a methadone program and a visiting physician, for as many as 35 per cent of the residents at the Portland Hotel who are HIV positive. There is an examination of Dutch policies where good social programs are considered the best prevention for drug problems.

9 Summary and Conclusions

This account of criminology has focused on classical and contemporary debates and controversies. This final chapter will briefly summarize the main points and research findings presented in the preceding chapters and comment on the implications of this material for social and criminal justice policy and for future research.

To study crime one must first define crime. The criminological community is not in complete agreement about how crime should be defined. Two general definitions are put forward: the objectivist-legalistic and the social-reaction perspective. For those endorsing the objectivist-legalistic approach, crime is defined according to legal statutes. In Canada this would mean that only behaviour cited in the *Criminal Code of Canada* would qualify as criminal behaviour. Research informed by the objectivist-legalistic perspective generally searches for the causes of rule-breaking behaviour. These causes could be biological, psychological, or sociological. Regardless of the specific causes of criminal behaviour, the objectivist-legalistic perspective regards criminals as abnormal, anti-social people.

Concern arose within the discipline because such a narrow definition assumes only legal definitions reflect widespread social consensus about what is criminal in society. The social-reaction perspective alerted us to the idea that crime can be understood as behaviour that is not inherently bad or immoral. Rather, crime may be viewed as behaviour that has been deemed wrong by those who have the power and legitimacy to create laws, maintain legal systems, and punish offenders. The creation of early drugs laws in Canada and the Ontario Safe Streets Act illustrate how illegal behaviour can be created without widespread social consensus.

The way in which crime is depicted in the mass media is an ever-present aspect of our culture. The mass media are the resources the public relies on for information about the level and character of crime in society. But, as a number of researchers have emphasized, the media's portrayal of crime does not correspond to how crime is measured by official crime statistics. Whether we are referring to crime dramas, documentaries, or news programs, television tends to portray most crime as brutal, interpersonal violence. Conversely, over three-quarters of the acts of crime that come to the attention of the police are non-violent.

Criminologists have reason for concern over the relationship between public fear of crime and the stereotypical way in which crime is presented in the mass media. Research generally shows that the impact of the mass media on the public's fear is neither simple nor direct. Factors such as age, gender, and where people reside are better predictors for explaining fear of crime than how much one views television. Nevertheless, because a police perspective is implicit in so much crime news reporting, law-and-order responses to crime dominate discussions about how crime should be managed (Sacco, 2000, p. 17).

Moral panic refers to a situation or a condition that generates widespread public concern because it threatens societal values. A moral panic is not so much about why certain behaviours are thought to be deviant, but about stereotypical images of "folk devils" and overreaction. Some criminologists suggest that moral panics are the outcome of poorly understood anxieties in society. One might even argue moral panics are metaphors for other, larger, more contentious social issues. Tanner (2001, p. 253) suggests that contemporary fears about gang violence, for example, are reflections of broader concerns about immigration policy and the shifting racial composition occurring throughout Canada, particularly in large urban areas.

The problems associated with an overreliance on the media as a basis of information about crime suggests other data sources are needed. Chapter 2 outlines how official police statistics are collected and analyzed. While these data are accessible to the public, and they present a fairly precise and detailed picture about crimes such as homicide, official statistics are quite limited for recording other types of crime. For this reason criminologists use other methods to study crime, which include self-report studies, victimization surveys, and observational accounts. Even though these alternative methods have limitations, if used properly, they can be extremely useful for testing and building criminological theory in a reliable and valid fashion.

A number of perspectives purport to explain crime. Notions about the causes of crime have a long pedigree. For example, archaeological research has unearthed human remains several thousand years old that indicate some abnormal behaviours were treated by boring holes into the skulls of the afflicted so that the demonic spirits holding the individuals' minds captive could be released. It was suggested that ideas about a generalized force of evil continue to be used to this day in accounting for certain types of criminal behaviour, especially cases that involve extremes of violence and depravity.

With the Renaissance, ideas about crime changed. The work of Beccaria and Bentham suggested that criminality can be understood on the basis of free will and rational decision making. According to the classical school of criminology, crime could be effectively deterred if society invoked reasonable punishments. This point of view continues to inform the logic used in virtually all Western criminal justice systems today, including Canada's.

One key issue discussed in Chapter 4 concerned the differences between sociological and non-sociological explanations of crime. Sociological theorizing about crime is primarily interested in understanding group action and patterns of group behaviour. For example, understanding how crime is related to gender, race, and social class are fundamental issues for sociological criminologists and played prominently in the theories reviewed in Chapters 4 and 5. This is why the concept of gender, for example, was discussed in several different chapters of the book. That most crime is committed by males and that approximately 9 out of every 10 prison inmates in Canadian prisons are men are not mere chance phenomena. Moreover, prison populations are overrepresented by visible racial minorities, especially blacks and Aboriginals, and by individuals with economically disadvantaged backgrounds.

Sociologists from the Chicago School proposed that crime was socially patterned according to social class. When police-reported street crime was plotted on a map of Chicago early in the twentieth century, researchers found crime to be concentrated in the poorer neighbourhoods of the growing city. Shaw and McKay (1942) argued that crime was more likely to be found in poorer communities for the reason that these inhabitants were socially disorganized. In other words, unemployment, alcohol abuse, and family breakdown caused community breakdown and a lack of social cohesion. Recent research on crime and social mapping relies upon more advanced technology, such as GIS (geographic information system, or spatial mapping).

Several other theories have been developed based on the idea that low social status is responsible for criminality. These views were clearly evident in the work of Robert Merton and Albert Cohen, but later challenged by Travis Hirschi and control theory. According to control theory, crime is not caused by low social status, but by weak bonds to important social institutions such as the family and the educational system. Sutherland's proposed differential association theory also questioned the class–crime connection by urging researchers to think about how criminal behaviour is learned in group-like settings, and that crime is not limited to lower-class individuals. Sutherland's work on corporate crime clearly challenged the crime–class connection.

But not all criminological theory is specifically interested in explaining the causes of offending. Critical theories, for instance, pay much more attention to lawmakers than to lawbreakers. Attention to how society reacts to crime is an important feature of the conflict approach. For example, Marxist criminology directs attention from an exclusive focus on "street crime" that is committed by working-class people and illuminates the social harms committed by the powerful. Moreover, this perspective argues that the crime committed by those who are powerless is heavily regulated, while the wrongdoing engaged in by those with power is not subject to nearly the same level of social censure. Feminist criminology introduces a body of thought that emerged by showing how invisible women were in most criminological theory. Feminist criminology has also been instrumental in drawing attention to issues of sexual assault and domestic violence, crimes where women are much more likely than men to be victimized.

Many sociological explanations have been developed over the years to explain crime, including recent developments that were introduced in Chapter 5. Quite a few of the theories explored in this chapter were evolutions of previous theories. For example, the general theory of crime proposed by Gottfredson and Hirschi (1990) was linked to Hirschi's early control theory (1969); Agnew's general strain theory was a development of Merton's earlier work on crime and anomie; rational choice theory was a derivative of the classical school; the life course approach to crime proposed by Sampson and Laub was closely connected to the pioneering work on juvenile delinquency carried out by Glueck and Glueck; and actuarial and risk criminology has its roots to conflict theory since the primary focus of this approach is about changes in how society regulates and controls crime.

These linkages suggest theoretical integration is taking place in the discipline, since attempts have been made to fuse or revise related theories. There is considerable debate within the field of theoretical criminology about just how one goes about identifying the commonalities of one or more theories (Akers, 1993). Upper-level courses in criminological theory often touch on this issue.

Crime and wrongdoing can occur in most levels and classes of society. Whether it is homeless youth stealing and selling drugs to survive, or wealthy corporate executives engaged in fraudulent business practices, rule-breakers are ubiquitous. Nevertheless, it is important to realize that the reasons for rule-breaking can vary, and that not all street youth are involved in crime, nor are all business people. Explanations for crime and victimization among marginalized groups are quite different from explanations for corporate offending. Indeed, different theories are often required to explain different types of crime.

How does society respond to crime? Even though billions of dollars are spent to maintain the police, courts, and correctional institutions—the main resources used to deal with crime—crime persists. Some people argue that if the system were made tougher, crime would decline. But the research evidence assessing "get-tough" measures of crime control does not give much support to that method. For example, in the United States, where capital punishment is legal in several jurisdictions, the homicide rate is several times greater than it is in Canada, a country that abolished capital punishment years ago. Furthermore, police crackdowns on "disorderly" people and the use of boot camps for delinquent youth do not seem to be answers to crime control, either.

Less punitive measures like harm reduction offer a promising alternative in dealing with the harms associated with drug use, and restorative justice initiatives, like sentencing circles, appear to be more effective at resolving certain kinds of interpersonal disputes. However, as innovative and effective as these approaches are, they do have limitations.

Future Directions in Criminology

The study of crime has come a long way since Cesare Lombrosso first examined the physical characteristics of Italian prisons over a century ago. Today the study of crime is a large-scale enterprise, and most colleges and universities all over the globe offer courses and degrees related to the study of crime. But what bodes for the future of criminology? Will the discipline continue to grow and expand? If so, what topics will criminologists be interested in studying in the future?

As far as growth is concerned—not taking into account the uncertainty of future government funding levels for universities and colleges in Canada—the study of crime will likely continue to grow for at least a couple of reasons. First, there is no sign that society's fascination with rule-breaking will diminish in the near future, and interested students will continue to be drawn toward the discipline. Relatedly, with the ever expanding web of technology, the public will likely be exposed to an increasing variety of sources of communication capable of transmitting information about the risks and fears associated with crime. Second, credentialism (requiring formal educational credentials for certain occupations) will also likely continue to grow and expand in the Canadian labour market of the future. Not that long ago, for instance, it was uncommon for public police officers in North America to hold degrees. Today it is estimated that 25 to 30 per cent of the state and local police officers in the United States have four-year degrees. In Canada, while most police agencies have a minimum educational requirement of Grade 12, many recruits also have diplomas or degrees. Moreover, to move up into the senior administrative ranks of Canadian police organizations—particularly larger ones—post-secondary credentials are virtually a necessity.

Not only will advances in technology arguably lead to a continued interest in the field of criminology within civil society, but such change will likely impact what criminologists study in the future. Take, for example, the study of tasers (a taser is advertised as a non-lethal self-defence weapon that uses compressed nitrogen to shoot two tethered needle-like probes at an assailant to deliver an electric shock). According to TASER International, the company that manufactures the device, tasers are used by 10,000 police forces in 40 countries. Tasers are promoted as a means to save lives since the devices are an alternative to lethal force (firearms). However, the device has raised considerable controversy. For example, Robert Dziekanski, a Polish citizen who came to Canada to visit his mother with the hopes of immigrating to Canada, was killed after being repeatedly tasered in the Vancouver airport after he was approached by four RCMP officers for allegedly causing a disturbance. The incident caused enough controversy that it led to a public inquiry headed by

Commissioner Thomas Braidwood. The second and final phase of the report was released to the public in 2010. Although the RCMP officers who were involved in the incident did not face criminal charges related to the death of Dziekanksi, they were charged for perjury in connection with the officers' testimony at the Braidwood inquiry. At the time of writing, the trials of the four offices had not taken place. Interestingly, according to report that appeared in the press, the police use of tasers in British Columbia has dropped by 87 per cent since the incident (*Globe and Mail*, 2012). Amnesty International, who have been a vocal critic in the use of tasers within the law enforcement community, has claimed that the devices have caused 300 deaths (White & Ready, 2009). Although a growing body of research has examined the physiological effects of tasers on animals and healthy human volunteers in laboratory settings, according to a recent review of the literature by White and Ready, "there has been virtually no empirical analysis of 'real-world' fatal and nonfatal taser cases simultaneously" (2009, p. 865). This, of course, would be an ideal topic for future evaluation research in criminology.

As the global economy becomes more and more integrated there will be a need for criminology to increasingly be attentive to international issues and comparative research. At present, most comparative research that criminologists have undertaken tends to be in the area of homicide studies. This limited focus is mainly because *valid* and *reliable* data that measure crimes other than homicide are simply unavailable at the international level. However, just as world economies have become subject to the forces of globalization, so too will there be a need to study crime, law, and social control across two or more cultures. At present, most of the theories about crime that have been presented in this text have, by and large, only been tested in the context of a limited number of Western countries.

The range of crime that would be appropriate for comparative analyses would include computer-based crimes, human trafficking, the human and animal organ trade, narcotics smuggling, transnational organized and corporate crime, international money laundering, environmental violations, and last, but not least, global terrorism.

Cybercrime is another area ripe for more criminological research. This would include illegal activities such as computer and network intrusion/hacking, identity theft, online child pornography, cyber bullying (although not technically criminal), and fraud. In 2008, the International Cybercrime Research Centre opened at Simon Fraser University in British Columbia and has begun to develop a cybercrime research program. For the most part, though, this research is currently at the developmental phase in Canada.

While program evaluations of crime prevention programs have always been of some interest to criminologists, until recently the academic criminological community has generally not been that interested in carrying out such evaluations. Part of this reluctance is due, in part, to the lack of criminological theory used in many program evaluations. This reluctance, however, may be changing. This is particularly the case with the study of inmate reintegration. Given the fact that the United States puts so many people in prison, and since most inmates eventually are released back into the community, inmate reintegration is an import policy issue for Americans today. Researchers are interested in better understanding the challenges that released inmates face when they attempt to re-join society. Studies on the factors that help and hinder reintegration has been explored in the United States, and this research is often informed by life course and social bonding theories (Lynch, 2006), which were reviewed earlier in the text. Canadian research on this topic, however, is in its relative infancy and would be an idea focus for future research, especially since the federal government has recently put into place mandatory minimum sentences which will likely have the effect of keeping more people in prison for longer time periods.

How Should Crime Be Responded to in Canada?

Two scenarios come to mind. If Canadians really wanted to take a slice out of crime they could accept living in a society that is dominated by a totalitarian government where human rights would be severely curtailed. In such a society there would be zero tolerance to all forms of behaviour outlawed by the state. Rule-breaking of any type would not be tolerated. As a result, many rule-breakers could face capital punishment, others would spend long terms in prison, while the rest of the population would live in a constant state of fear of state repression.

In a second scenario, Canadians could create a social system where social and economic inequality would be virtually eliminated—where no one would be socially excluded and where the reasons why people want to break the rules would be addressed before the problem arose. While Canadians presently do have access to universal health care, to affordable housing, to post-secondary education, and to rewarding employment, these benefits are not equally accessible.

Both of these scenarios would likely be reasonably effective for reducing crime, but the likelihood of either becoming a reality, at least in the foreseeable future, is doubtful: Crime will not be eliminated, whether it is corporate offending, police misconduct, domestic violence, or the use of illegal drugs and the conflicts that follow in their wake. Society must come to terms with the fact that human beings are prone to rule-breaking behaviour. But if Canada is moving in a direction of crime control that is on the punitive side of the spectrum, where "cutting costs" and "getting tough on criminals" and retribution are more important than addressing fundamental human needs, then we should be mindful of these words of Mohandas K. Gandhi: "An eye for eye only ends up making the whole world blind."

Glossary

A General Theory of Crime   A theoretical perspective proposed by Gottfredson and Hirschi (1990) contending that crime and other analogous behaviours are the result of low self-control. Their theory is considered by some researchers to be founded on tautological (circular) reasoning.

administrative law   A form of public law that governs the relationships between individuals and the state by regulating the activities of organizations dealing with matters such as unemployment insurance, labour relations, and landlord–tenant relations.

Agnew's revision of general strain theory   Several types of negative experiences (not just economic ones, although economic ones exacerbate many strains) can lead to stress that prevents individuals from attaining socially valued goals. Three forms of negation are: (a) the denial or undermining of ability to achieve such goals; (b) the loss or potential loss of valued elements in the environment; and (c) threats to valued elements in the environment with various forms of negation.

anomie   Durkheim's anomie is a social condition causing the individual to feel lost or in a predicament of normlessness. Merton's anomie occurs when societies inadvertently bring to bear pressure, or strain, on individuals that can lead to rule-breaking behaviour. This strain is caused by the discrepancy between culturally defined goals, such as the acquisition of wealth, and the institutionalized means (education and employment) available to achieve these goals.

bad-apple theory   The adage is "one rotten apple spoils the whole barrel." The idea is that a little police corruption spreads like rot among apples. The counterclaim by the police is that one rotten apple can be removed and the rest of the organization protected.

boot camps   Correctional institutions where inmates, often youth offenders, are treated like army cadets.

British Home Office   The part of the government for England and Wales called the Home Office is responsible, among many other things, for compiling statistics on crime.

Canadian Centre for Justice Statistics (CCJS)   The CCJS is the agency responsible for gathering and analyzing the reports submitted by police forces from across the country. In Canada, about 1,200 separate police detachments, representing about 230 police forces, submit crime data to the CCJS in Ottawa.

capital punishment   Execution of a criminal by the state is called capital punishment, the most severe penalty exacted from a person for breaking the law, usually for having committed murder. Canada abolished capital punishment in 1976.

Chicago School   Also called the *ecological school of criminology*, the urban researchers of the 1920s from the University of Chicago discovered that crime was not randomly distributed across the population. Similar to Durkheim's earlier findings pertaining to the distribution of suicide, Robert Park and Ernest Burgess (1967) provided evidence that levels of crime in Chicago were geographically patterned.

civil law The branch of the legal system that deals with arrangements between individuals, such as property disputes, wills, and contracts.

classical school of criminology The human capacity for rational thinking informed the writings of Englishman Jeremy Bentham and Italian Cesare Beccaria, scholars who today are credited with forming what we look back to as the classical school of criminology.

cognitive behaviour approach Cognitive, meaning "thoughtful," behaviour is taught under this approach to youth to prevent crime. Social skills training programs directed at problem youth 13 and older have been shown to be effective in reducing anti-social behaviour; that is, teaching social skills such as starting a conversation, giving a compliment, entering an ongoing play group, and establishing and maintaining friendships.

control theory Society is a set of institutions that acts to *control* and *regulate* rule-breaking behaviour. Humans, by nature, are egocentric and risk-takers, so that to satisfy their desires by the easiest means possible, if social bonds are broken or weak, they may resort to criminal behaviour. However, if an individual is properly bonded to society, then he or she will not engage in crime.

conditional sentences Also called intermediate sentences, conditional sentences fall between incarceration and probation with the purposes of denunciation, individual deterrence, and rehabilitation. Introduced in 1996 to reduce the prison populations, they include such requirements as attending drug or alcohol treatment programs in addition to curfews, house arrest, and electronic monitoring.

corporation The legal form of organization for both capitalist and public enterprise, whereby a group of people function under the law as one "person," with control apparently or actually in the hands of a managerial elite. Corporations are deemed persons under the law, but are not subject to laws pertaining to persons, a circumstance that gives them great power with few controls regarding responsibility to the societies in which they flourish.

crime opportunity Grasmick et al. (1993) found that crime opportunity was just as strong a predictor of fraud and aggression as was low self-control.

Crime Prevention through Environmental Design (CPTED) The premise that proper design of the physical environment can be effective in preventing crime (e.g., the installation of lighting in outdoor areas that are frequented by women during hours of darkness) is expressed in the CPTED approach to crime prevention.

Crime in the United States This book, compiled by the FBI, is a compilation of crime data provided by nearly 17,000 law enforcement agencies across the United States.

Crime rate The number of police-reported criminal events, usually per 100,000 population.

The Criminal Code of Canada An Act that codifies criminal offences and procedures in Canada, which forms a section of the Constitution Act of 1867.

criminal division of provincial courts The criminal division hears all summary convictions, that is, less serious offences that carry a maximum of a $2,000 fine or six months of incarceration, and indictable offences under section 533 of the *Criminal Code* (e.g., prostitution-related offences and driving while disqualified).

criminal law   Rules made by a society that define what behaviours are "crimes," that is, what may be determined to have happened and can be punished by the state.

criminologist   One who studies what society deems to be criminal offences, why the society has so deemed them, and what other approaches society might take to such behaviours.

critical criminology   Based on Karl Marx's ideas regarding class conflict, critical criminology regards capitalist societies as marked by the struggle between the powerful and less powerful classes. Laws do not reflect socially agreed-on norms and values, therefore criminology should focus not only on the rule-breakers, but also on the rule-makers.

cyber bullying   Refers to the use of the Internet and other digital technology to threaten, humiliate or embarrass another person.

decriminalization   is another policy alternative to criminalizing drug use. If drug use were to be decriminalized then there would be an end to criminal penalties for certain acts. Decriminalized acts are no longer crimes, but they may still be the subject of regulation. In addition, unlike legalization, drug production and distribution would not be the responsibility of the state.

deterrence   Legal measures aimed to discourage certain acts or to place restrictions on the rational choices of people are called deterrents. As a crime control strategy, the notion of deterrence finds expression in attempts to reduce motivation for crime by increasing the perceived certainty, severity, and swiftness of penalties.

deviance   For sociologists, deviance is not related to "a type of person" but to a pattern of norm violation relative to the society in which it occurs. There is no fixed agreement about the substance of deviance—even murder and incest have been accepted in certain societies at certain times. When labels are applied to people instead of classes of behaviour, people can become devalued, discredited, and excluded.

differential association theory   Edwin Sutherland (1939) suggests that criminal behaviour is learned behaviour: A person is more likely to become embedded in criminal activity if surrounded by an excess of socializing definitions favourable toward norm-violation over definitions that are unfavourable to the violation of social norms.

domestic violence   Domestic violence is so named for taking place in the domicile, or home, and means any act or omission to a partner "that is perceived as psychologically, socially, economically, or physically harmful" (DeKeseredy & Schwartz, 1996).

empirical reality   The systematic collection of observable data finds what is empirical reality.

expressive crime   Is often impulsive and emotional such that people who commit these acts are not likely to be concerned at the time of their commission with the future implications of these actions. Examples of expressive crime include non-premeditated murder and assault.

federal penitentiary   A federal prison is for criminals sentenced to a term of two years or greater. Those sentenced to terms of two years less a day are incarcerated in provincial correctional facilities. Canada's rate of imprisonment ranks fifth highest out of 16 leading industrialized countries, with 116 inmates per 100,000 population in 2003.

femicide   The murder of women by men because they are females. This can include honour killings and witch lynching.

feminist criminology   Feminist criminology emerged during the 1970s as a response to the discipline's having ignored women's involvement in crime, both as victims and as perpetrators. Feminist criminology has helped raise awareness around women who are victims of male violence, including intimate partner violence.

first-degree murder   Homicide that is planned and deliberate. A person may also be convicted of first-degree murder if he or she is found guilty of killing an on-duty police officer or correctional officer. A murder that is committed during the course of other criminal acts, such as hijacking, kidnapping, forcible confinement, and sexual assault, is also designated as first degree.

folk devils   This term is employed most famously by Stanley Cohen in his study of the moral panic surrounding the mods and rockers subcultures in England during the 1960s. Cohen suggests that society creates a gallery of social types to show its members which roles should be avoided and which should be emulated. The groups portrayed as deviant, and of which society disapproves, occupy a constant position as folk devils: visible reminders of what should not be.

fundamentalist evangelist   From the Greek *euaggelion*, meaning "gospel" or good news (of the life of Jesus), an evangelist is a fundamentalist when the speaker for Christianity emphasizes literalistic interpretations of the Bible, impassioned preaching, and personal conversion from wrongdoing to holy living through acceptance of the teachings of Jesus Christ.

gang   According to Miller (1975) a gang is "a group of recurrently associating individuals with identifiable leadership and internal organization, identifying with or claiming control over territory in the community, and engaging either individually or collectively in violent or other forms of illegal behavior." More recent analyses of gangs, particularly in North America, have focused on the racial and gender dimensions of gangs.

General Social Survey (GSS)   The GSS is a large population survey ongoing in Canada since 1985 that surveys many issues, including family and work life, education, use of information technology, and criminal victimization.

green criminology   The study of environmental damage caused by human activity which is viewed through a criminological lens.

harm reduction   Most often used within the context of illegal drug use, harm reduction is a set of practical strategies that attempts to reduce the negative consequences of drug use by incorporating a spectrum of strategies from safer use to managed use to abstinence.

hate crime   When crimes are directed to individuals simply because they are or seem to be part of a particular minority group, whether racial, religious, or sexual, they are designated as "hate crimes." Recently, anti-discrimination laws have been enacted to protect minority groups such as Jews, blacks, gays and lesbians.

homicide   Homicide means the killing of a person and is recognized in the law as first-degree murder, second-degree murder, manslaughter, or infanticide.

homeless youth   Any young male or female is considered homeless when the street (in the widest sense of the word, including unoccupied dwellings, parks, rooftops, shelters for homeless youth, etc.) has become his or her habitual abode or source of livelihood, and when they are inadequately protected, supervised, or directed by responsible adults.

human trafficking   The Canadian government defines human trafficking as ". . . the recruitment, transportation, harbouring and/or exercising control, direction or influence over the movements of a person in order to exploit that person, typically through sexual exploitation or forced labour" (Public Safety Canada, 2012).

infanticide   A wilful act or omission by a female that causes the death of her newly born child (under the age of 12 months, and the mother must not have fully recovered from the effects of childbirth; psychiatrists are usually given the responsibility of making this determination).

instrumental crime   These involve some planning and weighing of risks and include offences such as break and enter, accounting fraud, and embezzlement.

John Howard Society   John Howard led prison reform. Between 1775 and 1790 Howard made several trips across Western Europe in search of a more humane prison system. A century later, the John Howard Society was formed and is dedicated to the humane treatment of prisoners. In Canada, the John Howard Society is active in all of Canada's 10 provinces and the Northwest Territories.

labelling theory   A form of symbolic interactionism developed by Frank Tannenbaum (1938), labelling theory considers that being identified as an outsider, or social deviant, can cause a person to start thinking about him or herself as "a bad person," which can lead to the formation of a deviant persona. Unlike most other criminological theories that assume the crime leads to social control (labelling), the line of causal relationship is reversed: Social control (labelling) leads to crime.

law-and-order   The law-and-order approach supports a strict criminal justice system: the police, the courts, and prisons. A tough on crime approach to crime control is in keeping with deterrence theory that the fear of harsh punishment is the most effective way to deter crime, but is not supported by sociological research.

left realism   Highlighting the fact that most victims of street crime are people with working-class backgrounds, left realism, a critical branch of criminology, attempts to explain why this is the case.

legalization   A policy alternative to criminalizing a drug, where drug use would be legal. Much like how alcohol and tobacco are regulated in Canada today, drugs would be available for purchase by the public, albeit with certain restrictions (e.g., minimum age restrictions).

life course theory   Some research indicates that problem behaviours, including criminality, are age-related and may be impeded by certain events in the life cycle, including the birth of a child, marriage, divorce, and retirement.

Magna Carta   The document considered to provide the foundation of constitutional law. It was drawn up by his nobles and signed by English King

John in 1215. It guaranteed traditional land rights to the barons, certain guarantees under the law to freemen, and the protection of religious rights and local customs.

manslaughter A murder committed in the heat of passion or by sudden provocation.

media accounts of crime The way in which crime is portrayed in the mass media. This includes television, Internet blogs, radio, newspapers, and magazines.

moral panic When a condition, episode, person, or group of persons emerges to become defined as a threat to the societal values and interests.

moral entrepreneur Becker defines a moral entrepreneur as an enterprising person (or group of people) who want to bring a particular non-criminalized behaviour under the purview of criminal behaviour, whether or not there is societal consensus on its dangers

moral regulation Michel Foucault's view, in keeping with the social-reaction definition of crime, is that the social regulation of behaviour is not based on consensus but is mediated by a complex system of social institutions that reward and punish people, thus defining what is right and what is wrong for society, encouraging certain forms of behaviour while discouraging others.

nasty-girl phenomenon An idea perpetrated in the mass media recently that a new breed of female criminal has emerged and is on the rise; a form of "folk devil."

objectivist-legalistic criminology This standpoint understands the definition of crime to be factual and precise; it defines crime as "something that is against the law."

observational accounts In this style of reporting, the researcher interacts with individuals on a face-to-face basis in a natural setting to gather accounts of crime within the context where crime or victimization occurs. Normally takes place on a relatively small scale so that a deeper understanding and appreciation of crime and victimization can be achieved.

occupational crime Crime committed by employees within the course of their employment; the two most common forms are theft and fraud, such as insider trading.

occupational death The third leading cause of death in Canada is due to accidents and hazardous conditions in the workplace.

organized transnational crime Organized criminal activity that occurs across national boundaries.

overrepresentation The disproportionate presence of a minority group, for example, in a prison population, compared to the numbers of that group in the population as a whole. For example, Aboriginal people are overrepresented in the criminal justice system as 17 per cent of the federal inmate populations and 19 per cent of inmates in provincial institutions are Aboriginal, but only 3 per cent of the total Canadian population is Aboriginal (Roberts & Melchers, 2003). Criminologists study overrepresentation to try to determine its causes.

Physical Assault Level 1 According to the *Criminal Code of Canada*, physical assault at Level 1 is pushing, slapping, punching, and face-to-face threats (Sauvé, 2005).

police misconduct Situations of police misconduct occur when the actions of police officers are "inconsistent with the officer's legal authority, organizational authority, and standards of ethical conduct" (Goff, 2004).

Police-Reported Crime Severity Index (PRCSI) A measure where more serious crimes in Canada are assigned higher weights and less serious offences lower weights. As a result, when all crimes are included, more serious offences have a greater impact on changes in the index.

political crime Crimes committed against the state (treason), such as acts of terrorism, and crimes committed by the state, such as fraudulent dealings with corporations that cheat the tax-paying citizens or that are oppressive measures contrary to the Constitution and laws.

Ponzi scheme A form of fraudulent investment that pays returns to investors from their own money or money from other investors and not from profits earned.

positivist criminology An approach to crime that applies the principles of the scientific method to understanding the causes of crime, which are believed to reside in the physical, genetic, psychological, or moral makeup of offenders. This perspective rejects the view of classical criminology, where criminals are deemed to be rational actors who are exercising free will.

power control theory Researchers have been able to explain differences in self-reported male and female misconduct by comparing the gender roles and parental control mechanisms in two different types of families, patriarchal and egalitarian.

provincial police forces The three provincial police forces found in Canada are the Ontario Provincial Police, the Sûreté du Quebec, and the Royal Newfoundland Constabulary.

price-fixing An illegal activity where individuals from different companies get together and agree to fix prices on goods and services that are sold on the open market.

psychoanalytic theory A psychological theory of deviant behaviour proposed by Sigmund Freud which argues that unresolved conflicts between the id, ego, and superego cause deviant behaviour—particularly sexual misconduct.

psychological theories Psychological theories of human behaviour suggest that criminal behaviour is created by a child's upbringing and by influences in the environment. Unlike some biologists, who would support the view that criminals are born, psychology suggests that criminals are created by the society.

psychopathy Stemming from the psychological study of human personality, this term is used to describe criminals who share impulsive and aggressive traits and are incapable of showing remorse for their violent behaviour.

racial profiling Racial profiling refers to the practice by some members of the police force in systematically targeting, stopping, and interrogating members of racial groups on the basis of a perceived criminal proclivity of the whole group; racial profiling is most commonly directed toward visible minority groups.

rational choice theory Early theories considered criminal behaviour to be the result of conscious decision making based on the "expected utility" principle in economic theory. Criminals are assumed to make calculated choices so as to make the most of their profits or benefits and reduce their costs or losses—influenced by variations in opportunity, environment, target, and risk of detection. This thinking persists in the legal and prison systems prevalent today.

recidivism   A term which refers to inmates who re-offend after they are released into the community from correctional institutions.

reliability   Data are reliable if they can be replicated by applying the research procedure again. If the research method produces the same result when applied repeatedly, the method is also considered to be reliable.

remand custody   Holding those who await further court appearances in custody in correctional facilities.

restorative justice   Restorative justice is a consensus method of dealing with crime rather than retribution and punishment. It emphasizes remedies and restoration; often involves crime victims, offenders, and the wider community; and is less costly and more effective and constructive than the prison system. Restorative justice offers compensation or even assistance to victims; it takes crime seriously without increasing repression and exclusion (McEvoy & Mika, 2002).

risk theory and actuarial criminology   A postmodern view that the social world is not easily knowable analyzes crime with no effort to explain the causes of rule-breaking behaviour, but instead seeks to understand emerging forms of social control.

Royal Canadian Mounted Police (RCMP)   Detachments of the RCMP are found in all of Canada's provinces and territories. The RCMP is responsible for enforcing all federal statutes, including the Controlled Drugs and Substances Act. In many small communities throughout Canada, RCMP detachments are engaged in the day-to-day policing under contract from provincial governments.

routine activity theory   Relating their reasoning to rational choice theory, Cohen and Felson (1979) suggest that changes in levels of crime in society are associated with changing lifestyles.

second-degree murder   All murder that is not first-degree is second-degree murder and most likely is a murder with a lower degree of intent legally attached to it than a first-degree murder.

self-report surveys   Questionnaires that seek anonymous reports from respondents about offences they have committed over a selected period of time to capture information about crimes that may not have come to the attention of the police; they also seek information about the demographic characteristics of participants, such as age and gender profiles.

sentencing   Judges' reasoned decisions on how to punish convicted criminals. It is based on the philosophy of deterrence, incapacitation, justice, and rehabilitation and is influenced by the precedents for punishing similar offences recorded from past legal judgments.

sexual assault   According to the *Criminal Code of Canada*, sexual assault at Level 1 pertains to acts involving the least amount of physical injury and can include acts short of sexual penetration such as unwanted sexual touching. Level 2 sexual assaults must involve a weapon, or the threat of a weapon, or result in bodily harm to the victim. Level 3, also known as aggravated sexual assault, results in the wounding, maiming, disfiguring, or endangering of the life of the victim (Sauvé, 2005).

social consensus Gottfredson and Hirschi (1990), for example, suggest that crime is based on a social consensus and that those who break the law do so because they lack self-control; crime and crime control are considered to be objective phenomena.

social contract Thomas Hobbes's view of the development of social behaviour, expressed in his book *Leviathan* (1651), described a "natural state" of humanity where life in a pre-social state of nature was "nasty, brutish, and short." He thought that fear of violent death forces human beings into a "social contract" with each other that leads to the formation of the state.

social control Social processes—norms and rules—operate generally to regulate or control the behaviour of individuals in groups in line with those norms and to define and punish deviance that departs from them.

social constructionism A school of thought in sociology which believes that social phenomena are produced, institutionalized, and made into custom by human interaction.

social Darwinism The application to sociology of Charles Darwin's theory of natural selection suggests that those individuals who are better suited to their environments survive ("survival of the fittest").

social disorganization In such neighbourhoods as the zone of transition, social controls break down as a result of the immigrant population in these areas having few social ties and at the same time being disadvantaged (especially economically) in the means of effective parental control over their children.

social exclusion Defined by Walker and Walker (1997) as "the process of being shut out, fully or partially, from any of the social, economic, political, or cultural systems that determine the social integration of a person in society, social exclusion may, therefore, be seen as the denial (or non-realization) of the civil, political, and social rights of citizenship."

social norms Norms are the kinds of behaviour expected within a cultural group that are considered desirable and appropriate. Norms have the rigid quality of rules, but do not have their formal status.

social-reaction (to crime) The meaning of crime varies across social and cultural contexts. Behaviour considered criminal in one society may be acceptable to people in a different society.

sociobiology The premise for criminological investigation that human behaviour results from genetic encoding that has been subjected to the Darwinian process of natural selection.

sociological criminologists These are criminologists interested in studying the types of behaviours that characterize individuals acting as groups, for example, studying why the majority of prison inmates in Canada are from lower-class social backgrounds.

state–corporate crime Kramer and Michalowski define this term as "illegal or socially injurious actions that occur when one or more institutions of political governance pursue a goal in direct co-operation with one or more institutions of economic production and distribution" (cited in McMullan & Smith, 1997).

subculture Subcultures form in reaction to problems the members experience in relating to the dominant culture. Subcultures may be composed primarily of youth who adapt or reinvent the symbols and values of the culture they are reacting to.

Supreme Court of Canada The Supreme Court hears federal cases on civil, criminal, and constitutional matters and is the last court of appeal. It is applied to in criminal cases when there has been disagreement on a subject of law from provincial courts of appeal, as in the Latimer case.

symbolic interactionism The theory that investigates the ways meanings emerge through interaction is symbolic interactionism. Its preoccupation is everyday life, and its methods entail close observation of the familiar.

trial division of the provincial superior courts The trial division hears more serious indictable offences, such as murder. Rarely, the Supreme Court of Canada hears criminal cases when there has been disagreement on a subject of law from provincial courts of appeal.

UCR 2 Survey This survey is an alternative method of data collection for Canadian police; a separate statistical record is created for each criminal incident, and it is known as an "incident-based" reporting system.

Uniform Crime Reporting (UCR) data Crimes known by the police to have taken place are reported on the UCR data collection forms and relayed to Statistics Canada. The UCR includes violent crime, property crime, and other *Criminal Code* violations.

Uniform Crime Reporting (UCR) system Most countries have official crime-reporting systems based on reports of crime by the police. Thus, crime is measured under the objectivist-legalistic definition. In theory, whatever crime comes to the attention of the police is reported by the police to their government's statistical agencies.

utilitarianism Another block in the foundation of the classical school, influenced by Jeremy Bentham, is called utilitarianism and refers to the belief that reason requires decisions to be made according to what will procure the greatest good for the greatest number.

validity Validity is the property of being genuine; a true reflection of attitudes, behaviour, or characteristics. A questionnaire or other testing instrument is considered valid if it is generally regarded as successful in measuring the concept or property it claims to measure.

victimization survey A tool used by researchers to collect information on the victimization experiences of a population.

white-collar crime "Crime that is committed by a person of respectability and high social status in the course of his [*sic*] occupation" (Sutherland, 1939).

Youth Criminal Justice Act In 2003 this Act replaced the Young Offenders Act as the legislation defining and dealing with crimes committed by persons from 12 to 17 years of age.

zero tolerance policing This style of policing, said to be important for "the maintenance of order," occurs when the police target those individuals they perceive to be the most important causes of "disorder" for special attention, whether or not they appear to have broken any laws.

References

Adler, F. (1975). *Sisters in crime*. New York, NY: McGraw-Hill.

Agnew, R. (1992). Foundation for a general strain theory of delinquency. *Criminology, 30*, 47–87.

———. (1999). A general strain theory of community differences in crime rates. *Journal of Research in Crime and Delinquency, 36*, 123–55.

———. (2002). Experienced, vicarious, and anticipated strain: An exploratory study focusing on physical victimization and delinquency. *Justice Quarterly, 19*, 603–32.

———. (2012). *Foundation for a unified criminology: Assumptions about the nature of crime, people, society, and reality*. New York: New University Press.

———, & Brezina, T. (1997). Relational problems with peers, gender and delinquency. *Youth and Society, 29*, 84–111.

———, & Broidy, L. (1997). Gender and crime: A general strain theory perspective. *Journal of Research in Crime and Delinquency, 34*(3), 275–306.

Akers, R. (1993). Criminological theories: Introduction and evaluation. Los Angeles, CA: Roxbury.

Alcántara, A. (2012). Great debate: Human trafficking. Retrieved from http://www.themorningsidepost.com/2012/12/04/great-debate-human-trafficking/

Allen, K. (2010, 3 November). KKK costume wins first prize at Legion Halloween party. *Toronto Star*, A8.

Anderson, C., & Bushman, B. (2001). Effects of violent video games on aggressive behavior, aggressive cognition, aggressive affect, physiological arousal, and pro-social behavior: A meta-analytic review of the scientific literature. *Psychological Science, 12*, 353–9.

Andrade, J.T. (2008). The inclusion of anti-social behavior in the construct of psychopathy: A review of the research. *Aggression and Violent Behavior, 13*, 328–35.

Anglican Church of Canada. (2008). A living apology. *Ministry Matters*. Retrieved from http://www.anglican.ca/rs/apology/index.htm.

Armstrong, J. (2012, 19 July). Mayor Rob Ford voted against "hug a thug" initiatives for at-risk youth. *Global News*. Retrieved from http://globalnews.ca/news/268081/mayor-rob-ford-voted-against-hug-a-thug-initiatives-for-at-risk-youth/.

Australian Institute of Criminology. (2010). Charges and offences of money laundering. Retrieved from http://www.aic.gov.au/publications/current%20series/tcb/1-20/tcb004.aspx.

Bala, N., Carrington, P., & Roberts, J. (2009). Evaluating the Youth Criminal Justice Act after five years: A qualified success. *Canadian Journal of Criminology and Criminal Justice, 51*(2), 131–67.

Balakrishnan, T.R., Jarvis, G.K. (1991). Is the concentric zonal theory of spatial differentiation still applicable to urban Canada? *Canadian Review of Sociology and Anthropology, 28*, 526–39.

Bandura, A. (1973). *Aggression: A social learning analysis*. Englewood Cliffs, NJ: Prentice-Hall.

Baron, S. (1989). The Canadian west coast punk sub-culture: A filed study. *Canadian Journal of Sociology, 14*(3), 289–316.

———. (2003). Self-control, social consequences and criminal behaviour: Street youth and the general theory of crime. *Journal of Research in Crime and Delinquency, 40*, 403–15.

———, & Hartnagel, T. (1997). Attributions, affect and crime: Street youth's reactions to unemployment, *Criminology, 35*(3): 409–34.

Barrett, S. (1987). *Is God a racist?* Toronto, ON: University of Toronto Press.

Barron, C., & Lacombe, D. (2005). Moral panic and the nasty girl. *Canadian Review of Sociology and Anthropology, 41*(1), 51–70.

Bartol, A. (2001). While collar crime. In Nicole Hahn Rafter (Ed.), *Encyclopedia of women and crime* (pp. 284–85). Phoenix, AZ: Oryx Press.

Bates, K., Bader, C., & Mencken, F. (2003). Family structure, power-control theory, and deviance: Extending power-control theory to include alternate family forms.

Western Criminological Review, 4(3), 170–90.

Beare, M. (2003). Critical reflections on transnational organized crime, money laundering, and corruption. Toronto, ON: University of Toronto Press.

Beattie, K. (2005). Adult correctional services in Canada. *Juristat 25*(8). Ottawa, ON: Statistics Canada.

Beaver, K., DeLisi, M., Vaughn, M.G., & Barnes, J.C. (2009). Monoamine oxidase A genotype is associated with gang membership and weapon use. *Comprehensive Psychiatry, 51*(2), 130–4.

Beccaria, C. (1995). *Essays on crimes and punishments and other writings*, R. Bellamy (Ed.) & R. Davies, (Trans.) with V. Cox & R. Bellamy. New York, NY: Cambridge University Press.

Beck, U. (1992). Risk society: Towards a new modernity. London, UK: Sage.

Becker, H. (1963). *Outsiders: Studies in the sociology of deviance.* New York, NY: Free Press.

Beirne, P., & Messerschmitt, J. (1991). *Criminology.* New York, NY: Harcourt.

———, & ———. (2006). *Criminology*, 4th ed. Los Angeles, CA: Roxbury.

Belanger, B. (2001). Sentencing in adult criminal courts, 1999/00. *Juristat 21*(10). Ottawa, ON: Statistics Canada.

Benson, M.L., & Moore, E. (1992). Are white-collar offenders and common criminals the same? An empirical and theoretical critique of a recently proposed general theory of crime. *Journal of Research in Crime and Delinquency, 29,* 251–72.

Bentham, J. (1973 [1780]). *An introduction to the principles of morals and legislation.* Garden City, NY: Anchor Press Doubleday.

Ben-Yehuda, N. (1986). The sociology of moral panics: Toward a new synthesis. *Sociological Quarterly 4,* 495–513.

Berger, A. (1995). *Essentials of mass communications theory.* Thousand Oaks, CA: Sage.

Berger, P., & Luckmann, T. (1966). *The social construction of reality.* London, UK: Allen Lane.

Berk, R.A. (1990). Thinking about hate-motivated crimes. *Journal of Interpersonal Violence, 5,* 334–49.

Best, J. (1989). *Images of issues: Typifying social problems.* Hawthorne, NY: Aldine de Gruyter.

Binns, J. (2005). Social exclusion and homicide: A cross-national approach. MA thesis, University of Guelph.

Black, D., & Reiss, A. (1970). Police control of juveniles. *American Sociological Review, 35,* 63–77.

Bonger, W. (1916). *Criminality and economic conditions.* Boston, MA: Little, Brown.

Bonta, J., Wallace-Capretta, S., & Rooney, J. (2000). Can electronic monitoring make a difference? An evaluation of three Canadian programs. *Crime and Delinquency, 46*(1), 61–75.

Bowlby, J., & McMullen, K. (2002). At a crossroads: First results for the 18–20-year-old cohort of the youth in transition survey. Ottawa, ON: Human Resources Development Canada.

Boyd, N. (1991). *High society: Legal and illegal drugs in Canada.* Toronto, ON: Key Porter Books.

———. (1995). *Canadian law: An introduction.* Toronto, ON: Harcourt Brace.

———. (2007). *Canadian law: An introduction* 4th ed. Toronto, ON: Thompson.

Brownfield, D., & Sorenson, A.M. (1993). Self-control and juvenile delinquency: Theoretical issues and an empirical assessment of selected elements of a general theory of crime. *Deviant Behavior, 14,* 243–64.

Burtch, B. (2003). The sociology of law: Critical perspectives on social control, 2nd ed. Toronto, ON: Thomson Nelson

Byers, L., Menzies, K., & O'Grady, W. (2004). The impact of computer variables on the viewing and sending of sexually explicit material on the Internet: Testing Cooper's triple-A engine. *Canadian Journal of Human Sexuality, 13*(3/4), 157–69.

Campbell, A. (1990). *The girls in the gang*, 2nd ed. New York, NY: Blackwell.

Canada Online. (2003, 26 May). Issue: Decriminalization of marijuana in Canada. Retrieved from http://canadaonline.about.com/library/issues/blimj.htm.

Canadian Press. (2012a, 5 June). Conservatives seek ban on "bath salts" drug after grisly US face eating attack. *Vancouver Sun.* Retrieved from http://www.vancouversun.com/opinion/editorials/Conservatives+seek+bath+salts+drug+after+grisly+face+eating+attack/6732275/story.html.

———. (2012b, 28 March). McClintic's shoes found after Tori Stafford's death.

CBC News. Retrieved from http://www.cbc.ca/news/canada/story/2012/03/28/stafford-rafferty-trial-wednesday.html.

Cardinal, M. (1998). *First Nations police services in Alberta: Review.* Edmonton, AB: Minister of Justice and Attorney General.

Carrington, P., & Schulenberg, J. (2005). The impact of the Youth Criminal Justice Act on police charging practices with young persons: A preliminary statistical assessment. Ottawa, ON: Report to the Department of Justice.

Carson, E.A, & Sabol, W.J. (2012). *Prisoners in 2011.* Washington, DC: US Department of Justice Bureau of Justice Statistics, Dec. Retrieved from http://bjs.ojp.usdoj.gov/content/pub/pdf/p11.pdf.

Carstairs, C. (2005). Jailed for possession: Illegal drug use, regulation and power in Canada, 1920 to 1961. Toronto, ON: University of Toronto Press.

CBC News. (2004, 27 October). Point for point: Canada's needle exchange program. *In Depth.* Retrieved from http://www.cbc.ca/news/background/drugs/needleexchange.html.

———. (2007). Panhandling charges soar in 2007: Toronto police. Retrieved from http://www.cbc.ca/canada/toronto/story/2007/08/17/panhandlers-police.html.

———. (2009, 1 December). Manitoba anti-gang ads sell prevention. Retrieved from http://www.cbc.ca/canada/manitoba/story/2009/12/01/man-gangs-swan-first.html.

CBC News Online. (2006). The WorldCom Story. Retrieved from http://www.cbc.ca/news/background/worldcom.

———. (2010). Dangerous offender: What the label means. Retrieved from http://www.cbc.ca/news/canada/story/2010/10/21/f-dangerous-offender.html.

———. (2012). Exorcist expertise sought after Saskatoon "possession". Retrieved from http://www.cbc.ca/news/canada/saskatchewan/story/2012/04/12/sk-church-priest-experience-120412.html.

Chambliss, W. (1975). Types of deviance and the effectiveness of legal sanctions. In William Chambliss (Ed.), *Criminal law in action* (pp. 398–407). Santa Barbara, CA: Hamilton Publishing Company.

———, & Seidman, R. (1971). *Law, order and power.* Reading, MA: Addison-Wesley.

Chesney-Lind, M., & Hagedorn, J., eds. (1999). *Female gangs in America: Essays on girls, gangs, and gender.* Chicago, IL: Lakeview Press.

Cheung, Y., Erickson, P.G., & Landau, T. (1991). Experience of crack use: Findings from a community based study in Toronto. *Journal of Drug Issues, 21*(1), 121–40.

City of Toronto. (2008). SafeCitySafer. *Our Toronto.* Retrieved from http://www.toronto.ca/ourtoronto/fall2008/safecitysafer/article01.utf8.htm.

City of Vancouver. (2009). Downtown Eastside Crime Prevention/Community Development Project (1999–2006). Retrieved from http://www.city.vancouver.bc.ca/commsvcs/planning/dtes/project.htm.

Clark, L., & Lewis, D. (1977). *Rape: The price of coercive sexuality.* Toronto, ON: Women's Press.

Clarke, A. (1986). *Summary—public hearing proceeding: Background report.* Royal Commission on Employment and Unemployment. St John's, NF: Queen's Printer.

Clarke, R., ed. (1997). *Situational crime prevention: Successful case studies,* 2nd ed. New York, NY: Harrow and Heston.

Clear, T. (1994, 21 December). Tougher is dumber. *New York Times.*

Cleckley, H. (1964). *The mask of insanity,* 4th ed. St Louis, MI: Mosby.

Clement, W. (1975). The Canadian corporate elite: An analysis of economic power. Toronto, ON: McClelland & Stewart.

Cohen, A. (1955). *Delinquent boys: The culture of the gang.* Chicago, IL: Free Press.

Cohen, L., & Felson, M. (1979). Social change and crime rates: A routine activities approach. *American Sociological Review, 44,* 588–608.

Cohen, S. (1973). *Folk devils and moral panics.* London, UK: Paladin.

———. (1985). *Visions of social control.* Cambridge, UK: Polity Press.

Coleman, J. (2002). *The criminal elite: Understanding white-collar crime.* New York, NY: Worth.

Controlled Drugs and Substances Act, S.C. 1996, c. 19. (2005, 22 March). Regulations Amending the Controlled Drugs and Substances Act (Police Enforcement) Regulations, SOR/2005–72.

Cooley, C. (1964 [1902]). *Human nature and the social order.* New York, NY: Schocken Books.

Corbett, C., & Simon, F. (1992). Decisions to break or adhere to the rules of the road, viewed from a rational choice perspective. *British Journal of Criminology, 30*(4), 537–49.

Correctional Service of Canada. (2012). Methadone maintenance treatment, specific guidelines for. Retrieved from www.publicsafety.gc.ca/cnt/rsrcs/pblctns/2012-ccrs/#e3

Corrigan, P. (1990). On moral regulation: Some preliminary remarks. In P. Corrigan (Ed.), *Social form, human capacities.* London, UK: Routledge.

Coy, M., Kelly, L., & Foord, J. (2007). Map of gaps: The postcode lottery of violence against women support services in Britain. London, UK: End Violence Against Women.

Cross, P. (2005, 27 May). Criminal court outcomes in intimate partner homicide cases. Ontario Women's Justice Network. Retrieved from http://www.owjn.org/owjn_2009/index.php?option=com_content&view=article&id=186:criminal-court-outcomes-in-intimate-partner-homicide-cases&catid=56:criminal-law.

CRTC. (2007). http://www.crtc.gc.ca/eng/cancon/t_facts.htm.

———. (2009, 5 August). CRTC issues second annual report on the communications industry. Retrieved from http://www.crtc.gc.ca/eng/com100/2009/r090805.htm.

———. (2011, 28 July). CRTC report shows more Canadians are adopting broadband Internet and wireless services. Retrieved from http://www.crtc.gc.ca/eng/com100/2011/r110728.htm.

CTV National News. (2001). Prisoners with FAS. Retrieved from http://www.come-over.to/FAS/PrisonersFAS.htm.

CTV News. (2006). Harper considers legal action over Adscam funds. Retrieved from http://www.ctv.ca/CTVNews/Canada/20060511/tories_adscam_060511/.

Currie, E. (1993). Reckoning: Drugs, the cities, and the American future. New York, NY: Hill and Wang.

Daly, K. (1989). Gender and varieties of white-collar crime. *Criminology, 27,* 769–93.

Daly, M., Singh, L.S., & Wilson, M. (1993). Children fathered by previous partners: A risk factor for violence against women. *Canadian Journal of Public Health, 84,* 209–10.

Darwin, C. (1929 [1859]). *On the origin of species by means of natural selection,* 6th ed. London, UK: Watts.

Dauvergne, M. (2005). Homicide in Canada, 2004. *Juristat 25*(6). Ottawa, ON: Statistics Canada.

Davidson, S. (2009, 16 December). Activists urge tough sentence for man convicted in assault against Asian fishermen. *National Post.* Retrieved from http://network.nationalpost.com/np/blogs/toronto/archive/2009/12/16/activists-urge-tough-sentence-for-man-convicted-in-assault-against-asian-fishermen.aspx.

Dawe, A. (1978). Theories of social action. In T. Bottomore & R. Nisbet (Eds.), *A history of sociological analysis* (pp. 362–417). London, UK: Heinemann.

DeKeseredy, W., Alvi, S. Schwartz, M., & Tomaszewski, A. (2003). *Under siege: Poverty and crime in a public housing community.* New York, NY: Lexington.

———, & Schwartz, M. (1991). British left realism on the issue of women: A critical appraisal. In R. Quinney & H. Pepinsky (Eds.), *Criminology as peacemaking* (pp. 154–71). Bloomington, IN: Indiana University Press.

———, & ———. (1996). *Contemporary criminology.* Belmont, CA: Wadsworth.

Department of Justice Canada. (2003). Anti-terrorism Act. Retrieved from http://laws-lois.justice.gc.ca/PDF/A-11.7.pdf.

Dickie, M. (1990, March). The art of intimidation: Sexism and destiny at Queen's. *This Magazine.* Retrieved from http://www.rapereliefshelter.bc.ca/dec6/thismag.html.

Dickson-Gilmore, J., and LaPrairie, C. (2005). Will the circle be unbroken? Aboriginal communities, restorative justice, and the challenges of conflict and change. Toronto, ON: University of Toronto Press.

DiManno, R. (2005, 28 December). There's no going back to what we once were. *Toronto Star* A6.

Dobash, R., & Dobash, R. (2003). Violence in intimate relationships. In W. Heitmeyer and J. Hagan (Eds.), *International handbook of violence research* (pp. 737–52). London, UK: Kluwer.

Donzelot, J. (1979). *The policing of families.* London, UK: Hutchinson.

Doob, A., & Cesaroni, C. (2004). *Responding to youth crime in Canada.* Toronto, ON: University of Toronto Press.

Doob, A.N., & Sprott, J.B. (2004). Changing models of youth justice in Canada. In M. Tonry & A. Doob (Eds.), *Crime and justice: A review of the research*, Vol. 31. Chicago, IL: University of Chicago Press.

Douglas, J. (1967). *The social meanings of suicide*. Princeton, NJ: Princeton University Press.

Dowden, C., & Brennan, S. (2012). Police-reported hate crime in Canada, 2010. *Juristat* no. 85-002, 12 April.

Dowler, K. (2003). Media consumption and public attitudes toward crime and justice: The relationship between fear of crime, punitive attitudes and perceived police effectiveness. *Journal of Criminal Justice and Popular Culture*, 10(2), 109–26.

Doyle, K., & Lacombe, D. (2003). Moral panic and child pornography: The case of Robin Sharp. In Debra Brock (Ed.), *Making normal: Social regulation in Canada*. Toronto, ON: Thompson.

Driedger, L. (1991). *The urban factor: Sociology of Canadian cities*. Toronto, ON: Oxford University Press.

Dumas, M. (2003). Punk in drublic: Gender, politics, resistance and producing punk rock in a small Canadian town. MA thesis, University of Guelph.

Durkheim, E. (1951 [1897]). *Suicide: A study in sociology*. New York, NY: Free Press.

———. (1982 [1895]). *The rules of sociological method*. S. Lukes (Ed.) & W.D. Hall (Trans). New York: Free Press.

———. (1997 [1893]). *The division of labor in society*. L.-A. Coser (Ed.) & W.D. Hall (Trans). New York: Free Press.

Edmonton Journal. (2006, 2 September). Hate-monger gets 16 months. *Edmonton Journal*. Retrieved from http://www.canada.com/story.html?id=0f7a6de8-cb5d-4165-9a7d-f7443d4817d2.

Ehrlich, I. (1975). The deterrent effect of capital punishment: A question of life and death. *American Economic Review*, 65, 397–414.

Ekblom, P., & Tilley, N. (2000). Going equipped: Criminology, situational crime prevention and the resourceful offender. *British Journal of Criminology*, 40, 376–98.

Elliott, D., & Ageton, S.S. (1980). Reconciling race and class differences in self-reported and official estimate of delinquency. *American Sociological Review*, 4(1), 95–110.

Environment Canada. (2004, 13 December). Atlantic Region News Release.

Ericson, R. (1981). *Making crime: A study of detective work*. Toronto, ON: Butterworths.

———. (1982). *Reproducing order: A study of police patrol work*. Toronto, ON: University of Toronto Press.

———, & Doyle, A. (2004). Criminalization in private: The case of insurance fraud. In Law Commission of Canada (Ed.), *What is crime? Defining criminal conduct in contemporary society* (pp. 99–124). Vancouver, BC: University of British Columbia Press.

Erikson, K. (1966). Wayward Puritans: A study in the sociology of deviance. New York, NY: Wiley.

Ernst, T., & President of the Canadian Bar Association. (2011, 14 November). 10 reasons to oppose Bill C-10. *Toronto Star*. Retrieved from http://www.thestar.com/opinion/editorialopinion/2011/11/14/10_reasons_to_oppose_bill_c10.html.

Faith, K. (1993). Unruly women: The politics of confinement and resistance. Vancouver, BC: Press Gang.

Farrington, D.P., & Burrows, J.N. (1993). Did shoplifting really decrease? *British Journal of Criminology*, 33(1), 57–69.

———, & Painter, K. (2004). *Gender differences in risk factors for offending (findings 1996)*. London, UK: Home Office, Research, Development and Statistics Directorate.

Faulkner, E. (2003). Hate crime in Canada: An overview of issues and data sources. *International Journal of Comparative Criminology*, 2(2), 239–61.

FBI. (n.d.) Uniform crime reports. Retrieved from www.fbi.gov/ucr/ucr.htm.

Felson, M. (1994). Out of sync youth. In *Crime and everyday life*, 2nd ed. (pp. 95–125). Thousand Oaks, CA: Pine Forge Press.

Felt, L., Sinclair, P. (1995). Living on the edge: The great northern peninsula of Newfoundland. St John's, NF: ISER.

Fischer, B., Oviedo-Joekes, E., Blanken, D., Haasen, C., Schechter, M.T., Strand J. & Vanden Brink, W. (2007). Heroin-assisted treatment (HAT) a decade later: A brief update on science and politics. *Journal of Urban Health: Bulletin of the New York Academy of Medicine*, 84(4), 552–62.

Fishman, M. (1978). Crime waves as ideology. *Social Problems*, 25, 531–43.

Foucault, M. (1991). Governmentality. In G. Burchell, C. Gordon, and P. Miller (Eds.), *The Foucault effect: Studies in governmentality*. Chicago, IL: University of Chicago Press.

Flood, M. & Dyson, S. (2007). Sport, athletes, and violence against women. *NTV Journal*, Summer, pp. 37–46.

Fountain, J.W. (2000, 28 November). Exorcists and exorcisms proliferate across US *New York Times*. Retrieved from www.rickross. com/reference/general/general315.html.

Gabor, T. (2004). Inflammatory rhetoric on racial profiling can undermine police services. *Canadian Journal of Criminology, 46*, 457–66.

———, & Roberts, J. (1990). Rushton on race and crime: The evidence remains unconvincing. *Canadian Journal of Criminology, 32*, 335–43.

Gaetz, S. (2004). Safe streets for whom? Homeless youth, social exclusion, and criminal victimization. *Canadian Journal of Criminology and Criminal Justice* (July), 423–56.

———, & O'Grady, B. (2002). Making money: Exploring the economy of young homeless workers. *Work, Employment and Society, 16*(3), 433–56.

———, ———, & Vaillancourt, B. (1999). *The Shout Clinic report on youth homelessness and employment*. Toronto, ON: Central Toronto Community Health Centres.

Gannon, M., & Mihorean, K. (2005). Criminal victimization in Canada, 2004. *Juristat, 25*(7). Ottawa, ON: Statistics Canada Catalogue no. 85–002.

Gazze, M. (2013, 28 February). 16-year sentence for Toronto 18 terror ringleader. *The Globe and Mail*. Retrieved from http://m. theglobeandmail.com/news/national/16-year-sentence-for-toronto-18-terror-ringleader/article4262949/?service=mobile.

George-Cosh, D. (2006, 15 September). Gill attracted to gun violence. *National Post*.

Gibbons, D. (1968). *Society, crime and criminal careers*. London, UK: Prentice-Hall.

Gibbs, C., Gore, M., McGarrell, E.F., & Rivers, L. (2010). Introducing Conservation Criminology: Towards Interdisciplinary Scholarship on Environmental Crimes and Risks. *British Journal of Criminology, 50*(1), 124–44.

Gibson, K. (2011). *Street kids: Homeless youth, outreach, and policing New York's streets*. New York: New York University Press.

Globe and Mail. (2012, 16 October). Braidwood "impressed" that B.C. is heeding Taser inquiry warnings. *The Globe and Mail*.

Retrieved from http://www.theglobeand mail.com/news/british-columbia/braidwood-impressed-that-bc-is-heeding-taser-inquiry-warnings/article4616230/? service=print.

Goff, C. (1978). *Corporate crime in Canada: A critical analysis of anti-combines legislation*. Scarborough, ON: Prentice-Hall of Canada.

———. (2004). *Criminal justice in Canada*, 3rd ed. Toronto, ON: Thompson.

Gordon, R. (2000). Criminal business organizations, street gangs and "wanna-be" groups: A Vancouver perspective. *Canadian Journal of Criminology* (January): 39–60.

Goring, C. (1913). *The English convict: A statistical study*. Montclair, NJ: Patterson Smith.

Gottfredson, M., Hirschi, T. (1990). *A general theory of crime*. Stanford, CA: Stanford University Press.

Grasmick, H.G., Tittle, C.R., Bursik Jr., R.J., & Arneklev, B.J. (1993). Testing the core empirical implications of Gottfredson and Hirschi's general theory of crime. *Journal of Research in Crime and Delinqeuency, 30*(1), 5–29.

Graves, J.L. (2004). The race myth: Why we pretend race exists in America. New York, NY: Plume.

Greaves, L., Hankivsky, O., & Kingston-Riechers, J. (1995). *Selected estimates of the costs of violence against women*. London, ON: Centre for Research on Violence Against Women and Children.

Greenwald, G. (2009). Drug decriminalization in Portugal: Lessons for creating fair and successful drug policies. Washington, DC: CATO Institute.

Griffiths, C. (2007). *Canadian criminal justice*, 3rd ed. Toronto, ON: Thompson.

Hagan, J. (1974). Criminal justice and Native people: A study of incarceration in a Canadian province. *Canadian Review of Sociology and Anthropology* (Special Issue), 220–36.

———. (1985). *Modern criminology: Crime, criminal behaviour and its control*. Toronto, ON: McGraw-Hill.

———. (1991). *The disreputable pleasures: Crime and deviance in Canada*, 3rd ed. Toronto, ON: McGraw-Hill.

———, Gillis, R., & Simpson, J. (1979). Class in the household: A power-control theory of gender and delinquency. *American Journal of Sociology, 92*, 788–816.

———, & McCarthy, B. (1997). *Mean streets: Youth crime and homelessness.* Cambridge, UK: Cambridge University Press.

Hagedorn, J.M. (1998). *People and folks: Gangs, crime, and the underclass in a rust-belt city,* 2nd ed. Chicago, IL: Lakeview Press.

Hall, J. (1952). *Theft, law and society.* Indianapolis, IN: Bobbs-Merrill.

Hall, S., Critcher, C., Jefferson, T., Clarke, J., & Roberts, B. (1978). *Policing the crisis: Mugging, the state, and law and order.* London, UK: Macmillan.

Hare, R.D., McPherson, L.M., & Forth, A.E. (1988). Male psychopaths and their criminal careers. *Journal of Consulting and Clinical Psychology, 56,* 710–14.

Harris, M. (1990). *Unholy order: Tragedy at Mount Cashel.* Markham, ON: Penguin.

Harrison, P., & Beck, A. (2005). *Prisoners in 2004.* Washington, DC: US Department of Justice, Bureau of Justice Statistics.

Henry, S., & Lanier, M. (2001). *What is crime? Controversies over the nature of crime and what is to be done about it.* Lanham, MD: Rowman & Littlefield.

Hermer, J., & Mosher, J. (2002). *Disorderly people: Law and the politics of exclusion in Ontario.* Halifax, NS: Fernwood.

Hindelang, M., Hirschi, T., & Weiss, J.G. (1979). *Measuring delinquency.* Beverly Hills, CA: Sage.

Hirschi, T. (1969). *Causes of delinquency.* Berkeley, CA: University of California Press.

———, & Gottfredson, M. (1983). Age and the explanation of crime. *American Journal of Sociology, 89,* 552–84.

Hofstadter, R., & Wallace, M. (Eds.). (1970). *American violence: A documentary history.* New York, NY: Dover.

Horley, S. (1991). *The charm syndrome.* London, UK: Macmillan.

Howard, M., Williams, J.H., Vaughn, M.G., & Edmond, T. (2004). Promises and perils of a psychopathology of crime: The troubling case of juvenile psychopathy. *Journal of Law and Policy, 14,* 440–83.

Huff, R. (Ed.). (2002). *Gangs in America,* 3rd ed. Thousand Oaks, CA: Sage.

Humphries, L. (1970). *Tearoom trade: Impersonal sex in public places.* Chicago, IL: Aldine.

Hwang, S. (2001). Homelessness and health. *Canadian Medical Association Journal, 164,* 229–33.

Jacklin, A. (2009). Theorizing the effects of new and changing media routines on explanations crime in news. Unpublished paper. Department of Sociology and Anthropology. University of Guelph.

Jacobs, P.A., Brunton, M., & Melville, M. (1965). Aggressive behaviour, mental subnormality and the XYY male. *Nature, 208,* 351–2.

Jenkins, J.P., & Maier-Katkin, D. (1992). Satanism: Myth and reality in a contemporary moral panic. *Crime, Law and Social Change: An International Journal, 17*(1).

Jenkins, P. (1994). *Using murder: The social construction of serial homicide.* New York, NY: Aldine de Gruyter.

Jensen, G.F., & Brownfield, D. (1983). Parents and drugs. *Criminology, 21,* 543–44.

Joe, K., & Chesney-Lind, M. (1998). "Just every mother's angel": An analysis of gender and ethnic variations in youth gang membership. In K. Daly and L. Maher (Eds.), *Criminology at the crossroads: Feminist readings in crime and justice* (pp. 87–109). New York, NY: Oxford University Press.

John Howard Society of Canada. (2010). Services across Canada. Retrieved from http://www.johnhoward.ca/services-across-canada.

Johnson, H., & Pottie Bunge, V. (2001). Prevalence and consequences of spousal violence in Canada. *Canadian Journal of Criminology, 43*(1), 27–45.

Johnson, H., & Dawson, M. (2011). Violence Against Women in Canada: research and policy perspectives. Toronto: Oxford University Press.

Johnson, M.P., & Ferraro, K. (2000). Research on domestic violence in the 1990s: Making distinctions. *Journal of Marriage and the Family, 62,* 948–63.

Johnson, S. (1995). *The AAP and gender differences.* Research Report for the Scottish Office Education Department.

Jones, T., MacLean, B., & Young, J. (1986). *The Islington crime survey.* London, UK: Routledge.

Karabanow, J. (2009). How young people get off the street: Exploring paths and processes. In J.D. Hulchanski, P. Campsie, S. Chau, S. Hwang, & E. Paradis (Eds.), *Finding home: Policy options for addressing homelessness in Canada* (Chapter 3.6). Toronto, ON: Cities Centre, University of Toronto. Retrieved from http://www.homelesshub.ca/FindingHome.

Katz, J. (1999). Ten things men can do to prevent gender violence. Retrieved from http://www.jacksonkatz.com/wmcd.html.

Kauri, V. (2012, 17 July). Toronto shooting "a terrible case," but not the worst. *National Post.* Retrieved from http://news.nationalpost.com/2012/07/17/toronto-shooting-a-terrible-case-but-not-the-worst/.

Keene, Carl. (1993). Drinking and driving, self-control and gender: Testing a general theory of crime. *Journal of Research in Crime and Delinquency, 30*(1), 30–46.

Kelling, G., & Wilson, J.Q. (1982). Broken windows: The police and neighbourhood safety. *The Atlantic Monthly, 249*(3), 29–38.

Knapp Commission. (1973). *Knapp Commission report on police corruption.* New York, NY: Braziller.

Krahn, H., Lowe, G., & Hughes, K. (2007). *Work, industry and Canadian society,* 5th ed. Toronto, ON: Thompson.

LaPrairie, C. (1987). Native women and crime in Canada: A theoretical model. In E. Adelberg & C. Currie (Eds.), *Too few to count: Canadian women in conflict with the law.* Vancouver: Press Gang.

———. (2002). Aboriginal over-representation in the criminal justice system: A tale of nine cities. *Canadian Journal of Criminology, 44*(2), 181–208.

Laqueur, T. (2000, 28 September). Festival of punishment: The American way of death. *London Review of Books.* Retrieved from http://www.guardian.co.uk/books/2000/sep/28/londonreviewofbooks.

Laub, J., & Sampson, R. (2003). *Shared beginnings, divergent lives.* Cambridge, MA: Harvard University Press.

Lazarsfeld, P., Berelson, B., & Gaudet, H. (1968). *The people's choice: How the voter makes up his mind in a presidential campaign.* New York, NY: Columbia University Press.

Lea, J., & Young, J. (1984). *What is to be done about law and order?* London, UK: Penguin.

Lemert, E. (1969). Primary and secondary deviation. In D. Cressey & D. Ward (Eds.), *Delinquency, crime and social process.* New York, NY: Harper and Row.

Leuner, P. (1977). Feminism. In A. Bullock & O. Stallybrass (Eds.), *The Harper dictionary of modern thought.* New York, NY: Harper and Row.

Levin, J., & McDevitt, J. (1993). *Hate crimes: The rising tide of bigotry and bloodshed.* New York, NY: Plenum Press.

Levitt, C, & Shaffir, W. (1978). *The riot at Christie Pits.* Toronto, ON: Lester & Orpen Dennys.

Leyton, E. (1975). *Dying hard: The ravages of industrial carnage.* Toronto, ON: McClelland & Stewart.

———. (1992). The theatre of public crisis. In E. Leyton, W. O'Grady, & J. Overton, *Violence and public anxiety: A Canadian case.* St John's, NF: ISER.

Lilly, J.R., Cullen, F.T., & Ball, R.A. (1995). *Criminological theory: Context and consequences.* Thousand Oaks, CA: Sage.

Lloyd, S. (1997). The effects of domestic violence on women's employment. *Law and Policy, 19,* 139–67.

Lombroso, C. (1911 [1861]). *Criminal man, according to the classification of Cesare Lombroso, briefly summarized by his daughter Gina Lombroso-Ferrero.* New York, NY: Putnams.

——— & Ferraro, G. (2004 [1895]). *Criminal woman, the prostitute, and the normal woman.* N. Rafter (Ed.) & M. Gibson (Trans). Durham, NC: Duke University Press.

Longshore, D., Turner, S., & Stein, J.A. (1998). Reliability and validity of self-control measure: Rejoinder. *Criminology, 34,* 175–82.

Loseke, D. (2003). *Thinking about social problems: An introduction to constructionist perspectives.* Piscataway, NJ: Transaction Publishers.

MacDonald, N. (2009, 12 March). Look out victims, the government wants its share now. *CBC News.* Retrieved from http://www.cbc.ca/world/story/2009/03/12/.

Mack, K., & Leiber, M. (2005). Race, gender, single-mother households, and delinquency: A further test of power-control theory. *Youth and Society, 37,* 115–44.

MacCharles, T. (2012, 23 October). Federal Prison Population in Canada Growing. *The Toronto Star.* N1.

Mackenzie, D., & Souryal, C. (1995). Inmates' attitude change during incarceration: A comparison of boot camp with traditional prison. *Justice Quarterly, 12*(2), 325–53.

Macmillan, R. (2000). Adolescent victimization and income deficits in early adulthood: Rethinking the costs of criminal victimization from a life course perspective. *Criminology, 38*(2), 553–88.

MADD Canada. (2006). MADD Canada calls for new impaired driving legislation. Retrieved from http://www.madd.ca/english/news/pr/p06jun12bkgrnd.htm.

Maestro, M. (1973). *Cesare Beccaria and the origins of penal reform.* Philadelphia, PA: Temple University Press.

Maidment, M. (2002). Toward a "woman-centered" approach to community-based corrections: A gendered analysis of electronic monitoring (EM) in eastern Canada. *Women & Criminal Justice, 13*(4), 47–68.

Mann, E., & Lee, J.A. (1979). *RCMP vs the People.* Don Mills, ON: General Publishing.

Martin, B. (2005, June 23). Hold a cover-up in the open. *Sydney Morning Herald,* p. 15.

McCarthy, B. (2002). New economics of sociological criminology. *Annual Review of Sociology, 28,* 417–42.

———, Hagan, J., & Woodward, T. (1999). In the company of women: Structure and agency in a revised power-control theory of gender and delinquency. *Criminology, 37,* 761–88.

McClennen, J.C. (2005). Domestic violence between same-gender partners: Recent findings and future direction. *Journal of Interpersonal Violence, 20*(2), 149–54.

McCorkle, R., & Miethe, T. (2002). *Panic: The social construction of the street gang problem.* Upper Saddle River, NJ: Prentice-Hall.

McEvoy, K., & Mika, H. (2002). Punishment, policing and praxis: Restorative justice and non-violent alternatives to paramilitary punishments in Northern Ireland. *Policing and Society, 11*(1), 359–82.

McMahon, M. (1995). *The persistent prison? Rethinking decarceration and penal reform.* Toronto, ON: University of Toronto Press.

McMullan, J.L. (2006). *News truth and crime: The Westray disaster and its aftermath.* Halifax, NS: Fernwood.

McMullan, J., & Smith, S. (1997). Toxic steel: State corporate crime and the contamination of the environment. In J. McMullan, D. Perrier, S. Smith, & P. Sawn (Eds.), *Crimes, laws and communities.* Halifax, NS: Fernwood.

McRobbie, A., & Thorton, S. (1995). Rethinking "moral panic" for multi-mediated social worlds. *British Journal of Sociology, 66*(4), 559–75.

Mead, G. (1967 [1934]). *Mind, self, and society from the standpoint of a social behaviorist.* Chicago, IL: University of Chicago Press.

Mellor, B., MacRae, L., Pauls, M., & Hornick, J. (2005). *Youth gangs in Canada: A preliminary review of programs and services.* Calgary, AB: Canadian Research Institute for Law and the Family.

Merton, R. (1938). Social structure and anomie. *American Sociological Review, 3,* 672–82.

Miller, W. (1975). Violence by youth gangs and youth groups as a crime problem in major American cities. Washington, DC: US Department of Justice.

Monier-Williams, E. (2006, 20 April). *News at the University of Toronto.* Retrieved from http://www.news.utoronto.ca/bin6/060420-2218.asp.

Moore, D., & Valverde, M. (2003). Party girls and predators: "Date rape drugs" and chronotopes of gendered risk. In Debra Brock (Ed.), *Making normal: Social regulation in Canada.* Toronto, ON: Thompson.

Moyer, S. (2005). A comparison of case processing under the Young Offenders and the first six months of the Youth Criminal Justice Act: A report to the Ministry of Justice. Ottawa, ON: Ministry of Justice.

Muffels, R., & Fouarge, D. (2001). Social exclusion and poverty: Definition, public debate and empirical evidence in the Netherlands. In D. Mayes, J. Berghman, & R. Salais (Eds.), *Social exclusion and European policy.* Northampton, MA: Edward Elgar.

Nagin, D., & Paternoster, R. (1994). Personal capital and social control: The deterrence implications of a theory of individual differences in criminal offending. *Criminology, 32*(4), 581–602.

Nairne, D. (1996, 29 March). Teen faces 'net hate charges. *Winnipeg Free Press.*

NAJCD (National Archive of Criminal Justice Data). (n.d.). National crime victimization survey resource guide. Retrieved from http://www.icpsr.umich.edu/NACJD/NCVS/.

Neuman, L., Wiegand, B., & Winterdyk, J. (2004). *Criminal justice research methods: Qualitative and quantitative approaches* (Canadian ed.). Toronto, ON: Pearson.

Newburn, T. (1999). *Understanding and preventing police corruption: Lessons from the literature.* London, UK: Home Office, Research Development and Statistics Directorate.

Newman, O. (1972). Defensible space: Crime prevention through urban design. New York, NY: Macmillan.

Novac, S., Hermer, J., Paradis, E., & Kellen, A. (2006). *Justice and injustice: Homelessness, crime, victimization and the criminal justice system.* Toronto, ON: Centre for Urban and Community Studies, University of Toronto.

Nuwer, P. (2009). High school hazing page. Retrieved from http://hazing.hanknuwer.com/hs2.html.

Native Women's Association of Canada. (1992, 25 February). The Canadian Human Rights Act: Changes required by behalf of the NWAC.

O'Connor, C. (2008). What research tells us about effective interventions for juvenile offenders. *What Works, Wisconsin Fact Sheet.* Madison, WI: University of Wisconsin–Madison/Extension.

O'Grady, W. (1992). Criminal statistics and stereotypes: The social construction of violence in Newfoundland. In E. Leyton, W. O'Grady, & J. Overton (Eds.), *Violence and public anxiety: A Canadian case.* St John's, NF: ISER Books.

———, Asbridge, M., & Abernathy, T. (2000). Illegal tobacco sales to youth: A view from rational choice theory. *Canadian Journal of Criminology, 42*(1), 1–20.

———, & Bright, R. (2002). Squeezed to the point of exclusion: The case of Toronto squeegee cleaners. In J. Hermer & J. Mosher (Eds.), *Disorderly people: Law and the politics of exclusion in Ontario.* Halifax, NS: Fernwood.

———, ———, & Cohen, E. (1998). Sub-employment and street youths: An analysis of the impact of squeegee cleaning on homeless youth. *Elsevier, Security Journal, 10*(4), 315–23.

———, & Gaetz, S. (2004). Homelessness, gender and subsistence: The case of Toronto street youth. *Journal of Youth Studies, 7*(4), 397–416.

———, ———, & Buccieri, K. (2011). *Can I see your ID? The policing of youth homelessness in Toronto.* Toronto: JFCY & Homeless Hub.

Oliveira, M. (2011, 13 June). Fewer Canadians using Facebook, *The Toronto Star.* Retrieved from http://www.thestar.com/business/2011/06/13/fewer_canadians_using_facebook.html.

Paglia-Boak, A., Mann, R.E., & Adlaf, E.M. (2011). *Drug use among Ontario students 1977–2011.* CAMH Research Document Series # 33. Toronto, ON: Centre for Addiction and Mental Health.

Park, R., & Burgess, E. (1967). *The city.* Chicago, IL: University of Chicago Press.

Parker, H., & Kirby, P. (1996). *Methadone maintenance and crime reduction in Merseyside.* Crime Detection and Prevention Series Paper 72. London, UK: Home Office Police Research Group.

Parkinson, G. (2008). Recovering the early history of Canadian criminology: Criminology at the University of British Columbia, 1951–1959, *Canadian Journal of Criminology and Criminal Justice, 50*(5), 589–620.

Parnaby, P. (2003). Disaster through dirty windshields: Law, order and Toronto's squeegee kids. *Canadian Journal of Sociology, 28*(3), 281–307.

———. (2006). Crime prevention through environmental design: Discourses of risk, social control, and a neo-liberal context. *Canadian Journal of Criminology and Criminal Justice, 48*(1), 1–30.

Paternoster, R., & Simpson, S. (1996). Sanction threats and appeals to morality: Testing a rational choice model of corporate crime. *Law and Society Review, 30*(3), 540–80.

———, & ———. (2001). A rational choice theory of corporate crime. In N. Shover & J. Wright (Eds.), *Crimes of privilege: Readings in white-collar crime,* (pp. 194–209). New York, NY: Oxford University Press.

Pearson, G. (1983). *Hooligan.* London, UK: Macmillan.

Perry, B. (1998). *In the name of hate: Understanding hate crimes.* New York, NY: Routledge.

Petersilia, J. (2003). *When prisoners come home: Parole and prisoner reentry.* New York, NY: Oxford University Press.

Pfohl, S. (1985). *Images of deviance and control: A sociological history.* New York, NY: McGraw-Hill.

Pile, S. (1999). What is a city? In D. Massey, J. Allen, & S. Pile (Eds.), *City worlds.* New York, NY: Routledge.

Platt, A. (1969). *The child savers.* Chicago, IL: University of Chicago Press.

Porter, R. (1989). *Health for sale: Quackery in England, 1660–1850.* Manchester, UK: Manchester University Press.

Porter, D., & Calverley, D. (2011). Trends in the use of remand in Canada. *Juristat.* Retrieved from http://www.statcan.gc.ca/pub/85-002-x/2011001/article/11440-eng.htm.

Porterfield, A. (1943). Delinquency and its outcome in court and college. *American Journal of Sociology, 49,* 199–208.

Pratt, T., & Cullen, F. (2000). The empirical status of Gottfredson and Hirschi's general theory of crime. *Criminology, 38,* 931–64.

Public Safety Canada. (2012). Human trafficking. Retrieved from http://www.publicsafety.gc.ca/prg/le/ht-tp-eng.aspx.

Quinney, R. (1970). *The social reality of crime.* Boston, MA: Little, Brown.

Rankin, J., Winsa, P., & Ng, H. (2013). Sucked into the criminal justice system. *The Toronto Star,* 2 March, IN 1 & 4.

Reasons, C., Ross, L., & Patterson, C. (1981). *Assault on the worker: Occupational health and safety in Canada.* Toronto, ON: Butterworths.

Reiman, J. (2004). *The rich get richer and the poor get prison: Ideology, class and criminal justice,* 5th ed. Boston, MA: Allyn and Bacon.

Reimer, B. (2004). Social exclusion in a comparative context. *Sociologica Ruralis, 44*(1), 76–94.

Reinarman, C., & Levine, H. (1989). Crack in context: Politics and media in the making of a drug scare. *Contemporary Drug Problems, 16*(4), 535–77.

Reiner, R., & Livingstone, S. (1997). *Discipline or desubordination: Changing media images of crime.* Final Report ERSC Grant L210252029.

Rennie, R. (2005). The historical origins of an industrial disaster: Occupational health and labour relations at the fluorspar mines, St. Lawrence, Newfoundland, 1933–1945. *Labour/Le Travail, 55,* 107–42.

Rigakos, G. (1999). Hyperpanoptics as commodity: The case of the parapolice. *Canadian Journal of Sociology, 24*(3), 381–409.

Robert, M. (2002). Mother and drugs: The governance of pregnancy. Unpublished paper available from author.

Roberts, J.V. (1995). *Disproportionate harm: Hate crime in Canada. An analysis of recent statistics.* Ottawa, ON: Department of Justice.

——, & Melchers, R. (2003). *The incarceration of Aboriginal offenders: Trends from 1978 to 2001.* Ottawa, ON: Department of Justice.

Rose, N. (2000). The biology of culpability: Pathological identity and crime control in a biological culture. *Theoretical Criminology, 4,* 5–34.

Rousmaniere, K., Dehli, K., & de Coninck-Smith, N. (Eds.). (1997). *Discipline, moral regulation and schooling: A social history.* London, UK: Garland Press.

Royal Canadian Mounted Police (RCMP). (2013). Frequently asked questions on human trafficking. Retrieved from http://www.rcmp-grc.gc.ca/ht-tp/q-a-trafficking-traite-eng.htm#q1.

Rugge, T., Bonta, J., & Wallace-Capretta, S. (2005). *Evaluation of the collaborative justice project: A restorative justice program for serious crime.* Ottawa, ON: Public Safety and Emergency Preparedness Canada, User Report 2005–02.

Rushton, P. (1995). *Race, evolution and behaviour.* Piscataway, NJ: Transaction Publishers.

Sacco, V. (2000). Media constructions of crime. In R. Silverman, J. Teevan, & V. Sacco, *Crime in Canadian society,* 6th ed. Toronto, ON: Harcourt Brace.

Sampson, R., & Laub, J. (1993). *Crime in the making: Pathways and turning points through life.* Cambridge, MA: Harvard University Press.

Satzewich, V., & Shaffir, W. (2009). Racism versus professionalism: Claims and counter-claims about racial profiling. *Canadian Journal of Criminology and Criminal Justice, 51*(2), 199–226. Reproduced with the permission of University of Toronto Press.

Saulitis, A. (1979). Chromosomes and criminality: The legal implications of XXY syndrome. *Journal of Legal Medicine, 23*(1), 269–91.

Sauvé, J. (2005). Crime statistics in Canada, 2004. *Juristat, 25*(5). Ottawa, ON: Statistics Canada.

Schissel, B. (1997). *Blaming children: Youth crime, moral panics and the politics of hate.* Halifax, NS: Fernwood.

Schoolfile. (2010). The national longitudinal survey of children and youth. Retrieved from http://www.schoolfile.com/cap_start/nlscy12.htm.

Schwartz, M., Dunfee, T., & Kline, M. (2005). Tone at the top: Ethics code for directors? *Journal of Business Ethics, 58,* 79–100.

Sears, R.R., Maccoby, E.E., & Levin, H. (1957). *Patterns of childrearing.* Evanston, IL: Row, Peterson, and Co.

Serin, R.C., & Amos, N.L. (1995). The role of psychopathy in the assessment of dangerousness. *International Journal of Law and Psychiatry, 18*, 231–8.

Shalla, V. (2011). *Working in a global era: Canadian perspectives*, 2nd ed. Toronto, ON: Canadian Scholars Press.

Shaw, C., & McKay, H. (1942). *Juvenile delinquency and urban areas*. Chicago, IL: University of Chicago Press.

Shaw, H. (2006). More common than cancer: The sexual abuse of kids has gotta stop. Retrieved from http://sadlynormal.word press.com/2006/12/12/more-common-than-cancer-the-sexual-abuseof-kids-has-gotta-stop-by-hank-shaw.

Shearing, C. (2005). *Paradigms for policing*. Centre for the Study of Violence and Reconciliation, Criminal Justice Conference Proceedings. Retrieved from http://www.csvr.org.za/cjspeak.

Sheldon, W. (1940). *Atlas of men: A guide for somatotyping the adult male at all ages*. New York, NY: Harper.

Sheppard, M. (1998, 24 October). Teen gangs: Fear in our schools. *The Toronto Star*. A1.

Sher, G. (2003). On the decriminalization of drugs. *Criminal Justice Ethics, 22*(1), 30–3.

Sherman, L. (1974). Becoming bent: Moral careers of corrupt policemen. In L.W. Sherman (Ed.), *Police corruption: A sociological perspective* (pp. 191–208). Garden City, NY: Anchor Books.

———. (1992). *Policing domestic violence*. New York, NY: Free Press.

———, & Berk, R. (1984). The specific deterrent effects of arrest for domestic assault. *American Sociological Review, 49*, 261–72.

Short, J., & Nye, F.I. (1958). Extent of unrecorded juvenile delinquency: Tentative conclusions. *Journal of Criminal Law and Criminology, 49*, 296–302.

Shover, N., & Wright, J. (2001). *Crimes of privilege: Readings in white-collar crime*. New York, NY: Oxford University Press.

Silver, W., Mihorean, K., & Taylor-Butts, A. (2004). Hate crime in Canada. *Juristat, 24*(4). Ottawa, ON: Statistics Canada.

Simon, D. (1996). *Elite deviance*, 5th ed. Boston, MA: Allyn and Bacon.

———. (2001). *Elite deviance*, 7th ed. Boston, MA: Allyn and Bacon.

Simon, R. (1975). *Women and crime*. Lexington, MA: Lexington Books.

Singer, S., & Levine, M. (1988). Power control theory, gender and delinquency:

A partial replication with additional evidence on the effects on peers. *Criminology, 26*(4), 627–47.

Sinha, M. (2013) Measuring violence against women: statistical trends. *Juristat*. no. 85-002.

Small, S.A. (2008). What research tells us about effective youth mentoring programs. *What Works, Wisconsin Fact Sheet*. Madison, WI: University of Wisconsin–Madison/Extension.

Smart, C. (1976). *Women, crime and criminology: A feminist critique*. London, UK: Routledge & Kegan Paul.

Snider, L. (1993). *Bad business: Corporate crime in Canada*. Toronto, ON: Nelson.

———. (2004). Resisting neo-liberalism: The poisoned water disaster in Walkerton, Ontario. *Social & Legal Studies 13*(2) June: 265–89.

Solomon, R., & Green, M. (1988). The first century: The history of non-medical opiate use and control policies in Canada, 1870–1970. In J. Blackwell & P. Erickson (Eds.), *Illicit drugs in Canada: A risky business* (pp. 88–104). Scarborough, ON: Nelson Canada.

Sprott, J. (1996). Understanding public views of youth crime and the youth criminal justice system. *Canadian Journal of Criminology, 38*(3), 271–91.

Statistics Canada. (2005, 31 March). *The Daily*.

Statistics Canada. (2005a, 16 December). *The Daily*.

Statistics Canada. (2008a, 20 February). *The Daily*.

Statistics Canada. (2008b, 23 October). *The Daily*.

Statistics Canada. (2009a, 21 July). *The Daily*.

Statistics Canada. (2009b, 28 October). *The Daily*.

Statistics Canada. (2009c). Victims and persons accused of homicide, by age and sex. Table 253-0003.

Statistics Canada. (2010). General Social Survey: Victimization. *The Daily*. Retrieved from http://www.statcan.gc.ca/daily-quotidien/100928/dq100928a-eng.htm.

Statistics Canada. (2011). Police personnel and expenditures. *The Daily*. Retrieved from http://www.statcan.gc.ca/daily-quotidien/111213/dq111213b-eng.htm.

———. (2012). Homicide in Canada, 2011. *The Daily*. Retrieved from http://www.statcan.gc.ca/daily-quotidien/121204/dq121204a-eng.htm.

"Stoning to death in Iran." (n.d.). Stoning women to death in Iran: A Special Case Study. Retrieved from http://www.iran-e-azad.org/stoning/women.html.

Surette, R. (1998). *Media, crime and criminal justice: Images are realities.* Belmont, CA: Wadsworth.

Sutherland, E. (1939). *Principles of criminology.* Philadelphia, PA: Lippincott.

T-3 Associates Training and Consulting. (2001). *Project turnaround outcome evaluation— final report.* Toronto, ON: Ministry of Correctional Services.

Tannenbaum, F. (1938). *Crime and the community.* New York, NY: Columbia University Press.

Tanner, J. (2001). *Teenage troubles: Youth and deviance in Canada.* Toronto, ON: Nelson.

———. (2010). *Teenage troubles: Youth and deviance in Canada,* 3rd ed. Toronto, ON: Oxford University Press.

———, Davies, S., & O'Grady, B. (1999). Whatever happened to yesterday's rebels? Longitudinal effects of youth delinquency on education and employment. *Social Problems, 47*(2), 250–74.

——— & Wortley, S. (2002). *The Toronto youth crime and victimization survey: Overview report.* Toronto, ON: Centre of Criminology.

Tappan, P. (1947). Who is the criminal? *American Sociological Review, 12,* 96–102.

Taylor, I., Walton, P., & Young, J. (1973). *The new criminology: For a social theory of deviance.* London, UK: Routledge & Kegan Paul.

Taylor-Butts, A. (2004). Private security and public policing in Canada in 2001. *Juristat, 24*(7). Ottawa, ON: Statistics Canada.

Taylor-Butts, A. (2010). When and where youth commit police-reported crimes, 2008. *Juristat. 30*(2). Ottawa, ON: Statistics Canada. Retrieved from http://www.statcan.gc.ca/pub/85-002-x/2010002/article/11241-eng.htm.

Thomas, W. (1923). *The unadjusted girl.* Boston, MA: Little, Brown.

Thompson, S., and Bucerius, S. (2012, 16 June). Regent Park revitalization: Has it created an "us versus them" dynamic? *The Toronto Star.* Retrieved from http://www.thestar.com/news/gta/article/1211654--regent-park-revitalization-has-it-created-an-us-versus-them-dynamic.

Thornberry, T., & Krohn, M. (2000). The self-report method for measuring delinquency and crime. *Criminal Justice* (Vol. 4). Washington, DC: US Department of Justice.

Thrasher, F. (1927). *The gang.* Chicago, IL: University of Chicago Press.

Toronto Police Services Board. (2008). Minutes of meeting held on March 27. Toronto.

Toronto Star. (2005, 25 December). Editorial. p. A26.

Toronto Star. (2006, 17 May). Girl gang members on the rise six per cent are female, say police — major change in the last five years.

Toronto Star. (2009, 12 June). Guilty verdict restored in Virk case. p. A1.

Trevethan, S., & Rastin, C. (2004). *A profile of visible minority offenders in the federal Canadian correctional system.* Ottawa, ON: Correctional Services Canada.

Turenne, M. (2005). *Racial profiling: Context and definition. Commission des Droits de la Personne et des Droits de la Jeunesse.* Quebec, QC: Ministry of Justice.

Turk, A. (1969). *Criminality and the legal order.* Chicago, IL: Rand McNally.

Unis, A.S., Cook, E.H., Vincent, J.G., Gjerde, D.K., Perry, B.D., Mason, C., & Mitchell, J. (1997). Platelet serotonin measures in adolescents with conduct disorder. *Biological Psychiatry, 42*(7), 553–9.

Varma, K. & Doob, A. (1998). Deterring economic crimes: The case of tax evasion. *Canadian Journal of Criminology, 40*(2), 165–84.

Varma, N. (n.d.). What can I do with an undergraduate degree in criminology? Student Counselling and Career Centre, University of Manitoba. Retrieved from http://www.umanitoba.ca/student/counselling/WhatCanIDo/criminology.html.

Visano, L. (1987). *The idle trade.* Concord, ON: VitaSana Books.

Vlemincx, K, & Berghman, J. (2001). Social exclusion and the welfare state: An overview of conceptual issues and policy implications. In D. Mayes, J. Berghman, & R. Salais (Eds.), *Social exclusion and European policy.* Northampton, MA: Edward Elgar.

Walker, A., & Walker, C. (1997). *Britain divided: The growth of social exclusion in the 1980s and 1990s.* London, UK: Child Poverty Action Group.

Walker, L. (1979). *The battered woman.* New York, NY: Harper and Row.

Walmsley, R. (2012). *World prison population list*, 9th ed. International Centre for Prison Studies, University of Essex.

Wareham, J., Cochran, J., Dembo, R., & Sellers, C. (2005). Community, strain, and delinquency: A test of a multi-level model of general strain theory. *Western Criminology Review*, 6(1), 117–33.

Warner, B, & Fowler, S.K. (2003). Strain and violence: Testing a general strain theory model of community violence. *Journal of Criminal Justice, 31*, 511–21.

Welsh, B., & Farrington, D. (2005). Evidence-based crime prevention: Conclusions and directions for a safer society. *Canadian Journal of Criminology and Criminal Justice, 47*(2) 337–54.

Whelan, B., & Whelan, C. (1995). In what sense is poverty multidimensional? In G. Room (Ed.), *Beyond the threshold: The measurement and analysis of social exclusion.* London, UK: Hobbs.

White, M.D., & Ready, J. (2009). Examining fatal and nonfatal incidents involving the TASER: Identifying predictors of suspect death reported in the media. *Criminology and Public Policy, 8*(4), 865–91.

White, R., & Haines, F. (2004). *Crime and criminology: An introduction*, 3rd ed. Melbourne, AU: Oxford University Press.

Whyte, W. (1943). *Street corner society: The social organization of a Chicago slum*, 2nd ed. Chicago, IL: University of Chicago Press.

Williams, Paul, & Dickinson, Julie. (1993). Fear of crime: Read all about it? The relationship between newspaper crime reporting and fear of crime. *British Journal of Criminology, 33*(1): 33–56.

Wilson, E.O. (1975). *Sociobiology: The new synthesis.* Cambridge, MA: Belknap Press.

———. (1998). *Consilience.* New York, NY: Random House.

Wilson, J. (1985). *Crime and human nature.* New York, NY: Simon & Schuster.

Witkin, H.A., et al. (1976). XYY and XXY men: Criminality and aggression. *Science, 193*, 547–55.

Wolf, D. (1991). *The rebels.* Toronto, ON: University of Toronto Press.

Wortley, S., & Tanner, J. (2005a). Inflammatory rhetoric? Baseless accusations? A response to Gabor's critique of racial profiling research in Canada. *Canadian Journal of Criminology and Criminal Justice, 47*(3), 581–609.

Wortley, S., & Tanner, J. (2005b). They got my back: Social support, respect and gang activity among socially alienated Toronto youth. Retrieved from http://www.toronto.ca/metropolis/metropolistoronto2005/pdf/wortley_714b.pdf.

Wortley, S., & Tanner, J. (2007). Criminal organizations or social groups? An exploration of the myths and realities of youth gangs in Toronto (First draft). Retrieved from http://ceris.metropolis.net/Virtual%20Library/EResources/WortleyTanner2007.pdf.

Wortley, S., & Owusu-Bempah, A. (2011). The usual suspects: Police stop and search practices in Canada. *Policing and Society, 21*(4), 395–407.

Wright, D., & Mays, L. (1998). Correctional boot camps, attitudes and recidivism: The Oklahoma experience. *Journal of Offender Rehabilitation, 28*(1/2), 71–87.

Wrong, D. (1961). The oversocialized conception of man. *American Sociological Review, 26*, 184–93.

Yessine, A.K. & Bonta, J. (2009). The offending trajectories of youthful Aboriginal offenders. *Canadian Journal of Criminology and Criminal Justice, 15*(4), 435–72.

Young, J. (1975). Working Class Criminology in Taylor, I.P. Walton and J. Young (Eds.) *Critical Criminology.* London, UK: Routledge & Kegan Paul.

———. (1999). *The exclusive society.* London, UK: Sage.

———. (2003). Merton with energy, Katz with structure. *Theoretical Criminology, 7*(3), 388–414.

———. (2007). *The vertigo of late modernity.* London, UK: Sage.

Zehr, H., & Mika, H. (1998). Fundamental concepts of restorative justice. *Contemporary Justice Review, 1*(1), 47–56.

Zeitlin, I. (1968). *Ideology and the development of sociological theory.* Englewood Cliffs, NJ: Prentice-Hall.

Index